Non-Western Educational Traditions
Indigenous Approaches to Educational
Thought and Practice

Third Edition

Sociocultural, Political, and Historical Studies in Education
Joel Spring, Editor

Non-Western Educational Traditions
Indigenous Approaches to Educational Thought and Practice

Third Edition

Timothy Reagan
Roger Williams University

 LAWRENCE ERLBAUM ASSOCIATES, PUBLISHERS
2005   Mahwah, New Jersey   London

Lawrence Erlbaum Associates, Inc., Publishers
10 Industrial Avenue
Mahwah, New Jersey 07430

Cover design by Kathryn Houghtaling Lacey

Library of Congress Cataloging-in-Publication Data

Non-Western Educational Traditions: Indigenous Approaches to Educational Thought
   and Practice, Third Edition, by Timothy Reagan.
      p.   cm.
   Includes bibliographical references and index.
   ISBN 0-8058-4857-6 (pbk : alk. paper).

Copyright information for this volume can be obtained
by contacting the Library of Congress.

Books published by Lawrence Erlbaum Associates are printed on acid-free paper,
and their bindings are chosen for strength and durability.

Printed in the United States of America
10 9 8 7 6 5 4 3 2 1

This book is dedicated to my father,
Gerald Reagan

Contents

10 Themes and Lessons in the Study of Non-Western Educational Traditions: Toward a Beginning   247

Bibliography   257

Author Index   291

Subject Index   295

List of Figures

Preface

In all societies, throughout human history, people have educated their children. Indeed, one of the fundamental characteristics of human civilization is a concern for the preparation of the next generation. From one generation to the next, we seek to pass on what we know and have learned, hoping to ensure not merely the survival of our offspring, but of our culture as well.

The history of education, as it has been conceived and taught in the United States (and generally in the West), has focused almost entirely on the ways in which our own educational tradition emerged, developed, and changed over the course of the centuries. This is, of course, understandable, but it means that we have ignored the many ways that other societies have sought to meet many of the same challenges. In this book, an effort is made to try to provide a brief overview of a small number of other, non-Western approaches to educational thought and practice. An understanding of the ways that other peoples have tried to educate their children, as well as what counted for them as "education," may help us to think more clearly about some of our own assumptions and values, as well as to help us to become more open to alternative viewpoints about important educational matters.

Unlike most areas traditionally included in the training of educators, very few individuals have had any real exposure to non-Western educational traditions, and so the audience for this book is a very broad and diverse one. The book was written to be accessible to both preservice and inservice teachers, but may also be of interest to advanced students in graduate programs as well as faculty members. Although both the book as a whole and particular sections of the book may be of considerable interest to educators in other societies, the book is written from the perspective of American readers and presupposes that readers are, at the very least, familiar with the Western educational tradition.

ORGANIZATION OF THE BOOK

Non-Western Educational Traditions: Indigenous Approaches to Educational Thought and Practice, Third Edition consists of ten chapters dealing with a wide variety of different, non-Western cultural and historical educational traditions. In chapter 1, a theoretical foundation and base for the study of non-Western educational traditions is offered. Chapter 2 provides an overview of the problematic concept of "culture," and then offers a brief overview of the culture of the DEAF-WORLD. In chapter 3, a broad overview of traditional, indigenous African educational thought and practice is offered. Chapters 4 and 5 move our focus away from Africa and onto indigenous educational thought and practice in two distinctive settings in the Americas. In chapter 4, an examination of the educational thought and practice of the Mayas and Aztecs is used as a case study of indigenous education in Mesoamerica, whereas in chapter 5, the indigenous North American experience is discussed. Traditional educational thought and practice in imperial China is the focus of chapter 6, with a special emphasis on the thought of Confucius and the role of the imperial examination system. Chapter 7 provides an overview of the educational tradition embedded in Hinduism and Buddhism. Chapter 8 presents an overview of educational thought and practice among the Rom. Although technically not non-Western in important ways, including its relation to the so-called "Judeo-Christian" tradition, the Muslim educational heritage is similarly excluded in large part from Western histories of educational thought and practice, and so its inclusion in a book of this sort is certainly defensible. Therefore, chapter 9 presents a survey of traditional Islamic educational thought and practice. Finally, the last chapter in *Non-Western Educational Traditions: Indigenous Approaches to Educational Thought and Practice, Third Edition* summarizes some of the major themes and issues discussed in the book and suggests future areas for scholarly exploration. At the end of each chapter, there are a number of questions for reflection and discussion, as well as recommendations for further readings.

NEW IN THE THIRD EDITION

This third edition of *Non-Western Educational Traditions: Indigenous Approaches to Educational Thought and Practice* has again allowed me the opportunity to revisit a number of areas, to expand and clarify points that I felt were not sufficiently clear in the first and second editions, to update chapters as needed, and to continue to improve the pedagogical usefulness of the text. Chapter 2 is new to this edition, and is a response to feedback about the problems inherent in our general discourse about "culture." In addition, it provides what I take to be an interesting example of a culture that is near to us but nevertheless alien: the case of the DEAF-WORLD. Chapter 9, which deals with Islam and traditional Muslim education, has also been substantially revised. The third edition also involves a change in terminology, reflected in the subtitle, from "alternative" approaches to educational thought and practice to "indigenous" approaches. This change in terminology reflects not so much a change in the emphases found in the book, but rather is a recognition of the growing popularity of scholarly interest in indigenous peoples, their languages, cultures, and histories.

ACKNOWLEDGMENTS

Writing a book is an undertaking like few others in that it is profoundly personal and individual, but at the same time it requires considerable patience and support from many others. I am deeply grateful to many colleagues for their help and assistance throughout the writing of this work. In particular, I would like to thank Naomi Tutu, Sharon Rallis, Patricia Weibust, Tom Jones, Chuck Case, Eva Díaz, Frank Stone, Kay Norlander, Cheryl Spaulding, and Tom DeFranco, all at the University of Connecticut, as well as Larry Klein and Daniel Mulcahy at Central Connecticut State University, Rose Morris at the Human Sciences Research Council in Pretoria, and Claire Penn at the University of the Witwatersrand. I am also very thankful for the insights and challenges provided by many of my doctoral students, and especially those of Beatrice Ndu Okwu, Terry A. Osborn, Hsiung-Huei Lee, Eliana Rojas, Sharon Wilson, Gerda Walz-Michaels, Joe Veth, Adama Sow, and Kamala Willey. The librarians at the University of Connecticut, as well as those at Central Connecticut State University, the University of Hartford, The Ohio State University, the Human Sciences Research Council, the University of the Witwatersrand, and the Pontificia Universidad Católica de Chile were incredibly supportive as well, tracking down difficult-to-find material and making every effort to be helpful. My friends Tammy Wood and Ann Randall provided many cups of coffee and worthwhile discussion on many of the topics covered in this book, and I am also more grateful to them than I can say. Naomi Silverman, at Lawrence Erlbaum Associates, has been a wonderful friend and supporter from the beginning of this project. Over the course of three editions, the reviewers of the manuscript provided many useful and helpful ideas and questions, and I would like to thank Maenette Benham, Michigan State University; Robert H. Kim, Western Washington University; Patricia K. Kubow, Bowling Green State University; Tove Skutnabb-Kangas, The University of Roskilde, Denmark; and Ruth Thomas, University of Minnesota. Finally, and as always, I want to thank Jo Ann, Joshua, Bryan, and Kimberly.

—*Timothy Reagan*

It is not for him to pride himself who loveth his own country,
but rather for him who loveth the whole world.
The earth is but one country, and mankind its citizens.

—Bahá'u'lláh

1

An Introduction to the Study of Non-Western and Indigenous Educational Traditions: A Philosophical Starting Point

> *We find it pedagogically tragic that various indigenous knowledges of how action affects reality in particular locales have been dismissed from academic curricula. Such ways of knowing and acting could contribute so much to the educational experiences of all students; but because of the rules of evidence and the dominant epistemologies of Western knowledge production, such understandings are deemed irrelevant by the academic gatekeepers. . . . Our intention is to challenge the academy and its "normal science" with the questions indigenous knowledges raise about the nature of our existence, our consciousness, our knowledge production, and the "globalized" future.*
> —Semali and Kincheloe (1999, p. 15)

I fully concur with the sentiments expressed so clearly by Ladislaus Semali and Joe Kincheloe, and this book is a result of roughly the same impetus that drove them to produce their book, *What Is Indigenous Knowledge? Voices from the Academy.*[1] Most books and courses that deal with the history and philosophy of education include few, if any, references to indigenous educational ideas and practices in Africa and the Americas, and relatively few references to those of Asia. Although for some time now there have been calls for the inclusion of the perspectives of women and people of color in studies of the history and philosophy of education, such efforts, where they have taken place, have often entailed little more than the addition of vignettes indicating the contributions of members of such groups to the Western tradition. In other words, the idea that there might be valuable insights to be gained from a serious examination of non-Western educational traditions themselves—indeed, that these traditions might be fully comparable to the Western tradition in their unique richness and diversity—is one that rarely has been voiced. Furthermore, where non-Western educational ideas and practices have been discussed, they are often subjected to a treatment roughly comparable to the

1

"Orientalism" discussed by the late Edward Said with regard to the Western (and specifically, Anglo-French-American) response to Islam and the Islamic world. According to Said:

> Orientalism can be discussed and analyzed as the corporate institution for dealing with the Orient—dealing with it by making statements about it, authorizing views of it, describing it, by teaching it, settling it, ruling over it: in short, Orientalism as a Western style for dominating, restructuring, and having authority over the Orient. . . . European culture gained in strength and identity by setting itself off against the Orient as a sort of surrogate and even underground self.[2]

In other words, when scholars do try to examine non-Western educational thought and practice, all too often they tend to do so through a lens that not only colors what they see, but also one that reifies the object of study—making it, in essence, part of "the Other" and hence alien. Reification results not only in the distortion of what one is trying to understand, but also in its subjugation to one's own preexisting values and norms. This problem is not, of course, unique to the study of educational thought and practice; it is a common criticism of Western scholarship about the non-Western world in general. For example, in his discussion of the study of indigenous African religions by Western scholars, the Ugandan poet Okot p'Bitek wrote of the "systematic and intensive use of dirty gossip" in place of solid and sensitive scholarship.[3] In a similar vein, the anthropologist Adam Kuper wrote of *The Invention of Primitive Society* by 19th- and 20th-century anthropologists and social theorists in the West.[4] In terms of traditional African educational practices, A. Babs Fafunwa commented that "because indigenous education failed to conform to the ways of the Westernised system, some less well-informed writers have considered it primitive, even savage and barbaric. But such contentions should be seen as the product of ignorance and due to a total misunderstanding of the inherent value of informal education."[5] At the present time, there is perhaps no better place to see this tendency at work than in the examination and treatment of the Muslim world and Islamic tradition in the West. As Joshua Cohen and Ian Lague noted in their "Preface" to Kaled Abou El Fadl's recent book, *The Place of Tolerance in Islam*:

> Since September 11, Western discussions of Islam have typically been conducted through a contest of caricatures. Some analysts present Islamic extremism as a product of a "clash of civilizations" that pits Eastern despotism against Western individualism. Others see such extremism as a grim "blowback" of America's cold-war foreign policy. Engagement with the Muslim faith commonly takes the form of simplistic pronouncements about [the] "essence" of Islam: Osama bin Laden either represents the true message of the Prophet or corrupts a "religion of peace" . . . . These discussions are driven more by West-

ern concerns—"are Muslims dangerous or not?"—than by a serious effort to understand Islam and the place of toleration and moral decency in its conception of a proper human life.[6]

Such simplistic misunderstandings and misrepresentations remain all too common as we seek to understand the Other, and it is as a challenge to such misunderstandings, in part, that this book has been written.

The same, of course, can be argued with respect to Western treatment of indigenous educational ideas and practices in Asia, the Americas, and elsewhere. In short, when we speak of the history of educational thought and practice, what we have actually meant in the past has been the history of *Western* educational thought and practice, and the effect of our meaning has been, in essence, to dismiss, or at the very least to delegitimatize, the many alternatives to the Western tradition that have developed, evolved, and thrived elsewhere in the world. In other words, it is discourse itself—the way that one talks, thinks about, and conceptualizes educational thought and practice— that is at issue. As Stephen Ball noted in a discussion of the work of the French philosopher Michel Foucault, "Discourse is a central concept in Foucault's analytical framework. Discourses are about what can be said and thought, but also about who can speak, when, and with what authority. Discourses embody meaning and social relationships, they constitute both subjectivity and power relations."[7]

The underlying purpose of this book, then, is to begin the process by which the existing discourse in the history of educational thought and practice can be expanded in such a way as to provide a starting point for the development of a more open and diverse view of the development of various approaches to educational thought and practice. Needless to say, this work is intended to be only a beginning. If the study of the various educational traditions discussed here is to be taken seriously, then these traditions (and many others as well) will require, and are certainly entitled to, the same sort of concern that has long been accorded the Western tradition. Furthermore, given their differences from the Western tradition, it is essential that we all learn to invite and listen to the "multiple voices" and perspectives that can enlighten our understanding of these traditions, just as we must learn to recognize that different groups may, as a consequence of their sociocultural contexts and backgrounds, possess ways of knowing that, although different from our own, may be every bit as valuable and worthwhile as those to which we are accustomed.[8] As Carol Gilligan suggested with respect to "woman's place in man's life cycle" in *In a Different Voice: Psychological Theory and Women's Development*:

At a time when efforts are being made to eradicate discrimination between the sexes in the search for social equality and justice, the differences between the sexes are being rediscovered in the social sciences. This discovery occurs when theories formerly considered to be sexually neutral in their scientific objectivity are found instead to reflect a consistent observational and evaluative bias. Then the presumed neutrality of science, like that of language itself, gives way to the recognition that the categories of knowledge are human constructions. The fascination with point of view that has informed the fiction of the twentieth century and the corresponding recognition of the relativity of judgment infuse our scientific understanding as well when we begin to notice how accustomed we have become to seeing life through men's eyes.[9]

A very similar kind of argument can be made with respect to the differences in perspective and worldview in various non-Western cultural and historic traditions. To be sure, at the present time, this argument remains largely speculative in nature with respect to many of the traditions to be discussed in this book, although in the case of women there is now a growing body of fairly compelling empirical evidence. My hope would be that others, from a wide array of different backgrounds, would challenge, modify, and add to the base that is offered here, and someday the study of the Aztec *calmécac* and *telpochcalli*, of the imperial Chinese examination system and its content, and the role of various African initiation schools, among others, might be as commonly taught in courses in the history of educational thought as the study of Plato, Rousseau, and Dewey is today. Having said this, I also want to stress that I am not arguing that Plato, Rousseau, and Dewey (among others) should be eliminated; they, and many others, are important figures in the development of our own historical tradition, and certainly merit serious study. My focus here is not on replacing the Western tradition, but rather on trying to expand our understanding of education, broadly conceived, through the examination and study of other approaches to educational thought and practice with which many of us tend to be less familiar. Ultimately, of course, as we better understand the educational traditions of other societies and cultures, we will also be forced to reexamine and to reflect on our own tradition in somewhat different ways—and this will be immensely beneficial to our understanding of our own traditions.

THE CHALLENGE OF ETHNOCENTRISM

As we begin the process of trying to broaden our perspectives on the history of educational thought and practice, it is important for us to understand that the activity in which we are engaged will inevitably involve challenging both our own ethnocentrism and the ethnocentrism of others. Basically, *ethnocentrism* refers to the tendency to view one's own cultural group as superior to others—a tendency common to most, if not all, human societies. However, in contemporary scholarly discourse, one seldom comes across such blatant ethnocentrism. Rather, what is far more common is simply the practice of using one's own society and sociocultural practices as the norm by which other societies are viewed, measured, and evaluated. Ethnocentrism of this kind takes two somewhat distinct forms: cultural ethnocentrism and epistemological ethnocentrism.[10]

Cultural ethnocentrism refers to manifestations of ethnocentrism in individual scholars and their work, as well as to the sociocultural context that has helped to form and support such individual and idiosyncratic biases. In other words, we see examples of cultural ethnocentrism when writers and scholars allow common biases, prejudices, and assumptions to color their work in various ways. Racism, sexism, linguicism, ageism, and so on, all contribute to cultural ethnocentrism, most often in ways that are unconscious. Thus, the topics that a scholar chooses to explore, the questions that are asked about the topic, the framework within which hypotheses are constructed, how conflicting evidence is weighed, and even what counts as evidence, can all be affected by personal biases.

This brings us to the second sort of ethnocentrism, *epistemological ethnocentrism*, which deals not so much with individual assumptions and biases, but rather with those common to an entire field of study. With epistemological ethnocentrism, we are concerned with what the philosopher of science Thomas Kuhn called the dominant "paradigm" in our own field of study.[11] A paradigm, on Kuhn's account, is far more than merely a model or a theory. As Patton explained:

> A paradigm is a world view, a general perspective, a way of breaking down the complexity of the real world. As such, paradigms are deeply embedded in the socialization of adherents and practitioners: paradigms tell them what is important, legitimate, and reasonable. Paradigms are also normative, telling the practitioner what to do without the necessity of long existential or epistemological consideration. But it is this aspect of paradigms that constitutes both their strength and their weakness—their strength in that it makes action possible, their weakness in that the very reason for action is hidden in the unquestioned assumptions of the paradigm.[12]

Thus, the dominant paradigm in a field of study at any given point in time essentially establishes the parameters within which "legitimate" discourse may take place. Kuhn explained the significance and power of the dominant paradigm in a field of study as follows:

> Scientists work from models acquired through education and through subsequent exposure to the literature often without quite knowing or needing to know what characteristics have given these models the status of community

paradigms. . . . That scientists do not usually ask or debate what makes a particular problem or solution legitimate tempts us to suppose that, at least intuitively, they know the answer. But it may only indicate that neither the question
nor the answer is felt to be relevant to their research. Paradigms may be prior
to, more binding, and more complete than any set of rules for research that
could be unequivocally abstracted from them.[13]

In the case of the study of the history and philosophy of education, the
dominant paradigm has focused almost entirely on a single educational tradition (albeit one with many branches), to the exclusion of virtually all others,
as was mentioned earlier in this chapter. The study of traditional, indigenous
educational practices has been reduced to the study of "socialization" and
"acculturation," and has been left to anthropologists and others. Because
scholars have tended to equate "education" with "schooling," and because
they have consistently focused on the role of literacy and a literary tradition,
many important and interesting—indeed, fascinating—traditions have been
seen as falling outside of the parameters of "legitimate" study in the history
and philosophy of education. Furthermore, even in the study of the Western
educational tradition itself, scholars have been somewhat remiss in examining aspects of the traditions that seem to fall outside the bounds of their expectations. For example, even recent works concerned with educational
thought and practice in classical antiquity generally ignore the formidable
work of Martin Bernal, who has, since the early 1980s, been arguing that the
civilization of classical Greece has deep and important roots in Afroasiatic
cultures.[14] Similarly, until fairly recently, the contributions of women to the
Western educational tradition were largely ignored, in part as a result of over-
looking the contributions of specific individual women, but even more, by
defining *education* in such a way as to eliminate from discussion what might
be called the "reproductive" (as opposed to the "productive") aspects of education.[15] Thus, although throughout virtually all of the Western historical tradition women have played the central role in raising children and in educating them, this was largely ignored in formal studies of the development of the
Western educational tradition.[16]

Although dangerous and pernicious, cultural ethnocentrism is actually
somewhat easier to challenge than epistemological ethnocentrism, because
individual scholars in a particular field at the same point in time may differ to
a considerable degree with respect to issues related to cultural ethnocentrism.
Thus, many scholars today are far more sensitive to issues of gender, race, and
ethnicity than others, while nonetheless working within the same epistemologically ethnocentric paradigm.

An example in which both cultural and epistemological ethnocentrism can
be clearly seen was written in the mid-1970s by H. M. Phillips, and is presented here:

In Africa, education was extremely limited and associated with the very small numbers who were in contact with Islam over the land routes and later with Europeans in the ports or administrative centres already starting to be set up in those parts of Africa which were colonized. But basically the continent as a whole was still completely underdeveloped and tribal. African potential, though great, was late in being mobilized.[17]

The epistemological ethnocentrism of this passage can be seen, for instance, in its conflation of "education" with "formal schooling" to the obvious detriment of traditional education in Africa, which has been informal in nature and closely tied to the social life of the community.[18] By assuming, as Phillips did, that "education" and "schooling" are synonymous constructs, one dramatically distorts the reality of the African experience. The passage also displays elements of cultural ethnocentrism, especially in its presentation of colonialism and imperialism (whether Islamic or Western) as essentially progressive in nature, whereas indigenous practices, ideals, and so on are seen as "underdeveloped" and "primitive"—spoken of only in terms of "potential," suggesting the need for "development."

In short, as one considers both cultural and epistemological ethnocentrism in the study of the history of educational thought and practice, there is good reason to believe that perhaps it is time to begin to challenge the dominant paradigm in the field. This might be done in roughly the same way that an increasing number of educational researchers have challenged the traditional, essentially positivistic, paradigm in educational research, seeking to replace it with or, at the very least, supplement it with a naturalistic, interpretivist qualitative paradigm.[19] In the case of the history and philosophy of education, the paradigmatic challenge must rest in large part on the reality of diversity, and the lack of any "universal" tradition—a theme discussed by Paul Ricoeur, in his book *History and Truth*: "When we discover that there are several cultures instead of just one and consequently at the time when we acknowledge the end of a sort of cultural monopoly, be it illusory or real, we are threatened with destruction by our own discovery. Suddenly it becomes possible that there are just *others*, that we ourselves are an 'other' among others."[20]

The recognition that one's own tradition is simply one among many (and not necessarily even *primus inter pares*,[21] at that) will for many be difficult to accept, and yet that is precisely what is required if the study of the history of educational thought and practice is to be more than a parochial artifact. Furthermore, in order to better understand the many educational traditions that exist and have existed in the world, it will be necessary to expand substantially the methodological tools at the disposal of scholars, using not only the standard methods of historical and philosophical scholarship, but increasingly, those of such disciplines as anthropology, cultural studies, linguistics, sociology, comparative literature, archeology, and others. Our scholarship, in short, must become far more interdisciplinary in both theory and practice than has been true in the past.

THE ROLE OF CONSTRUCTIVIST EPISTEMOLOGY
IN THE STUDY OF INDIGENOUS EDUCATIONAL TRADITIONS

As our discussion of ethnocentrism in general, and of epistemological ethnocentrism in particular, makes clear, a critical component of the study of non-Western educational traditions must necessarily be that of epistemology, especially with respect to our view of the *nature of knowledge*. In this book, two important assumptions are made about knowledge: First, knowledge is, to some degree, relative, in that it is both reasonable and indeed appropriate for us to talk about "multiple perspectives" on reality.[22] Thus, in order to make sense of the events and debates of the American Civil Rights Movement, for instance, one would need to understand the perspectives of the various actors in that movement: civil rights workers (both black and white), hard-core segregationists, politicians, and everyday black and white people living in different parts of the United States. It is important to note that although we need to recognize all of these perspectives (and indeed many others as well), that does not mean that we presuppose that all perspectives should be treated as equally valid. To grant the *legitimacy* of an individual's or a group's perspective is by no means the same as granting its *accuracy*.[23] In short, what we do when we accept the idea of "multiple perspectives" is to admit that a single event or set of events can be understood in very different ways by different groups and individuals—and that it is important to take into account as many of these different perspectives as possible in any serious examination of the event or events.

Second, an assumption is made here that knowledge is *constructed* by each individual.[24] In other words, "knowledge" is not something that is "out there" that we need to grasp or obtain; rather, it is something that we ourselves build based on our own background, experiences, prior understandings, and the data before us. This means that each of us will construct our own knowledge in what is inevitably a unique manner, and each of us will, therefore, have idiosyncratically derived understandings of reality (and, hence, we see the need for the recognition of "multiple perspectives"). It is important to stress here that constructivist epistemology is more than simply an alternative to other approaches to epistemology; rather, it entails a rejection of some of the core assumptions that have been shared by Western epistemology for some two and a half millennia.[25] As von Glasersfeld argued, "The crucial fact [in understanding constructivism is] that the constructivist theory of knowing breaks with the epistemological tradition in philosophy,"[26] which is why it has been labeled not merely postmodernist, but *postepistemological* by some writers.[27]

Up to this point, we have discussed constructivism as a single entity; in reality, it has become fairly commonplace in discussions of constructivism to distinguish between what are often taken to be two fundamentally distinct, competing *types* of constructivism.[28] The first type of constructivism, radical constructivism, is fundamentally an epistemological construct that has been most clearly and forcefully advocated in the work of Ernst von Glasersfeld.[29] Radical constructivism has its philosophical roots in Piaget's genetic epistemology,[30] and is essentially a cognitive view of learning in which "students actively construct their ways of knowing as they strive to be effective by restoring coherence to the worlds of their personal experience."[31] Radical constructivism is premised on the belief that an individual's knowledge can never be a "true" representation of reality (i.e., in an observer-independent sense), but is rather a construction of the world that the individual experiences. In other words, knowledge is not something that is passively received by the learner; it is, quite the contrary, the result of active mental work on the part of the learner. Thus, from a radical constructivist perspective, knowledge is not something that can merely be conveyed from teacher to student and any pedagogical approach that presumes otherwise must be rejected.

The alternative to radical constructivism is social constructivism, which has the work of Lev Vygotsky as its primary theoretical foundation.[32] Social constructivism, while accepting the notion that individuals do indeed construct their own knowledge, argues that the process of knowledge construction inevitably takes place in a sociocultural context, and therefore knowledge is in fact *socially* constructed. As Driver and her colleagues argued with respect to science education, "It is important . . . to appreciate that scientific knowledge is both symbolic in nature and also socially negotiated. . . . The objects of science are not phenomena of nature but constructs that are advanced by the scientific community to interpret nature."[33]

The tension between radical and social constructivism, between the personal and the social construction of knowledge, is to a significant extent more apparent than real, and in any event, is certainly amenable to resolution on a practical level, criticisms to the contrary notwithstanding.[34] As Paul Cobb asserted, "The sociocultural and cognitive constructivist perspectives each constitute the background for the other,"[35] and von Glasersfeld recognized that "we must generate an explanation of how 'others' and the 'society' in which we find ourselves living can be conceptually constructed on the basis of our subjective experiences."[36] Ultimately, even D. C. Phillips, a leading critic of the philosophical foundations of radical constructivism,[37] agreed:

> It is worth stressing that these philosophical issues do not have to be settled before the business of education can proceed. I suspect that von Glasersfeld and I

are very close in the kinds of educational attitudes and practices that we endorse. If you are about to undergo brain surgery, you do not have to wait until surgeons reach agreement about the thorny philosophical issues surrounding the body–mind problem. Similarly, a student can manipulate geological samples without having to settle upon a defensible philosophical account about the nature of the existence of these samples.[38]

Perhaps the most reasonable way to articulate the common, shared elements of radical and social constructivism is to talk about learning as "socially mitigated but personally constructed," a formulation that at the very least moves us away from a strong bifurcation of radical and social constructivism. Finally, it is important to keep in mind that not only is reality a social and individual construction in a certain sense, but further, that any academic discipline is itself the result of both personal and social construction.[39] As Gunnarsson argued:

> Scientific language and discourse emerge in a cooperative and competitive struggle among scientists to create the knowledge base of their field, to establish themselves in relation to other scientists and to other professional groups, and to gain influence and control over political and socioeconomic means. In every strand of human communication, language and discourse play a role in the formation of a social and societal reality and identity. This is also true both of the different professional and vocational cultures within working and public life and of the formation of different academic cultures.[40]

THE CONCEPT OF "TRADITION" AND ITS LIMITS

This book is about non-Western educational traditions, and throughout "tradition" is discussed in a number of different ways. Patricia Weibust compellingly argued that the concept of "tradition" is a far more complex one than is generally recognized. She suggested that "tradition" can come in three very different, and in fact logically distinct, forms: the historical tradition (i.e., what really took place historically), the defined tradition (i.e., what members of the culture believe to have taken place historically), and the contemporary tradition (i.e., the way in which the tradition is manifested in people's lives today), and furthermore, that "tradition" is best understood not in static terms, but rather as an ongoing process.[41] This distinction is a powerful and useful one as a heuristic device and analytic tool. However, in practice the three kinds of tradition are often far from distinct, and it is very difficult indeed to distinguish among them in many of the instances that we examine. Our task becomes even more complex in this regard when one considers that some of the traditions that we study here are living ones, whereas others continue to exist in very truncated forms, if at all. Thus, although we are concerned primarily with the historical tradition in each of the cases we examine, the defined tradition may well function as a limitation to our understanding, and in some cases, confusion may arise between the historical, defined, and contemporary traditions. Finally, as we talk about different traditions, it is important that we keep in mind that traditions are in fact processes that continually change, develop, and evolve and that, at best, we are looking at a snapshot of a tradition at a particular point in time.

THE WESTERN–NON-WESTERN DICHOTOMY

The title and organization of this book would appear to create a dichotomy between Western and non-Western traditions and practices. It is important that we note that such a dichotomy, although heuristically useful, is in fact misleading. As Swartz noted, "The categories 'Western' and 'Non-Western' are our creations, and reflect neither the diversity of beliefs (often mutually contradictory) that people hold, nor the commonalities that exist across apparently very different groups of people."[42] The problem is really one of oversimplification: Although there may be certain similarities from one non-Western culture to another, there are also bound to be significant and relevant differences, just as there are significant and relevant differences among different Western traditions. Furthermore, individuals often tolerate (and even thrive on) mutually contradictory beliefs—thus, people in Western traditions may well hold stereotypic non-Western beliefs, and vice versa. Finally, the distinction itself is potentially problematic ideologically, in that the terms "Western" and "non-Western" may (and often do) reflect biased and loaded assumptions. In other words, even the labels that we are using may lead us to errors akin to those identified by Said with respect to "Orientalism."

If the labels "Western" and "non-Western" are such a problem, then why use them? The answer to this very reasonable question is actually quite simple: The biases inherent in the terms are in fact a significant and telling component of the phenomenon that we are concerned with studying. The assumptions and stereotypes that need to be challenged are already present, and if our language reflects them, then it may be useful to recognize the biases that are inherent in the language that we use. Thus, what begins as a false dichotomy can emerge as an effective way of challenging and reforming racist and ethnocentric assumptions and biases, both conceptually and linguistically.

LEARNING FROM ORAL TRADITIONS

An important element in the process of expanding our perspectives on the history of educational thought and practice is learning more about the many ways in which different societies pass on their traditions, histories, and so on.

Although many of the societies that we will examine in this book do have written traditions, similar to those found in the Western tradition, others have relied primarily or exclusively on oral traditions. Written traditions have many advantages, but so do oral ones—advantages that our own society, for the most part, lost long ago. In his landmark work, *Oral Tradition as History*, Jan Vansina argued:

> The marvel of oral tradition, some will say its curse, is this: messages from the past exist, are real, and yet are not continuously accessible to the senses. Oral traditions make an appearance only when they are told. For fleeting moments they can be heard, but most of the time they dwell only in the minds of people. The utterance is transitory, but the memories are not. No one in oral societies doubts that memories can be faithful repositories which contain the sum total of past human experience and explain the how and why of present day conditions. *Tete are ne nne:* "Ancient things are today" or "History repeats itself".
> . . . How it is possible for a mind to remember and out of nothing to spin complex ideas, messages, and instructions for living, which manifest continuity over time, is one of the greatest wonders one can study, comparable only to human intelligence and thought itself. Because the wonder is so great, it is also very complex. Oral tradition should be central to students of culture, of ideology, of society, of psychology, of art, and, finally, of history.[43]

One might well add, of students of education, because education plays a key role both in the perpetuation of any oral tradition (as it does in the perpetuation of any written tradition) and in helping to determine the content of that tradition.[44]

It is important to understand that oral and written traditions are *different*, and each is useful and valuable in its own right. Neither is intrinsically superior to the other in all ways; each has its own strengths and each has its own limitations.[45] It is also important for us to bear in mind that much of the Western tradition has its origins in oral traditions—the epic poetry of Homer,[46] Anglo-Saxon heroic poetry,[47] the Irish epics,[48] even the synoptic Gospels,[49] all have their origins in oral, rather than written, traditions.[50]

Finally, the fact that we attempt to discuss oral traditions in a written text is itself something of a paradox. As Karl Kroeber commented about the study of American Indian tales, "One must ask if any *written* text can accurately produce an *oral* recitation."[51] The problem is that oral literature is, by its very nature, dependent on *performance*. As Ruth Finnegan explained in her discussion of oral literature in Africa:

> Oral literature is by definition dependent on a performer who formulates it in words on a specific occasion—there is no other way in which it can be realized as a literary product . . . without its oral realization and direct rendition by

singer or speaker, an unwritten literary piece cannot easily be said to have any continued or independent existence at all. In this respect the parallel is less to written literature than to music and dance; for these too are art forms which in the last analysis are actualized in and through their performance and, furthermore, in a sense depend on repeated performances for their continued existence.[52]

Thus, when we discuss oral traditions in a book like this one, we are at best dealing with a mere shadow of the true reality of the oral text (somewhat analogous to Plato's allegory of the cave). The risks of such an undertaking are made clear in the following story, an example of dissident humor in the former Soviet Union:

> Standing on Lenin's tomb in Red Square, Stalin was acknowledging the acclamation of the masses. Suddenly he raised his hands to silence the crowd.
> "Comrades," he cried. "A most historic event! A telegram of congratulations from Leon Trotsky!"
> The crowd could hardly believe its ears. It waited in hushed anticipation.
> "Joseph Stalin," read Stalin. "The Kremlin. Moscow. You were right and I was wrong. You are the true heir of Lenin. I must apologize. Trotsky."
> A roar erupted from the crowd.
> But in the front row a little Jewish tailor gestured frantically to Stalin. "Psst!" he cried. "Comrade Stalin."
> Stalin leaned over to hear what he had to say.
> "Such a message! But you read it without the right *feeling*."
> Stalin once again raised his hands to the still excited crowd. "Comrades!" he announced. "Here is a simple worker, a Communist, who says I did not read Trotsky's message with the right *feeling*. I ask that worker to come up on the podium himself to read Trotsky's telegram."
> The tailor jumped up on the podium and took the telegram into his hands. He read: "Joseph Stalin. The Kremlin. Moscow."
> Then he cleared his throat and sang out: "You were *right* and I was *wrong*? *You* are the true heir of Lenin? *I* must *apologize*?"[53]

Needless to say, the tailor's rendition of the telegram conveyed a radically different meaning to the text—a meaning disguised by the written text, and best made clear in an oral rendition. The use of italics in the text may help us to reproduce the oral event, but it requires a performance to really make sense. It is just such risks that we must be sensitive to when we examine any oral tradition or written rendering of an oral "text." In addition, it is essential that we keep in mind "that all texts are in some sense intertextual, all discourses interdiscursive, requiring a Foucaultian archaeology to uncover and explicate how it is that they are multiply formed."[54]

E.T., THE LOST CONTINENT OF ATLANTIS, AND CANNIBALISM:
SOME REFLECTIONS ON CREDIBILITY AND "OTHERNESS"

One of the more interesting aspects of studying non-Western cultures is the variety of ways in which the impressive accomplishments of such cultures and societies have often been either rejected altogether, diminished in importance, or attributed to other civilizations and sources. For example, the ruins and ancient mine shafts of Great Zimbabwe in southern Africa were claimed to have been the creation of some mysterious civilization in the distant past, perhaps related to the Carthaginians or some other ancient people, perhaps even the product of some extraterrestrial culture—*anyone*, in short, other than the ancestors of the indigenous Africans living in the area today.[55] It was simply inconceivable to many people that these incredible remnants of a once-great civilization could have been produced by people who were, in the words of the South African historian George McCall Theal, "fickle barbarians, prone to robbery and unscrupulous in shedding blood."[56] Such views were common in the late 19th and early 20th centuries, not just about Africa but also about the indigenous peoples of Asia and the Americas,[57] and might perhaps be dismissed as mere historical oddities, except that many of the elements of these views (and much of the work of the historians who proposed and supported them) has continued to be circulated, studied, and taught despite the overwhelming rejection of such ideas by academic historians and archeologists.[58]

The same tendency also appears, often overlapping "New Age" rhetoric and practice, in efforts to explain Mesoamerican and other non-Western civilizations by proposing ties to Atlantis, ancient Egypt, Stonehenge, and to various extraterrestrial sources. Such efforts date back at least to the 19th century,[59] but have become increasingly popular in the years following the initial publication of Erich von Däniken's *Chariots of the Gods*.[60] A quick trip to my local bookstore offered a selection of recent examples of such works, including not only a number of follow-up works by von Däniken,[61] but also Maurice Cotterell's *The Supergods: They Came on a Mission to Save Mankind*,[62] about the Maya; David Furlong's *The Keys to the Temple*,[63] which ties the pyramids in Egypt to Mayan temples and to Marlborough Downs; and José Argüelles' *The Mayan Factor: Path Beyond Technology*,[64] which purports to use Mayan sources to explain harmonic convergence (among other things). Although these works, and those like them, tend to include ties to Atlantis, ancient Egypt, the Mayas, and the Incas—and, of course, extraterrestrial contacts—they also share another common theme: They are all based, at least implicitly, on the idea that various aspects of human civilizations (almost always non-Western civilizations, interestingly enough) cannot be explained by "normal" human history, sociocultural development, and so on. Instead, they all posit some sort of *deus ex machina* who, it is asserted, must have been responsible for the emergence of the great non-Western civilizations. The problem with such explanations, apart from the fact that they are simply pseudoscience in the garb of scholarship[65]—no small problem in its own right, to be sure—is that they also serve to support and reinforce beliefs and ideologies that are demonstrably racist in both origin and nature. In short, to assume or presuppose that the indigenous peoples of Mesoamerica, for instance, needed help from escaping Atlanteans, planet-hopping extraterrestrials, or whomever, would inevitably seem to suggest that they were not themselves capable of creating the civilizations whose ruins and remnants remain so impressive even today. This, it seems to me, does these people, the civilizations they created, their descendants, and indeed, all of us as human beings, a serious injustice. It is far better, I would suggest, and certainly more credible in any meaningful sense of the term, to suppose that human beings in many different times and places have been able to create great civilizations, as well as architectural, artistic, musical, and literary feats.[66]

If there sometimes seems to be a reluctance to believe that various indigenous peoples, or their ancestors, could have been the creators of great civilizations, then there is no similar reticence in believing that such people might be capable of horrible atrocities of various sorts. To be sure, human beings in many times and places have behaved in awful ways and done things that certainly deserve condemnation (child sacrifice and abandonment, both not uncommon in the ancient world,[67] come to mind here, as does the Holocaust). However, it may be the case that we have been far too quick, and perhaps too gullible, in believing some of the more extreme claims about other peoples and societies. One example here is that of cannibalism. We know beyond any reasonable doubt that cannibalism has taken place in certain extreme situations; the question is whether there have been cultures in which ritualized cannibalism has been relatively commonplace. As Martin Gardner argued:

> No one denies that during life-and-death emergencies, such as starving after a shipwreck or airplane crash, or during times of extreme famine, individuals may choose to eat human corpses rather than die. No one denies that there have been occasions among primitive peoples when, after a military victory, the body of a once-feared enemy leader was ritually devoured, either out of revenge or out of a belief that the enemy's powers would be acquired by the eaters. . . . The big question is this: Has cannibalism ever been a *common* custom?[68]

Although some anthropologists continue to maintain that ritual cannibalism is indeed found among some groups,[69] other scholars have begun to reject such claims and to argue that they are in fact the result of "pure folklore, fabricated by the desire of one culture to feel superior to another."[70] Although this debate is still an active and unresolved one in anthropology, it nevertheless does provide us with a strong reason for being careful about believing claims of extreme practices on the part of other cultures, peoples, and societies.

COMMONALITY AND DIVERSITY IN INDIGENOUS TRADITIONS

The role of oral traditions is a common theme in many of the different societies examined in this book, and the commonality of this theme raises an important question. If different non-Western societies share many features, such as the role of an oral tradition, a communal approach to the education of children, a reliance on nonformal kinds of educational experiences, and so on, then to what extent are they really different traditions? Is it, in short, really necessary for us to study many different non-Western traditions, or would it not be sufficient for us to simply study one tradition in detail?

This is an important question, and one that does not have a simple answer. The different educational traditions that we explore in this book do indeed share many common features, but they also differ in significant ways. One way to think about this that may prove useful is to draw an analogy to a concept used in contemporary linguistics. Linguists distinguish among different kinds of linguistic "universals" (i.e., properties and characteristics common to all languages). The most important distinction made in linguistics in this regard is that between what are called "absolute universals," which "are properties all languages share," and "relative universals," which "are general tendencies in language."[71] In other words, there can be no exceptions to absolute universals, but there may be exceptions to relative universals. Furthermore, the way in which such universals are manifested in particular languages may differ dramatically. The study of non-Western educational traditions is in fact fairly similar to the study of the diverse languages used by human beings around the world. Although there are likely to be certain absolute universals (e.g., the goal of helping the child to become a "good person," albeit perhaps defined in different ways), and there are also likely to be relative universals (e.g., a concern with treating other people with respect), the ways in which such universals are in fact manifested in any particular culture—as well as the means by which the society seeks to accomplish these goals—will be very distinctive.

The purpose of studying non-Western educational traditions is both to help us understand the common principles that underlie all educational undertakings and to understand the different means that human beings have devised to accomplish these principles. Such understanding is of course valuable in its own right, but it may also have profound effects on the way in which we view diversity and difference writ large, and as it impacts our own personal and professional lives. An understanding of Aztec education, for instance, is unlikely to have an immediate and direct use for the classroom teacher—there is no likelihood whatsoever that a teacher will have to deal with a child whose parents wish him to be prepared to enter a *calmécac*. Nevertheless, an awareness of how the Aztecs educated their children, both in terms of the goals that guided their educational system and the means they used to achieve these goals, may well help each of us as educators to develop a more critical and sensitive understanding of the educational goals and methods used in our own society.

POSITIONALITY AND *NON-WESTERN EDUCATIONAL TRADITIONS*

In contrast to the pluralism and relativism inherent in constructivist views of knowledge discussed earlier in this chapter, traditional positivistic research has presupposed a very different view of both reality and of the nature of knowledge. In essence, positivism presupposes that reality is singular and objective. In addition, the purpose of scientific investigation is to provide data that allow us to come to understand and, at least in a weak sense, to know aspects of this reality. Thus, the role of researchers and that of the object of their research must be kept independent. In other words, the "knower" and the "known" are logically and practically distinct.[72] This means that in the context of any particular investigation, the researcher's background and presence should (at least ideally) be irrelevant in that it should have no effect whatsoever on the outcomes of the investigation. If our approach to knowledge generation assumes that research must be replicable, then it follows that it should make no difference who does the replicating.

This view of the investigator as a neutral observer has come under increasing fire in recent years from a number of different perspectives. Many researchers now believe that their background knowledge and experience influence not only their choice of research topic, but also their understanding of the topic. If knowledge is indeed socially constructed, then this makes a great deal of sense because the building blocks of knowledge must be individually distinct. Thus, in much post-positivistic research, we find that scholars and researchers will, as a sort of "truth in advertising," acquaint the reader with information about the researcher's own background. This process is referred to as identifying the author's "position," and includes relevant information about such factors as gender, language, race and ethnicity, nationality, academic training, ideology, and so on. This is not, of course, to justify bias in our writing; rather, it is to make any biases that appear all that much clearer to the reader. By explicating our "position" up front, we provide the reader with information that will be helpful in understanding and critiquing our own work. In short, the view of the researcher as a neutral observer is rejected as myth—and potentially dangerous myth, at that.

The recognition of one's "positionality," although important and valuable, does not determine the outcomes and findings of one's research. As Michael Apple, citing the work of Edward Said, argued, "Authors are not mechanically determined by ideology, or class, or history. However, authors are very much *in* the history of their societies, 'shaping and shaped by that history and their social experience.' "[73] Apple continued, making clear the tension that inevitably emerges as we focus on positionality in scholarly research and writing:

> Do not misconstrue what I am saying here. As so much feminist and postcolonial work has documented, the personal often is the absent presence behind even the most eviscerated writing, and we do need to continue to explore ways of heightening the sense of the personal in our "stories" about education. But, at the same time, it is equally crucial that we interrogate our own "hidden" motives here. Is the insistence on the personal, an insistence that underpins much of our turn to literary and autobiographical forms, partly a class discourse as well? The "personal may be political," but does the political end at the personal? Furthermore, why should we assume that the personal is any less difficult to understand than the "external" world? I cannot answer these questions for all situations, but I think that these questions must be asked by all of us who are committed to the multiple projects involved in struggling for a more emancipatory education.[74]

I believe that Apple is absolutely correct here, and the rhetoric and discourse of positionality can serve to mask as well as to unmask, to enlighten as well as to befog. This does not, however, mean that identifying one's position and background is not a good idea; rather, it simply reminds us that the reader must continue to be critical. So, with that said, who am I and why am I writing this book about non-Western educational traditions?

My background is largely that of what remains the norm for mainstream U.S. academics: I am white, male, middle-aged, and middle class. I was born and raised in the United States and received my university education at U.S. institutions. Unlike many of my colleagues, however, I am multilingual, and have spent a good deal of my adult life living and working in both Africa and the Middle East. This book is a product of my own curiosity and desire to understand the ways in which human beings have conceived of education and have structured experiences to educate their children in various times and places. Academically, the work is informed by my training in history, philosophy, and linguistics, as well as by my practical experiences teaching and working with other teachers in a wide range of settings. It is written from what is, basically, a U.S. perspective, and is intended primarily for others from this perspective—although, of course, the insights and perspectives of those from other societies are especially valuable because they can provide critiques as well as support for what is written here. Finally, my views and observations are those of a parent, and reflect my deep belief that whereas we may well differ about what is best for our children, virtually all parents—now and in the past—are concerned with providing the best possible life preparation for their children.

CONCLUSIONS

In short, this book proposes that it is neither idealistic nor unrealistic to suggest that we can learn much from non-Western and indigenous educational traditions. As Ali Mazrui argued in the first of his BBC Reith Lectures with respect to Africa and its relations with the West, "I cannot help feeling that it is about time Africa sent missionaries to Europe and America, as well as teachers, engineers, doctors and ordinary workers. . . . It is indeed time that Africa counter-penetrated the western world."[75] Perhaps it is time not only for Africa, but for the non-Western world in general, to begin penetrating the study of the history of educational thought and practice. It is with this goal in mind that this book was written.

QUESTIONS FOR REFLECTION AND DISCUSSION

1. What are the implications of Edward Said's notion of "Orientalism" for what should be taught in the public schools in our society? For what classroom teachers should know?

2. This chapter asserts that "schooling" and "education" are by no means synonymous concepts. In our own society, how do these concepts differ? What are the implications of these differences for "public education" and "public schooling"?

3. When Paul Ricoeur wrote that when "we acknowledge the end of a sort of cultural monopoly . . . we are threatened with destruction by our own discovery," what did he mean? What are the implications of this claim for the curriculum in the public schools? For the curriculum in teacher education programs?

4. Although our own culture is predominantly a written rather than an oral culture, one could nevertheless make a strong case for one or more oral traditions coexisting and paralleling the written tradition. What would the elements of such oral traditions be in our own society? How are these traditions passed on from one generation to the next? Are there some oral traditions in our society that are not transgenerational? What are the implications of your answers for the classroom teacher?

5. The concept of "multiple perspectives" is a very powerful one that can help us make sense of many different social, political, and cultural conflicts. Identify three current controversies in the news, and explain how the concept of "multiple perspectives" can assist us in understanding what is taking place in each of these controversies.

6. What are the implications of constructivist epistemology, as discussed in this chapter, for our understanding of history? What are its implications for teaching and learning in the classroom context? In informal educational settings? How does constructivist epistemology differ from that proposed by Plato?

7. In order to test the author's claim that even the terms "Western" and "non-Western" may contain hidden biases, construct a list of adjectives that seem to you to intuitively fit in each of these two categories. What conclusions can you draw from this experience?

8. What does it mean when we say that, "To grant the *legitimacy* of an individual's or a group's perspective is by no means the same as granting its *accuracy*"? Can you provide examples of legitimate perspectives that may not be accurate? How is this possible?

9. In a recent book, critical of "pseudoscientific" claims about history and archeology, Francis Harrold and Raymond Eve wrote that many popular books, articles, movies, and so on, about historical issues (and especially about human origins and past civilizations) "make claims about the past which are simply wrong—sometimes spectacularly so."[76] Can such a claim be reconciled to the notion of "multiple perspectives" and constructivist epistemology, and if so, how?

10. Do you think that Ali Mazrui was serious when he called for Africa to send missionaries to Europe and America? If you think he was serious, what kinds of messages do you think that such missionaries might carry? If you think that he was speaking metaphorically, what are the implications of the metaphor?

RECOMMENDED FURTHER READINGS

The late Edward Said's book *Orientalism* (New York: Vintage, 1978) provides a powerful and challenging perspective on how cultural expectations and biases can influence and distort the way that we make sense of the "Other," as does his more recent *Culture and Imperialism* (New York: Vintage, 1993). Also quite useful in helping us to understand traditions different from our own is Jan Vansina's *Oral Tradition as History* (Madison: University of Wisconsin Press, 1985). With respect to education in particular, two recent books provide wonderful introductions: Ladislaus Semali and Joe Kincheloe (eds.), *What Is Indigenous Knowledge? Voices from the Academy* (New York: Falmer Press, 1999), and Maenette Kape'ahiokalani Padeken Ah Nee-Benham, with Joanne Cooper (eds.), *Indigenous Educational Models for Contemporary Practice: In Our Mother's Voice* (Mahwah, NJ: Lawrence Erlbaum Associates, 2000). A fascinating perspective on the concept of democracy as it has emerged in various non-Western societies is provided in Raul Manglapus' *Will of the People: Original Democracy in Non-Western Societies* (New York: Greenwood, 1987). Finally, although dealing with issues of mental health rather than education, *Culture and Mental Health: A Southern African View* (Cape Town: Oxford University Press, 1998), by Leslie Swartz, is an incredibly powerful example of the kind of critical response to Western biases in scholarship and practice that is being advocated here.

NOTES

1. Ladislaus Semali and Joe L. Kincheloe (eds.), *What Is Indigenous Knowledge? Voices from the Academy* (New York: Falmer Press, 1999).

2. Edward Said, *Orientalism* (New York: Vintage, 1978), 3. Also relevant and useful in this regard are Lisa Lowe, *Critical Terrains: French and British Orientalisms* (Ithaca, NY: Cornell University Press, 1991); Bryan Turner, *Orientalism, Postmodernism, and Globalism* (London: Routledge, 1994); John J. Clarke, *Oriental Enlightenment: The Encounter Between Asian and Western Thought* (London: Routledge, 1997); Robert Young, *White Mythology: Writing History and the West* (London: Routledge, 1990); Gyan Prakash, "Writing Post-Orientalist Histories of the Third World: Perspectives from Indian Historiography," *Comparative Studies in Society and History* 32 (1990): 383–408.

3. Okot p'Bitek, *African Religions in Western Scholarship* (Nairobi, Kenya: East African Literature Bureau, 1971), 22.

4. Adam Kuper, *The Invention of Primitive Society: Transformations of an Illusion* (London: Routledge, 1988). Also of interest in this regard is Henrika Kuklick, *The Savage Within: The Social History of British Anthropology, 1885–1945* (Cambridge, England: Cambridge University Press, 1991).

5. A. Babs Fafunwa, *A History of Education in Nigeria* (London: Allen & Unwin, 1974), 17. See also Alan Williamson, "Decolonizing Historiography of Colonial Education: Processes of Interaction in the Schooling of Torres Strait Islanders," *International Journal of Qualitative Studies in Education* 10, 4 (1997): 407–423.

6. Joshua Cohen and Ian Lague, "Editor's Preface," in Khaled Abou El Fadl, *The Place of Tolerance in Islam* (Boston: Beacon Press, 2002), vii.

7. Stephen Ball (ed.), *Foucault and Education: Disciplines and Knowledge* (London: Routledge, 1990), 2.

8. Mary Field Belenky, Blyth McVicker Clinchy, Nancy Rule Goldberger, and Jill Mattuck Tarule, *Women's Ways of Knowing: The Development of Self, Voice, and Mind* (New York: Basic Books, 1986).

9. Carol Gilligan, *In a Different Voice: Psychological Theory and Women's Development* (Cambridge, MA: Harvard University Press, 1982), 6.

10. See V. Mudimbe, *The Invention of Africa: Gnosis, Philosophy, and the Order of Knowledge* (London: Currey, 1988), 19.

11. See Thomas Kuhn, *The Structure of Scientific Revolutions*, 2nd enlarged ed. (Chicago: University of Chicago Press, 1970); Thomas Kuhn, *The Essential Tension: Selected Studies in Scientific Tradition and Change* (Chicago: University of Chicago Press, 1977).

12. Michael Patton, *Utilization-Focused Evaluations* (Beverly Hills, CA: Sage, 1978), 203.

13. Kuhn, *The Structure of Scientific Revolutions*, 46.

14. See Martin Bernal, *Black Athena: The Afroasiatic Roots of Classical Civilization, volume 1: The Fabrication of Ancient Greece, 1785–1985* (New Brunswick, NJ: Rutgers University Press, 1987); Martin Bernal, *Black Athena: The Afroasiatic Roots of Classical Civilization, volume 2: The Archeological and Documentary Evidence* (New Brunswick, NJ: Rutgers University Press, 1991). See chapter 3 for a detailed examination of the issues surrounding Afrocentrism and Afrocentric perspectives in contemporary American education.

15. Jane Roland Martin, "The Ideal of the Educated Person," in Daniel DeNicola (ed.), *Philosophy of Education: 1981* (Normal, IL: Philosophy of Education Society, 1982), 3–20.

16. See Jane Roland Martin, *Reclaiming a Conversation: The Ideal of the Educated Woman* (New Haven, CT: Yale University Press, 1985). An outstanding analysis and critique of Roland Martin's work is found in D. G. Mulcahy, *Knowledge, Gender, and Schooling: The Feminist Educational Thought of Jane Roland Martin* (Westport, CT: Bergin & Garvey, 2002).

17. H. M. Phillips, quoted in Niara Sudarkasa, "Sex Roles, Education and Development in Africa," *Anthropology and Education* 13, 3 (1982): 281.

18. Traditional African educational thought and practice is discussed in detail in chapter 3.

19. See Yvonna Lincoln and Egon Guba, *Naturalistic Inquiry* (Newbury Park, CA: Sage, 1985); Michael Patton, *Qualitative Evaluation and Research Methods*, 2nd ed. (Newbury Park, CA: Sage, 1990). An interesting example of a scholarly effort to challenge epistemological ethnocentrism is Robbie Davis-Floyd and Carolyn Sargent (eds.), *Childbirth and Authoritative Knowledge: Cross-Cultural Perspectives* (Berkeley: University of California Press, 1997).

20. Paul Ricoeur, *History and Truth* (Evanston, IL: Northwestern University Press, 1965), 278.

21. "First among equals"—the way in which the role of the Pope with respect to the other bishops of the church is traditionally discussed.

22. See Lincoln and Guba, *Naturalistic Inquiry*, 70–91; David Erlandson, Edward Harris, Barbara Skipper, and Steve Allen, *Doing Naturalistic Inquiry: A Guide to Methods* (Newbury Park, CA: Sage, 1993), 5–28. See also Jonathan Jansen (ed.), *Knowledge and Power in South Africa: Critical Perspectives Across the Disciplines* (Johannesburg: Skotaville, 1991), for a detailed examination of the role of epistemology and perspective in critical scholarship. The complexity of constructivism as an epistemol-

ogy is explored cogently and in detail in Ian Hacking, *The Social Construction of What?* (Cambridge, MA: Harvard University Press, 2001).

23. See Harvey Siegel, *Rationality Redeemed? Further Dialogues on an Educational Ideal* (New York: Routledge, 1997), 130–133. This point also leads to the issue of the trustworthiness of observations in general, and of naturalistic research in particular. See Lincoln and Guba, *Naturalistic Inquiry*, 289–331. A fascinating and powerful example of the phenomena being discussed here is provided in Marshall Sahlins' book, *How "Natives" Think: About Captain Cook, for Example* (Chicago: University of Chicago Press, 1995).

24. See Catherine Fosnot (ed.), *Constructivism: Theory, Perspectives, and Practice* (New York: Teachers College Press, 1996); Hacking, *The Social Construction of What?*; Yasmin Kefai and Mitchel Resnick (eds.), *Constructionism in Practice: Designing, Thinking, and Learning in a Digital World* (Mahwah, NJ: Lawrence Erlbaum Associates, 1996); Thomas Duffy and David Jonassen (eds.), *Constructivism and the Technology of Instruction* (Hillsdale, NJ: Lawrence Erlbaum Associates, 1992); Virginia Richardson (ed.), *Constructivist Teacher Education: Building a World of New Understandings* (London: Falmer Press, 1997); Ricardo Baquero, Alicia Camilloni, Mario Carretero, José Castorina, Alicia Lenzi, and Edith Litwin, *Debates contructivistas* (Buenos Aires: Aique, 1998); and Nel Noddings, *Philosophy of Education* (Boulder, CO: Westview, 1995), 115–119. Two recent works in the philosophy of mathematics are outstanding examples of the implications of constructivist epistemology for how we conceptualize various fields of study: see Stanislas Debaene, *The Number Sense: How the Mind Creates Mathematics* (New York: Oxford University Press, 1997); Reuben Hersh, *What Is Mathematics, Really?* (New York: Oxford University Press, 1997). For a powerful and critical theoretical examination of social constructivism, see Finn Collin, *Social Reality* (London: Routledge, 1997).

25. See Kenneth Gergen, *Towards Transformation in Social Knowledge* (New York: Springer-Verlag, 1982). Also of relevance here is Kenneth Gergen, "Social Construction and the Educational Process," in Leslie Steffe and Jerry Gale (eds.), *Constructivism in Education* (Hillsdale, NJ: Lawrence Erlbaum Associates, 1995), 17–39.

26. Ernst von Glasersfeld, "A Constructivist Approach to Teaching," in Leslie Steffe and Jerry Gale (eds.), *Constructivism in Education* (Hillsdale, NJ: Lawrence Erlbaum Associates, 1995), 6.

27. See Nel Noddings, "Constructivism in Mathematics Education," in Robert Davis, Carolyn Maher, and Nel Noddings (eds.), *Constructivist Views on the Teaching and Learning of Mathematics* (Reston, VA: National Council of Teachers of Mathematics, 1990), 7–18.

28. See Paul Cobb, "Where Is the Mind? Constructivist and Socioculturalist Perspectives on Mathematical Development," *Educational Researcher* 23 (1994): 13–20; Paul Cobb, "Where Is the Mind? A Coordination of Sociocultural and Cognitive Constructionist Perspectives," in Catherine Fosnot (ed.), *Constructivism: Theory, Perspectives, and Practice* (New York: Teachers College Press, 1996), 34–52; L. Magadla, "Constructivism: A Practitioner's Perspective," *South African Journal of Higher Education* 10 (1996): 83–88.

29. Among Ernst von Glasersfeld's works, the most helpful in this regard include "An Introduction to Radical Constructivism," in Paul Watzlawick (ed.), *The Invented Reality: How Do We Know What We Believe We Know?* (New York: Norton, 1984), 17–40; "Cognition, Construction of Knowledge, and Teaching," *Synthese* 80 (1989):

121–140; "Questions and Answers about Radical Constructivism," in Kenneth Tobin (ed.), *The Practice of Constructivism in Science Education* (Hillsdale, NJ: Lawrence Erlbaum Associates, 1993), 23–38; "A Constructivist Approach to Teaching"; *Radical Constructivism: A Way of Knowing* (London: Falmer Press, 1995); "Footnotes to 'The Many Faces of Constructivism,'" *Educational Researcher* 25 (1996): 19.

30. Jean Piaget, *L'epistémologie génétique*, 3rd ed. (Paris: Presses Universitaires de France, 1979); H. Sinclair, I. Berthoud, J. Gerard, and E. Venesiano, "Constructivisme et psycholinguistique génétique," *Archives de Psychologie* 53 (1985): 37–60.

31. Cobb, "Where Is the Mind? A Coordination of Sociocultural and Cognitive Constructionist Perspectives," 34.

32. Lev Vygotsky, *Mind in Society: The Development of Higher Psychological Processes* (Cambridge, MA: Harvard University Press, 1978); Lev Vygotsky, *Thought and Language* (Cambridge, MA: MIT Press, 1986). See also Luis Moll (ed.), *Vygotsky and Education: Instructional Implications and Applications of Sociocultural Psychology* (Cambridge, England: Cambridge University Press, 1990); Ricardo Baquero, *Vigotsky y el aprendizaje escolar* (Buenos Aires: Aique, 1997).

33. Rosalind Driver, Hilary Asoko, John Leach, Eduardo Mortimer, and Philip Scott, "Constructing Scientific Knowledge in the Classroom," *Educational Researcher* 23 (1994): 5.

34. See, e.g., William Cobern, "Contextual Constructivism: The Impact of Culture on the Learning and Teaching of Science," in Kenneth Tobin (ed.), *The Practice of Constructivism in Science Education* (Hillsdale, NJ: Lawrence Erlbaum Associates, 1993), 51–69; Jere Confrey, "How Compatible Are Radical Constructivism, Sociocultural Approaches, and Social Constructivism?" in Leslie Steffe and Jerry Gale (eds.), *Constructivism in Education* (Hillsdale, NJ: Lawrence Erlbaum Associates, 1995), 185–225; R. E. Young, "The Epistemic Discourse of Teachers: An Ethnographic Study," *Anthropology and Education Quarterly* 12, 2 (1981): 122–144.

35. Cobb, "Where Is the Mind? A Coordination of Sociocultural and Cognitive Constructionist Perspectives," 48.

36. von Glasersfeld, "A Constructivist Approach to Teaching," 12.

37. See Denis C. Phillips, "The Good, the Bad, and the Ugly: The Many Faces of Constructivism," *Educational Researcher* 24 (1995): 5–12.

38. Denis C. Phillips, "Response to Ernst von Glasersfeld," *Educational Researcher* 25 (1996): 20.

39. See Britt-Louise Gunnarsson, Per Linell, and Bengt Nordberg (eds.), *The Construction of Professional Discourse* (London: Longman, 1997).

40. Britt-Louise Gunnarsson, "On the Sociohistorical Construction of Scientific Discourse," in Britt-Louise Gunnarsson, Per Linell, and Bengt Nordberg (eds.), *The Construction of Professional Discourse* (London: Longman, 1997), 99. For extensions of the implications of this argument, see Eva Krugly-Smolska, "An Examination of Some Difficulties in Integrating Western Science into Societies with an Indigenous Scientific Tradition," *Interchange* 25, 4 (1994): 325–334; Janice Raymond, "Medicine as Patriarchal Religion," *Journal of Medicine and Philosophy* 7 (1982): 197–216.

41. See Patricia Weibust, "Tradition as Process: Creating Contemporary Tradition in a Rural Norwegian School and Community," *International Journal of Qualitative Studies in Education* 2, 2 (1989): 107–122.

42. Leslie Swartz, *Culture and Mental Health: A Southern African View* (Cape Town: Oxford University Press, 1998), 92.

43. Jan Vansina, *Oral Tradition as History*, rev. ed. (Madison: University of Wisconsin Press, 1985), xi.

44. See Louis-Jean Calvert, *La tradition orale* (Paris: Presses Universitaires de France, 1984), 9–25. See also David Olson, *El mundo sobre el papel: El Impacto de la Escritura y la Lectura en la Estructura del Conocimiento* (Barcelona: Editorial Gedisa, 1998); David Olson and Nancy Torrance (eds.), *Cultura escrita y oralidad* (Barcelona: Editorial Gedisa, 1998); Eldred Jones, Eustace Palmer, and Marjorie Jones (eds.), *Orature in African Literature Today* (London: James Currey, 1992); Russell Kaschula (ed.), *Foundations in Southern African Oral Literature* (Johannesburg: Witwatersrand University Press, 1993); Graham Furniss and Liz Gunner (eds.), *Power, Marginality and African Oral Literature* (Cambridge, England: Cambridge University Press, 1995); Gary Gossen, *Chamulas in the World of the Sun: Time and Space in a Maya Oral Tradition* (Prospect Heights, IL: Waveland, 1974); Isidore Okpewho, *African Oral Literature: Backgrounds, Character, and Continuity* (Bloomington, IN: Indiana University Press, 1992).

45. See Russell H. Kaschula (ed.), *African Oral Literature: Functions in Contemporary Contexts* (Cape Town: New Africa Books, 2001). The relation between written and oral texts and traditions is also of considerable interest in this regard. See Jack Goody, *The Interface Between the Written and the Oral* (Cambridge, England: Cambridge University Press, 1987); Anita Rampal, "A Possible 'Orality' for Science?" *Interchange* 23, 3 (1992): 227–244.

46. See Geoffrey Horrocks, *Greek: A History of the Language and Its Speakers* (London: Longman, 1997), 17–23; Maurice Balme and Gilbert Lawall, *Athenaze: An Introduction to Ancient Greek, Book I* (New York: Oxford University Press, 1990), 74–75.

47. See James Hulbert, *Bright's Anglo-Saxon Reader* (New York: Henry Holt, 1935), cvi–cxv. Also relevant here are Robert Diamond, *Old English: Grammar and Reader* (Detroit, MI: Wayne State University Press, 1970); Richard Hamer, *A Choice of Anglo-Saxon Verse* (London: Faber & Faber, 1970); Bruce Mitchell, *An Invitation to Old English and Anglo-Saxon England* (Oxford, England: Blackwell, 1995); Bruce Mitchell and Fred Robinson, *A Guide to Old English*, 5th ed. (Oxford, England: Blackwell, 1992).

48. Colin Graham, *Ideologies of Epic: Nation, Empire, and Victorian Epic Poetry* (Manchester, England: Manchester University Press, 1998).

49. See Vansina, *Oral Tradition as History*, 159–160.

50. See Colin Renfrew, *Archeology and Language: The Puzzle of Indo-European Origins* (Cambridge, England: Cambridge University Press, 1987), 21–23; in contrast, see Mzo Sirayi, "Oral African Drama in South Africa: The Xhosa Indigenous Drama Forms," *South African Theatre Journal* 10, 1 (1996): 49–61. For an outstanding discussion of the role of rhetoric and oratory in a contemporary setting, see Philippe-Joseph Salazar, *An African Athens: Rhetoric and the Shaping of Democracy in South Africa* (Mahwah, NJ: Lawrence Erlbaum Associates, 2002).

51. Karl Kroeber, "The Art of Traditional American Indian Narration," in Karl Kroeber (ed.), *Traditional Literatures of the American Indian: Texts and Interpretations* (Lincoln: University of Nebraska Press, 1981), 2.

52. Ruth Finnegan, *Oral Literature in Africa* (Nairobi, Kenya: Oxford University Press, 1970), 2. See also Ruth Finnegan, "Reflecting Back on *Oral Literature in Africa*: Some Reconsiderations after 21 Years," *South African Journal of African Languages* 12, 2 (1992): 39–47.

53. Joseph Telushkin, *Jewish Humor* (New York: Morrow, 1992), 121–122.

54. Christopher Candlin, "General Editor's Preface," in Britt-Louise Gunnarsson, Per Linell, and Bengt Nordberg (eds.), *The Construction of Professional Discourse* (London: Longman, 1997), ix.

55. This was the view promulgated, e.g., in Richard Hall's *Ancient Ruins of Rhodesia: Monomotapae Imperium*, 2nd ed. rev. and enlarged (New York: Negro Universities Press, 1969) (original publication 1904). See Christopher Saunders, *The Making of the South African Past: Major Historians on Race and Class* (Cape Town: David Philip, 1988), 36–37; Stephen Howe, *Afrocentrism: Mythical Pasts and Imagined Homes* (London: Verso, 1998), 117–119; Erik Hornung, *The Secret Lore of Egypt: Its Impact on the West* (Ithaca: Cornell University Press, 2001), 173–188.

56. Quoted in Ken Smith, *The Changing Past: Trends in South African Historical Writing* (Johannesburg: Southern, 1988), 37.

57. In the North American case, it was a commonplace belief in the 19th century that Native Americans were descended from the lost tribes of Israel. One variation of this view is represented, e.g., in the *Book of Mormon* (see Jan Shipps, *Mormonism: The Story of a New Religious Tradition* [Urbana: University of Illinois Press, 1985], 25–39). Others, most notably DeWitt Clinton, during the same period argued that the Indians had more likely come from Asia, perhaps with a possible link to the ancient Scythians, or had ties to the seafaring Carthaginians and Phoenicians. See Evan Cornog, "American Antiquity: How DeWitt Clinton Invented Our Past," *The American Scholar* 67 (1998): 53–61.

58. Theal's work, e.g., was widely cited and utilized by conservative historians well into the 1970s and 1980s, and its influence is clearly present in such works as C. F. J. Muller's *Five Hundred Years: A History of South Africa*, 5th ed. (Pretoria: Academica, 1986); and F. A. van Jaarsveld's *From Van Riebeeck to Vorster, 1652–1974* (Pretoria: Perskor, 1975). See also Saunders, *The Making of the South African Past*; Smith, *The Changing Past*. A significant exception and alternative to such works, albeit in a broader context, worth mentioning here is Raul Manglapus' book, *Will of the People: Original Democracy in Non-Western Societies* (New York: Greenwood, 1987).

59. See, e.g., Ignatius Donnelly's *Atlantis: The Antediluvian World* (New York: Dover, 1976), which was originally published in 1882.

60. Erich von Däniken, *Chariots of the Gods: Unsolved Mysteries of the Past* (New York: Berkley, 1968).

61. Erich von Däniken, *The Return of the Gods* (Shaftesbury, Dorset: Element, 1995); Erich von Däniken, *The Eyes of the Sphinx* (New York: Berkley, 1996); and Erich von Däniken, *Arrival of the Gods* (Shaftesbury, Dorset: Element, 1997).

62. Maurice M. Cotterell, *The Supergods: They Came on a Mission to Save Mankind* (London: Thorsons, 1997).

63. David Furlong, *The Keys to the Temple* (London: Piatkus, 1997).

64. José Argüelles, *The Mayan Factor: Path Beyond Technology* (Sante Fe, NM: Bear & Co., 1987).

65. See Francis Harrold and Raymond Eve (eds.), *Cult Archaeology and Creationism: Understanding Pseudoscientific Beliefs About the Past*, expanded ed. (Iowa City: University of Iowa Press, 1995).

66. This is not, of course, to deny the obvious and significant influences that different societies and civilizations have had on one another. The issue raised here is simply the need to distinguish between those cases where contact and the historical and archeological record make such influences possible or likely, and those instances where it is less likely or not at all likely. Demonstrating *possibilities*, especially in cases where the evidence is scarce to begin with, can obviously be done. Virtually anything is *possible*; the question is whether a claim is likely, probable, or credible.

67. See, e.g., John Boswell, *The Kindness of Strangers: The Abandonment of Children in Western Europe from Late Antiquity to the Renaissance* (New York: Pantheon, 1988), especially part I.

68. Martin Gardner, "Is Cannibalism a Myth?" *Skeptical Inquirer* 22, 1 (1998): 14, my emphasis.

69. See Eli Sagan, *Cannibalism: Human Aggression and Cultural Form* (Santa Fe, NM: FirstDrum, 1993); Garry Hogg, *Cannibalism and Human Sacrifice* (London: Hale, 1990).

70. Gardner, "Is Cannibalism a Myth?" 14. For a clear and cogent articulation of this position, see William Arens, *The Man-Eating-Myth: Anthropology and Anthropology* (New York: Oxford University Press, 1979).

71. David Crystal, *A Dictionary of Linguistics and Phonetics*, 3rd ed. (Oxford, England: Blackwell, 1991), 367.

72. See Lincoln and Guba, *Naturalistic Inquiry*, 93–94.

73. Michael Apple, *Cultural Politics and Education* (New York: Teachers College Press, 1996), ix. The quote is from Edward Said, *Culture and Imperialism* (New York: Vintage, 1993), xxii.

74. Apple, *Cultural Politics and Education*, xiv.

75. Ali Mazrui, *The African Condition: The Reith Lectures* (London: Heinemann, 1980), 16.

76. Harrold and Eve (eds.), *Cult Archaeology and Creationism*, ix.

2

Conceptualizing Culture:
"I, We, and the Other"

Culture is an invention, tied up with the invention of anthropology. . . .
Unlike earlier generations of anthropologists who thought of culture in
essentialist terms, we now realize that it is a creation on our part, and
one which may become increasingly poeticized—in fact and in text. . . .
Whether construed in the singular, and denoting a philosophic counter-
point to nature, or in the plural, designating sociological entities, we can
no longer claim culture to be an objective fact.

—Hastrup (1995, p. 16)

Words, the primary tools that human beings use to communicate with one
another, are incredibly powerful, but are also potentially problematic and difficult. Nearly half a century ago, the historian Carl Becker wrote:

> Now, when I meet with a word with which I am entirely unfamiliar, I find it a
> good plan to look it up in the dictionary and find out what someone thinks it
> means. But when I have frequently to use words with which everyone is per-
> fectly familiar—words like "cause" and "liberty" and "progress" and "govern-
> ment"—when I have to use words of this sort which everyone knows perfectly
> well, the wise thing to do is to take a week off and think about them.[1]

The word "culture" is perhaps the prime case of a "week-off word"; as Raymond Williams noted, culture is "one of the two or three most complicated
words in the English language."[2] We use the word culture in a wide variety of
contexts with an equally wide range of meanings. Sometimes the term is used
to speak about aspects of what is also called "high culture," which refers primarily to aesthetic manifestations of social life: literature, music, visual art,
and so on. Although examples of popular culture might be included here,[3] in
general the emphasis is on the work of writers, poets, musicians, and artists
who have been identified, over time, as "great," or at least "good" or perhaps

"meritorious." The term can also be used to discuss intellectual or spiritual developments in a society, as when we talk about the cultural development of western Europe with a concern for the evolution of religious and philosophical thought. Finally, and of greatest relevance to us here, the term *culture* is used to refer to what Young Pai and Susan Adler described as "that pattern of knowledge, skills, behaviors, attitudes and beliefs, as well as material artifacts, produced by a human society and transmitted from one generation to another."[4] Although certainly a useful starting point, such a definition still leaves much to be desired as we try to make sense of the construct of "culture" and its role in the history of humanity. In this chapter, we will explore this complex and often perplexing construct, and try to establish a foundation for discussing cultures and traditions in a variety of times and places throughout human history.

UNDERSTANDING CULTURE: THE ROLE OF ANTHROPOLOGY

The academic discipline that has had as its principle focus and purpose the study and understanding of human cultures is anthropology. A product of the 19th century, from its inception in the 1860s and 1870s, anthropology was closely tied to popular scientific, pseudo-scientific, and ideological beliefs and values about the peoples and groups studied. Further, in its formative period, much anthropological work was focused on the study of "primitive" cultures and peoples. As Adam Kuper noted:

> The idea of primitive society is intimately related to other potent and beguiling notions concerning primitive mentality, primitive religion, primitive art, primitive money, and so on. . . . The rapidity with which the anthropological idea of primitive society was worked out is very striking, but its persistence is perhaps yet more extraordinary. . . . The persistence of this prototype for well over a hundred years is the more remarkable since empirical investigation of tropical "primitive" societies only began in a systematic way and on any scale in the last decade of the nineteenth century.[5]

The normative element in anthropology, which sought to place relative values on different cultures and cultural practices, is no longer a part of mainstream academic anthropology. Indeed, professional academic anthropologists would reject the characterization of any human society as "primitive" out of hand. As Gardner and Lewis explained, anthropology at its best:

> promotes an attitude and an outlook: a stance which encourages those working in development to listen to other people's stories, to pay attention to alternative points of view and to new ways of seeing and doing. This outlook continually questions generalised assumptions that we might draw from our own culture and seek to apply elsewhere, and calls attention to the various alternatives

that exist in other cultures. Such a perspective helps to highlight the richness and diversity of human existence as expressed through different languages, beliefs and other aspects of culture. Anthropology tries to show the interconnectedness of social and economic life and the complex relationships which exist between people under conditions of change. Finally, anthropology encourages us to dig as deeply as possible, to go beyond what is immediately apparent, and to uncover as much of the complexity of social and economic life that we can.[6]

Underlying such a view is, in some form, the notion of cultural relativism, a widely cited and nearly as widely misunderstood construct itself. In its most basic form, cultural relativism can be formulated in two very distinct ways: elementary cultural relativism and empirical cultural relativism.[7] *Elementary cultural relativism*, as it was articulated by William Graham Sumner, argues that "in the folkways, whatever is, is right."[8] *Empirical relativism* offers a somewhat more nuanced and sophisticated understanding of cultural diversity, noting instead that "the ethical judgments supported by different . . . groups are often different and conflicting in a very fundamental way."[9] The difference between these two formulations is very significant, because the former results in *ethical* as well as cultural relativism, whereas the latter does not.[10] Claude Lévi-Strauss, one of the greatest French anthropologists, has insightfully noted that "cultural relativism affirms that no culture has any absolute criteria for judging the activities of another culture as 'low' or 'noble.' However, every culture can and should apply such judgment to its own activities, since its members are actors as well as observers."[11] On an even deeper level, however, cultural relativism as a doctrine is useful in reminding us to be wary of making judgments about cultural differences. It does *not*, however, prevent such judgments altogether. As Clifford Geertz suggested, "The truth of the doctrine of cultural (or historical—it is the same thing) relativism is that we can never apprehend another people's or another period's imagination neatly, as though it were our own. The falsity of it is that we can therefore never genuinely apprehend it at all. We can apprehend it well enough, at least as well as we apprehend anything else not properly ours; but we do so not by looking *behind* the interfering glosses that connect us to it but *through* them."[12] In other words, cultural relativism can be a valuable tool in helping us to recognize our own epistemological lenses and limitations, but does not actually make it impossible to study and even to understand the Other.

Contemporary anthropologists define culture in a variety of ways.[13] In part because of its problematic history, in part because of its lack of a clearly agreed on meaning, it is even considered by some anthropologists to be, perhaps, more trouble than it is worth. And yet, it remains a widely used and useful construct. As Geertz explained:

The term "culture" has by now acquired a certain aura of ill-repute in social anthropological circles because of the multiplicity of its referents and the studied vagueness with which it has all too often been invoked. . . . In any case, the culture concept to which I adhere has neither multiple referents nor, so far as I can see, any unusual ambiguity: it denotes an historically transmitted pattern of meanings embodied in symbols, a system of inherited conceptions expressed in symbolic forms by means of which men [sic] communicate, perpetuate, and develop their knowledge about and attitudes toward life.[14]

Geertz provides us with a very valuable starting point in conceptualizing culture. Culture, on his account, is systematic, communal, and dynamic. It is learned rather than inherited, and it is necessarily permeable. Indeed, cultural identity is inevitably plural to some extent: Each of us belongs to a variety of cultural communities. For instance, ethnic identity, religious identity, gender identity, age identity, political identity, social class identity, professional identity, and so on, can all relate to or be grounded in different (albeit perhaps overlapping) cultures. These cultural communities are not of equal importance for us, of course, and our membership in them is often context and time specific. Indeed, we often distinguish between "cultures" and "subcultures," or "microcultures," as a way of indicating relative importance, although this practice can also unfortunately indicate the very sorts of value judgments about different cultures that we wish to avoid. Among the characteristics that can distinguish one cultural community from another are language, behavioral norms, cultural artifacts, family and kinship patterns, gender roles, religious and spiritual beliefs and practices, attitudes and values, and so on. Although far from perfect, this attempt to define culture at the very least provides us with a useful heuristic device for studying and discussing different cultures.

Culture actually exists in a contextual framework that mediates between the universal aspects of human nature and the specific aspects of individual personality, as well as between learned and inherited characteristics. As Geert Hofstede,[15] using the analogy of computer programming to explicate human patterns of thinking and behavior, explained:

> *Human nature* is what all human beings, from the Russian professor to the Australian aborigine, have in common: it represents the universal level in one's mental software. It is inherited with one's genes. . . . The human ability to feel fear, anger, love, joy, sadness, the need to associate with others, to play and exercise oneself, the facility to observe the environment and talk about it with other humans all belong to this level of mental programming. However, what one does with these feelings, how one expresses fear, joy, observations, and so on, is modified by culture. . . . The *personality* of an individual, on the other hand, is her/his unique personal set of mental programs which (s)he does not share with any other human being. It is based upon traits which are partly inherited with the individual's unique set of genes and partly learned.[16]

Culture, in short, however difficult it may be to define and demarcate, is nonetheless an inextricable and essential component of both individual and social identity.

THE MISREPRESENTATION OF CULTURE

It would not be unreasonable at this point for the reader to wonder why all of this talk about culture really matters. After all, even if there are different meanings for the term, there is certainly an everyday understanding of the concept of culture, and such an everyday understanding could surely suffice for our purposes here. The response to this argument is that the way in which we conceptualize culture does, in fact, make a huge difference both in how we analyze and how we understand cultures other than our own, and further, that our everyday conceptualization of culture may well contain in it the very biases that we are seeking to avoid. As Christopher Hutton recently demonstrated in his masterful work *Linguistics and the Third Reich*, many of the fundamental constructs used in modern linguistics are far from neutral historically and, in fact, overlap much of the history of 19th- and 20th-century European nationalism.[17] Likewise, particular conceptions of culture have not only reflected, but have also guided and informed government, social, and educational policies. Such applications of anthropological concepts and constructs have had, and in many settings continue to have, important consequences for the daily lives of groups and individuals—and especially of dominated and oppressed groups and individuals.

Perhaps there is no better example of the misuse and misapplication of anthropological concepts than was found in 20th-century South Africa. Social anthropology was first introduced as an academic discipline in South Africa at the University of Cape Town in 1921, and rapidly became a significant intellectual endeavor. Not only were many of the early South African anthropologists internationally recognized and admired scholars who did important work on indigenous South African societies and cultures (including Isaac Schepera, Monica Wilson, Hilda Kuper, and Eileen and Jack Krige), but others—especially those involved in what came to be called *Volkekunde* at Afrikaans universities—provided invaluable intellectual and scholarly support for the development and maintenance of apartheid. Just as intellectuals and scholars in Nazi Germany provided important support for the National Socialist régime,[18] so too did many academics in South Africa offer their support to the apartheid régime.

The key academics involved in the development and articulation of *Volkekunde*, especially in the period following World War II, were W. M. Eiselen, Pieter Schoeman, P. J. Coertze, J. A. Engelbrecht, A. J. Van Schalkwyk, and F. J. Language. As W. D. Hammond-Tooke clearly demonstrated in his powerful and critical history of anthropology in South Africa, "There is no doubt that these Afrikaner academics, and others who followed them, sought to justify their essentially political claims by the fact that they were anthropologists—scientists and so-called experts on 'the life of the Natives' (this was a ploy often used by Eiselen in his various defences of apart-

heid)."[19] These individuals not only supported apartheid, but more important, they provided much of its intellectual and ideological foundation.
Although *Volkekunde* is generally translated simply as "ethnology," it is in fact
a fairly complex term and quite difficult to translate accurately. It is not the
study of ethnic groups, as "ethnology" might suggest, but rather the study of
different *Volke*. This Afrikaans term has the same meaning as the German
Volk, and is every bit as ideologically bounded as the German term. P. J.
Coertze, in his introductory text *Inleiding tot die Algemene Volkekunde,* explained the concept of *Volk,* as opposed to "culture," as follows:

> A *Volk* is not an accidental number of individuals living together in a particular
> area. The members of a *Volk* form an organized unit. However, a *Volk* is not or-
> ganized by people. It has come into existence through a growth process and is
> therefore a type of organic unit. The members of a *Volk* are, so to say, cells in a
> greater organism which is linked together in a particular way. . . . The members
> of a *Volk* also stand in a special relationship to one another, each with his own
> status and playing his role within the greater whole. The structural relationship
> in which they are ordered lies locked in the cultural pattern. It is the experience
> of, and conformity with, a particular shared culture that binds a number of in-
> dividuals into an organic whole. Among people who have lived together from a
> long period, there occurs a biological tie caused by intermarriage. In addition,
> a spiritual unification takes place, which binds people together on the spiritual
> level. This is expressed in the unfolding of a unified language, and a single form
> of life and thought, i.e., a one and only culture. The structural form of such a
> *Volk* is therefore contained in its cultural pattern. This is why a *Volk* and its cul-
> ture is a two-fold unity. The term "*Volk*" refers to the ordering of relationships
> in a closed unity (people), while the term *"culture"* refers to the structure of re-
> lationships, the pattern of thought, attitudes, interactions and the result of the
> labor of the members of such a *Volk.*[20]

Using the essentialist concept of *Volk* rather than culture, these scholars
argued that only by separating the different *Volke* present in South Africa
could real social justice be achieved. As early as 1943, Afrikaans anthropologists were engaged in describing an apartheid-based "solution" to the "Native
Problem," as R. D. Coertze noted as recently as 1991:

> What was here advocated in 1943, five years before the coming to power of the
> National Party, was a policy of "radical and total apartheid" which must be re-
> alized in practice through a strong central government over a period of 50–100
> years. The implications of such a policy must be worked out in the social, polit-
> ico-administrative, educational, religious and economic spheres. The core of
> the exposition involved the propagation of a foundation of separate political
> bonds for the different black groups, each with an area in which the population
> could enjoy a decent economic existence. . . . [This] is the only policy that
> could . . . guarantee tranquility and peace in South Africa.[21]

Apartheid, on such an account, was a utopian vision as well as an incredibly complex effort at social engineering. In the educational sphere, for instance, this vision was manifested in separate educational systems for the different *Volke,* justified by the educational theories of *"fundmentele pedagogiek"* ("fundamental pedagogics"):

> Perhaps the central article of faith of fundamental pedagogics is that different cultural groups have different "philosophies of life," and that, in turn, appropriate educations for different cultural groups must therefore be grounded in significantly different philosophies of education. . . . Fundamental pedagogics does not, however, serve merely to mystify the process and content of education. It is an integral component of the ideological foundation of apartheid, and it thus functions to both justify and legitimate the reality of separate educational systems. By asserting that different ethnolinguistic, cultural and racial groups have different "philosophies of life" and "worldviews," the fundamental pedagogicians in essence deny the possibility of a unified, integrated educational system in South Africa. In short, fundamental pedagogics provides an intellectual and "scientific" justification for racist and separatist educational policies.[22]

The misrepresentation of cultures is hardly unique to the South African experience, however. Somewhat closer to home, the traditional representations of Native American cultures are in many ways just as problematic. In an essay documenting how Native Americans are presented in contemporary museums as both unidimensional and essentially ahistorical and disembodied from the local past, James Nason commented:

> Few exhibitions about Native Americans have anything to do with the contemporary world. Indians are virtually always presented as elements from the community's past—elements that no longer have any importance or bearing on current life in the community. Indian culture is seen as a relic of the past. This disassociation between the community's past and present essentially "disembodies" the reality of a continuing Indian presence by the simply expedient of denying it. Even the exhibition of historic photographs of Native Americans serves to reinforce this deadly notion, as these photographs present a fading glimpse of bygone days, and thus of long-gone people.[23]

Nason went on to suggest that such exhibitions inevitably influence both the attitudes and perceptions of visitors, and further, that the exhibitions convey important (albeit, perhaps, arguably unintentional) messages and lessons:

> I believe these exhibitions convey several messages. First, "real" Indians are gone, regardless of what one reads of "Indians" in today's newspapers. Second, "real" Indian culture and life are also past, and their material products are of

no more importance than their nonexistent values, beliefs, and perceptions. Third, there is no such thing as Indian history, and therefore no contribution by Indians to "progress" or "significance" in the lives of present-day people. Fourth, the "real" Indians who once existed are interesting only as an extinguished footnote or as obstacles that had to be removed from the "real" progress that characterizes the history of the community or the nation.[24]

Such concerns about the messages conveyed about Native Americans are especially timely in many parts of the United States, including my home state of Connecticut, as tribes seek federal recognition (often, at least in part, in order to construct casinos). The arguments against such federal recognition are complex, and rely on a variety of different kinds of evidence.[25] An important assumption of many such arguments, however, is all too often precisely the sort of view articulated by Nason.

ISSUES OF CULTURE, POWER, AND DOMINANCE

Examples such as those already cited make clear that the study of culture takes place in a broader ideological context. To be sure, such misunderstandings and misrepresentations are not unique to anthropologists; virtually all of the social sciences have comparable cases that could be cited, as of course do biology, genetics, and many other fields.[26] What is really at stake here is not so much academic or intellectual endeavors per se, but rather the uses and misuses of such undertakings in social, political, ideological, and economic contexts. When dealing with issues of culture, cultural difference, and cultural diversity in particular, it is important to keep in mind the warning offered by the Australian scholar Brian Bullivant, who noted that programs designed and intended to encourage ethnic and cultural identification, including many multicultural education programs, "are ideal methods of controlling knowledge/power, while appearing through symbolic political language to be acting solely from the best of motives in the interests of the ethnic groups themselves."[27] Issues of power and dominance, in short, are closely related to issues of culture, and we need to be aware of this nexus even as we seek to explore and to understand various cultures.

WHAT IS "WESTERN" CULTURE?

This book is about non-Western cultures, which of course immediately raises the prior question of what we mean by "Western" culture. There is no easy answer to this question, as was implied in chapter 1 when we discussed the apparent dichotomy between "Western" and "non-Western." Although there is certainly an historical, intellectual, aesthetic, and religious chain linking the Classical Greek period (and even before) to the present in Europe and the areas of the world colonized and settled by Europeans, such a "Plato-to-NATO" perspective inevitably involves considerable distortion. There is no single "Western" culture in any really meaningful sense; rather, there are many different and distinct cultures that share certain elements of a common historical background that are manifested in different ways in the present. There are, in addition, popular cultures that parallel and overlap more traditional conceptions of culture in all of these different settings, as well as an almost infinite variety of "subcultures" and "microcultures." Although presumably intended to be a tongue-in-cheek comment, Mahatma Gandhi's attributed response to a reporter's question about what he thought of "Western civilization" comes to mind here: Gandhi said that he thought it would be a good idea. Such humor aside, however, it is far easier to talk about "Western" culture than it is to actually define it, and it is interesting to note that this is a task that many of the most vociferous advocates of the "Western" cultural heritage seem to avoid.[28] Beyond this problem is another, which is in fact even more telling: Although the "Western" cultural heritage is often seen as a kind of "umbrella" under which different Western cultures coexist, in reality this coexistence is itself often very problematic, as any number of major wars *among* groups that presumably share this common cultural heritage make clear. Even today, the noticeable divisions within the so-called "Western" world are often at least as great as those between "Western" and "non-Western" societies.[29]

THE CULTURE OF THE DEAF-WORLD

At this point, we can turn to an examination of a particular culture in order to understand how the study of cultures other than our own can be both interesting and useful. The culture that I have chosen for this exercise is one that coexists with the cultural world in which most of us live, and that even touches our world from time to time, but nonetheless remains largely unknown and alien. In discussions about the complex relations that can and do exist between language and identity, Deaf people stand out as an exceptionally complicated and intriguing case.[30] As Charlotte Baker recently observed, "Deaf people do not necessarily identify with the hearing world and increasingly regard the hearing world as a different language community. Rather than allowing themselves to be defined by the majority hearing group, Deaf people are progressively expressing and valuing their own self-constructed identity."[31] Since the 1970s, there has been a growing recognition that many individuals identify themselves as members of a common Deaf cultural community (in American Sign Language, or ASL, this concept is expressed in the sign DEAF-WORLD[32]). Such a cultural conceptualization of deafness presents a significant challenge to the more popular view among hearing people of deafness as a disability. The difference is not merely a semantic one; it is fundamental to one's conception of what deafness is, what it means to be deaf/Deaf, and how both individuals and society as a whole ought to address deafness. As Lane, Hoffmeister, and Bahan noted in their powerful book, *A Journey into the DEAF-WORLD,* "When hearing people think about Deaf people, they project their concerns and subtractive perspective onto Deaf people. The result is an inevitable collision with the values of the DEAF-WORLD, whose goal is to promote the unique heritage of Deaf language and culture. The disparity in decision-making power between the hearing world and the DEAF-WORLD renders this collision frightening for Deaf people."[33]

The complexities of the situation become even greater when one takes into account the fact that not all deaf people are Deaf. Audiological deafness and cultural Deafness are distinct and different conditions. The deaf population can be subdivided into a wide range of different groups, distinguished in part by degree of hearing loss, but also by language preference, educational experience, and relative integration into either the DEAF-WORLD or the hearing world.[34] Among the different subgroups within the deaf population, then, are those who:

- use ASL as their primary language and identify with the Deaf cultural community;
- communicate primarily through speech (i.e., in a spoken language) and identify with the hearing community;
- became deaf later in life, as a result of the aging process (i.e., the elderly deaf);
- do not know either ASL or English, but rather communicate through gestures, mimes, and their own "home" signing systems; and
- have normal hearing but (generally as a result of family ties to deaf people) understand and use ASL and integrate with the Deaf cultural community.

Our focus here will be on understanding the multiple, competing conceptions of deafness that divide the DEAF-WORLD and hearing world, with emphasis on the dominant constructions of deafness that exist in each of these worlds. It is important to note at the outset, then, that the concern here is primarily with *Deaf* people rather than with *deaf* people. As Harlan Lane observed in his book *The Mask of Benevolence,* "Most Americans who have impaired hearing are not members of the American deaf community. They were acculturated to hearing society, their first language was a spoken one, and they became hard of hearing or deaf in the course of their lives, often late in life. This book is not about them; it is about people who grow up deaf, acculturated to the manual language and society of the deaf community."[35] Although there are many interesting issues that might be addressed with respect to the identities of deaf people, as well as with regard to the complex identities of the hearing children of both deaf and Deaf people, these issues are beyond the bounds to be discussed here.[36] It is, nevertheless, important to recognize that the dichotomy separating the hearing and Deaf worlds is in fact a false one; rather than two completing distinct identities, the reality of deafness is one of a continuum of multiple identities ranging from "hearing" to "Deaf."

At issue here is the broader issue of disability. As numerous scholars have explored in detail in recent years, "disability" is a social construct grounded in cultural, political, ideological, and economic assumptions and biases.[37] In the case of Deaf people, the relative emphasis and importance accorded to audiological versus social factors is the central feature of differentiation between what can be labeled the etic and emic views of deafness.[38] At stake, ultimately, is the question of who defines "deafness": the dominant hearing world or the DEAF-WORLD. It is, at a fundamental level, the relation between power and discourse that is at stake.

Deaf constructions of Deaf identity, which are grounded in the experiences and history of the DEAF-WORLD, stress the sociocultural and linguistic aspects of deafness.[39] As Carol Padden and Tom Humphries wrote at the start of their book *Deaf in America: Voices from a Culture*:

> The traditional way of writing about Deaf people is to focus on the fact of their condition—that they do not hear—and to interpret all other aspects of their lives as consequences of this fact. . . . In contrast to the long history of writings that treat them as medical cases, or as people with "disabilities," who "compensate" for the deafness by using sign language, we want to portray the lives they live, their art and performances, their everyday talk, their shared myths, and the lessons they teach one another. We have always felt that the attention given to the physical condition of not hearing has obscured far more interesting facets of Deaf people's lives.[40]

Describing this same phenomenon, and attempting to explain the emic construction of deafness in an essay published in *The Atlantic*, Edward Dolnick wrote:

> Lately . . . the deaf community has begun to speak for itself. To the surprise and bewilderment of outsiders, its message is utterly contrary to the wisdom of centuries: Deaf people, far from groaning under a heavy yoke, are not handicapped at all. Deafness is not a disability. Instead, many deaf people now proclaim, they are a subculture like any other. They are simply a linguistic

minority (speaking American Sign Language) and are no more in need of a cure than are Haitians or Hispanics.[41]

In short, emic constructions of deafness focus primarily on Deaf people as a cultural and linguistic minority community (and, indeed, on that community as an oppressed one). The Deaf cultural community is, from this perspective, characterized by the same sorts of elements that might characterize any cultural community, including the following:

- a common, shared language
- a literary and artistic tradition
- a shared awareness of Deaf cultural identity
- endogamous marital patterns
- distinctive behavioral norms and patterns
- cultural artifacts
- a shared historical knowledge and awareness
- a network of voluntary, in-group social organizations.

The single most significant element of Deaf cultural identity in the United States is, without a doubt, communicative competence in ASL.[42] ASL serves multiple roles within the Deaf community, functioning not only as the community's vernacular language, but also as an indicator of cultural group membership.[43] It is important to note here, however, that this applies only to ASL; other types of signing commonly used in the United States (including both the contact sign language normally employed by hearing signers and the artificially constructed manual sign codes) fulfill very different functions and are viewed very differently by members of the Deaf community.[44] For instance, contact sign language is viewed as an appropriate means of communication with hearing individuals, whereas manual sign codes are often rejected by the Deaf community as awkward efforts to impose the structures of a spoken language on sign.

ASL plays an important role in the construction of what could be termed the DEAF-WORLD worldview—that is, the way in which Deaf people make sense of the world around them. It does this in two distinct ways: first, through its role as linguistic mediator, and second, as an identifying facet of cultural identity. For instance, ASL mediates experience in a unique way, as of course do all languages. The structures and vocabulary of ASL provide the framework within which experience is organized, perceived, and understood, and this framework is inevitably distinct from the frameworks employed by other languages. For example, in ASL if one describes a person as VERY HARD-OF-HEARING, then it means that the person has substantial residual hearing, whereas A LITTLE HARD-OF-HEARING would suggest far less residual hearing. In other words, the concepts themselves are based on different norms than would be the case in English (where the meanings of these two expressions would be reversed).

The use of ASL as one's primary vernacular language is arguably the single most important element in the construction of Deaf cultural identity. Deaf cultural identity presupposes communicative competence in ASL, and is impossible without it. As Jerome Schein has explained, "Being deaf does not in itself make one a member of the deaf community. To understand this, one has to remember that the distinguishing feature of membership in the deaf community is how one communicates."[45] It is not merely signing that is necessary, however—it is, specifically, the use of ASL. Many hearing people sign, but relatively few are competent in ASL. ASL has historically functioned as a "language of group solidarity" for Deaf people, serving both as a badge of ingroup membership and as a barrier to those outside the cultural community. Recently, as more hearing people have begun to learn ASL, new complications have arisen with respect to issues of "ownership" of ASL.[46] As one leader in the U.S. Deaf community noted,

> I have asked a number of deaf individuals how they feel about hearing people signing like a native user of ASL. The responses are mixed. Some say that it is acceptable for hearing people to use ASL like a deaf person on one condition. The condition is that this hearing person must make sure that the deaf person knows that s/he is not deaf. Some people resent the idea of seeing hearing people signing like a native ASL user. Those who are resentful may feel sociolinguistic territorial invasion by those hearing people.[47]

The role of ASL in the construction of Deaf identity, then, is quite complex—it is clearly a *necessary* condition for Deaf cultural identity, but (as is demonstrated in the cases of hearing individuals who use ASL fluently) not a *sufficient* condition for group membership. Indeed, for nongroup members, use of ASL can present significant challenges to one's credibility and status as a sympathetic outsider, and it is far from uncommon to find Deaf people who seek to "protectively withhold from hearing people information about the DEAF-WORLD's language and culture."[48]

Members of the Deaf cultural community identify themselves as socially and culturally Deaf, maintaining a clear-cut distinction between audiological deafness and sociocultural deafness—a phenomenon sometimes referred to as "attitudinal deafness."[49] Thus, within an emic construction of deafness, the fact of audiological deafness is actually neither a necessary nor a sufficient condition for cultural deafness. Hearing children of Deaf people, who grow up with ASL as their first language, are (at least in some significant ways) potential members of the Deaf culture, just as older hearing people who lose their hearing are, under normal circumstances, not Deaf—they are, rather, hearing people who can no longer hear. It is interesting to note that in ASL there is actually a very pejorative and insulting sign ("HEAFIE") used to denigrate a deaf person who "thinks like a hearing person." Further, a common facet of cultural identity for many ethnic groups is the presence and maintenance of endogamous marital patterns, and the same is true in the case of Deaf people. Indeed, estimates of the rate of in-group marriage in the Deaf community range from 86 to over 90 percent—a remarkably high rate in contemporary American society.[50] This high rate of in-group marriage is certainly facilitated by the role of the residential schools for the deaf, but is also tied to the common, shared language of Deaf people as well as to the power of the concept of attitudinal deafness.

This concept of attitudinal deafness is, further, a key element in understanding much of Deaf humor.[51] Jokes and funny stories abound in the DEAF-WORLD, and many involve the presumed difference between Deaf people and the DEAF-WORLD and hearing people and the hearing world— almost inevitably, as one would expect, with the punch line focusing on hearing people's ignorance of signing, deafness, and Deaf people. One story, for instance, involves a hearing man who is hitch-hiking, and is given a ride by a Deaf man. As they drive along, the Deaf driver exceeds the speed limit, and is stopped by a police officer. The police officer comes to the car, and the Deaf man signs to him, indicating that he is deaf. Unable to communicate with the driver, the police officer just says, "Oh, never mind—just slow down!" Some time later, the hearing man offers to drive so that the Deaf man can rest. The Deaf driver accepts the offer, and the hearing man begins driving. Before too long, they are again stopped by a police officer. The hearing man, recalling what occurred before, copies what he saw the Deaf man sign to the police officer. This police officer, however, immediately signs back, "Oh, you're deaf? So are my parents. So why are going so fast, anyway?" The joke, of course, is on the hearing man, who had tried, for selfish reasons, to "pass" as a Deaf person.

There are also differences with respect to behavioral norms between the hearing world and the DEAF-WORLD. Most notable here would be differences in eye contact patterns, rules governing the permissibility of physical contact of various sorts (including touching to gain attention), the use of facial expressions, gesturing, and so on.[52] Similarly, the cultural artifacts of the Deaf community are primarily technological devices designed in recent years to facilitate the ability of the deaf to function in the hearing world. The key difference between the audiologically deaf and culturally Deaf with respect to the use of such technologies is that there is a reluctance on the part of many culturally Deaf people to utilize technological devices (e.g., hearing aids) that focus primarily on *hearing*. For the most part, other kinds of technological innovations, such as TDD/TTYs, which allow the deaf to use the telephone, television decoders for closed-captioned programs, doorbells and alarms tied to lights, and so on, although to some extent cultural artifacts, are widely and commonly used both within the Deaf culture and by those who are audiologically deaf but not culturally Deaf. Cultural artifacts emphasizing membership in the Deaf culture (e.g., jewelry, T-shirts, bumper stickers, etc.), which often involve visual images of signs, are additional artifacts that are somewhat more likely to be found among culturally Deaf people, although such artifacts are also used more generally by both deaf and hearing people with an interest in deafness—sometimes even inappropriately, as Tom Willard articulated in a wonderful short essay entitled, "I've had enough of the I-LOVE-YOU sign, thanks."[53]

Members of the Deaf community have a strong sense of the history of their community, and this awareness has been passed from generation to generation largely through "oral" means in the past. However, the 1981 publication of Jack Gannon's *Deaf Heritage: A Narrative History of Deaf America*[54] has contributed to a broader access to the historical awareness of the Deaf community, and more recently, there have been a number of outstanding scholarly works on the history of Deaf people that are also reinforcing pride in the community's history and heritage.[55]

Finally, there is an extensive voluntary network of social organizations serving Deaf people, which work to maintain the cohesiveness of the Deaf community and provide, to a very significant extent, for the companionship needs of group members. This network includes local deaf clubs, the state and national organizations of the deaf (e.g., the National Association of the Deaf), sports associations, the National Theatre of the Deaf, and so on.

It is clear, in an anthropological sense, that the DEAF-WORLD is a legitimate and viable culture. Thus, attempts medically to "cure" or "remediate" audiological deafness are seen as not merely misguided, but as culturally and linguistically oppressive as well. This point was made quite vividly by I. King Jordan, the president of Gallaudet University, in a recent interview. Jordan was asked by the interviewer if he would like to have his hearing restored, to which Jordan replied, "That's almost like asking a black person if he would rather be white. . . . I don't think of myself as missing something or as incomplete. . . . It's a common fallacy if you don't know deaf people or deaf issues. You think it's a limitation."[56] From within the Deaf culture, this response was appropriate, meaningful, and indeed relatively uncontroversial; from outside the culture, it no doubt strikes many hearing people as somewhat bizarre. Precisely the same situation, albeit in reverse, can be found in the following quote from a chairperson of a National Institutes of Health planning group in *The New York Times*: "I am dedicated to curing deafness. That puts me on a collision course with those who are culturally Deaf. That is interpreted as genocide of the Deaf."[57] It is the tension between the two kinds of constructions of deafness that is at stake here, and it is this tension that is, on a fundamental level, probably irreconcilable.

Perhaps the clearest contemporary manifestation of this tension has been the debate about the use of cochlear implants in young children. Cochlear implants do not restore hearing; rather, they can create the perception of sound that, coupled with effective rehabilitation, can assist some hearing impaired individuals to function more effectively. In the case of young children, advocates of cochlear implants argue that "early implantation of deaf children should be considered as a way to expose them to the spoken word, enable them to learn spoken languages, and develop better speech skills."[58] Implantation involves a three- to four-hour surgical procedure:

> The hospitalized child is placed under general anesthesia. . . . The surgeon cuts the skin behind the ear, raises the flap, and drills a hole in the bone. Then a wire carrying electrodes is pushed some twenty-five millimeters into the coiled inner ear. The tiny endings of the auditory nerve are destroyed and electrical fields from the wire stimulate the auditory nerve directly. A small receiver coil connected to the wire is sutured to the skull and the skin is sewn over it. A small microphone worn on an ear piece picks up sound and sends signals to a processor worn on a belt or in a pocket. The processor sends electrical signals back to the implanted receiver via a transmitter mounted behind the ear, and those signals stimulate the auditory nerve.[59]

In short, the cochlear implant functions as a kind of hearing aid. There is no doubt that cochlear implants can be helpful for some late-deafened individuals, for whom the procedure was originally designed. The debate is not about the choice of adults to seek cochlear implants; it is about whether the procedure is appropriate for very young children.[60] From an outsider's perspective, the arguments in favor of cochlear implants for young deaf children are fairly compelling. The procedure does have the potential to help the hearing impaired individual function more effectively in the hearing world, offering if not a cure for deafness, then at least the possibility of the individual acquiring the skills necessary to "pass" as hearing and, hence, as "normal."[61]

It is this very conception of what constitutes "normal" that is at the heart of much of the resistance to such procedures in the Deaf community. Just as Michel Foucault made clear the epistemological power of socially established norms, whether in terms of mental illness, punishment, or sexuality, so too is the challenge to the conception of "normal" and its equation with "hearing" important in understanding this topic. It is, in Foucault's words, necessary for us to examine "the power of normalization and the formation of knowledge in modern society."[62] Returning once again to Harlan Lane's observation, from a Deaf perspective it is clear that:

> if the birth of a Deaf child is a priceless gift, then there is only cause for rejoicing, as at the birth of a black child, or an Indian one. Medical intervention is inappropriate, even if a perfect "cure" were available. Invasive surgery on healthy children is morally wrong. We know that, as members of a stigmatized minority, these children's lives will be full of challenge but, by the same token, they

have a special contribution to make to their own community and the larger society.[63]

Although the tension between the dominant hearing and Deaf constructions of deaf identity may well be irreconcilable on a conceptual level, it is nevertheless important to recognize that the reality of deaf experience is more complex and less clear than this might suggest. The vast majority of Deaf people become members of the Deaf culture relatively late in comparison with membership in most cultures. This is the case because most Deaf people have hearing parents and are introduced to the Deaf culture not by adults but rather by peers, most often in the context of residential schools for the deaf. Further, membership in the Deaf culture is not really an either–or proposition: Individual Deaf people identify as culturally Deaf in different ways and to different extents. Perhaps the clearest example of this complexity is manifested in the case of the hard-of-hearing, for whom membership in the Deaf culture is related to often conflicting attitudes about deafness itself. The extent to which the process of normalization of deafness to hearing norms (or "hearization") is accepted or rejected is key here, as Nover made clear: "Hearization leads many deaf children into wishing or thinking they will become hearing some day. Others prefer to be called 'hearing impaired' or 'hard-of-hearing' rather than deaf. Unfortunately, deaf and hard-of-hearing children may learn to view hearing people as superior to those who are deaf."[64]

The cultural and linguistic identity of individuals who are hard-of-hearing is, in short, both potentially and practically ambiguous,[65] as indeed is the identity of many other individuals who straddle multiple cultural and linguistic worlds. It is this ambiguity that makes simple descriptions of cultural identity misleading, not only in the case of the deaf, but with respect to virtually all minority cultural and linguistic groups.[66]

CONCLUDING THOUGHTS

The academic study of other cultures, especially as it has been manifested in anthropology, although unquestionably useful and valuable, has from its very inception been closely tied to colonialism and imperialism. As Katy Gardner and David Lewis noted:

> The utilisation by anthropologists of opportunities for fieldwork within colonial administrations has subsequently been subject to considerable criticism. The best-known critique is by Talal Asad and colleagues, who mounted a powerful retrospective attack on the aims and motivations of these anthropologists and indeed upon anthropology itself, based upon what Asad sees as the sub-

ject's colonial origins. It was the unequal encounter between Europe and the Third World, it was argued, which gave the West the opportunity to gain access to the types of cultural information upon which anthropology depends. Anthropology itself became part of this act of domination, though Asad recognizes that anthropology simultaneously—as part of what he terms "bourgeois consciousness"—provided ideas and activities which did not reflect the ideology of the colonial administration.[67]

Such critical views of anthropology[68] were all too often justified, as we have seen, although it would be easy to overemphasize the actual impact of anthropological scholarship in many colonial and postcolonial settings. At the same time, anthropology has provided us with the essential tools and vocabulary necessary to study and understand cultures other than our own, and, indeed, even to more accurately understand our own culture.

In this chapter, we have explored the complex nature of the construct of culture, as well as some of the ways in which this construct has been used and misused. We have also examined an unusual culture with which most of us are not terribly familiar, and seen how the application of what are essentially anthropological perspectives can enhance and strengthen our understanding of this culture. It is precisely in the same manner that anthropological perspectives, concepts, and constructs will be utilized in the remainder of this book—that is, as valuable but very much two-edged tools.

QUESTIONS FOR REFLECTION AND DISCUSSION

1. This chapter begins with a discussion of what the historian Carl Becker called "week-off words." Generate a list of such words that are common in educational discourse, and then try to explain why such terms are significant for teachers, students, and the public to understand.

2. One of the fundamental debates in U.S. education in recent years has been the role of the school in cultural reproduction. In essence, the debate is about whether the school should seek to inculcate a common national culture in all students, or whether it should rather emphasize and celebrate the cultural diversity of our society. What are the advantages and disadvantages of each view? What do you believe the school should do with respect to addressing cultural diversity?

3. What are the implications of the concept of "cultural relativism" for the classroom teacher? For the curriculum? For the organization of the school? For the connection between the school and the community?

4. As we have seen, Geert Hofstede distinguished among human nature, culture, and personality. Based on your own experience working with children, give examples of each of these constructs, and explain whether it is in

some sense an inherited or innate characteristic, or whether it is a learned or experienced characteristic. What are the implications of your answer for classroom practice?

5. "Fundamental pedagogics" is one of the educational manifestations of *Volkekunde,* as it is explained in this chapter. Its basic, core belief is that different cultural groups have different worldviews, and thus require different kinds of education and educational experiences. How does this view differ, both in principle and in practice, from contemporary multicultural education in the United States?

6. Consider Brian Bullivant's claim that programs designed and intended to encourage ethnic and cultural identification, including many multicultural education programs, "are ideal methods of controlling knowledge/power, while appearing through symbolic political language to be acting solely from the best of motives in the interests of the ethnic groups themselves." Do you agree or disagree with his assessment? Why?

7. How would you define "Western" culture? What criteria for inclusion and exclusion are you applying? Can you identify any borderline cases that are difficult to label as either "Western" or "non-Western"?

8. This chapter makes a case for the DEAF-WORLD constituting a distinctive cultural group. To what extent do you believe that comparable arguments might be made for other commonly identified "disabled" groups (e.g., the blind, individuals with mental retardation, etc.)? In what ways would these arguments be similar to those used in the case of the DEAF-WORLD, and in what ways would they be different?

9. According to Harlan Lane, "If the birth of a Deaf child is a priceless gift, then there is only cause for rejoicing, as at the birth of a black child, or an Indian one. Medical intervention is inappropriate, even if a perfect 'cure' were available." Do you agree or disagree with his view? Why?

10. In your own words, explain what the author means when he said that culture is a "valuable, but very much two-edged, tool." As an educator, how can the concept of culture be usefully and appropriately applied? What are the risks involved with the concept?

RECOMMENDED FURTHER READINGS

There are any number of excellent introductions to anthropology and the critical issues raised with respect to anthropology. Clifford Geertz's *The Interpretation of Culture* (New York: Basic Books, 1973) and his *Local Knowledge: Further Essays in Interpretive Anthropology* (New York: Basic Books, 1983) are now widely regarded as classics. More recent works worth reviewing, in my view, include Kirsten Hastrup's *A Passage to Anthropology: Between Experi-*

ence and Theory (London: Routledge, 1995), Bruce Knauft's *Genealogies for the Present in Cultural Anthropology* (New York: Routledge, 1996), and Katy Gardner and David Lewis' *Anthropology, Development and the Post-Modern Challenge* (London: Pluto Press, 1996). For readers interested in the culture of the DEAF-WORLD, the best available works include Harlan Lane's *The Mask of Benevolence: Disabling the Deaf Community* (New York: Knopf, 1992); Harlan Lane, Robert Hoffmeister, and Ben Bahan's *A Journey into the DEAF-WORLD* (San Diego, CA: DawnSign Press, 1996); and Carol Padden and Tom Humphries' *Deaf in America: Voices from a Culture* (Cambridge, MA: Harvard University Press, 1988). Finally, for an excellent discussion of disabilities studies as a distinct kind of cultural studies, see James Charlton, *Nothing About Us Without Us: Disability Oppression and Empowerment* (Berkeley: University of California Press, 1998), as well as Lennard Davis' edited collection, *The Disability Studies Reader* (New York: Routledge, 1997).

NOTES

1. Carl Becker, "What Are Historical Facts?" *Western Political Quarterly* 7 (1955): 328.

2. Raymond Williams, *Keywords* (London: Fontana, 1983), 87.

3. See John Storey, *An Introduction to Cultural Theory and Popular Culture*, 2nd ed. (Athens, GA: University of Georgia Press, 1998).

4. Young Pai and Susan A. Adler, *Cultural Foundations of Education*, 3rd ed. (Upper Saddle River, NJ: Merrill Prentice-Hall, 2001), 21.

5. Adam Kuper, *The Invention of Primitive Society: Transformation of an Illusion* (London: Routledge, 1988), 1.

6. Katy Gardner and David Lewis, *Anthropology, Development and the Post-Modern Challenge* (London: Pluto Press, 1996), 167–168.

7. Robert Ennis, *Logic in Teaching* (Englewood Cliffs, NJ: Prentice-Hall, 1969), 412–417.

8. William G. Sumner, *Folkways* (Boston: Ginn and Co., 1940, original publication 1906), 28.

9. Richard Brandt, *Value and Obligation* (New York: Harcourt, Brace & World, 1961), 433.

10. Although cultural relativism can be an immensely valuable tool in anthropology and other social sciences, its application in the field of ethics is considerably more controversial, as indeed it is when applied as an epistemological strategy (see chap. 1). See, e.g., James Harris, *Against Relativism: A Philosophical Defense of Method* (LaSalle, IL: Open Court, 1992), and F. C. White, *Knowledge and Relativism: An Essay in the Philosophy of Education* (Assen, The Netherlands: Van Gorcum, 1983).

11. Claude Lévi-Strauss and Didier Eribon, *De près et de loin* (Paris: Editions Odile Jacob, 1988), 229, my translation.

12. Clifford Geertz, *Local Knowledge: Further Essays in Interpretative Anthropology* (New York: Basic Books, 1983), 44.

13. See, e.g., Geert Hofstede, *Culture's Consequences,* 2nd ed. (Thousand Oaks, CA: Sage, 2001), 1–40.

14. Clifford Geertz, *The Interpretation of Cultures* (New York: Basic Books, 1973), 89.

15. Hofstede, *Culture's Consequences,* as well as his *Cultures and Organizations: Software of the Mind* (New York: McGraw-Hill, 1997).

16. Hofstede, *Cultures and Organizations,* 5–6.

17. See Christopher M. Hutton, *Linguistics and the Third Reich: Mother-Tongue Fascism, Race and the Science of Language* (London: Routledge, 1999); also of interest here is Dirk Scholten, *Sprachverbreitungspolitik des nationalsozialistischen Deutschlands* (Frankfurt, Germany: Peter Lang, 2000).

18. Max Weinreich, *Hitler's Professors: The Part of Scholarship in Germany's Crimes Against the Jewish People* (New Haven, CT: Yale University Press, 1999, original publication 1946).

19. W. D. Hammond-Tooke, *Imperfect Interpreters: South Africa's Anthropologists, 1920–1990* (Johannesburg: University of the Witwatersrand Press, 1997), 129; see also Saul Dubow, *Illicit Union: Scientific Racism in Modern South Africa* (Cambridge, England: Cambridge University Press, 1995); R. Gordon, "Serving the Volk with Volkekunde: On the Rise of South African Anthropology," in J. Jansen (ed.), *Knowledge and Power in South Africa: Critical Perspectives Across the Disciplines* (Johannesburg: Skotaville, 1991), 79–97.

20. P. J. Coertze, in his introductory text *Inleiding tot die Algemene Volkekunde* (Johannesburg: Voortrekkerpers, 1959), 61–62, my translation.

21. R. D. Coertze, "Aanvang van Volkekunde aan Afrikaanstalige universiteite in Suid-Afrika," *South African Journal of Ethnology* 14 (1991): 31, my translation.

22. Timothy Reagan, "Philosophy of Education in the Service of Apartheid: The Role of 'Fundamental Pedagogics' in South African Education," *Educational Foundations* 4, 2 (1990): 65–66.

23. James D. Nason, " 'Our' Indians: The Unidimensional Indian in the Disembodied Local Past," in *The Changing Presentation of the American Indian: Museums and Native Cultures* (Seattle and Washington, DC: National Museum of the American Indian, Smithsonian Institution, in association with the University of Washington Press, 2000), 37.

24. Nason, " 'Our' Indians," 38–39.

25. See, e.g., Jeff Benedict, *Without Reservation: How a Controversial Indian Tribe Rose to Power and Built the World's Largest Casino* (New York: Perennial, 2001), and Kim Eisler, *Revenge of the Pequots: How a Small Native American Tribe Created the World's Most Profitable Casino* (New York: Simon & Schuster, 2001).

26. There is in fact a growing body of very powerful historical work dealing with the misuses of science in various contexts. In the U.S. setting, perhaps among the most horrific examples of such misuse, driven by racism, is documented in James H. Jones, *Bad Blood: The Tuskegee Syphillis Experiment,* expanded ed. (New York: The Free Press, 1993). The case of Nazi Germany is similarly well-documented; see, e.g., Götz Aly, Peter Chroust, and Christian Pross, *Cleansing the Fatherland: Nazi Medicine and*

Racial Hygiene (Baltimore, MD: John Hopkins University Press, 1994), and Robert Lifton, *The Nazi Doctors: Medical Killing and the Psychology of Genocide* (New York: Basic Books, 2000). The Soviet case is discussed in Vadim J. Birstein, *The Perversion of Knowledge: The True Story of Soviet Science* (Cambridge, MA: Westview, 2001).

27. Brian Bullivant, *The Pluralist Dilemma in Education: Six Case Studies* (Sydney: Allen & Unwin, 1991), 291.

28. A noteworthy exception to this claim is provided in the work of E. D. Hirsch, who indeed attempted to articulate what is to be included in the concept of "Western culture." See E. D. Hirsch, *Cultural Literacy: What Every American Needs to Know* (New York: Vintage, 1988), as well as his more recent *The Schools We Need and Why We Don't Have Them* (New York: Doubleday, 1996). The problem with Hirsch is not that he avoided the problem of articulating the content of Western culture, but rather, that his conception of what is to be included (and, by extension, what is to be excluded) is both idiosyncratic and atheoretical. There are extensive critical analyses of Hirsch's work available. See, e.g., Michael Apple, *Official Knowledge: Democratic Education in a Conservative Age,* 2nd ed. (New York: Routledge, 2000); Michael Apple, *Educating the "Right" Way: Markets, Standards, God, and Inequality* (New York: RoutledgeFalmer, 2001); D. G. Mulcahy, *Knowledge, Gender and Schooling: The Feminist Educational Thought of Jane Roland Martin* (Westport, CT: Bergin & Garvey, 2002).

29. See, e.g., Jean-François Revel, *L'obsession anti-américaine: Son fontionnement, ses causes, ses inconséquences* (Paris: Editions Plon, 2002).

30. See Jennifer Harris, *The Cultural Meaning of Deafness: Language, Identity and Power Relations* (Aldershot, England: Ashgate, 1995), and Ila Parasnis (ed.), *Cultural and Language Diversity and the Deaf Experience* (Cambridge, England: Cambridge University Press, 1998). I have attempted to follow the common practice of distinguishing between audiological *deafness,* which is represented with a lowercase "d," and cultural *Deafness,* which is represented with an uppercase "D." It is also important to note that the discussion here focuses on the specific case of the Deaf community in the United States, but that comparable cases exist worldwide.

31. Colin Baker, "Sign Language and the Deaf Community," in Joshua Fishman (ed.), *Handbook of Language and Ethnic Identity* (New York: Oxford University Press, 1999), 129.

32. The use of all capital letters here is deliberate. This is the normal practice for indicating when signs rather than words are being employed. Thus, DEAF-WORLD represents a specific sign in ASL. This convention is especially important in instances in which ASL has a sign that cannot be adequately or easily translated into English.

33. Harlan Lane, Robert Hoffmeister, and Ben Bahan, *A Journey into the DEAF-WORLD* (San Diego, CA: DawnSign Press, 1996), 371.

34. See A. Hagemeyer, *The Red Notebook* (Silver Spring, MD: National Association of the Deaf, 1992).

35. Harlan Lane, *The Mask of Benevolence: Disabling the Deaf Community* (New York: Knopf, 1992), xi.

36. The identity issues of the hearing children of Deaf adults are explored in a number of recent works. See, e.g., Lennard Davis, *My Sense of Silence: Memoirs of a Childhood with Deafness* (Urbana: University of Illinois Press, 2000), P. Preston,

MOTHER FATHER DEAF: Living Between Sound and Silence (Cambridge, MA: Harvard University Press, 1994).

37. See Len Barton, "Blaming the Victims: The Political Oppression of Disabled People," in Russell Farnen and Heinz Sünker (eds.), *The Politics, Sociology and Economics of Education: Interdisciplinary and Comparative Perspectives* (Houndsmills, England: Macmillan, 1997), 63–72; James Charlton, *Nothing About Us Without Us: Disability Oppression and Empowerment* (Berkeley: University of California Press, 1998); Lennard Davis, *Enforcing Normalcy: Disability, Deafness, and the Body* (London: Verso, 1995); Lennard Davis (ed.), *The Disability Studies Reader* (New York: Routledge, 1997); Simi Linton, *Claiming Disability: Knowledge and Identity* (New York: New York University Press, 1998); Phillip Safford and Elizabeth Safford, *A History of Childhood and Disability* (New York: Teachers College Press, 1996); Joseph Shapiro, *No Pity: People with Disabilities Forging a New Civil Rights Movement* (New York: Times Books, 1993). With respect to the Deaf community's response to the oppression of the disabled, see Katherine Jankowski, *Deaf Empowerment: Emergence, Struggle, and Rhetoric* (Washington, DC: Gallaudet University Press, 1997). Perhaps the most extreme examples of the oppression of the Deaf/deaf took place in Nazi Germany as part of the ongoing eugenics efforts that constituted an important part of Nazi ideology and policy. See, e.g., Donna Ryan and John Schuchman (eds.), *Deaf People in Hitler's Europe* (Washington, DC: Gallaudet University Press, in association with the United States Holocaust Memorial Museum, 2002), and Horst Biesold, *Crying Hands: Eugenics and Deaf People in Nazi Germany* (Washington, DC: Gallaudet University Press, 1999).

38. See Susan Gregory and Gillian Hartley (eds.), *Constructing Deafness* (London: Pinter Publishers, in association with the Open University, 1991).

39. See, e.g., Yerker Andersson, "The Deaf World as a Linguistic Minority," in Siegmund Prillwitz and Tomas Vollhaber (eds.), *Sign Language Research and Application* (Hamburg, Germany: Signum Press, 1990), 155–161; Yerker Andersson, "Deaf People as a Linguistic Minority," in Inger Ahlgren and Kenneth Hyltenstan (eds.), *Bilingualism in Deaf Education* (Hamburg, Germany: Signum Press, 1994), 9–13; Jim Kyle, "The Deaf Community: Custom, Culture and Tradition," in Prillwitz and Vollhaber, *Sign Language Research and Application*, 175–185; Paddy Ladd, *Understanding Deaf Culture: In Search of Deafhood* (Clevedon, England: Multilingual Matters, 2003); Peter Paul and Dorothy Jackson, *Toward a Psychology of Deafness: Theoretical and Empirical Perspectives* (Boston: Allyn & Bacon, 1993); Dora Quintela, Irene Ramírez, Ximena Robertson, and Ana Pérez, ¿Por qué una educación bicultural bilingüe para las personas sordas? *Revista de la Universidad Metropolitana de Ciencias de la Educación* 3 (1997): 43–52; Timothy Reagan, "Cultural Considerations in the Education of Deaf Children," in Donald Moores and Kathryn Meadow-Orlans (eds.), *Educational and Developmental Aspects of Deafness* (Washington, DC: Gallaudet University Press, 1990), 73–84; Timothy Reagan, "The Development and Reform of Sign Languages," in István Fodor and Claude Hagège (eds.), *Language Reform: History and Future* (Hamburg, Germany: Buske Verlag, 1990), 253–267; Timothy Reagan, "A Sociocultural Understanding of Deafness: American Sign Language and the Culture of Deaf People," *International Journal of Intercultural Relations* 19 (1995): 239–251; Oliver Sacks, *Seeing Voices: A Journey into the World of the Deaf* (Berkeley: University of California Press, 1989); Jerome Schein, *At Home Among Strangers: Exploring the Deaf*

Community in the United States (Washington, DC: Gallaudet University Press, 1989); McCay Vernon and Jean Andrews, *The Psychology of Deafness* (New York: Longman, 1990); Sherman Wilcox (ed.), *American Deaf Culture: An Anthology* (Burtonsville, MD: Linstok Press, 1989).

40. Carol Padden and Tom Humphries, *Deaf in America: Voices from a Culture* (Cambridge, MA: Harvard University Press, 1988), 1.

41. Edward Dolnick, "Deafness as Culture," *The Atlantic* 272 (1993): 37.

42. See Lane, Hoffmeister, and Bahan, *A Journey into the DEAF-WORLD*; Jerome Schein and David Stewart, *Language in Motion: Exploring the Nature of Sign* (Washington, DC: Gallaudet University Press, 1995); Clayton Valli and Ceil Lucas, *Linguistics of American Sign Language: An Introduction,* 3rd ed. (Washington, DC: Gallaudet University Press, 2000).

43. An indication of the important role of American Sign Language in the establishment and maintenance of cultural identity can be seen in the use of "name signs." Name signs constitute a special category of signs in American Sign Language (and in other natural sign languages), and "seem to develop wherever a group of Deaf people have extended contact with each other and use sign language as their vernacular language. They are created for individuals within each generation or social grouping of Deaf people. Most typically, name signs originate in deaf school settings where Deaf children form an autonomous social world beyond the gaze of teachers. . . . The name signs that Deaf adults bestow on each other later in life are determined by Deaf social norms and visual language structures rather than those of the 'outside' hearing society." Further, "the acquisition of a name sign may mark a person's entry to a signing community, and its use reinforces the bond of shared group history and 'alternative' language use (in relation to mainstream society)." For more extended discussions of the role of name signs in various natural sign languages, see Tomas Hedberg, "Name Signs in Swedish Sign Language: Their Formation and Use," in Carol Erting, Robert Johnson, Dorothy Smith, and Bruce Snider (eds.), *The Deaf Way: Perspectives from the International Conference on Deaf Culture* (Washington, DC: Gallaudet University Press, 1994), 416–424; Samuel Supalla, *The Book of Name Signs: Naming in American Sign Language* (San Diego, CA: DawnSign Press, 1992); Shunchiu Yau, "Creation d'anthroponumes gestuels par une sourde amérindienne isolée," *Amérindia: Revue d'Éthnolinguistique Amérindienne* 7 (1982): 7–22; Shunchiu Yau, "Lexical Branching in Sign Language," in Susan Fischer and Patricia Siple (eds.), *Theoretical Issues in Sign Language Research: Linguistics* (Chicago: University of Chicago Press, 1990), 261–278; and Shunchiu Yau and Jinxian He, "How Do Deaf Children Get Their Name Signs During Their First Month in School?," in W. Edmondson and F. Karlsson (eds.), *SLR '87: Papers from the Fourth International Symposium on Sign Language Research* (Hamburg, Germany: Signum Press, 1990), 242–254.

44. See Ceil Lucas (ed.), *The Sociolinguistics of the Deaf Community* (San Diego: Academic Press, 1989); Ceil Lucas and Clayton Valli, *Language Contact in the American Deaf Community* (San Diego, CA: Academic Press, 1992); Timothy Reagan, " 'Neither Easy to Understand Nor Pleasing to See': The Development of Manual Sign Codes as Language Planning Activity," *Language Problems and Language Planning* 19 (1995): 133–150; Timothy Reagan, "But Does It *Count?* Reflections on 'Signing' as a Foreign Language," *Northeast Conference on the Teaching of Foreign Languages* 48 (2000): 16–26.

45. Jerome Schein, *Speaking the Language of Sign: The Art and Science of Signing* (Garden City, NY: Doubleday, 1984), 130.

46. See Lane, Hoffmeister, and Bahan, *A Journey into the DEAF-WORLD*, 70–77; Jack Levesque, "Let's Return ASL to Deaf Ownership," in Lois Bragg (ed.), *DEAF-WORLD: A Historical Reader and Primary Sourcebook* (New York: New York University Press, 2001), 116–117.

47. Quoted in Schein and Stewart, *Language in Motion*, 155.

48. Lane, Hoffmeister, and Bahan, *A Journey into the DEAF-WORLD*, 71.

49. See Valerie Janesick and Donald Moores, "Ethnic and Cultural Considerations," in Thomas Kluwin, Donald Moores, and Martha Gaustad (eds.), *Toward Effective Public School Programs for Deaf Students: Context, Process, and Outcomes* (New York: Teachers College Press, 1992), 49–65; Reagan, "Cultural Considerations in the Education of Deaf Children."

50. See Reagan, "Cultural Considerations in the Education of Deaf Children."

51. See M. J. Bienvenu, "Reflections of Deaf Culture in Deaf Humor," in Erting, Johnson, Smith, and Snider, *The Deaf Way*, 16–23; Guy Bouchauveau, "Deaf Humor and Culture," in Erting, Johnson, Smith, and Snider, *The Deaf Way*, 24–30.

52. See Sara Kersting, "Balancing Between Deaf and Hearing Worlds: Reflections of Mainstreamed College Students on Relationships and Social Interactions," *Journal of Deaf Studies and Deaf Education* 2 (1997): 252–263.

53. T. Willard, "I've Had Enough of the I-LOVE-YOU Sign, Thanks," *Silent News* 25 (1993): 2.

54. Jack Gannon, *Deaf Heritage: A Narrative History of Deaf America* (Silver Spring, MD: National Association of the Deaf, 1981).

55. See, e.g., Douglas Bayton, *Forbidden Signs: American Culture and the Campaign Against Sign Language* (Chicago: University of Chicago Press, 1996); Bragg, *DEAF-WORLD*; Robert Buchanan, *Illusions of Equality: Deaf Americans in School and Factory, 1850–1950* (Washington, DC: Gallaudet University Press, 1999); Nora Groce, *Everyone Here Spoke Sign Language: Hereditary Deafness on Martha's Vineyard* (Cambridge, MA: Harvard University Press, 1985); Harlan Lane (ed.), *The Deaf Experience: Classics in Language and Education* (Cambridge, MA: Harvard University Press, 1984); Harlan Lane, *When the Mind Hears: A History of the Deaf* (New York: Random House, 1984); Lane, *The Mask of Benevolence*; Jonathan Reé, *I See a Voice: Deafness, Language and the Senses—A Philosophical History* (New York: Metropolitan Books, 1999); John Van Cleve (ed.), *Deaf History Unveiled: Interpretations from the New Scholarship* (Washington, DC: Gallaudet University Press, 1993); John Van Cleve and Barry Crouch, *A Place of Their Own: Creating the Deaf Community in America* (Washington, DC: Gallaudet University Press, 1989); Richard Winefield, *Never the Twain Shall Meet: Bell, Gallaudet, and the Communications Debate* (Washington, DC: Gallaudet University Press, 1987).

56. Quoted in Harlan Lane, "Cochlear Implants: Their Cultural and Historical Meaning," in van Cleve, *Deaf History Unveiled*, 288.

57. Quoted in Lane, Hoffmeister, and Bahan, *A Journey into the DEAF-WORLD*, 379.

58. Kathryn Woodcock, "Cochlear Implants vs. Deaf Culture?" in Mervin Garretson (ed.), *Viewpoints on Deafness: A Deaf American Monograph, Vol. 42* (Silver Spring, MD: National Association of the Deaf, 1992), 151.

59. Lane, Hoffmeister, and Bahan, *A Journey into the DEAF-WORLD*, 388.

60. A. Philip Aiello and Myrna Aiella, "Cochlear Implants and Deaf Identity," in Bragg, *DEAF-WORLD*, 406–407; Marylyn Howe, "Untruths in Advertising: Cochlear Implants," in Garretson, *Viewpoints on Deafness*, 67–68; Harlan Lane, "Cochlear Implants Are Wrong for Young Deaf Children," in Garretson, *Viewpoints on Deafness*, 89–92; Harlan Lane, "Reproductive Control of Deaf People and the Deaf Search for a Homeland," in Mervin Garretson (ed.), *Deafness: Life and Culture II: A Deaf American Monograph, Vol. 45* (Silver Spring, MD: National Association of the Deaf, 1995), 73–78; Lane, Hoffmeister, and Bahan, *A Journey into the DEAF-WORLD*, 386–407; Woodcock, "Cochlear Implants vs. Deaf Culture?"

61. See Woodcock, "Cochlear Implants vs. Deaf Culture?"

62. Michel Foucault, *Surveiller et punir: Naissance de la prison* (Paris: Gallimard, 1975), 360.

63. Harlan Lane, "The Medicalization of Cultural Deafness in Historical Perspective," in Renate Fischer and Harlan Lane (eds.), *Looking Back: A Reader on the History of Deaf Communities and Their Sign Languages* (Hamburg, Germany: Signum Press, 1993), 490–491.

64. Steven Nover, *Our Voices, Our Vision: Politics of Deaf Education.* Paper presented at the 1993 CAIS/CEASD Convention, Baltimore, Maryland.

65. See S. Benson, *Ambiguous Ethnicity* (Cambridge, England: Cambridge University Press, 1981).

66. See also, e.g., S. Fordham and John Ogbu, "Black Students' School Success: Coping with the 'Burden of Acting White.' " *The Urban Review* 18 (1986): 176–206; M. Motoyoshi, "The Experience of Mixed-Race People: Some Thoughts and Theories," *Journal of Ethnic Studies* 18 (1990): 77–94.

67. Gardner and Lewis, *Anthropology, Development and the Post-Modern Challenge*, 32–33.

68. See Talal Asad (ed.), *Anthropology and the Colonial Encounter* (London: Ithaca, 1973).

3

"A Wise Child Is Talked to in Proverbs": Indigenous African Educational Thought and Practice

> *Africa has never been cut off from the crosscurrents of world history. It was the source of the earliest human biological and cultural developments and the point from which some of the most essential elements of human society and growth were derived. . . . As early as the first millennium A.D., Africans participated in a busy Indian Ocean trading system dealing with distant places in Arabia, India, Persia, and China, and they exported gold and other commodities across the Sahara Desert to Europe. The Middle East and Europe were also in contact with Africa, exchanging scholars and ideas with important centers of learning in the Arabic-speaking world. Thus, long before the better-known contacts between Europe and Africa that started in the fifteenth century, parts of Africa had interacted continuously with other world areas for centuries.*
> —Martin and O'Meara (1995, p. 6)

Africa is immense, not only in terms of its size and geographic diversity but, more important, with respect to the cultural, linguistic, and ethnic diversity that characterizes the people who live in its various parts. As Richard Olaniyan observed, "With almost a thousand separate language groups, a variety of climatic regions and greatly different levels of social and economic development . . . Africa is a continent of bewildering diversity and extraordinary dynamism."[1] This immensity and diversity might lead one to believe that it is not possible for us to discuss traditional "African" educational thought and practice in any meaningful way because there is bound to be considerable variation on such a topic from one group to another throughout the continent. This is an important issue, as Meyer Fortes made clear:

> Take, to begin with, the idea of African culture: by what criteria can we include, under this rubric, both the culture of the Kung Bushmen of the Kalahari— those gentle, peaceful, propertyless, hunting and collecting folk who have been

so aptly described as "the harmless people" by Lorna Marshall—and the traditional patterns of life and thought of the sophisticated, materially wealthy, politically and socially complex, militarily organized kingdoms of West Africa—Ashanti and Benin, Yoruba and Hausa.[2]

To assume that such diversity makes impossible any discussion of "African" culture (an assumption that Fortes did not, in fact, make), however, would ignore, or at the very least distort, the many commonalities that unite the African experience. As Molefi and Kariamu Asante argued:

> Africa . . . is one cultural river with numerous tributaries characterized by their specific responses to history and the environment. In this way we have always seen Europe after the Christian manifestations. England, Norway, Ireland, France, Belgium, Germany, etc., were one culture although at the same time they were different. Asante, Yoruba, Mandinka are also one, though different in the historical sense. When we speak of unity in Africa, we are speaking of the commonalities among the people. Thus, a Yoruba who is different from an Ibo or Asante still shares more in common culture with them than with Thais or Norwegians. To the degree that the material conditions influence the choices people make, we Africans share similarities in behavior, perceptions, and technologies.[3]

In short, what we must seek in an examination of traditional African educational thought and practice[4] is what Cheikh Anta Diop, in *The Cultural Unity of Negro Africa*, called the "profound cultural unity still alive beneath the deceptive appearance of cultural heterogeneity" present in Africa.[5] The Organization of African Unity, in its 1969 "Pan-African Cultural Manifesto" issued in Algiers, made clear its commitment to the ongoing presence and importance of this cultural unity when it noted that "African culture, art and science, whatever the diversity of their expression, are in no way essentially different from each other. They are but the specific expression of a single universality."[6] In this chapter, an attempt is made to identify and discuss some of the common characteristics and assumptions shared by much traditional education in Africa, while at the same time noting differences and variations that are related to sociocultural and geographic context.

THE HISTORY OF AFRICA: A BRIEF OVERVIEW

It is both interesting and telling that one of the classic treatments of world history, Will and Ariel Durant's eleven-volume *The Story of Civilization*, contains virtually no references to indigenous Africa or to African civilizations whatsoever, with the notable exception of ancient Egypt, which is dealt with in the first volume (*Our Oriental Heritage*) under the section labeled "The

Near East." This exclusion of Africa from "the story of civilization" is, of course, partially a product of the era during which the Durants were writing (from the mid-1930s until the mid-1970s), and also mirrors to some extent the more general view in our society of African history as primarily colonial and postcolonial in nature. However, this in fact radically distorts not only the very real history of Africa and her many peoples, but also the history of humanity itself. Africa is not, after all, peripheral to the development of our species; in fact, it is central. Modern human beings first evolved in Africa and then spread to the rest of the world. Further, Africa has been the home to a number of remarkable and impressive civilizations, only one of which—ancient Egypt—is commonly studied as a part of the public school social studies curricula in the United States. Whereas a thorough treatment of the history of Africa is obviously not possible here, it is important that a brief overview of the precolonial history of Africa be provided before we move on to our discussion of indigenous African educational thought and practice.

Human Origins and Prehistory

In his outstanding study of the history of Africa, *The African Experience,* Roland Oliver began by noting that "it seems that we all belong, ultimately, to Africa. Almost certainly, the Garden of Eden, in which our ancestors grew gradually apart from their nearest relatives in the animal kingdom, lay in the highland interior of East Africa, where the equatorial forest belt is broken by mountains and high savanna parklands running south from Ethiopia to the Cape."[7] Although the earliest emergence, development, and spread of our species will probably always remain somewhat uncertain and ambiguous in its precise details, the broad outlines of our ancestors' origins are fairly clear. As early as 1871, Charles Darwin, impressed by the similarities between human beings and the great apes of Africa, proposed that Africa might well be the birthplace of humanity.[8] Contemporary analyses of the DNA of modern human beings and apes suggest that Darwin was correct; in fact, the genetic evidence would seem to support a closer relationship between human beings and other primates than is generally reflected in biological taxonomies. As Peter Mitchell noted,

> Supporting Darwin's claim for an African origin for humanity . . . studies show that humans and chimpanzees share over 98 per cent of their DNA, with gorillas only marginally less closely related. This kind of distance is common among very closely related species, although traditionally African apes and humans are placed in separate families. These analyses force a radical reassessment of primate taxonomy. From the standpoint of genetic or molecular systematics, chimpanzees, gorillas and humans are *all* hominids. . . . Comparison of blood

proteins and DNA shows that chimpanzees and humans last shared a common ancestor no more than 8–6 million years ago.[9]

In any event, it is clear that genetic evidence supports the view of a relatively recent African origin for human beings. Some 100,000 to 250,000 years ago, anatomically modern human beings first emerged; more recently, only 40,000 to 50,000 years ago, we begin to see evidence for human beings who functioned cognitively much as modern humans, and it is to this period that human language and organized human culture is most often dated.[10] Although there remains considerable controversy about when human beings migrated out of Africa, the best evidence at this point in time would seem to suggest that the major exodus of modern humans took place around 60,000 to 70,000 years ago.[11]

The late Pleistocene era saw the gradual replacement of middle stone age cultures with later stone age cultures, which in turn entailed the development of "subsistence-settlement strategies and forms of social relations."[12] Both hunter-gatherer and subsistence farming cultures emerged and, in turn, a number of more complex and sophisticated societies evolved throughout Africa, as they did elsewhere in the world. As Basil Davidson explained, what followed was "a gradual emergence of specialization in the use of tools and weapons, as one or other branch of humanity adjusted itself to the particular environment in which it lived. The almost universal hand-axe of a million years ago gave way, in short, to a far better armoury of tools and weapons wielded by different types of men for different purposes in difference places. By the dawn of the Neolithic this diversification was already far advanced."[13]

Indigenous Political Systems in Africa

Broadly speaking, there were four major types of indigenous political organizations in precolonial Africa: stateless societies, chiefdoms, kingdoms, and empires.[14] Perhaps most puzzling to Western colonizers, and indeed even for many of us today, is the "stateless society." In Western political thought, the existence of the state has generally been taken as a given (albeit perhaps a "necessary evil"),[15] and the concept of a "stateless society" thus verges on being a contradiction. And yet, in the African context, a number of societies essentially ensured against autocracy and tyranny by eliminating centralized political authority, generally replacing it with strong social and cultural mores and practices related to communal governance. Among the better known examples of "stateless societies" have been the Igbo and Fulani of Nigeria, the Somali, the Gikuyu and the Mbeere of Kenya, the Kru of Liberia, the Jie of Uganda, and the !Kung of the Kalahari.[16] As Williams commented:

It was therefore in the societies without chiefs or kings where African democracy was born and where the concept that the people are sovereign was as natural as breathing. And this is why in traditional Africa, the rights of the individual never came before the rights of the community. . . . These self-governing people did not have a Utopian society in any idealistic sense. Theirs was a practical society in every way. Their laws were natural laws, and order and justice prevailed because the society could not otherwise survive. Theirs was, in fact, a government of the people; theirs was, in fact, not a theory, but a government by the people; and it was, in fact, a government for the people.[17]

Chiefdoms probably constituted the majority of specific political entities in precolonial Africa, and as a result, varied extensively in terms of their organizational structure, size, degree of independence and/or subjugation to other groups, and so on. The nucleus of a chiefdom was, of course, the chief—although the term *chief* is somewhat problematic, and has been used to refer not only to a village leader but even to a king or simply an honored person.[18] In addition, the relatives and supporters of the chief played significant social and political roles as well. Most typically, chiefdoms were village-based. Chiefs were selected on the basis of lineage and popular selection, most often by some sort of council of elders. Examples of chiefdom-based groups in Africa include the Fanti of Ghana, the Yoruba of Nigeria, and the Swazi and Zulu of South Africa.[19] Population pressures, coupled with other demographic factors, ecological factors, political factors, and so on, often led to the fragmentation of chiefdoms and the establishment of new chiefdoms. Indeed, one of the characteristics of the chiefdom-type political organization has been its tendency to change over time as the processes of abandonment, migration, conquest, and overlordship all played themselves out.[20]

Kingdoms in Africa constituted an important but paradoxical approach to governance. As one would expect, there was considerable diversity with respect to the characteristics and organization of different kingdoms. As George Ayittey noted:

The sizes of African kingdoms varied enormously and dispersed geographically although there were some regional concentrations. For example, most of East African kingdoms were located north and west of Lake Victoria, while small chiefdoms and self-governing lineages predominated over much of present-day Kenya, Tanzania, and northern Uganda. In some kingdoms, there were no provinces, and the political entity did not amount to much. Nevertheless, nearly all the societies of central Africa had kingdoms.[21]

Common to most of the African kingdoms, and quite unlike the situation in both the stateless societies and chiefdoms, was the metaphysical view of the King as "the actual embodiment of the kingdom, and [the related idea] that there is a mystical union between the two."[22] In other words, kingdoms were

generally based on a "divine kingship" model, not unlike the European concept of the "divine right of kings," but also by no means the same as that concept.[23] In the African case, "divine kingship" also entails legitimacy grounded
in the popular acceptance of the king.[24] As Kopytoff explained:

> The crucial point in Africa was that legitimacy had been conferred by the peo-
> ple by way of the "consent" of their symbols . . . being the creation of subjects,
> the African ruler's legitimacy rested on an implicit contract that could be with-
> drawn. . . . Under a satisfactory ruler, who had lived up to his nurturing obliga-
> tions, the subjects would present the patrimonial perspective on rulership, in
> which the ruler is the absolute "owner" of everything. Similarly, the good ruler
> would state publicly that his rule rested on the happiness of the people and on
> their consent.[25]

This two-way obligation was not just theoretical in nature; the very real op-
tion of regicide played an important role in many African kingdoms. The
king "was expected by his non-kin subjects to live up to his side of the bar-
gain, and the subjects were not interested in his motives but in his performance. This indifference to motivation was congruent with the fact that many
of the taboos which the ruler might breach were quite beyond his volitional
control—taboos against physical weakness, illnesses, and old age . . . while the
sacredness of the king made him 'divine,' it also made him into a 'scapegoat
king.' "[26]

Finally, Africa has been the home of a number of highly centralized imperial states. Apart from that of ancient Egypt, Africa has also witnessed the rise
and fall of more than a dozen major empires, including those of Great Zimbabwe (Mwene Mutapa), Kuba, Lunda, Kanuri, Benin, Oyo, Asante, Mali,
Wolof, Ghana, Zande, and Zulu, among others,[27] as well as the Mandinka
Empire, which was itself a result of the expansion of Islam into Africa. These
empires were urbanized, economically complex, and politically and culturally
sophisticated, and in their times, some were among the most impressive civilizations in the world. Although the study of each of these empires is both fascinating and significant, what is especially intriguing, I would suggest, has
been their absence from our conception of "the story of civilization." With
this very brief overview of the precolonial history of Africa as background, we
are now ready to turn to our discussion of indigenous African educational
thought and practice.

THE GOALS OF INDIGENOUS AFRICAN EDUCATION

It is possible to identify a number of different goals that traditional indigenous African educational practices seek to achieve. For instance, Fafunwa,
in his *A History of Education in Nigeria*, discussed what he termed the "seven

cardinal goals of traditional African education," which included the following:

- to develop the child's latent physical skills;
- to develop character;
- to inculcate respect for elders and those in position of authority;
- to develop intellectual skills;
- to acquire specific vocational training and a healthy attitude toward honest labor;
- to develop a sense of belonging and to participate actively in family and community affairs; and
- to understand, appreciate, and promote the cultural heritage of the community at large.[28]

Taken together, these educational goals constitute a descriptive inventory of the characteristics of the "good person" for traditional African societies. Such an individual, on Fafunwa's account, will be one who "is honest, respectable, skilled, cooperative and conforms to the social order of the day."[29] Although much can be said in favor of such individuals, there is also a risk involved in encouraging conformity in societies that are no longer purely traditional in nature as is, of course, the case in most of contemporary Africa. It is such people, in fact, about whom the Nigerian novelist Chinua Achebe wrote rather critically in *A Man of the People*:

> Overnight everyone began to shake their heads at the excesses of the last regime, at its graft, oppression and corrupt government: newspapers, the radio, the hitherto silent intellectuals and civil servants—everybody said what a terrible lot; and it become public opinion the next morning. And these were the same people that only the other day had owned a thousand names of adulation, whom praise-singers followed with song and talking-drum wherever they went.[30]

Traditional African educational thought and practice is characterized not only by its concern with the "good person," however, but also by its interweaving of social, economic, political, cultural, and educational threads together into a common tapestry. In his book *Education in Africa*, Abdou Moumouni argued that traditional education in Africa is distinguished by the following four features:

- the great importance attached to it, and its collective and social nature;
- its intimate tie with social life, both in a material and a spiritual sense;
- its multivalent character, both in terms of its goals and the means employed; and

- its gradual and progressive achievements, in conformity with the successive stages of physical, emotional, and mental development of the child.[31]

Education, then, in the traditional African setting cannot (and indeed, philosophically should not) be separated from life itself. It is a natural process by which the children gradually acquire skill, knowledge, and attitudes appropriate to life in their community. Furthermore, in precolonial settings, such education was generally highly effective. As Moumouni argued:

> The effectiveness of this education was possible because of its very close relationship with life. It was through social acts (production) and social relationships (family life, group activities) that the education of the child or adolescent took place, so that he was instructed and educated simultaneously. To the extent that a child learned everywhere and all the time, instead of learning in circumstances determined in advance as to place and time, outside of the productive and social world, he was truly in the "school of life," in the most concrete and real sense.[32]

An important facet of education conceived of in this way is that all adults in the community become, in essence, teachers for any child with whom they have contact. Thus, writing about traditional education among the Igbo, Ambrose Okeke noted that "education in the wider sense of the term has all along been an essential factor in the way of life of the Igbo man. Parents, guardians, relatives and a wider circle of kinsmen in Igboland consider it a sacred trust of discharging their obligations as it concerned the socialization of the Igbo child. As a matter of fact, the entire village took part in this socialization process."[33] Children learn adult roles, as well as the skills necessary for survival, in short, by imitating adults engaged in their daily activities, and by assisting parents and other adults as they engage in such activities.[34] Much is learned by the child through play and imitative games, as Duminy noted:

> The work and ways of the adult provided the material for the play of the child. Often, especially among girls, the imitative games (spontaneous imitation at first) gradually passed through a phase of diverted imitation to serious work. In various South African tribes (e.g., Sotho and Venda) it was customary for young children to build small houses and play at being grown up, imitating all the actions they had seen their elders do. Young girls were grinding soft stones between harder ones and young boys went through the whole ritual of their fathers "stock-farming" with their clay oxen.[35]

In fact, in the traditional African social context, it is often virtually impossible to distinguish between "play," "learning," and other kinds of social activities: "Among all peoples children learn by imitating their elders in play so that it is often difficult to distinguish between learning and play: the San boy is given a miniature bow and arrow as soon as he is able to handle them. The arrows are not poisoned and he plays at hunting, shooting field-mice, birds and hares; but when he kills a little duiker he is deemed ready to handle poisoned arrows."[36] Furthermore, from early childhood, the African child in a traditional society is expected to participate in the economic life and activities of the community. As de Villiers and Hartshorne commented:

> Among peoples having non-specialized cultures children begin to participate at an early age in the economic activities of the adults according to their strength and skill. The Zulu girl tends her younger siblings, fetches water and firewood, cleans the home and, as she grows older, increasingly shares in the tasks she will one day perform as an adult. What she learns thus has a direct bearing on the knowledge and skills she will require in adulthood.[37]

With this general background to traditional African educational thought and practice in mind, we can now turn to more detailed discussions of several key components of such education. Specifically, we examine the role and place of the oral tradition in education, traditional education as moral education, the process of initiation, and the vocational aspects of traditional African education.

THE ORAL TRADITION IN INDIGENOUS AFRICAN EDUCATION

Traditional African societies are, by and large, oral ones, and this is true even where an established written literary tradition exists, as in the cases of such languages as Swahili, Zulu, Xhosa, and so on.[38] Writing about traditional education in East Africa, Mazrui and Wagaw noted:

> Yet another characteristic of most indigenous systems of education in East Africa is that they are based on the oral tradition rather than the written one. This is not to suggest that the written tradition has been entirely absent. On the contrary, both the Amharic literary culture and the Kiswahili literary culture are centuries old. But most "tribal" educational systems in Eastern Africa operated on the basis of the supremacy of the oral tradition, with only a minor role for the written word.[39]

An important aspect of traditional education in the African context has, therefore, been concerned with teaching children the oral tradition, as well as helping them to learn to use language creatively and effectively. In essence, such learning is a central feature of the intellectual training of the African child. With specific reference to traditional educational practice in Igboland, Okeke commented:

> The proverbs, the riddles, the ideation of "*chi*" and "*anyanwu la eseelu*," the ability to distinguish between a killing herb and a healing one—all these constitute a veritable storehouse of intellectual exercise. Proverbs and riddles are used to hide a saying from the ordinary turn of mind. They help in selecting and analysing issues and problems of the moment. Traditional education exposed the Igbo to this training. So too do tongue-twisters used to train the child's capacity to retain the sequence of events.[40]

Proverbs feature prominently in virtually all traditional African cultures, and play important communicative and educational roles, as Boateng explained:

> Another means by which traditional education promoted intergenerational communication was through proverbial sayings. Proverbial sayings are widespread throughout Africa, and their themes bear strong similarity to one another. The educative and communicative power of proverbs in traditional Africa lies in their use as validators of traditional procedures and beliefs. Children are raised to believe strongly that proverbial sayings have been laid down and their validity tested by their forefathers.[41]

Furthermore, Fajana argued that "proverbs which constituted an important intellectual mode of communication were used to develop the child's reasoning power and skill, and in expressing the deeper thoughts most essential in settling disputes and in decision-making processes. They had to be mastered if the child was to be fully developed and be able to cope with the various occasions when they had to be used."[42]

The basic idea underlying proverbs is that such sayings provide succinct, easily remembered summaries of important ideas and experiences that are part of the shared cultural knowledge of the community. Borland, writing about the oral culture of the Shona, noted that "*tsumo* [proverbs] embody the wisdom and experience of a people lacking written records in a concise, quotable and often amusing form. The free use of *tsumo* is the accepted way of winning an argument, and *tsumo* are therefore an integral part of Shona legal procedure which is conducted by argument."[43]

Proverbs can be used to discuss virtually any aspect of social life; in his discussion of Zulu proverbs, for instance, Nyembezi classified Zulu proverbs as falling into ten categories, which are also applicable to proverbs found in most other African languages. The categories suggested by Nyembezi, together with examples of each type of proverb, are presented in Fig. 3.1.

Examples of proverbs from traditional African contexts abound, and many of them provide us with insight into both traditional education and social and

Category of Proverb	Content of Proverbs	Examples
Ubuntu	Treatment of people, good and bad behaviour, pride, ingratitude, etc.	A kindness is reciprocted The stomach of a traveller is small.
Ukwethembeka Nokungethembeki	Faithfulness and unfaithfulness, deception, cunning, etc	He cries with one eye. A crime is always denied.
Ubuhlobo Nobutha	Friendship and enmity.	The harshness of young people is repaid. The one offended never forgets; it is the offender who forgets.
Impumelelo, Inhlanhla, Namashwa	Good fortune, misfortune, troubles, uncertainty, despair, futile labour, failure and encouragement.	She has married her lover. To see once is to see twice.
Ubuqhawe Nobugwala	Bravery and cowardice.	An elephant is stabbed by all before it falls.
Emakhaya	Home life, marriage, heredity, relatives, child–parent relationships, etc.	A small pot is like the big one. A minister does not beget a minister.
Ukewedlula Kwemihla	Passage of time, aging, etc.	Old age does not announce itself. Death has no modesty.

FIG. 3.1.   Categories of Zulu proverbs.

cultural values and mores.[44] Consider, for instance, the Swahili proverb, "*Mgeni siki mbili, siku ya tatu mpe jembe*" [Your guest is a guest for two days; after that, give him a hoe], which conveys both practical advice and considerable insight into interpersonal relationships. A great deal can also be learned by examining proverbs that relate to the relationship between parents and children, as in these Igbo examples:

- *Akukwo nnewu talu, ka nweya nata.* [The leaf that the big goat has eaten, will be eaten by his kids.]
- *Ezinkpolo nada ezinkpolo.* [From good seed falls good seed.]
- *Ainy elur ike ili owa iru nabo.* [We can't eat the world on two sides; i.e., you can't have both many children and a lot of money.][45]

For our purposes here, it is perhaps useful to consider proverbs common in southern Africa that relate directly to education:

- If you take a knife from a child, give him a stick.

- The teacher sometimes commits adultery himself.
- The dry stick kindles the green ones.[46]

These proverbs provide us with considerable insight into the educational philosophy that underlies traditional African education, although it is important to keep in mind that proverbs are often notoriously difficult to translate. As Taban lo Liyong noted about Acoli proverbs, "The meaning of deep Acoli proverbs are made very light by their rendition into English word for word, rather than sense for sense, or proverb for proverb."[47] Furthermore, the use of proverbs in educating children, as well as in indirect social communication in general is, by its very nature, context specific. Thus, if one sees two reasonably well-matched Zulu boys fighting, one might say, "*Kubamben' ingwe nengonyama*" [The leopard and the lion are fighting]. Similarly, to describe two children who simply do not get along, one would use a proverb contrasting two animals that are natural enemies, such as:

- *Yinkuku nempaka.* [It is a fowl and a wild cat.]
- *Yikati negundane.* [It is a cat and a mouse.]
- *Yinja nekati.* [It is a dog and a cat.][48]

In this way, vast amounts of information can be conveyed quickly and creatively, and the use of proverbs in childrearing is widespread throughout Africa. As the Twi say, after all, "A wise child is talked to in proverbs."[49]

Finally, proverbs are sometimes used in various types of wordplay. For example, speakers of Teke in the Congo often engage in a specialized kind of linguistic behavior called *Bisisimi*, which can be roughly translated as "the language of the wise."[50] *Bisisimi* involve the competitive chanting of proverbs, as opposed to their common use in everyday speech, and is found primarily in specialized settings, such as mourning ceremonies, festive gatherings, and acts of divination.[51] Nkara described the process of *Bisisimi* as follows:

> In most contexts, participants sit in a circle, in the *mbong* (sort of communal shed in villages), in the shade of a big tree and sometimes around a fire at night. To begin with, participants converse in everyday Teke. After an hour or so, depending on the occasion, they start using *Bisisimi*. . . . The addresser or initiator stands up and starts an *Isisimi*. The other participants chant either a part of it or the whole *Isisimi* as they clap hands following the rhythm of the chant. A small drum is sometimes beaten by one of them. As soon as any other participant realizes that he is the object of the *Isisimi* he responds immediately in kind. If he fails or happens to be in no position to respond, a friend or relative of his may come to his rescue.[52]

Furthermore, it is important to understand that, in some cases, *Bisisimi* may go far beyond being merely a game: "The use of *Bisisimi* . . . may be regarded as a contest of wits or a verbal game, but this game may also turn into a kind of occult fight when the use of *mpaana* [psychic power] is involved. In such cases, it is believed that the loser may suffer physically."[53]

Another example of the way in which oral cultures are transmitted and language used creatively in traditional African education is the use of riddles, word games, puzzles, and tongue-twisters. All of these activities, which are common throughout most of Africa, are examples of what we might call "critical thinking activities," encouraging as they do innovative, creative, and difficult uses of various symbol systems. For instance, in Shona culture *zvirahwe*, or riddles, are widely used by and with children. Examples of Shona riddles, and their correct responses, include:

- Question: *Nzira mbiri dzinoenda mugomo?* [Two paths lead up the mountain?]
  Answer: *Mhino.* [Nostrils.]
- Question: *Imba imiri nebango rimwe?* [The house is supported by one pole?]
  Answer: *Howa.* [Mushroom.]
- Question: *Shumba mbiri dzakaririra gomo?* [Two lions waited on the hill?]
  Answer: *Nzeve.* [Ears.][54]

Riddles can also be used to teach a great deal of information about the natural world, as these Ndebele riddles make clear:

- Question: *Ngabantwana bami bakha indlu banganamanzi?* [My children burning a house without water?]
  Answer: *Mmuhlwa.* [Termites.]
- Question: *Ngesitimela sami asikhambi esiporweni?* [By my train that does not go on the railway track?]
  Answer: *Lisongololo.* [Millipede.]
- Question: *Ngomntwa'mi unamehlo amakhulu usaba ukuqalana nomkhayo?* [By my person with big eyes who is afraid of facing the light?]
  Answer: *Sirhulurhulu.* [Owl.][55]

Finally, riddles can reinforce social and cultural knowledge, as the following Yoruba riddle demonstrates:

- Question: *A be ori, a be idi re, sibe-sibe o nsowo ola?* [We cut off the top and the bottom, yet it produces wealth?]
  Answer: *Ilu.* [Drum.][56]

Word games can include a wide variety of different kinds of linguistic activities, but are generally concerned with the players' speed and continuity, although such games can also depend heavily on knowledge of the social and natural worlds, as was the case with riddles. For example, a common word game is for children to quiz one another about the names for different kinds of trees, plants, animals, and so on.[57] Another common type of word game is one in which children must engage in repetition (or alteration) of words, either real or invented, in some series or sequence. Such a game strengthens the memory and helps to develop mental acuity and speed.

Similar games often serve to teach and reinforce mathematical concepts. For instance, "The Yoruba have developed a system of counting and have used a variety of human experiences to promote practice and dexterity in enumeration. The Yoruba child is introduced early in life to counting by means of concrete objects, counting rhymes, folklore, plays, and games, at home and on the farm."[58] The following is an example of one of the counting rhymes that Yoruba children are likely to learn, and that is fairly typical of such rhymes:

Rhyme	Translation
Eni bi eni	One is one
Eji bi eji	Two is two
Eta metagba	Three, spin calabash
Erin woroko	Four crooked
Arun igbodo	Five, pestle pounding
Efa ti ele	Six of ele
Aro nbaro	Cymbal, which cymbal?
Aro mbata	Cymbal, bata drum
B'oo da k'esan	If one is missing [out of ten fingers]
Gbangaba l'ewa	Ten exposed.[59]

Puzzles are also used in childrearing and education, and take several different forms. Two distinct examples of puzzles are "dilemma tales" and "arithmetic puzzles."[60] Although similar to proverbs in certain ways, both dilemma tales and arithmetic puzzles are distinctive in nature. Bascom explained the difference among riddles, arithmetic puzzles, and dilemma tales: "Put concisely, riddles are to be answered; arithmetic puzzles are to be solved; dilemma tales are to be resolved."[61] Kubik, writing about both dilemma tales and arithmetic puzzles among the Valuchazi in Eastern Angola and Northwestern Zambia, argued that dilemma tales are "a genre of oral literature; as a prose narrative that ends in an open question, a dilemma, for the audience to resolve. Thus, in contrast to ordinary folktales, a dilemma tale is not brought to a conclusion by the narrator, but it ends on a question which is followed by a lively discussion by the audience. . . . In dilemma stories the aim is to stimulate discussion. A problem has to be resolved."[62]

Arithmetic puzzles, on the other hand, are stories in which a logical or mathematical challenge is presented to the listener. As with dilemma tales, both children and adults can participate in the discussion. It is important to note here, as did Kubik, that despite its intellectual complexity (one arithmetical puzzle discussed by Kubik involved eleven steps) and potential metaphysical implications, "this is a leisure-time activity and arithmetic puzzles serve to stimulate the intellect and test the mathematical capabilities of the participants."[63]

Thus far, we have considered the oral nature of traditional African societies primarily in terms of its role in intellectual training, but also of great significance is the content of the oral tradition. It is through fables, myths, and legends that much of the history of the community, as well as its values and beliefs, is passed on from one generation to the next. As Boateng commented, "Myths played an active part in the African's everyday life and were a vital social force. . . . Myths and legends not only supplied accounts of the group's origin but related precedents to present-day beliefs, actions, and codes of behavior."[64]

The African child learns fables, myths, and legends in a variety of settings and from a host of different adults, including especially the village storyteller. As N. Uka explained:

By listening to the village story-teller [the child] acquires a knowledge of the past. Every tale is a parable; it is not just history but an educational story. The stories are manifestations of the tribal memory, the origin and history of the group, the deeds of their great men and women, their victories and defeats in war, their experiences which led to individual and group success and those which led to individual and group failure.[65]

Similarly, in describing the training of *bori* musicians among the Hausa, Besmer reported:

One common but informal institution for these lessons is the evening gossip sessions held inside or immediately in front of most Hausa compounds. A boy old enough to have "sense" (which the Hausa say should come to him by the time he is five or six years old) normally sits on the outside of the group presided over or attended by his father. Talking is the popular pastime and storytelling is an art, elderly bori musicians regularly claiming to be experts at both. The day's events are discussed and the society's problems solved during these sessions, and when spirits are the topic tale after tale is enjoyed by young and old alike. "Have I ever told you the secret of so-and-so's wealth?" or "Do you know the reason why such-and-such is a strange place?" an old man might ask. If his audience should reply "no" he would then ask them how many ears they had. Each listener would answer "two" and he would retort, "Well increase them to three and listen to this," the signal that a "true" story was about to be told.[66]

This oral tradition includes not only the history of the community, however, but also serves to "sustain morality, ritual, law, and sanctions against offenders."[67] It is manifested in everyday life in a variety of ways, none clearer than in the praise-songs or praise-poems (*izibongo*) that are sung to honor individuals, groups, and so on.[68] As Schapera noted:

> Praise-poems . . . are composed not only about chiefs, headmen, famous warriors, and other prominent tribesmen, but about ordinary commoners also, including women; there are, in addition, praise-poems of tribes and subdivisions of tribes (such as wards and lineages), of domestic animals (notably cattle), of wild animals (including birds and insects), of trees and crops, of rivers, hills, and other scenic features, and of such inanimate objects as divining-bones. In modern times some have even been composed about schools, railway trains, and bicycles.[69]

In order to understand many praise-poems, however, let alone to be able to compose one, an individual must possess a broad historical and cultural knowledge of the community, as well as a good grasp of the language of the community.[70] The recitation of such *izibongo* remains a way of maintaining and transmitting the oral tradition, and it is a feature of traditional African education to which we will return later in the chapter.

INDIGENOUS AFRICAN EDUCATION AS MORAL EDUCATION

One of the central features of traditional education throughout Africa is its concern with the formation of the child's character. Fafunwa, discussing the education of the Yoruba, described this concern with character formation as "the corner-stone of African education."[71] Furthermore, Moumouni argued:

> Moulding character and providing moral qualities are primary objectives in traditional African education. Almost all the different aspects of education of the child and adolescent aim towards this goal, to a greater or lesser degree. In the family, parents concern themselves with the bearing, manners, honesty and integrity of the child. Outside the house, games, the society of his friends in the same age group, and the demands they make on each other, constitute a real source of character-building. Sociability, integrity, honesty, courage, solidarity, endurance, ethics and above all the concept of honour are, among others, the moral qualities constantly demanded, examined, judged and sanctioned, in ways which depend on the intellectual level and capacities of the child and adolescent.[72]

The responsibility for teaching the child the moral and spiritual values of the community, as well as for ensuring his compliance with those values, as indicated in the previous passage, rests first of all with the child's mother and immediate family, but ultimately is the concern of the entire community.[73] As

Okeke noted with regard to the Igbo, "Everyone in the home, in the village and in the community wanted the Igbo child to be sociable, truthful, brave, humble, have stamina and be of unreproachable conduct at all times. For this reason, everyone joined in correcting or praising any child whenever and wherever he failed or succeeded in showing acceptable norms of behaviour."[74]

Among the more important aspects of character training common in traditional African education is its emphasis on respect for elders.[75] As Fafunwa commented in terms of the Nigerian experience:

> Age is an important element in the life of the African. Reverence for those who are older is particularly strong among the Yoruba. Seniority confers social and economic privileges, especially in the sharing of spoils, prizes, wealth, etc. The elder is assumed to be a man (or woman) of wisdom and is expected to demonstrate this in speech and action if he is to keep his position among those who look up to him for leadership. Age is such a vital factor among many . . . ethnic groups that a man (or woman) will overstate his age rather than understate it. Moreover, a young man or woman is not expected to look an elder straight in the face for this is considered a sign of disrespect.[76]

It is important to note that the concept "elders" here refers not only to those chronologically older than the individual, but also to "those who are in authority, particularly the chief, the cult leaders, the diviners, relatives (especially uncles) and older neighbours,"[77] and furthermore, that respect in this regard entails, among other things, obedience. It also involves appropriate forms of address and ritual greetings, which play an important role in many African societies,[78] and even distinct forms of language in some cases.[79]

THE PROCESS OF INITIATION

Perhaps the best-known, and arguably the most misunderstood, aspect of traditional African education is that of initiation. The process by which the adolescent is formally transformed, socially and spiritually, into an adult varies considerably from one African society to another, and a few traditional societies (e.g., the Akans[80] and the Shona[81]) do not even have a formal initiation process at all. Nonetheless, initiation remains a common, although less often observed, practice today as a result of increasing urbanization and Westernization, throughout much of eastern, western, and southern Africa, and traditional African initiation practices do share significant common features and characteristics. As Benjamin Ray argued in *African Religions*: "The most elaborate rites of passage usually concern the initiation of the young into adulthood. In this way a society not only socializes its young by outwardly moving them into new roles of social responsibility, but also transforms them inwardly by molding their moral and mental disposition towards the world.

This is what African societies consider to be the primary purpose of initiation rituals."[82]

African initiation ceremonies and practices are different from comparable rites of passage in the West, however, in that they make public what Westerners see as intensely private: "Besides being a test of courage and the completion of education, initiation is also a collective ceremony. In European societies, reaching puberty is a private matter. Each girl and boy goes through adolescence to sexual maturity alone. In Africa the long initiation ceremonials dramatize this change and make it a social ritual."[83]

Although the process of initiation is divided into different stages by various African societies, for most groups the initiation process includes the following components:

- separation of the initiates from the community, under the leadership of a specially selected adult;
- both formal and informal instruction about adult duties, responsibilities, and obligations;
- instruction in the folklore, legends, and history of the community;
- observation of selected food, behavioral, and sexual taboos and restrictions;
- instruction in aspects of sexuality and sexual relations in preparation for marriage;
- physical markings, commonly permanent in nature; and
- circumcision (often for both males and females).[84]

In addition, male initiation very often involves tests of physical and mental endurance, including various kinds of torture, which "is regarded as a test of fortitude and a conditioning to pain and discomfort which the new life in which the individual finds himself will bring in its train."[85]

Finally, a lasting feature of the initiation process in many societies is the establishment of a peer group, or "age-set."[86] Such age-sets are among the more important non-kin groupings found in traditional African societies and are found in virtually all parts of sub-Saharan Africa. In essence, such age-sets are male association groups based on contemporaneity and reinforced by the bonding that takes place during the initiation process. As Olaniyan explained:

A man belongs to that set of men who are his age mates, and their set moves through the several age-grades as the men go through life, beginning with their initiation into manhood as adolescents. Membership in an age set is not voluntary, and it carries with it both obligations and privileges. Typically, age sets pass through some four grades comprising (1) newly initiated men in a training period; (2) the warrior grade responsible for defence; (3) adult men responsible for governing; and (4) the society's elders.[87]

The initiation process, which in many ways is the pinnacle of traditional African educational practice, represents a huge investment on the part of the community. As Raum noted:

> The first thing that strikes an educationist is that initiation is a tremendous pedagogic effort. There is the ritual isolation of the company of initiands in a camp set apart "in the wilderness." There is the appointment of the requisite personnel: the master of the rite, or owner of the lodge, teachers of different rank, the operator, assistants and supervisors, the carriers of food to the camp. The master of the rite has to be a man of charisma to be able to transmit special qualities to the inmates of the camp; teachers and assistants must be ritually pure. The economic preparations for initiation are often on a grand scale.[88]

Although the initiation "school" and the ceremonials related to it are, then, clearly very important and costly to the community, they are also limited in their objectives. As van der Vliet observed, "The initiation schools . . . do not mark the final stage of the development of the individual; they do, however, equip and entitle him to accept the roles which maturity will bring."[89] In short, the process by which adolescents are initiated into adulthood serves a variety of functions in traditional African societies, including religious, political, psychological, and educational ones. The initiation schools do not, however, seek to address what might be called the vocational aspects of adulthood. As Blacking argued with respect to the Venda, "Formal . . . education in traditional Venda society was never intended to give people technological training for earning a living."[90] With this point in mind, we can now turn to a discussion of how the vocational needs of both the community and the individual are met in traditional African education.

VOCATIONAL ASPECTS OF INDIGENOUS AFRICAN EDUCATION

The preparation of children for their future economic roles in the society is an important element in traditional African educational thought and practice. To some extent, of course, many vocational skills and a great deal of knowledge related to and necessary for such skills are acquired simply by observation, imitation, and participation as children interact with their parents on an everyday basis. Such would, for instance, be the case for many agricultural and domestic types of activity. For other occupations in traditional societies, however, various kinds of apprenticeship are employed. Generally speaking, vocational preparation in traditional African education has been divided on the basis of type of occupation into three broad categories: agriculturally related occupations, trades and crafts, and the professions.[91]

Agricultural activities have been the basis for the vast majority of traditional agricultural societies, although some groups (e.g., the Masai in Kenya
and Tanzania) have relied on animal husbandry instead.[92] Agricultural knowledge and skills have been passed on from one generation to the next most often by involving children in all aspects of agricultural production from early
on. Gradually, the child is given increasing responsibilities as he becomes
proficient at the tasks related to agricultural production, often being given his
own small farm to tend. Here, Ishumi described the Yoruba custom:

> At the time the young farmer was learning these techniques, he would work
> with his guardian all day. But by about 12–15 years when he should have mas-
> tered these techniques he would be given some evenings free to work on his
> own farm. At first, it might be two evenings in the week, later this would be ex-
> tended to all afternoons. This in itself was a lesson in responsibility and the
> foundation for independent existence. From now, the boy had his own
> chicken, product of his own effort which he could dispose of according to his
> wishes. By the time he was married, between 20–25, he could stand on his own
> as a farmer.[93]

The experience of boys and girls in this regard differed somewhat, reflecting the later occupational division that would divide them as adults. As
Sudarkasa explained, however:

> Typically, in indigenous African societies, the occupational roles of women
> were different from but complementary to the roles of men. . . . Very often
> men and women worked in the same occupation (for example, in farming or
> trading), but the tasks undertaken tended to be sex specific (for example, pre-
> paring the land for farming versus tending the crops or trading in one line of
> goods as opposed to another). There does not seem to be a basis for holding
> that women's occupations were considered to be "inferior" to those of men, al-
> though such occupations were usually thought to be inappropriate for men,
> just as men's occupations were normally considered inappropriate for women.
> The point here is that the maintenance of separate occupational domains for
> the two sexes did not automatically imply a hierarchical relationship between
> those two domains.[94]

If agricultural and domestic occupations are learned largely from parents
through imitation and informal participation, and thus, as Sudarkasa noted,
"did not usually involve formal apprenticeships," more formal apprenticeship arrangements have been common for many crafts and professions in the
traditional African society.[95] Among the more common crafts learned
through some type of apprenticeship system are "weaving (for instance, bas-
kets and cloth), hunting, carving, sculpturing, painting and decorating, car-
pentry, building, hair-plaiting, dressmaking, boat-making, mat-making, dy-
ing, isusu-collecting (cooperative banking), food-selling, wine-tapping, and a

host of other trades and crafts."[96] It is important to note, however, that such craft skills and knowledge are generally passed on within specific families, as Callaway, writing about Nigeria, explained that "this vast apprenticeship training system began as a part of a wider educational process in which the indigenous societies of Nigeria passed on their cultural heritage from one generation to the next. The skills 'owned' by a family were highly valued, and in some lines such as native medicine, secrets were zealously guarded. . . . Evidence of the passing on of skills within families is still strong."[97]

Ogundijo noted several important features of indigenous apprenticeship practices, not the least of which are that "children were not free to choose the trade of the their liking, for they were bound to follow the guidance of their parents. For effective training, parents always apprenticed their children to their relatives, friends or competent craftsmen."[98]

Not only were trades and crafts learned through the apprenticeship system, but so too were the professional occupations of traditional African societies. Included under the general category of "professional occupations" are such social roles as "doctors, priests, witch doctors, civil servants, village heads, chiefs and kings, tax collectors, heralds, judges, councillors, police and messengers, shrine-keepers, soldiers, etc."[99] Unlike most trade and craft occupations, at least some of these professions have traditionally been what Nadel called "free professions," which means that one could become a member of the occupation not only through birth, but also through merit. As Nadel commented about the Nupe kingdom in Nigeria, "It is not surprising that a rich and complex culture like Nupe should possess its clearly defined 'free professions'—its professional scholars, scientists and artists, or, in a terminology more akin to the native conception, its mallams, barber-doctors, and drummers and dancers."[100]

An intriguing example of such "free professionals" in the traditional African context, and one that has important implications for many contemporary African societies as well, is that of traditional healers. Traditional healers in Africa provide an important alternative to Western medicine—both in terms of providing a kind of medical care where Western facilities are not available, and as socially and psychologically powerful alternatives and/or additions to Western medicine, especially, although by no means exclusively, in rural areas. Twumasi and Warren have divided traditional healers in Ghana and Zamiba into four main groups: traditional birth attendants, faith healers, herbalists, and spiritualists/diviners.[101] Although there are obviously variations in this model from one part of sub-Saharan Africa to another, these basic divisions work reasonably well to categorize different kinds of traditional healers. Traditional birth attendants actually have a far broader range of activities and responsibilities than the label would suggest: These individuals, almost universally women, serve not only as midwives, but also as specialists in obstetrics, sex education, and contraception. Their role is, in addition,

both medical and spiritual; it is quite common for them to function as god-
mothers for the children whom they deliver, and they also often have a role to
play in puberty ceremonies. Faith healers are generally tied to specific religious movements, such as the syncretic churches, millennial churches, and
thaumaturgical churches, and can be either Christian or Muslim in origin
and focus. Herbalists are traditional healers who make use of herbs in addressing medical problems; treatment procedures are generally fairly similar
to those employed in Western medical practice. Finally, spiritualist healers,
who are most often tied to particular shrines, are indigenous priests, priest-
esses, ritual, and cult leaders who specialize in divination and spiritual possession.[102] In many parts of Africa today, traditional healers are in the process of
organizing and gaining professional status,[103] and it is very important to keep
in mind that the services they provide are often valuable and effective—in
some instances, far more so than would be Western medical alternatives. A
powerful example of the way in which traditional and Western medical care
can overlap and coexist is provided by Leslie Swartz, who reported:

> At one time I was receiving three different treatments for a severe allergy: corti-
> sone (from biomedicine), a treatment based on anthroposophical medicine (a
> form of healing with a spiritual component), and homeopathic remedies. I had
> faith in none of the three approaches to help me on its own, and I knew that
> practitioners from the three approaches would not approve of my using all
> three simultaneously but, probably quite irrationally, I thought that if I tried
> everything at once, it might work. (It did!) At that time, my discomfort was
> such that I was not thinking logically. I was also not acting in terms of any
> worked-out ideology of care. I was simply desperate. And this need for treat-
> ment, of some kind or another, together with what happens to be reasonably
> accessible to people, will help determine how people use resources.[104]

Traditional healers are selected and trained in a wide variety of ways. In a
fascinating description of the process by which traditional healers acquire
their professional competence among the Zezuru in Zimbabwe, for instance,
Pamela Reynolds reported the following ten-stage "life cycle" for traditional
healers:

Childhood
  1. Prior to his death, a healer may designate his heir. The heir need not
     have been born yet; he or she is identified as, perhaps, the healer's son's
     first child of either sex.
  2. Special ties are established between the child and the healer, often be-
     tween grandparent and grandchild. Most children are taught to classify
     plants into three categories: poisonous plants, edible plants, and plants
     that must not be tampered with because they belong to the shades.

3. This instruction is enlarged upon from the age of nine. The healer instructs the child in the identification and naming of herbs. The child assists the healer in the preparation and administration of medicines. The child is expected to help during treatment sessions, including those in which the healer is possessed.

Young Adulthood

4. At about the age of thirteen, the child begins to collect herbs and prepare medicines alone. He may begin to gather herbs on his own initiative. While the healer is away, the child often treats patients, according to the healer's instructions.

5. The process of "matriculation" begins. It is characterised by illness and dreams, in which universal symbols like water, flying, and pythons appear, often as a test of courage. Western and traditional experts are consulted. The patient may stay with a healer for long periods, even for a number of years.

6. The spirit identifies itself, his demands are met and symptoms of illness fade away.

7. Soon thereafter the healer begins to treat in his own right. He gradually accumulates power and respect and a reputation for success in certain areas of divination and healing.

Middle Age

8. The healer is fully fledged. He begins to lead ritual occasions and bring out the spirits of others. In describing this stage of their life cycle, many healers admit training others but deny having been trained when they had their spirits brought out.

Old Age

9. A time of seniority follows. There is substantial evidence that grandchildren are trained to assume the healing role after the healer's death.

Death

10. Death is followed by the eventual possession of a kin member, often after a period of intense rivalry within the family.[105]

An interesting exception to the generally formal, apprenticeship-based training assumed for the professions is that of the *imbongi*, or praise-poet, among groups such as the Zulu and Xhosa in southern Africa.[106] The *imbongi* is in many ways a unique figure in traditional society; his role is part historian, part counselor, part social and political critic. The *imbongi* fulfills a role similar to that played by the medieval bard, relying both on the established oral tradition and his own ability to improvise in creating the appropriate *izibongo* (praise-poem) for the occasion. The *imbongi* is granted remarkable freedom in what he can say in his *izibongo*. As Opland explained, "It is generally accepted that the *imbongi* enjoys license in his poetry to use ribald language otherwise unacceptable in public. . . . Not only can the *imbongi* use ribald language, he also enjoys the license to criticize with impunity persons in positions of power."[107]

Technically not a "professional" because he is not actually paid for his services, the *imbongi* is, to a very great extent, born rather than made. As Opland noted about the Xhosa *imbongi*:

> There is no formal apprenticeship or training for an *imbongi*; he needs the tacit acceptance of the people to become an *imbongi*; rarely is he officially appointed *imbongi* by the chief, merely acknowledged or recognized if he chooses to present himself; and though he may associate himself intimately with the chief and the affairs of the great place, as *imbongi* he is never paid a salary by the chief. Aspirant *iimbongi* [plural] may listen to and learn from others, but they do not attach themselves to a practicing *imbongi* in order to learn their craft. The process is strictly informal: There are no guilds of poets; *iimbongi* do not form a separate class or caste; their status is not hereditary. . . . No amount of training can make an *imbongi* of a boy lacking a special talent.[108]

It must be remembered that the *imbongi*, however interesting as a social and cultural phenomenon, is atypical of the norm for vocational training in traditional African societies. Virtually all individuals in such societies learn occupational roles through either imitation of parents or apprenticeship training or, most commonly, a combination of the two.

AFROCENTRISM AND THE ROMANTICIZATION OF AFRICA

In recent years, especially in the United States, there has been a significant scholarly and academic movement advocating what has been called "Afrocentricity" or, more commonly in everyday discourse, the adoption and utilization of an "Afrocentric" worldview.[109] This movement has had a powerful impact on elements of public schooling in the United States, including contributing to the creation of curricular materials and even the establishment of entirely "Afrocentric" schools, and has, perhaps inevitably, resulted in considerable controversy and debate.[110] The fundamental focus of the emphasis on Afrocentrism is not so much on either historical or contemporary African reality, however, as much as it is on the articulation of a philosophical system containing its own historical framework for understanding the African past and present. Thus, for its supporters, Afrocentrism is not merely an interdisciplinary approach to the study of Africa, but is a unique discipline in its own right, whose rhetoric often seems almost evangelical in nature. In essence, the

Afrocentric movement, which is identified most closely and powerfully with the work of Molefi Asante,[111] is an example of what can be called "romantic nationalism." Romantic nationalism refers to the efforts of any particular national or ethnic group to create a favorable historical record of their past and is a commonplace development throughout the world. It is hardly surprising that various groups seek to understand their pasts in the most positive light, and it is just as understandable that we all look for heroes and wonderful accomplishments in our pasts. As Stephen Howe noted:

> Virtually every European state and ethnic group has drawn on and abused the discipline of archaeology in its search for historical roots, often involving straightforwardly racist ideas about the origins and destiny of itself and its neighbours. . . . In the cases I know best, those of Britain and Ireland, very long histories of utterly fantastic racial myth and ideas about the national pasts and origins can be traced, involving all the elements of mysticism, claims of racial primacy and superiority, and promiscuous borrowings from esoteric lore.[112]

There can be little doubt that the historical contributions of Africa in general, and of people of African descent in particular, have been overlooked, ignored, and even distorted. There should also be little question that much of this phenomenon, especially during the past two or three centuries, is a consequence of racism of various sorts and manifestations.[113] Recent efforts to raise such issues, and to help us come to a better, clearer, and more accurate picture of the African past and present, as well as of the contributions of that past and present to other civilizations (including our own), are very valuable and should be commended. At the same time, however, it is clear that there are elements of historical distortion and misrepresentation,[114] just as there are clear instances of pseudoscientific claims,[115] in parts of the growing Afrocentric literature. These concerns have been well-documented elsewhere[116] and need not be explored here. What does need to be emphasized, however, is that even if corrections and modifications of some of the claims of the Afrocentric movement are needed, this should in no way blind us to the very real need for serious consideration of and reflection on the contributions of Africa to world civilization. In order to accomplish this, it is important that we not overromanticize precolonial institutions and practices in Africa, as Mazrui noted in a critique of the "Négritude" movement common especially in Francophone Africa: "The mood of this branch of African romantic thought is one of nostalgia, yearning for an innocence which is eternally lost. All that can be done now is to make the best of a bad job, try to save some of the values of old Africa, and find a synthesis between these and the influences which have come with colonialism and modernity."[117]

CONCLUDING THOUGHTS

This chapter has presented an overview of several key components of traditional African educational thought and practice. Although such practices are
less and less commonly found in modern Africa, it is not at all clear that this is
due to any intrinsic flaw in either the theory or practices that underlie such
traditional conceptions of education. Rather, this is arguably the result of a
rejection of all things traditional in favor of Western models, a practice whose
risks are vividly evoked in p'Bitek's moving poem, "Song of Lawino":

> Listen Ocol, my old friend,
> The ways of your ancestors
> Are good,
> Their customs are solid
> And not hollow
> They are not thin, not easily
> breakable
> They cannot be blown away
> By the winds
> Because their roots reach deep
> into the soil.
> I do not understand
> The ways of foreigners
> But I do not despise their
> customs.
> Why should you despise yours?[118]

Although, as was noted earlier, it is important that we not take an overly
romantic or naive view of the African past, it is also important that this past
not be rejected wholesale. As Okeke persuasively argued, "It is my belief that
traditional education should serve as the springboard from which formal education takes off. Anything short of this shall continue to plague us and continue to make formal education non-functional and divorced from the social,
political and economic realities of Igboland."[119]

In short, much can be learned from the African educational tradition that
could benefit contemporary educational thought and practice throughout the
continent.[120] Indeed, there are useful and valuable lessons for non-Africans as
well. The communal responsibility for the education of the young, the effective use of the oral tradition in passing on various sorts of knowledge, the centrality of concerns with moral or character training in the education of the
young, the importance of a sense of belonging for the child, and the view of
education as an integral component of social life (rather than as something
separate from the daily lives of most adults) are all areas in which our own society might gain insight about the problems and challenges that we face today.

QUESTIONS FOR REFLECTION AND DISCUSSION

1. How does the focus in traditional African education with respect to moral education or character training differ from various contemporary Western approaches to and concerns about moral education? In what ways is the traditional African approach similar to calls for a return to "traditional values" in our own society?

2. Contemporary Western societies are, for the most part, literate, rather than oral, societies, and yet one could argue that the advent of much recent technology will change the way in which we view literacy. In what ways do we still possess an "oral culture," and how is that culture passed on to children? To what extent is modern technology utilized in this process? Do you believe that literacy will actually be necessary in the future, or will technological innovation make possible the development of a nonliterate but nonetheless "modern" society?

3. Does the concern in traditional African education with preparing children to accept and function in the status quo conflict with the goals of education for a democratic society? With the goal of producing "critical thinkers"?

4. What, in your view, are the greatest strengths of traditional African education? What are its greatest weaknesses?

5. What are the contemporary American equivalents of traditional African initiation schools? In what ways do we prepare individuals for and mark "rites of passage" in our own society?

6. How does the preparation and training of a traditional healer, as outlined in the chapter for the Zezuru in Zimbabwe, compare to that of the physician in the West? What are the similarities and differences between the two? How can these be explained?

7. One could argue that the social and political role played by the Xhosa *imbongi* is similar to that played historically by the court jester in the West. Is there a similar role or occupation in contemporary Western societies? If so, how does this role compare to the status of the *imbongi?*

8. "Romantic nationalism" is briefly mentioned in this chapter in the context of the discussion of Afrocentrism. How does this concept relate to issues raised in chapter 1? What are the implications of this idea for the study of non-Western societies and civilizations in general?

9. How many proverbs can you recall from your own childhood? Write as many of them down as you can, and then, using Fig. 3.1 (Categories and examples of Zulu proverbs) as a model, try to construct an organizational framework for proverbs in our own tradition. How might such a framework be used in a classroom setting?

10. What lessons can you draw for your own classroom practice from what you have learned about traditional African education?

RECOMMENDED FURTHER READINGS

There are a number of good general introductions to Africa and African studies broadly conceived. Especially useful are Basil Davidson's *Africa in History*, rev. and exp. ed. (New York: Macmillan, 1991); Davidson's edited *African Civilization Revisited: From Antiquity to Modern Times* (Trenton, NJ: Africa World Press, 1991); Philip Curtin, Steven Feierman, Leonard Thompson, and Jan Vansina's *African History: From Earliest Times to Independence*, 2nd ed. (London: Longman, 1995); and Sanford Ungar's *Africa: The People and Politics of an Emerging Continent*, rev. ed. (New York: Simon & Schuster, 1986). Also useful for students seeking a better understanding of life in Africa are novels, and among the best for this purpose are the works of the Nigerian author Chinua Achebe: *Things Fall Apart* (London: Heinemann, 1958), *No Longer at Ease* (London: Heinemann, 1960), *Arrow of God* (London: Heinemann, 1974), and *A Man of the People* (London: Heinemann, 1966), all of which are now easily obtainable in North America.

NOTES

1. Richard Olaniyan, "African History and Culture: An Overview," in Richard Olaniyan (ed.), *African History and Culture* (Lagos, Nigeria: Longman, 1982), 1.

2. Meyer Fortes, "Foreword," in Eric Ayisi (ed.), *An Introduction to the Study of African Culture*, 2nd ed. (London: Currey, 1979), vii. See also Jean Jolly, *Historie de continent Africain*, 2 vols. (Paris: Éditions l'Harmattan, 1989).

3. Molefi Asante and Kariamu Asante (eds.), *African Culture: Rhythms of Unity* (Trenton, NJ: Africa World Press, 1990), ix–x.

4. See the discussion of Patricia Weibust's work on the concept of "tradition" in chap. 1.

5. Cheikh Anta Diop, *The Cultural Unity of Negro Africa* (Paris: Presence Africaine, 1962), 7; the same point is made in Diop's later revision of this work, *The Cultural Unity of Black Africa* (London: Karnak House, 1989). See also Cheikh Anta Diop, *Civilization or Barbarism: An Authentic Anthropology* (Chicago: Hill, 1991); Kwame Appiah, *In my Father's House: Africa in the Philosophy of Culture* (New York: Oxford University Press, 1992); Heinz Kimmerle, *Philosophie in Afrika—Afrikanische Philosophie* (Frankfort/Main, Germany: Campus Verlag, 1991).

6. Quoted in George Ayittey, *Indigenous African Institutions* (Ardsley-on-Hudson, NY: Transnational Publishers, 1991), 1.

7. Roland Oliver, *The African Experience: From Olduvai Gorge to the 21st Century* (London: Phoenix Press, 1999), 1.

8. Charles Darwin, *The Origin of Species and the Descent of Man* (New York: Random House, 1871).

9. Peter Mitchell, *The Archeology of Southern Africa* (Cambridge, England: Cambridge University Press, 2002), 41.

10. For a fascinating discussion of the evolution of human language, and the relation of that evolution to biological evolution, see Robert Pennock, *Tower of Babel: The Evidence Against the New Creationism* (Cambridge, MA: MIT Press, 1999).

11. Mitchell, *The Archeology of Southern Africa*, 80.

12. Mitchell, *The Archeology of Southern Africa*, 107.

13. Basil Davidson, *Africa in History: Themes and Outlines*, rev. ed. (New York: Macmillan, 1991), 25.

14. Ayittey, *Indigenous African Institutions*, xvi.

15. See, e.g., Jean-Jacques Rousseau, *Discours sur l'origine et des fondements de l'inégalité parmi les hommes* (Paris: Garnier-Flammarion, 1971), as well as *Émile* (Paris: GF Flammarion, 1966).

16. Ayittey, *Indigenous African Institutions*, 72–73, 82–93.

17. Chancellor Williams, *The Destruction of Black Civilization* (Chicago: Third World Press, 1987), 170.

18. Ayittey, *Indigenous African Institutions*, 73.

19. Ayittey, *Indigenous African Institutions*, 72.

20. Ayittey, *Indigenous African Institutions*, 74–75.

21. Ayittey, *Indigenous African Institutions*, 151.

22. Ayittey, *Indigenous African Institutions*, 151.

23. Oliver, *The African Experience*, 167.

24. See Peter Schmidt, *Iron Technology in East Africa: Symbolism, Science and Technology* (Oxford, England: Currey, 1997), 30–36.

25. Quoted in Ayittey, *Indigenous African Institutions*, 152.

26. Quoted in Ayittey, *Indigenous African Institutions*, 153.

27. See Marq de Villiers and Sheila Hirtle, *Into Africa: A Journey Through the Ancient Empires* (Johannesburg: Jonathan Bell, 1997). Also useful are Collin McEvedy, *The Penguin Atlas of African History* (Harmmondsworth, England: Penguin, 1980); Pierre Bertaux, *Africa: Desde la prehistoria hasta los estados actuales*, 17th ed. (Madrid: Siglo Veintiuno de España Editores, 1997).

28. A. Babs Fafunwa, *A History of Education in Nigeria* (London: Allen & Unwin, 1974), 20. See also S. Nwosu, "Pedagogic Problems in Africa Today," in Joseph Okpaku, Alfred Opubor, and Benjamin Oloruntimehin (eds.), *The Arts and Civilization of Black and African Peoples: volume 6, Black Civilization and Pedagogy* (Lagos, Nigeria: Center for Black and African Arts and Civilization, 1986), 103–105; A. Okeke, "Traditional Education in Igboland," in F. Chidozie Ogbalu and E. Nolue Emenanjo (eds.), *Igbo Language and Culture*, vol. 2 (Ibadan, Nigeria: University Press, 1982), 15–26; Abiola Irele (ed.), *African Education and Identity* (Ibadan, Nigeria: Spectrum Books, 1992).

29. Fafunwa, *A History of Education in Nigeria*, 20.

30. Chinua Achebe, *A Man of the People* (Ibadan, Nigeria: Heinemann, 1966), 148.

31. Abdou Moumouni, *Education in Africa* (New York: Praeger, 1968), 15.

32. Moumouni, *Education in Africa*, 29.

33. Okeke, "Traditional Education in Igboland," 15.

34. Eric Ayisi, *An Introduction to the Study of African Culture* (London: Currey, 1979), 48–49.

35. P. Duminy, *African Pupils and Teaching Them* (Pretoria: van Schaik, 1973), 30–31.

36. Stephné de Villiers and S. Helena Hartshorne, "Education," in A. C. Myburgh (ed.), *Anthropology for Southern Africa* (Pretoria: van Schaik, 1981), 147–148.

37. de Villiers and Hartshorne, "Education," 147.

38. See, e.g., M. Katengo and G. Mwale, "Can Traditional Education Be Integrated with the Modern Educational System?" in Steven Moyo, Tobias Sumaili, and James Moody (eds.), *Oral Traditions in Southern Africa*, vol. 6 (Lusaka, Zambia: Division for Cultural Research, Institute for African Studies, University of Zambia, 1986), 456–481.

39. Ali Mazrui and Teshome Wagaw, "Towards Decolonizing Modernity: Education and Culture Conflict in Eastern Africa," in *The Educational Process and Historiography in Africa* (Paris: UNESCO, 1985), 40.

40. Okeke, "Traditional Education in Igboland," 19; Mary Bill, "Rhythmical Patterning of Tsonga Children's Traditional Oral Poetry," *South African Journal of African Languages* 11, 4 (1991): 133–143.

41. Felix Boateng, "African Traditional Education: A Tool for Intergenerational Communication," in Molefi Asante and Kariamu Asante (eds.), *African Culture: Rhythms of Unity* (Trenton, NJ: Africa World Press, 1990), 117. See also Mwambu Cabakulu, *Proverbios Africanos* (Buenos Aires: Ediciones del Sol, 2000).

42. A. Fajana, "Traditional Methods of Education in Africa: The Yoruba Example," in Joseph Okpaku, Alfred Opubor, and Benjamin Oloruntimehin (eds.), *The Arts and Civilization of Black and African Peoples: volume 6, Black Civilization and Pedagogy* (Lagos, Nigeria: Center for Black and African Arts and Civilization, 1986), 45.

43. C. H. Borland, "The Oral and Written Culture of the Shona," *LIMI: Bulletin of the Department of Bantu Languages, University of South Africa* 8 (1969): 8.

44. C. Nyembezi, *Zulu Proverbs* (Johannesburg: University of the Witwatersrand Press, 1974), 46–48; see also Northcote W. Thomas, *Proverbs, Narratives, Vocabularies and Grammar: Anthropological Report on the Ibo-Speaking Peoples of Nigeria, part III* (New York: Negro Universities Press, 1969).

45. Thomas, *Proverbs, Narratives, Vocabularies and Grammar*, 9.

46. Cited in O. F. Raum, "An Evaluation of Indigenous Education," in P. A. Duminy (ed.), *Trends and Challenges in the Education of the South African Bantu* (Pretoria: van Schaik, 1967), 103.

47. Taban lo Liyong, *The Last Word* (Nairobi, Kenya: East Africa Publishing House, 1969), 141.

48. Nyembezi, *Zulu Proverbs*, 91.

49. Boateng, "African Traditional Education," 117.

50. See J. Nkara, "*Bisisimi* or the Language of the Wise," *South African Journal of African Languages* 12, 4 (1992): 144.

51. Nkara, "*Bisisimi* or the Language of the Wise," 144.

52. Nkara, "*Bisisimi* or the Language of the Wise," 145.

53. Nkara, "*Bisisimi* or the Language of the Wise," 144.

54. Borland, "The Oral and Written Culture of the Shona," 9.

55. D. Mahlangu, "*Imiraro*: Ndebele Riddles," *South African Journal of African Languages* 8 (Suppl. 1) (1988): 154–155.

56. Fajana, "Traditional Methods of Education in Africa," 54.

57. See Borland, "The Oral and Written Culture of the Shona"; Okeke, "Traditional Education in Igboland." For an excellent examination of the meanings and metaphors related to many common Zulu words, e.g., see Adrian Koopman, *Zulu Names* (Pietermaritzburg: University of Natal Press, 2002).

58. Fafunwa, *A History of Education in Nigeria*, 28.

59. Fajana, "Traditional Methods of Education in Africa," 55.

60. See William Bascom, *African Dilemma Tales* (The Hague: Mouton, 1975); Gerhard Kubik, "*Visimu vya mukatikati*: Dilemma Tales and 'Arithmetical Puzzles' Collected among the Valuchazi," *South African Journal of African Languages* 10, 2 (1990): 59–68; Gerhard Kubik, "A Luchazi Riddle Session: Analysis of Recorded Texts in a South-Central African Bantu Language," *South African Journal of African Languages* 12, 2 (1992): 51–82.

61. Bascom, *African Dilemma Tales*, 12.

62. Kubik, "*Visimu vya mukatikati*," 60–61.

63. Kubik, "*Visimu vya mukatikati*," 67.

64. Boateng, "African Traditional Education," 113.

65. N. Uka, "Continuity and Change: A Challenge to African Educators," in Joseph Okpaku, Alfred Opubor, and Benjamin Oloruntimehin (eds.), *The Arts and Civilization of Black and African Peoples: volume 6, Black Civilization and Pedagogy* (Lagos, Nigeria: Center for Black and African Arts and Civilization, 1986), 131.

66. Fremont Besmer, *Horses, Musicians, and Gods: The Hausa Cult of Possession-Trance* (Zaria, Nigeria: Ahmadu Bello University Press, 1983), 44.

67. Boateng, "African Traditional Education," 115.

68. For a distinction between *izibongo* and *izithakazelo*, or clan praises among the Zulu, see D. Mzolo, "Social Function of Clan Praises," in A. Nkabinde (ed.), *African Linguistics and Literature* (Johannesburg: Lexicon, 1988), 132–138; also of interest here is Liz Gunner and Mafika Gwala (eds.), *Musho: Zulu Popular Praises* (Johannesburg: Witwatersrand University Press, 1991).

69. I. Schapera, *Praise-Poems of Tswana Chiefs* (Oxford, England: Oxford University Press, 1965), 1; see also Daniel Kunene, *Heroic Poetry of the Basotho* (Oxford, England: Oxford University Press, 1971).

70. See Schapera, *Praise-Poems of Tswana Chiefs*, 25.

71. Fafunwa, *A History of Education in Nigeria*, 21.

72. Moumouni, *Education in Africa*, 22.

73. See Nathaniel Fadipe, *The Sociology of the Yoruba* (Ibadan, Nigeria: Ibadan University Press, 1970).

74. Okeke, "Traditional Education in Igboland," 18.

75. See Fafunwa, *A History of Education in Nigeria*, 24–26; Nwosu, "Pedagogic Problems in Africa Today"; Virginia van der Vliet, "Growing Up in a Traditional Society," in W. Hammond-Tooke (ed.), *The Bantu-Speaking Peoples of Southern Africa* (London: Routledge & Kegan Paul, 1974), 224.

76. Fafunwa, *A History of Education in Nigeria*, 19.

77. Fafunwa, *A History of Education in Nigeria*, 25.

78. See Fafunwa, *A History of Education in Nigeria*; Borland, "The Oral and Written Culture of the Shona"; S. Guma, *The Form, Content and Technique of Traditional Literature in Southern Sotho*, 2nd ed. (Pretoria: van Schaik, 1977).

79. See Rosalie Finlayson, "*Hlonipha*: The Women's Language of Avoidance among the Xhosa," *South African Journal of African Languages* (Suppl. 1) (1982): 35–59; Rosalie Finlayson, "Linguistic Terms of Respect among the Xhosa," in Peter Raper (ed.), *Names 1983: Proceedings of the Second South African Names Congress* (Pretoria: Human Sciences Research Council, 1986), 128–138.

80. See Ayisi, *An Introduction to the Study of African Culture*, 47.

81. See Borland, "The Oral and Written Culture of the Shona."

82. Benjamin Ray, *African Religions: Symbol, Ritual, and Community* (Englewood Cliffs, NJ: Prentice-Hall, 1976), 91. Also of interest here are John Mbiti, *African Religions and Philosophy*, 2nd ed. (Oxford, England: Heinemann, 1989), 118–129; Geoffrey Parrinder, *Religion in Africa* (Harmondsworth, England: Penguin, 1969); E. Adegbola (ed.), *Traditional Religion in West Africa* (Nairobi, Kenya: Uzima, 1983).

83. Jacques Macquet, quoted in P. Boe, "Circumcision: The Rites of Manhood in the Bille Tribe," in E. Adegbola (ed.), *Traditional Religion in West Africa* (Nairobi, Kenya: Uzima Press, 1983), 88.

84. The practice of "female circumcision" has become increasingly controversial in recent years. It is important to note that the term itself is problematic, and that what is entailed is considerably more extreme than male circumcision (the routine practice of which has also become controversial in many Western nations).

85. Ayisi, *An Introduction to the Study of African Culture*, 47.

86. See Ayisi, *An Introduction to the Study of African Culture*, 46; also relevant here is Olaniyan, *African History and Culture*, 30–31.

87. See Ayisi, *An Introduction to the Study of African Culture*, 46; Olaniyan, *African History and Culture*, 30–31.

88. Raum, "An Evaluation of Indigenous Education," 99–100.

89. van der Vliet, "Growing Up in a Traditional Society," 241.

90. Blacking, quoted in van der Vliet, "Growing Up in a Traditional Society," 235.

91. See Fafunwa, *A History of Education in Nigeria*, 30–31. See also Olaitan Obanewa, *Education of the Children and Youth in Ile-Ife: A Comparison of Formal and Non-Formal Systems of Education* (M.Ed. thesis, University of Ife, Nigeria, 1973), and Okeke, "Traditional Education in Igboland," 20–22.

92. See A. Ishumi, "Black Civilization and Pedagogy: A Search for Modern Methods," in Joseph Okpaku, Alfred Opubor, and Benjamin Oloruntimehin (eds.), *The Arts and Civilization of Black and African Peoples: volume 6, Black Civilization and Pedagogy* (Lagos, Nigeria: Center for Black and African Arts and Civilization, 1986), 67.

93. Ishumi, "Black Civilization and Pedagogy," 51.

94. Niara Sudarkasa, "Sex Roles, Education and Development in Africa," *Anthropology and Education* 13, 3 (1982): 280.

95. See Sudarkasa, "Sex Roles, Education and Development in Africa," 280–281.

96. Okeke, "Traditional Education in Igboland," 21.

97. Quoted in Fafunwa, *A History of Education in Nigeria*, 30.

98. M. Ogundijo, *Indigenous Education in the Ejigbo District of Oshun Division in the Pre-Colonial Days and the Coming of the Missionaries* (B.A. thesis, Faculty of Education, University of Ife, Nigeria, 1970), 11–12.

99. Fafunwa, *A History of Education in Nigeria*, 30; see also Okeke, "Traditional Education in Igboland," 21.

100. Quoted in Fafunwa, *A History of Education in Nigeria*, 37.

101. Patrick Twumasi and Dennis Warren, "The Professionalisation of Indigenous Medicine: A Comparative Study of Ghana and Zambia," in Murray Last and C. L. Chavunduka (eds.), *The Professionalization of African Medicine* (Manchester, England: Manchester University Press, 1986), 118.

102. Twumasi and Warren, "The Professionalisation of Indigenous Medicine," 118.

103. See Murray Last and C. L. Chavunduka (eds.), *The Professionalization of African Medicine* (Manchester, England: Manchester University Press, 1986). There is a growing recognition of the value of many indigenous medical practices and beliefs in many parts of the world. See, e.g., Arthur Kleinman, *Patients and Healers in the Context of Culture: An Exploration of the Borderland Between Anthropology, Medicine, and Psychiatry* (Berkeley: University of California Press, 1980); Charles Leslie and Allen Young (eds.), *Paths to Asian Medical Knowledge* (Berkeley: University of California Press, 1992); Paul Brodwin, *Medicine and Morality in Haiti: The Contest for Healing Power* (Cambridge, England: Cambridge University Press, 1996); Susan S. Campbell, *Called to Heal: Traditional Healing Meets Modern Medicine in Southern Africa Today* (Halfway House, South Africa: Zebra, 1998).

104. Leslie Swartz, *Culture and Mental Health: A Southern African View* (Cape Town: Oxford University Press, 1998), 92. Also relevant here is Robin Horton, "African Traditional Thought and Western Science," in Bryan Wilson (ed.), *Rationality* (New York: Harper & Row, 1970), 131–171.

105. Pamela Reynolds, "The Training of Traditional Healers in Mashonaland," in Murray Last and C. L. Chavunduka (eds.), *The Professionalization of African Medicine* (Manchester, England: Manchester University Press, 1986), 170–172.

106. See Jeff Opland, *Xhosa Oral Poetry: Aspects of a Black South African Tradition* (Cambridge, England: Cambridge University Press, 1983); Jeff Opland, *Xhosa Poets and Poetry* (Cape Town: David Phlip, 1998); Jeff Opland, "Xhosa *izibongo*: Improvised Line," *South African Journal of African Languages* 10, 4 (1990): 239–251; Russell Kaschula (ed.), *African Oral Literature: Functions in Contemporary Contexts* (Claremont, South Africa: New Africa Books, 2001); Russell Kaschula, "The Role of the Xhosa Oral Poet in Contemporary South African Society," *South African Journal of African Languages* 11, 2 (1991): 47–54; Trevor Cope (ed.), *Izibongo: Zulu Praise Poems* (Oxford, England: Oxford University Press, 1968); David Rycroft and A. Bhekabantu Ngcobo, *Say it in Zulu* (Pietermaritzburg: Language and Reading Laboratories, University of Natal, 1981), part II, appendix I; Noleen Turner, "Comparison of the *Izibongo* of the Zulu Royal Women, Mnkabayi and Nandi," *South African Journal of African Languages* 8, 1 (1988): 28–33; W. J. Pretorius, "A Comparative Look at the Development of Heroic Poetry in Northern Sotho," *South African Journal of African Languages* 10, 3 (1990): 125–131.

107. Opland, *Xhosa Oral Poetry*, 66–67.

108. Opland, *Xhosa Oral Poetry*, 64–65.

109. See Molefi Asante, *Afrocentricity*, rev. ed. (Trenton, NJ: Africa World Press, 1988); Molefi Asante, *Kemet, Afrocentricity and Knowledge* (Trenton, NJ: Africa World Press, 1990). Perhaps the most extensive articulation of Afrocentrism (although one with serious limitations as well) is Marimba Ani, *Yurugu: An African-Centered Critique of European Cultural Thought and Behavior* (Trenton, NJ: Africa World Press, 1994). For a fascinating historical study of the evolution of Afrocentrism, see Wilson J. Moses, *Afrotopia: The Roots of African American Popular History* (Cambridge, England: Cambridge University Press, 1998).

The Afrocentric literature should be distinguished from more general African scholarship, especially with respect to philosophic scholarship. See, e.g., P. H. Coetzee and A. P. Roux (eds.), *The African Philosophy Reader* (London: Routledge, 1998); Emmanuel Chukwudi Eze (ed.), *African Philosophy: An Anthology* (Oxford, England: Blackwell, 1998); and J. Chukwuemeka Ekei, *Justice in Communalism: A Foundation of Ethics in African Philosophy* (Lagos, Nigeria: Realm Communications Ltd., 2001).

110. Although much of the debate has taken place in the popular media, there has also been a critical scholarly response to Afrocentrism. This critical scholarly response includes Mary R. Lefkowitz and Guy MacLean Rogers (eds.), *Black Athena Revisited* (Chapel Hill: University of North Carolina Press, 1996); Mary Lefkowitz, *Not Out of Africa: How Afrocentrism Became an Excuse to Teach Myth as History* (New York: Basic Books, 1996); Stephen Howe, *Afrocentrism: Mythical Pasts and Imagined Homes* (London: Verso, 1998).

111. Molefi Asante is professor and chairperson of the Department of African American Studies at Temple University, and one of the most prolific Afrocentric scholars. In addition to Asante's own work, see Howe, *Afrocentrism: Mythical Pasts and Imagined Homes*, chap. 17. A more sympathetic treatment of Asante's work, especially in terms of its pedagogical implications, can be found in Joel Spring, *The Intersection of Cultures: Minority Education in the United States* (New York: McGraw-Hill, 1995), 135–141.

112. Howe, *Afrocentrism: Mythical Pasts and Imagined Homes*, 7.

113. This has been one of the more significant contributions of Martin Bernal's work, for instance. See Martin Bernal, *Black Athena: The Afroasiatic Roots of Classical Civilization, volume 1: The Fabrication of Ancient Greece, 1785–1985* (New Brunswick, NJ: Rutgers University Press, 1987); Martin Bernal, "Animadversions on the Origins of Western Science," *Isis* 83 (1992): 596–607.

114. See Howe, *Afrocentrism: Mythical Pasts and Imagined Homes*; Lefkowitz, *Not Out of Africa.*

115. See, e.g., Bernard Ortiz de Montellano, "Multiculturalism, Cult Archaeology, and Pseudoscience," in Francis Harrold and Raymond Eve (eds.), *Cult Archaeology and Creationism* (Iowa City: University of Iowa Press, 1995), 134–151; Howe, *Afrocentrism: Mythical Pasts and Imagined Homes*, 259–264; Robert Palter, "*Black Athena*, Afrocentrism, and the History of Science," in Mary R. Lefkowitz and Guy MacLean Rogers, *Black Athena Revisited* (Chapel Hill: University of North Carolina Press, 1996), 209–266. Martin Bernal offered powerful rejoinders to many of his critics that are also worth noting here. See, e.g., Martin Bernal, "Response," *Journal of*

Women's History 4, 3 (1993): 119–135; Martin Bernal, "Response to Edith Hall," *Arethusa* 24, 2 (1991): 203–214.

116. See Howe, *Afrocentrism: Mythical Pasts and Imagined Homes.*

117. Ali Mazrui, *The African Condition: The Reith Lectures* (London: Heinemann, 1980), 11.

118. Okot p'Bitek, *Song of Lawino and Song of Ocol* (Ibadan, Nigeria: Heinemann, 1967), 41.

119. Okeke, "Traditional Education in Igboland," 25.

120. See, e.g., Waly Diouf, Barry Sheckley, and Marijke Kehrhahn, "Adult Learning in a Non-Western Context: The Influence of Culture in a Senegalese Farming Village," *Adult Education Quarterly* 51, 1 (2000): 32–44.

4

Training "Face and Heart":
The Mesoamerican Educational Experience

Today, the search for the Aztecs goes far beyond national interests. The story of this remarkable people forms one of the most extraordinary chapters of cultural evolution in the Americas. Fearless warriors and pragmatic builders, the Aztecs ruthlessly created an empire . . . that was surpassed in size only by that of the Incas in Peru. The sacrificial aspect of their religion, with its seeming indifference to human life, appalled and repelled the Spaniards. But . . . beyond the ritual violence there were more easily appreciated achievements: the formation of a highly special-ized and stratified society and an imperial administration; the expan-sion of a trading network as well as a tribute system; the development and maintenance of a sophisticated agricultural economy, carefully ad-justed to the land; and the development of an intellectual and religious outlook that was in intimate contact with the earth, the sky, and the sea-sons.

—Townsend (1992, p. 11)

Mesoamerica has been the home of a number of distinct, but related, civiliza-tions since human beings first began settling in the area millennia ago. Al-though there is evidence of human habitation in Mesoamerica at least as far back as 25,000 years ago, it is possible that people were living in the area as early as 40,000 years ago.[1] By 1500 B.C.E., we know that the indigenous peo-ples of Mesoamerica had undergone the transition from hunter and gathering societies to settled agricultural village societies,[2] and it is with this develop-ment that Mesoamerican history (rather than prehistory) can be said to have begun. The history of Mesoamerica can, in turn, be divided into four very broad stages: the Formative Period (1500 B.C.E. to 150 C.E.), the Classic Pe-riod (from around 150 C.E. to around 900 C.E.), the Early Post-Classic Pe-riod (from around 900 C.E. to 1250 C.E.), and the Late Post-Classic Period (from 1250 C.E. to 1519 C.E.).[3] It was during the Formative Period that the elaboration of a set of core cultural beliefs and practices emerged. This set of core cultural beliefs and practices was first manifested in the Olmec civilization, which Jacques Soustelle called the "mother civilization" of Meso-america,[4] but was modified, reformulated, changed, and developed over the history of Mesoamerican civilizations.[5] As Adams argued, "The Olmec . . . did invent and diffuse much of the cultural equipment used and reformulated in later cultures."[6] Indeed, it was the Olmecs who provided the cultural matrix within which Mesoamerican civilization developed and evolved:

> The touching continuity of indigenous Mexican civilization in spite of the of-ten bloody upheavals of its history, and the indelible imprint still preserved in the depths of its nature despite the changes of the modern era, are ample justi-fication for the attempt being made by archaeologists to return to the earliest sources of this autochthonous civilization. With the Olmecs we catch a glimpse of the decisive mutation that made Mexico and Mesoamerica a cultural high-pressure area. . . . Pre-Conquest Mexico would not have been what it was—and even the Mexico of the twentieth century would not be what it is—if these men of long ago had not begun to erect their stelae and to sculpt their bas-reliefs in the depths of torrid jungles, more than three thousand years ago.[7]

Among the civilizations that developed in Mesoamerica were not only the Olmecs, but the Toltecs, the Mayas, and the Aztecs, among others.[8] Jacques Soustelle provided a vivid analogy for understanding the relationships among these groups: "The Aztecs have often been compared to the Romans, the Ma-yas to the Greeks. It has been said that the Toltecs played in Amerindian an-tiquity a role comparable to that of the Etruscans in Italy. The Olmecs, for their part, remind us of the Sumerians: like them long unknown, like them precursors, like them buried beneath ruins many thousands of years old and hidden from our eyes by the traces of peoples who succeeded them."[9] Al-though a powerful description, this analogy is only valid in part, because the cultural relationship among the peoples of Mesoamerica was far closer than that among the comparison civilizations that Soustelle identified. Further-more, the relationship among these different civilizations was one that was recognized by the members of the societies themselves, as can be seen in the following passage taken from the *Códice Matritense de la Real Academia*, which describes the development of Nahuatl philosophy from the Toltec pe-riod to that of the Aztecs:

> Those who
> carried with them
> the black and red ink,
> the manuscripts and the pictures,
> wisdom [*tlamatiliztli*].
> They brought everything with them:
> the song books and the music of the flutes.[10]

In any event, Mesoamerica presents us with a fascinating collection of related cultures that emerged, grew, developed, and—to some extent—disappeared over a period of some three millennia. Although it would be impossible for us to examine seriously and in detail the educational thought and practice of each of these civilizations, we can focus our attention on two of the civilizations of Mesoamerica. First, we will examine what little is known of Classic Mayan educational thought and practice, and then we will turn to the more abundant literature concerned with educational thought and practice in Aztec society.

EDUCATIONAL THOUGHT AND PRACTICE
IN CLASSIC MAYAN SOCIETY

In recent years, our knowledge about and understanding of classical Mayan society and civilization have undergone dramatic changes. As Michael Coe wrote in the late 1980s:

> The past two decades have seen great advances in our knowledge of Maya civilization in both the Preclassic and Classic epochs, often in ways that earlier generations of scholars would not have approved. From a picture of the Maya that emphasized peaceful theocracies led by priest astronomers, ruling over relatively empty "ceremonial centers," we now have highly warlike city-states led by grim dynasts obsessed with human sacrifice and the ritual letting of their own blood. Although traditional "dirt" archeology has contributed to our current view of the ancient Maya, the contributions of epigraphy and art history have been, in my opinion, truly revolutionary.[11]

This revolutionary rethinking of both the general nature and the details of ancient Mayan society has continued up to the present time.[12] If we know a great deal more today about the history and politics of the Maya, however, our knowledge about their views about childrearing and education, as well as of their specific educational practices and institutions, remains largely conjectural in nature.[13] What we do know, or at least what we now believe, is based largely on assumptions about the general nature of ancient Mayan society. For instance, according to Norman Hammond:

> We now have abundant evidence that Classic Maya society was divided into a number of layers, with rulers at the top and common people, some of them peasants, at the base of the social pyramid. It has become clear that this complex and many-layered society must have had a great many specialists and that any one layer in the pyramid could have embraced a range of occupations, many pursued as full-time economic specialties.[14]

To Hammond's observations we can add the presence of a highly complex written literature, produced by scribes, as well as obvious evidence of architectural, engineering, mathematical, and astronomical knowledge, not to mention what were clearly highly ritualized religious practices—all of which would strongly suggest the operation of some sort of formal educational system for at least some individuals in ancient Mayan society.[15] This formal educational system need not have been schooling as we understand it, however, as Robert Sharer explained, "There is no evidence that the ancient Maya had formal schools. But it is certain that children selected on the basis of social status or aptitude were trained for specialized roles in society by an apprentice system. Scribes, priests, artists, masons, and other occupational groups recruited novices and trained them."[16]

In addition to such conjectural sources, we also know something about the way in which the Maya lived at the time of the Conquest, largely due to the work of the second Bishop of Yucatán, Diego de Landa. De Landa recorded, in considerable detail, the society and way of life of the indigenous peoples of the Yucatán, based both on his own observations and information he received from native informants, in his work *Relación de las cosas de Yucatán*.[17] Such information provides us with invaluable insights into the kinds of child-rearing practices that were carried over from the time of the Classic Mayan civilization (many of which continue even to the present). We also possess a limited number of Mayan codices,[18] as well as the *Popol Vuh*,[19] a work of great literary and historical value that has been called "the Sacred Book of the ancient Quiché Maya."[20] Whereas these sources by no means provide us with a clear picture of ancient Mayan educational thought and practice, they do provide some limited insight into the role played by education in Mayan society, and the purposes that the ancient Maya believed should be served by child-rearing and education.[21]

For the ancient Maya, education was, at its heart, religious in nature. As Ana Luisa Izquierdo argued in *La educación maya en los tiempos prehispánicos*:

> The destiny of Mayan man and his role on earth find their ultimate plenitude through religious fulfillment. Attainments such as wisdom, social integration or personal success are only recognized when they are geared toward the fulfill-ment of the intrinsic and spiritual mission. So, if all the vital actions of Mayan man had a religious orientation, likewise education had its long-term and short-term objectives, as well as its ultimate goal, in sacred fulfillment. Because of this, the ways of shaping children and adolescents were deeply entrenched in the religious meaning of life, and were characterized by it.[22]

Mayan childrearing and education were clearly grounded in a fairly conservative social and educational agenda. The point of proper education, from a Mayan perspective, was conformity to one's society and an acceptance of one's place within that society.[23] Custom and religion governed virtually all parts of an individual's life cycle, and both formal and informal education were no exception to this rule.[24] This was achieved by learning from the priests and elders in society, generally orally.[25] Thus, "for the Mayas, the process through which it was assured that an individual made a concept, an idea, or a value his own, was the memorization of the words contained in it."[26] Such an approach to learning might have many advantages, but it was clearly not oriented to encouraging what we would today call critical thinking.

An interesting aspect of Mayan educational thought is that of its epistemology and implicit learning theory. In the *Popol Vuh*, the creation of the first human beings is described in considerable detail. Four human beings were created by the gods Tepeu and Gucumatz in order to nourish, sustain, and worship the gods. When first created, these men had all of the characteristics of the gods themselves:

> They had the appearance of men, they were men; they talked, conversed, saw and heard, grasped things; they were good and handsome men, and their figure was the figure of a man. They were endowed with intelligence; they saw and instantly they could see far, they succeeded in seeing, they succeeded in knowing all that there is in the world. When they looked, instantly they saw all around them, and they contemplated in turn the arch of heaven and the round face of the earth. The things hidden they saw all, without first having to move; at once they saw the world, and so, too, from where they were, they saw it. Great was their wisdom; their sight reached to the forests, the rocks, the lakes, the seas, the mountains, and the valleys. In truth, they were admirable men.[27]

The gods, however, were not entirely pleased with their creation; they were concerned that men could know all and see all, as they themselves could, and so decided to impose some limits on their creations. Thus, according to the *Popol Vuh*, "The Heart of Heaven blew mist into their eyes, which clouded their sight as when a mirror is breathed upon. Their eyes were covered and they could see only what was close, only that was clear to them. In this way the wisdom and all the knowledge of the four men, the origin and beginning, were destroyed."[28] This account is fascinating on a number of grounds, not the least of which are the intriguing parallels to the biblical account of the destruction of the Tower of Babel as well as to the theory of knowledge expounded by Plato.

THE AZTEC CASE

When Hernán Cortés and his men first arrived in Mexico in 1519, they were astounded by the civilization that greeted them. Unlike earlier contacts between Europeans and indigenous peoples in the Western hemisphere, in their introduction to the Aztec civilization,[29] Cortés and his followers faced a highly sophisticated urban culture in full flower—a civilization, in fact, that in many ways compared favorably to that of any 16th-century European society. As Cortés himself wrote to the Spanish king, "These people live like those in Spain, and in as much harmony and order as there, and considering that they are barbarous and so far from the knowledge of God and cut off from all civilized nations, it is truly remarkable to see what they have achieved in all things."[30] This was remarkably high praise from the man who was, more than any other single individual, responsible for the destruction of the Aztec world—or, as the Aztecs themselves would have termed it, the "time of the fifth sun."[31]

Education, both formal and informal, was an important and well-developed part of Aztec society.[32] As Miguel León-Portilla commented, "The written sources on the educational practices of the Nahuas are so abundant that a book could be written on that subject alone. Such a book might reconstruct—as did Jaeger's *Paideia* for the ancient Greeks—through the educational system all the richness and profundity of the Nahuatl concept of man."[33] And yet, despite its noteworthy successes, no mention whatever of the educational thought and practice of the Aztecs appears in the standard works in the history of education in the English-speaking world. Although a thorough analysis of education in the "time of the fifth sun" is far beyond the scope of this chapter, it is possible to present a general overview of Aztec education as it existed at the time of the arrival of the Spanish in the early 16th century.

THE AZTEC WORLD

The Aztecs were relative latecomers to the valley of Mexico, building their society on the cultural, religious, and intellectual foundations, as well as on the architectural ruins, of earlier civilizations, especially that of the Toltecs. Furthermore, their rise to prominence was, in the words of Muriel Weaver, "a dramatic rags-to-riches tale."[34] The Aztecs first arrived in the area of the Valley of Mexico in the early 13th century, by which time the more desirable areas around the lakeshore were already settled by other Nahuatl- and Otomí-speaking peoples, as well as by the descendants of earlier refugees from Teotihuacán and Tula, among others.[35] Indeed, the awareness of their late arrival, as well as of their status as outsiders, remained with the Aztecs until the arrival of the Spanish. Cortés himself recorded that Monteuczoma, in their first conversation together, commented, "From the records which we have long possessed and which are handed down from our ancestors, it is known that no one, neither I nor the others who inhabit the land of Anahuac, are native to it. We are strangers and we came from far outer parts."[36]

The new arrivals were not greeted with open arms by those already settled in the area, and in the early years after their arrival in the Valley of Mexico, the

Aztecs were driven from one area to another around the western part of the lake. As Jon Manchip White wrote:

> They were looked upon as little more than squatters. . . . Nor was it simply the case that they were backward and brutish: they were downright squalid. Their little uncouth tribal war-god, Huitzilopochtli, was already notorious for the number of fresh, bleeding hearts he required, and his worshippers did not seem to be particular about where they got them. They gained a reputation for every kind of murder and brutality.[37]

Finally, the Aztecs arrived at Culhuacan, one of the established cities in the Valley. The Culhua permitted the Aztecs to settle at Tizapan, about 6 miles west of Culhuacan, in an inhospitable area where they fully expected that the Aztecs would "perish . . . eaten by the serpents, since many dwell in that place."[38] Instead, the Aztecs prospered, ultimately acquiring not only access to the cultural heritage of the Toltecs, but also to claims of Toltec lineage as a result of intermarriage with the inhabitants of Culhuacan. The Aztecs also became mercenaries for the Culhua, and were so successful in this role that they eventually came to represent a serious threat to the Culhua. The tensions between the Culhua and the Aztecs were forced to a head when the Aztecs requested:

> the hand of one of Culhuacan's rulers, a beautiful girl whom they promptly killed and flayed. Her father arrived to attend her wedding, only to be confronted by a priest dancing in her flayed skin. Fighting broke out at once, and the [Aztecs] retreated into the swamps of the lagoon, finally reaching the safety of a reed-covered island near the center of what is now Mexico City. There they rested. Huitzilopochtli [the Aztec war god] appeared before one of the priests, ordering him to search for a cactus where a great eagle perched. This, said the god, was a place he had named Tenochtitlán, the "Place of the Fruit of the Prickly Pear Cactus."[39]

Thus was Tenochtitlán, the capital city of the Aztec Empire, established, probably around 1345.[40] The Aztecs now experienced a period of growth and consolidation, culminating in the defeat of the city of Azcapotzalco in 1428, which "established the Aztecs as the dominant power in the Basin of Mexico."[41]

By the time of the arrival of Cortés and his men, the Aztec Empire was in many ways at its height,[42] consisting of some 15 million people and 489 tributary towns, which were in turn divided into 38 provinces for administrative purposes.[43] It was in actuality not so much an "empire" as it was a loose collection of culturally related but distinct principalities sharing (for the most part) a common language[44] and united primarily by the paying of tribute to Tenochtitlán.[45] Under the Aztecs, local rulers continued to govern their communities, albeit under the auspices of the Aztecs. Characteristic of the Aztec approach to imperium was its emphasis on control of urban centers:

> Because of the nature of Mesoamerican warfare and the limitations on political consolidation, conquest did not mean complete territorial control. Rather, conquest was of political centers. Control of territory per se was not a major consideration. Once a political center was dominated, so too were its dependencies, and tribute, flowing from dependency to cabecera to provincial capital, could be drained from an entire region simply by dominating the center.[46]

The empire was held together, in short, not by the establishment of military garrisons throughout its territories, nor by overt control from Tenochtitlán, but rather by tribute to be paid to Tenochtitlán and well-developed commercial ties.[47] The paying of tribute, as well as the commercial ties, were both strengthened by what might be termed *ideological hegemony*. As Hassig noted:

> The Aztecs' reliance on hegemonic rather than territorial control produced an empire of distinctive character and vast expanse but loose control. Mesoamerican technological constraints limited the size, strength and duration of forays outside the empire, and such engagements took on strategic characteristics that varied with the political nature of the target. Furthermore, the Aztec Empire was essentially an alliance, and was expectedly fraught with rebellion. Nevertheless, the system functioned admirably within its cultural context, and through it the Aztecs expanded their domain to a size unprecedented in Mesoamerica.[48]

By 1519, Tenochtitlán was a large, thriving urban metropolis of some 200,000 people, with at least as many living in the satellite cities that surrounded it, making it far larger than any European city of the time.[49] The city was connected to the mainland by three elevated causeways, and was provided fresh water by a series of carefully engineered aqueducts.[50] Food came to the capital not only as tribute from the provinces, but also, and more important, from the *chinampas*, the island-gardens that made possible the intensive agricultural cultivation that supported the urban civilizations of the Valley of Mexico.[51]

The spiritual heart of the Aztec Empire was the Templo Mayor, the largest structure in the central plaza of Tenochtitlán,[52] which represented not only the ritualistic center of the empire, but even more, in its architecture itself was the embodiment of the Aztec view of the universe, as Eduardo Matos Moctezuma noted: "The Templo Mayor thus becomes the fundamental center where all sacred power is concentrated and where all the levels intersect. I propose that it not only occupies a privileged location but that in its architecture, form, and particular characteristics it also represents the entire Mexica conception of the cosmos."[53]

Aztec society was hierarchical in nature, characterized by rank and kin-ship.[54] The population was broadly divided into those of noble birth and those of common birth, although some degree of social mobility did exist—primarily as a result of success in commerce, military success, or entrance into the priesthood.[55] Gender also played a key role in individual identity in Aztec society,[56] as did ethnicity for those of non-Aztec ancestry. Central to so-cial status in Aztec society, however, was military rank. As Hassig explained, "Military ranking was intimately tied to the overall social structure of Aztec society, and social ranking was intimately tied to political offices, the latter defining rights and requiring the holder to have a specified status."[57]

It is interesting to observe that although, as Nicholson noted, "the sharply aristocratic bias of the society as a whole, naturally correlated with a high de-gree of social stratification,"[58] this social stratification was manifested in prac-tice by far greater expectations of those at higher social levels. For example, Muriel Weaver argued that "an interesting concept of Aztec law was that the se-verity of punishment was measured in accordance with the offender's station in life. A high priest would be put to death for a crime that might be tolerated if committed by a bondsman. That is, a man of high office assumed greater moral responsibilities and his conduct was expected to be beyond reproach."[59]

Also important in terms of the organization of Aztec society was the role played by the *calpulli*, the ancient territorial kinship groups to which every member of the society belonged. The *calpulli* "served as the interface between the citizens and the government,"[60] as well as maintaining religious and edu-cation institutions and communally holding a certain amount of land.[61] As Fagan commented, "The *calpulli* was probably the most important social in-stitution in Aztec society. It provided a mechanism by which people cooper-ated with one another and gave a large measure of security to everyone. The state used it not only to govern a teeming and diverse urban and rural popula-tion, but to recruit large numbers of people at short notice for public works or armies of conquest."[62]

Underlying virtually all aspects of Aztec society were the two closely inter-related pillars of Aztec society, militarism and religion.[63] For the Aztecs, war-fare was a means not only of gaining personal glory, social status, and ulti-mately tribute and expanding territorial control, but also a kind of sacrificial activity. In fact, warfare involved two kinds of sacrifice, as one of the terms used by the Aztecs to refer to war makes clear: *teoatl tlachinolli*, which trans-lates literally as "divine liquid and ashes."[64] The term itself incorporates a vast wealth of meaning:

> The first element signifies "blood," and the second is a shorthand statement for the practice of cremating dead warriors on the battlefield, a Toltec custom that released the fortunate soul like a sunburst to ascend into the heavens. War meant the spilling of human blood, which was by definition a liquor destined

for the support of the gods; war, in other words, was an act of sacrifice carried out voluntarily by those who killed as well as by those who were killed.[65]

Indeed, the need for such sacrifice was so great that when real warfare was not possible or advisable, the Aztecs engaged in what was called a *xochiya-oyotl*, or "war of flowers."[66] The *xochiyaoyotl* was a ritual military contest, "in which the two sides set out to capture the maximum number of sacrificial victims from the other while inflicting a minimum of damage in other respects."[67]

Sacrifice was essential in the Aztec religious system, because it was the shedding of human blood that ensured "the continued existence of the cosmos."[68] The sun itself, as well as the other deities of the Aztec pantheon, were nourished by human blood.[69] As Davies suggested, "In general terms, the religion of the Aztecs was an elaborate defence mechanism, born not out of hope but of anxiety. Every aspect, and in particular human offering, implies a struggle to ward off disaster, whether immediate catastrophes such as crop failure or the ultimate doom of the Fifth, and last, Sun."[70] Such an understanding is also consistent with the Aztec view of history, as the noted scholar Miguel León-Portilla maintained:

> It was believed that the present sun, moon, stars and earth integrate the fifth universe within a series of ages, known to the Nahua people as "Suns." Four other Suns had emerged and come to an end through the machinations of the gods: the ages of Earth, Air, Water, and Fire. The present is that of *Olintonatiuh*, "The Sun of Movement," which began to exist and to move thanks to a primeval sacrifice of the gods, who, with their own blood, brought it into being and thus also gave life to a new generation of humans. This fifth age not only may perish but actually carries within itself the very principle of death and destruction.[71]

Another view of the role of sacrifice in Aztec religious thought is that offered by López Austin, who, on the account of Bernard Ortiz de Montellano, "claimed that the relationship between god and man was mercantilistic: man gave blood, hearts, and fire to the gods, and was given in return crops, water, and freedom from disease and plagues. This claim is supported etymologically. The word for sacrifice to the gods is *nextlahualiztli* ('the act of payment'), and the offering of fire to the gods, *tlenamaca*, means 'to sell fire.' "[72]

Such sacrifice occurred, of course, not only on the battlefield, but in the temples and in everyday life as well. The role of human sacrifice, and the related practice of ritual cannibalism, in Aztec society has been well documented,[73] and it is clear that such sacrifice involved both males and females, adults and children,[74] and as many as 20,000 human sacrifices a year may have taken place by the time of the arrival of Cortés.[75] Also important in Aztec life, however, was the practice of autosacrifice, which involved personal bloodletting. As Cecelia Klein argued, "In Aztec society, from all reports, virtually everyone, regardless of age, sex, or social class, was expected to bleed himself."[76] The practice of such autosacrifice, which the Aztecs believed to have originated with the god Quetzalcoatl, was in fact closely related to human sacrifice, and it appears to have served as a symbolic substitute for human sacrifice in some instances.[77]

Aztec religious thought entailed far more than just sacrifice, of course. Religion played a central role in social life in general, touching every aspect of the society.[78] In addition to the rituals performed in the temples, their religion provided the Aztecs with a well-developed creation mythology, a powerful moral code, the basis for their political and economic social order, a complex view of life after death, a priesthood responsible for the maintenance of both the oral and written traditions of their society, the calendrical system used not only to maintain records but to make predictions, a highly developed astrological system, and the foundations for a metaphysical and ultimately philosophical worldview.[79] Thus, it is hardly surprising that religious concerns are in many ways at the heart of the Aztec notion of the educated person, the concept to which we now turn.

THE AZTEC CONCEPTION OF THE "EDUCATED PERSON"

The development of the individual's personality, which the Aztecs called "face and heart,"[80] played an important role in their conception of *education* and the *educated person*, although the primary focus of education was "the assimilation of individuals into the life and highest ideals of the community."[81] As one ancient text described what we would today call the "educated person":

> *In omacic oquichtli,*
> *Yollotetl, yollotlaquavac,*
> *ixlamati,*
> *ixehyollo,*
> *Mozcalia.*

> The mature man
> is a heart solid as a rock,
> is a wise face.
> Possessor of a face, possessor of a heart,
> he is able and understanding.[82]

The core values that were expected to guide the behavior of all individuals in Aztec society, regardless of social station, and provide a clear indication of the Aztec view of what the "educated person" might look like include: maintenance of control and discipline; fluency of speech and good manners; composed and reserved attitude; a sense of responsibility for the common people;

respect for one's elders; interest in and knowledge of the gods; and courage, submission to one's fate, a desire to die a heroic death rather than to die without having made a serious effort to expand and strengthen the Aztecs' supremacy.[83]

These core values are clearly intended to promote the general good of society, and have a social rather than individual focus, as one would expect. This focus can be seen vividly in the following model homily delivered by an Aztec father to his son:

> Revere and greet your elders; console the poor and the afflicted with good works and words. . . . Follow not the madmen who honour neither father nor mother; for they are like animals, for they neither take nor hear advice. . . . Do not mock the old, the sick, the maimed, or one who has sinned. Do not insult or abhor them, but abase yourself before God and fear lest the same befall you. . . . Do not set a bad example, or speak indiscreetly, or interrupt the speech of another. If someone does not speak well or coherently, see that you do not the same; if it is not your business to speak, be silent. If you are asked something, reply soberly and without affectation or flattery or prejudice to others, and your speech will be well regarded. . . . Wherever you go, walk with a peaceful air, and do not make wry faces or improper gestures.[84]

Such homilies were common in Aztec society, and a number, especially targeting the children of the elite, have been preserved. Among the kinds of advice and instruction provided in these homilies are such warnings as:

> "Do not throw thy feet much, nor raise thy feet high, nor go jumping, lest it be said of thee, lest thou be named fool, shameless."

> "Thou art not to speak hurriedly, nor to pant, nor to squeak, lest it be said that thou art a groaner, a growler, a squeaker."

> "Ignore [gossip]. Pretend not to understand the words. If thou canst not ignore it, respond not. And speak not; only listen, let what is said remain as said."

> "Be not called twice, like the wind art thou to go."

> "Thou art not to array thyself fantastically . . . neither art thou to put on rags, tatters, an old loosely-woven cape."[85]

Similar messages were conveyed less directly, but perhaps more effectively, to children in Aztec society through the use of proverbs, conundrums, and metaphors.[86] For example, typical proverbs that children might hear include the following, reported in the *Florentine Codex*:

- *Nonouian.* Here, there and everywhere. (This is said about a person who enters where he should not enter, sticks his hand where he should not stick his hand, and quickly takes part in whatever others are doing.)[87]
- *Ayac xictili in tlalticpac.* No one on earth is an umbilical cord (i.e., to be thrown away). (We should not sneer at anyone; meaning, we should not disdain anyone even though he appears to warrant disdain, as he might be a wise man, or learned, or able.)[88]
- *Tlacoqualli in monequi.* Moderation is proper. (We should not dress in rags, nor should we overdress. In the matter of clothing, we should dress with moderation.)[89]

The conundrums that characterized much of the verbal play of Aztec children, as Sullivan noted, "are like conundrums everywhere—charming, simple, and concerned with everyday things."[90] The following are some interesting examples of common conundrums, again drawn from the *Florentine Codex*:

- *Zazan tleino, icuitlaxcol quiuilana, tepetozcatl quitoca. Aca quittaz tozazaniltzin, tla ca nenca uitzmallotl.* (What is it that drags its intestines as it ambles along the foothills of the mountain? Someone is sure to guess our riddle; it is a sewing needle.)[91]
- *Zazan tleino, tezcatzintli acxoyacaletica. Tixtelolo.* (What is a little mirror in the middle of fir trees? Our eyes.)[92]
- *Zazan tleino, tepetlamimilolli yitic ameia. Toyac.* (What is a mountainside that has a spring of water in it? Our nose.)[93]
- *Zazan tleino, quauhtla calaqui nenepilotiuh. Tepuztli.* (What is it that goes into a tree and its tongue is hanging out? An ax.)[94]

The purpose of Aztec education, in short, was largely to promote socially appropriate, and basically conformist, behavior, and in this objective it is clear that Aztec education was remarkably successful.[95] As the Jesuit José de Acosta noted in the latter part of the 16th century, "Nothing caused me so much admiration and seems to me more worthy of praise and remembering than the care and discipline with which the Mexicans raised their children. In effect, it would be quite difficult to find a nation which in its times of paganism gave more attention to this element of highest importance to the state."[96]

We turn now to an examination of how the Aztecs accomplished the making of such "educated persons," first looking at the child's earliest years at home, and then at the formal educational institutions of Aztec society.

THE EDUCATIONAL FUNCTIONS OF THE FAMILY IN AZTEC SOCIETY

As Fagan commented, "From the moment of birth, an Aztec child became aware that the world was a place of hard work and suffering."[97] Early childhood education for the Aztecs was guided by the twin concerns of teaching self-control and accommodation to adversity on the one hand and self-knowledge and introspection on the other.[98] By age four, both boys and girls were performing chores around the home; boys began by carrying water and accompanying their fathers to work and the market, girls by helping their mothers in various household activities.[99] The nature of the activities in which children were engaged became increasingly sophisticated as they grew older and were given more responsibility; for girls, such training was intended to prepare them for their futures as wives and mothers, whereas for boys, the focus was increasingly on learning their father's craft.[100] Children also learned the importance of learning to control their appetites during this early period—a lesson reinforced by the relatively small food ration they were allowed.[101] Boys learned to tolerate not only hunger, but also extremes of heat and cold, as preparation for their later lives as warriors.[102] Indeed, one of the goals of such experiences was to develop in each individual "a heart of stone" (*yolotetl*), a necessary outcome for a society such as that of the Aztecs.[103]

Much of the concern of parents for their children during this early period in their children's upbringing concerned what might be called "character education," with punishments for inappropriate behavior ranging from mere scolding to beatings, being pricked with maguey spines, and, perhaps as a last result, being forced to inhale the fumes of burning chilis—punishments vividly portrayed in the Aztec manuscript, the *Codex Mendoza*.[104]

FORMAL SCHOOLING IN AZTEC SOCIETY

The first taste of formal schooling outside of the home that Aztec children had took place between ages twelve and fifteen, when both boys and girls attended the *cuicacalli* ("the House of Song").[105] Each *calpulli* maintained its own *cuicacalli*, in which the elderly members of the community taught the songs, dances, and music with which everyone in Aztec society needed to be familiar.[106] The *cuicacalli* took place toward the end of the day, about an hour before sunset, and children learned "the correct songs and orations for every major religious ceremony on the Aztec calendar. These incantations spoke of the Aztec cosmos, the creation, and the great migrations of the ancestors. They dealt with the roles of mortals on earth, and of the relationships between gods and humans. At the *cuicacalli* everyone learned about their cultural heritage and about the mystical and highly symbolic world that surrounded them."[107]

Attendance at the *cuicacalli* was, for all intents and purposes, compulsory, and absences were punished by law. In addition, it is clear that attendance at the *cuicacalli* was not left to chance or to the responsibility of the individual. Rather, as Fray Diego Durán explained, "certain elders were appointed to pick up and lead the children to their classes. They were elected exclusively for this task in all the wards and were known as *teaanque*, which means 'men who conduct boys.' Old women appointed by the wards went to fetch the girls; these were called *cihuatepixque*, which means 'keepers of the maidens.' "[108] These same elders were then responsible for returning the children to their homes or schools, and for ensuring that nothing inappropriate took place during the journey.

For the sons of the common people, additional schooling normally took place in the *telpochcalli* (the "House of Youth"), in which the curriculum included the study of history, religion, ritual, proper behavior, and music, singing, and dancing.[109] The *telpochcalli*, however, was primarily concerned with preparing their charges for war, and the students in the *telpochcalli* engaged in extensive military training and even participation in real battles on occasion.[110] As Hassig explained:

> Beyond greater numbers, the Aztecs also had a fully professional corps of soldiers, the result of a formal educational system. Initially, the Aztecs offered formal military training only to the elite, but within two decades of their emergence as an independent power, King Monteuczomah Ilhuicamina instituted training for all males. . . . The commoners' schools [the *telpochcalli*], located in each of the city's wards, were responsible for educating all the youths therein between the ages of fifteen and twenty years. . . . Each commoners' school had a staff of accomplished veteran soldiers who trained the youths in military skills. Youths . . . accompanied the army on its campaigns to teach them about battle, usually as burden bearers.[111]

Boys slept at the *telpochcalli* at night, and were required to perform a variety of different kinds of physical work necessary to the maintenance of the *telpochcalli*, but they ate their meals at home with their families, and spent part of their day with the fathers, continuing to learn the vocational skills they would someday need to support themselves.[112]

The sons of the nobility, on the other hand, generally attended the *calmécac*, which were attached to the temples and were under the direct control of the religious authorities.[113] The *calmécac* provided an academically superior education, focusing not only on the military skills needed by all Aztec males, but also on religious instruction, history, painting, music, law, astrology, mathematics, government, and architecture.[114] Also important in a *calmécac* education was learning to speak well; the Aztecs valued the ability to use what they called *qualli tlatolli* ("good language"), by which they meant noble (as opposed to common) speech, and even distinguished between *macehuallatolli* ("the language of the common people") and *tecpil-latolli* ("lordly language").[115]

The Aztec writing system was "not a transliteration of spoken words but an elaborate code that was reserved to those who had learned its intricacies and the orations behind it,"[116] so students at the *calmécac* spent much of their time memorizing vast quantities of historical and religious material.[117] This limitation of the Aztec literary tradition turned out to have significant benefits for us today as we try to understand more fully the Aztecs. As John Cornyn noted:

> The great body of the national literature was memorized in the Aztec schools over a period of scholastic life that was almost as long as our own. To this fact we owe the preservation of the very considerable body of Aztec metric compositions which have come down to us, for, had the Aztecs been able to write their literature, it would all have disappeared in the ruthless destruction of Indian libraries wrought by the Spanish conquerors and their native allies in the first few years after the conquest.[118]

Unlike in the *telpochcalli*, students in the *calmécac* lived at the school, in what has been suggested to have been an environment "more like that of a monastery than an ordinary school."[119] It was from the *calmécac* that the priests of Aztec society were drawn, as well as the senior government officials, military leaders, judges, and so on, and thus, the *calmécac* served an important role in "the spread of elite dogma and the consolidation of belief" in Aztec society.[120] Interestingly, whereas the patron god of the *telpochcalli* was Tezcatlipoca, the war god, the patron god of the *calmécac* was Quetzalcoatl, the Creator god who was also "the god of learning and culture, of ancient lore, the god of civilization itself."[121]

Although attendance at the *telpochcalli* and the *calmécac* was largely determined by social class background, there was nevertheless a certain degree of choice involved in the selection of the school one's son would attend.[122] It is well established that children of non-noble backgrounds attended the *calmécac*, primarily to become priests, just as it is documented that some children of the nobility attended the *telpochcalli*.[123] In any event, all young men in Aztec society, regardless of their social background, attended one or the other of these institutions.[124]

Although all boys went on for further schooling, the *cuicacalli* was the end of formal schooling for many, and perhaps most, girls. There were, however, equivalent institutions to both the *telpochcalli* and the *calmécac* available for girls,[125] which were in fact located in the same complex as their male counterparts,[126] as we read about in the "Bancroft Dialogues":

> Likewise within the houses, where the ladies were in their quarters, the girls were taught all the different things women do: sweeping, sprinkling, preparing

food, making beverages, grinding (maize), preparing tortillas, making tamales, all the different things customarily done among women; also (the art of) the spindle and the weaver's reed and various kinds of embroidery; also dyeing, how rabbit down or rabbit fur was dyed different colors. And in the same way (as with the boys) those who did something wrong or did not take care were severely punished. And they were all well cared for: no men, no matter who, entered there; taking care of them was the exclusive domain of the elderly noblewomen. . . . And the commoners were raised in the same way; the youths were raised in the school at the youths' house, and the girls at the women's temple, where the female penitents were enclosed and fasted.[127]

CONCLUSIONS

Formal schooling in Aztec society was well developed and effective. Perhaps most impressive was the fact that at a time when in virtually every European society schooling of any sort was limited to a small elite, in the Aztec world mandatory universal schooling for both boys and girls, regardless of social class, was an established fact.[128] Furthermore, for the Aztecs, "education" entailed a variety of different attributes; in fact, the Aztecs had two very distinct words for "education": *neixtlamachiliztli* ("the act of giving wisdom to the face") and *tlacahuapahualiztli* ("the art of strengthening or bringing up men").[129] Given this model of *education* and the *educated person*, it could certainly be argued that the Aztecs were far more successful in achieving their educational aims than are many contemporary societies.

QUESTIONS FOR REFLECTION AND DISCUSSION

1. We know virtually nothing about the Olmecs and Toltecs with respect to their educational thought and practice. However, because they are part of the same broad cultural tradition as the Maya and the Aztecs, what kinds of generalizations do you think could be made about education and childrearing among these peoples?

2. Consider the account offered in the *Popol Vuh* of the creation of human beings. If one accepts this account, then what are the social and educational implications? How would this account affect one's conception of what constitutes an "educated person"?

3. In this chapter, it is suggested that ancient Maya education was profoundly religious in nature. What are the parallels to other systems of education that are deeply religious? How did the Mayan experience differ from other religious approaches to education? How can you account for these differences?

4. Social class clearly played an important role in both informal and formal education in Aztec society. To what extent, and in what ways, was the educational system open to social class mobility, and how might this have strengthened Aztec society?

5. The Aztec conception of the *educated man* is discussed in detail in this chapter. What, given your knowledge of Aztec society, would have been the Aztec conception of the *educated woman*? How does this conception fit with the passage from the "Bancroft Dialogues" presented in the chapter?

6. In many ways, Aztec educational goals and practices are similar to those of a number of other societies historically. For example, what are the similarities to and differences from Spartan education? What about the educational ideals and institutions of Nazi Germany? How might the similarities that you have identified be explained?

7. Aztec schooling sought to promote the social status quo and to reproduce Aztec society. To what extent, and in what ways, is this true for contemporary schooling as well? Is this, in your view, a reasonable goal for schooling?

8. Music played a very important role in Aztec education. What purposes did music serve in Aztec schooling and society? How do these purposes compare to those offered for the study of music in our own society?

9. Because the Aztec writing system was "not a transliteration of spoken words but an elaborate code that was reserved to those who had learned its intricacies and the orations behind it," it was necessary for students to learn to use the written text as a support for the recall of memorized information. Can you think of any learning techniques that you have used that are similar to this one? What kind of learning is best promoted by such techniques?

10. This chapter concludes by noting that Aztec education may have been more effective than many contemporary systems of education. If this is true, then is it in fact desirable? With what issues other than effectiveness might one be concerned in evaluating educational thought and practice?

RECOMMENDED FURTHER READINGS

An excellent overview of Aztec society for the beginner is Richard Townsend's *The Aztecs* (London: Thames and Hudson, 1992), while a somewhat more sophisticated account is provided in Inga Clendinnen's *Aztecs: An Interpretation* (Cambridge, England: Cambridge University Press, 1991). Among the best works describing the intellectual and cultural world of the Aztecs are Miguel León-Portilla's *Aztec Thought and Culture* (Norman: University of Oklahoma Press, 1963) and his *The Aztec Image of Self and Society: An Introduction to Nahua Culture* (Salt Lake City: University of Utah Press, 1992). Finally, both Davíd Carrasco, with Scott Sessions, *Daily Life of the Aztecs: People of the Sun and Earth* (Westport, CT: Greenwood, 1998), and Robert Sharer, *Daily Life in Maya Civilization* (Westport, CT: Greenwood, 1996), provide very good summaries of many educationally relevant aspects of Aztec life.

NOTES

1. Richard E. Adams, *Prehistoric Mesoamerica*, rev. ed. (Norman: University of Oklahoma Press, 1991), 22.

2. Adams, *Prehistoric Mesoamerica*, 23.

3. Adams, *Prehistoric Mesoamerica*, 24. See also Nigel Davies, *The Ancient Kingdoms of Mexico* (Harmondsworth, England: Penguin, 1982), 11–20.

4. Jacques Soustelle, *The Olmecs: The Oldest Civilization in Mexico* (Norman: University of Oklahoma Press, 1979), 1; Davies, *The Ancient Kingdoms of Mexico*, 61–62.

5. This cultural continuity can be seen, e.g., in the development of Mesoamerican religious thought. See Davíd Carrasco, *Religions of Mesoamerica: Cosmovision and Ceremonial Centers* (San Francisco: HarperSanFrancisco, 1990).

6. Adams, *Prehistoric Mesoamerica*, 85.

7. Soustelle, *The Olmecs*, 194.

8. See, e.g., Ronald Spores, *The Mixtecs in Ancient and Colonial Times* (Norman: University of Oklahoma Press, 1984).

9. Soustelle, *The Olmecs*, 1.

10. *Códice Matritense de la Real Academia*, VIII, fol. 192, r; quoted in Miguel León-Portilla, *Aztec Thought and Culture: A Study of the Ancient Nahuatl Mind* (Norman: University of Oklahoma Press, 1963), 23.

11. Michael D. Coe, *The Maya*, 4th ed. (London: Thames and Hudson, 1987), 7.

12. For recent scholarship on Mayan civilization, see Linda Schele and Peter Mathews, *The Code of Kings: The Language of Seven Sacred Maya Temples and Tombs* (New York: Simon & Schuster, 1998); Anthony Aveni (ed.), *The Sky in Mayan Literature* (New York: Oxford University Press, 1992); Michael Coe, *Breaking the Maya Code* (London: Thames and Hudson, 1992); David Freidel, Linda Schele, and Joy Parker, *Maya Cosmos: Three Thousand Years of the Shaman's Path* (New York: William Morrow, 1993); Charles Gallenkamp, *Maya: The Riddle and Rediscovery of a Lost Civilization*, 3rd ed. (New York: Penguin, 1985); Linda Schele and David Freidel, *A Forest of Kings: The Untold Story of the Ancient Maya* (New York: William Morrow, 1990); Robert Sharer, *The Ancient Maya*, 5th ed. (Stanford, CA: Stanford University Press, 1994); Robert Sharer, *La civilización maya* (México: Fondo de Cultura Económica, 1998). The classic presentation of the older "peaceful priest-astronomers" view of the Maya is given by Eric Thompson, *The Rise and Fall of Maya Civilization* (Norman: University of Oklahoma Press, 1954); see also Sylvanus Morley, *The Ancient Maya*, 3rd ed. (Stanford, CA: Stanford University Press, 1956); Paul Gendrop, *Les mayas* (Paris: Presses Universitaires de France, 1978).

13. That such claims are largely conjectural, however, has not prevented a number of scholars from speculating about educational matters in ancient Mayan civilization. See, e.g., Ana Luisa Izquierdo, *La educación maya en los tiempos prehispánicos* (México:

Universidad Nacional Autónoma de México, 1983); Carlos Orellana, *Historia de la educación en Guatemala*, 5th ed. (Guatemala: Editoria Universitaria, Universidad de San Carlos de Guatemala, 1997), 19–39.

14. Norman Hammond, *Ancient Maya Civilization* (New Brunswick, NJ: Rutgers University Press, 1988), 180.

15. See, e.g., Robert Sharer, *Daily Life in Maya Civilization* (Westport, CT: Greenwood Press, 1996); Robert Sharer, *The Ancient Maya*, 5th ed. (Stanford, CA: Stanford University Press, 1994); Robert Sharer, *La civilización maya*; Mary Ellen Miller, *The Art of Mesoamerica from Olmec to Aztec* (London: Thames and Hudson, 1986).

16. Sharer, *Daily Life in Maya Civilization*, 118.

17. Diego de Landa, *Relación de las cosas de Yucatán* (México: Editorial Porrua, 1959).

18. See Gualberto Alonzo, *An Overview of the Mayan World*, 11th ed. (Mérida, México: Author, 1993), 50–52; Nelly Solana, *Códices de México: Historia e interpretación de los grandes libros pintados prehispánicos* (México: Panorama Editorial, 1990).

19. An excellent Spanish version is Ermilo Abreu Gomez, *Popol Vuh* (Mérida, México: Producción Editorial Dante, 1996); for English, see Della Goetz and Sylvanus Morley, trans., *Popol Vuy: The Sacred Book of the Ancient Quiché Maya* (Norman: University of Oklahoma Press, 1950).

20. Goetz and Morley, *Popul Vuh*, ix.

21. See Orellana, *Historia de la educación en Guatemala*, 27–29.

22. Izquierdo, *La educación maya en los tiempos prehispánicos*, 13, my translation. Also very useful here are Alfredo López Austin, *La educacíon de los antiguos nahuas*, 2 vols. (México: Secretaría de Educacíon Pública-Caballito, 1985), and Pablo Escalante, *Educacíon e ideologia en el México antiguo* (México: Secretaría de Educacíon Pública-Caballito, 1985).

23. Izquierdo, *La educación maya en los tiempos prehispánicos*, 17.

24. See Sharer, *Daily Life in Maya Civilization*, 117–129; Sharer, *The Ancient Maya*, 481–488; Sharer, *La civilización maya*, 458–468.

25. See the discussion of the role of oral traditions in education in chap. 1.

26. Izquierdo, *La educación maya en los tiempos prehispánicos*, 18.

27. Goetz and Morley, *Popol Vuh*, 168.

28. Goetz and Morley, *Popol Vuh*, 169.

29. There is something of a terminological problem involved in discussing the Aztecs. First, as Fagan quite correctly noted, "At the time of the Spanish Conquest, the Aztecs called themselves either Tenocha Mexica or Tlatelolca Mexica, depending on which part of the capital they lived in. 'Mexica' could also be used alone, depending on the context" (Brian Fagan, *The Aztecs* [New York: Freeman, 1984], x). Furthermore, the Aztecs were but one group among the closely related Nahuatl groups in Mesoamerica, and so one might also quite properly use the term "Nahuatl" to refer to them—as, indeed, did Miguel León-Portilla. However, "Aztec" is the most commonly and easily understood term used today for the people about whom I am writing, and so I have chosen to take the easiest way out for the benefit of the reader, as have many other writers on the Aztecs.

30. Quoted in Ross Hassig, *Trade, Tribute, and Transportation: The Sixteenth Century Political Economy of the Valley of Mexico* (Norman: University of Oklahoma Press, 1985), 4.

31. From the Aztec perspective, of course, the "time of the fifth sun" did not actually end with the Spanish Conquest—technically speaking, only the end of the world as we know it, on a predetermined date, would constitute the end of the "time of the fifth sun." However, in a very real social and political sense, the world of the Aztecs did indeed end in the early 16th century, as Brundage and others seem to implicitly recognize in utilizing the phrase "the fifth sun" to refer solely to the world of the Aztecs. See Burr Brundage, *The Fifth Sun: Aztec Gods, Aztec World* (Austin: University of Texas Press, 1979).

32. See Ruben Campos, *La producción literaria de los Aztecas* (México: Talleres Gráficos del Museo Nacional de Arqueología, Historia y Ethnografía, 1936), 65–72; F. Infante, *La educación de los Aztecas* (México: Panorama Editorial, 1983); Mina Markus, "Estudio comparativo entre la educación nahuatl y la griega," *Estudios de Cultura Náhuatl* 4 (1963): 281–292; P. Aizpuro, *Historia de la educación en la época colonial: El mundo indígena* (México: El Colegio de México, 1990); Jacqueline Sáenz, "Reto y educación en el México prehispánico," in J. Kathryn Josserand and Karen Dakin (eds.), *Smoke and Mist: Mesoamerican Studies in Memory of Thelma D. Sullivan, Part II* (Oxford, England: B.A.R., 1988), 681–695.

33. León-Portilla, *Aztec Thought and Culture*, 135. See also Miguel León-Portilla, *La filosofía Nahuatl: Estudio en sus fuentes* (México: Universidad Nacional Autónoma de México, 1966); Miguel León-Portilla, *Trece poetas del mundo azteca* (México: Universidad Nacional Autónoma de México, Instituto de Investigaciones Históricas, 1967).

34. Muriel Weaver, *The Aztecs, Maya, and Their Predecessors: Archeology of Mesoamerica*, 2nd ed. (New York: Academic, 1981), 420; see also Betty Bell (ed.), *Indian Mexico: Past and Present* (Los Angeles: University of California at Los Angeles, Latin American Center, 1967); Burr Brundage, *Two Heavens, Two Earths: An Essay Contrasting the Aztecs and the Incas* (Albuquerque: University of New Mexico Press, 1975); Davíd Carrasco, *Quetzalcoatl and the Irony of Empire: Myths and Prophecies in the Aztec Tradition* (Chicago: University of Chicago Press, 1982).

35. See Davies, *The Ancient Kingdoms of Mexico*, 167–171; John Thompson, *Mexico Before Cortez: An Account of the Daily Life, Religion, and Ritual of the Aztecs and Kindred Peoples* (New York: Scribner's, 1933), 23–27; Weaver, *The Aztecs, Maya, and their Predecessors*, 420; Jacques Soustelle, *Les aztèques*, 6th ed. (Paris: Presses Universitaires de France, 1991).

36. Quoted in Burr Brundage, *A Rain of Darts: The Mexica Aztecs* (Austin: University of Texas Press, 1972), 22.

37. Jon Manchip White, *Cortés and the Downfall of the Aztec Empire: A Study in a Conflict of Cultures* (New York: St. Martin's Press, 1971), 93.

38. Quoted in Fagan, *The Aztecs*, 57–58.

39. Fagan, *The Aztecs*, 58.

40. See Davies, *The Ancient Kingdoms of Mexico*, 171; Weaver, *The Aztecs, Maya, and their Predecessors*, 421.

41. Weaver, *The Aztecs, Maya, and their Predecessors*, 422.

42. Although in many ways the Aztec Empire was indeed at its height in 1519, in other ways it was profoundly troubled. As Benjamin Keen noted:

Was Aztec society going through a moral crisis, a *crise de conscience*, on the eve of the Conquest? Certainly the native chronicles reveal a state of jangled nerves, of profound insecurity on the part of the Aztec leadership. Economic and social factors undoubtedly contributed to this state of affairs: chronic discontent of conquered peoples under the mounting burden of tribute demands, perhaps population pressure on exhausted soils, dissension between warrior nobles and increasingly powerful merchants, a decline of tribal solidarity as a result of growing inequalities of wealth and status. Yet ideological factors also played their part. . . . Aztec civilization has reached an impasse that perhaps could have been overcome only by a decisive advance in technology, of the kind that attended the invention of ironworking in the Old World. (see Benjamin Keen, *The Aztec Image in Western Thought* [New Brunswick, NJ: Rutgers University Press, 1971], 47–48).

43. Warwick Bray, *The Everyday Life of the Aztecs* (New York: Dorset, 1968), 25.

44. Throughout Mesoamerica, Nahuatl, the language of the Aztecs and related peoples, functioned as a *lingua franca*. See James Andrews, *An Introduction to Classical Nahuatl* (Austin: University of Texas Press, 1975); Jorge Suárez, *The Mesoamerican Indian Languages* (Cambridge, England: Cambridge University Press, 1983); Gunter Lanczkowski, *Aztekische Sprach und Überlieferung* (Berlin: Springer-Verlag, 1970).

45. See Frances Berdan, "La organización del tributo en el imperio azteca," *Estudios de Cultura Náhuatl* 12 (1976): 185–195; Hassig, *Trade, Tribute and Transportation*, 276–280.

46. Hassig, *Trade, Tribute and Transportation*, 104.

47. See Weaver, *The Aztecs, Maya, and Their Predecessors*, 451–455; see also Hassig, *Trade, Tribute and Transportation*.

48. Ross Hassig, *Aztec Warfare: Imperial Expansion and Political Control* (Norman: University of Oklahoma Press, 1988), 26; see also Ross Hassig, *Trade, Tribute and Transportation*, 92–103.

49. Fagan, *The Aztecs*, 109; Bray, *The Everyday Life of the Aztecs*, 98.

50. See Bray, *The Everyday Life of the Aztecs*, 98.

51. Fagan, *The Aztecs*, 84–89.

52. Fagan, *The Aztecs*, 99–103; Elizabeth Boone (ed.), *The Aztec Templo Mayor: A Symposium at Dumbarton Oaks, 8th and 9th October 1983* (Washington, DC: Dumbarton Oaks Research Library and Collection, 1987).

53. Eduardo Matos Moctezuma, "Symbolism of the Templo Mayor," in Elizabeth Boone (ed.), *The Aztec Templo Mayor: A Symposium at Dumbarton Oaks, 8th and 9th October 1983* (Washington, DC: Dumbarton Oaks Research Library and Collection, 1987), 191. See also Jacques Soustelle, *El universo de los aztecas* (México: Fondo de Cultura Económica, 1996).

54. Diane Chase and Arlen Chase (eds.), *Mesoamerican Elites: An Archeological Assessment* (Norman: University of Oklahoma Press, 1992); Nigel Davies, *The Aztec Empire: The Toltec Resurgence* (Norman: University of Oklahoma Press, 1987), 106–116;

Fagan, *The Aztecs*, 137–138; Friedrich Katz, *Situación social y económica de los Aztecas durante los siglos XV y XVI* (México: Universidad Nacional Autónoma de México, Instituto de Investigaciones Históricas, 1966), 123–149; H. Nicholson, "The Efflorescence of Mesoamerican Civilization: A Resume," in Betty Bell (ed.), *Indian Mexico: Past and Present* (Los Angeles: University of California at Los Angeles, Latin American Center, 1967), 46–71.

55. Hassig, *Aztec Warfare*, 28.

56. See Anna-Britta Hellbrom, *La participación cultural de las mujeres: Indias y mestizas en el México precortesiano y postrevolucionario* (Stockholm, Sweden: The Ethnographic Museum, Monograph Series, Publication 10, 1967); Susan Kellogg, "Cognatic Kinship and Religion: Women in Aztec Society," in J. Kathryn Josserand and Karen Dakin (eds.), *Smoke and Mist: Mesoamerican Studies in Memory of Thelma D. Sullivan, Part II* (Oxford, England: B.A.R., 1988), 665–681.

57. Hassig, *Aztec Warfare*, 28.

58. Nicholson, "The Efflorescence of Mesoamerican Civilization," 64.

59. Weaver, *The Aztecs, Maya, and Their Predecessors*, 446.

60. Fagan, *The Aztecs*, 146; see also Claude Davies, *Los mexicas: Primeros pasos hacia el imperio* (México: Universidad Nacional Autónoma de México, Instituto de Investigaciones Históricas, 1973), 81–83; Jane Day, *Aztec: The World of Moctezuma* (Niwot, CO: Denver Museum of Natural History and Roberts Rinehart Publishers, 1992), 8–9.

61. See Katz, *Situación social y económica de los Aztecas durante los siglos XV y XVI*, 117–121; Day, *Aztec*, 8.

62. Fagan, *The Aztecs*, 148.

63. See Cecilia Klein, "The Ideology of Autosacrifice at the Templo Mayor," in Elizabeth Boone (ed.), *The Aztec Templo Mayor: A Symposium at Dumbarton Oaks, 8th and 9th October 1983* (Washington, DC: Dumbarton Oaks Research Library and Collection, 1987), 293–370; Brundage, *A Rain of Darts*, 96–102; White, *Cortés and the Downfall of the Aztec Empire*, 113–115.

64. Brundage, *A Rain of Darts*, 97.

65. Brundage, *A Rain of Darts*, 97.

66. Brundage, *A Rain of Darts*, 99–101.

67. Davies, *The Aztec Empire*, 93; see also R. Hassig, *War and Society in Ancient Mesoamerica* (Berkeley: University of California Press, 1992), 147–148.

68. Fagan, *The Aztecs*, 228.

69. Bray, *The Everyday Life of the Aztecs*, 171–175.

70. Davies, *The Ancient Kingdoms of Mexico*, 229–230.

71. Miguel León-Portilla, *Fifteen Poets of the Aztec World* (Norman: University of Oklahoma Press, 1992), 46.

72. Bernard Ortiz de Montellano, *Aztec Medicine, Health, and Nutrition* (New Brunswick, NJ: Rutgers University Press, 1990), 41.

73. See Brundage, *A Rain of Darts*, 101–107; Davies, *The Ancient Kingdoms of Mexico*, 228–231; Fagan, *The Aztecs*, 228–237; M. Othón de Mendizábal, "La cultura azteca y los sacrificios humanos," in Miguel León-Portilla (ed.), *De Teotihuacán a los Aztecas: Antología de fuentes e interpretaciones históricas* (México: Universidad Nacional

Autónoma de México, Instituto de Investigaciones Históricas, 1971), 208–214; White, *Cortés and the Downfall of the Aztec Empire*, 119–121.

74. See Juan Berrelleza, "Offering 48 of the Templo Mayor: A Case of Child Sacrifice," in Elizabeth Boone (ed.), *The Aztec Templo Mayor: A Symposium at Dumbarton Oaks, 8th and 9th October 1983* (Washington, DC: Dumbarton Oaks Research Library and Collection, 1987), 131–143; Brundage, *The Fifth Sun*, 212–214; Davies, *The Aztec Empire*; Fagan, *The Aztecs*, 232; Miguel León-Portilla (ed.), *Ritos, sacerdotes y atavíos de los dioses: Textos de los informantes de Sahagun, 1* (México: Universidad Nacional Autónoma de México, Instituto de Historia, 1958).

75. Brundage, *The Fifth Sun*, 215; Fagan, *The Aztecs*, 230; see also Davies, *The Aztec Empire*, 218–221, for a description of the inflationary nature of human sacrifice in Aztec society.

76. Klein, "The Ideology of Autosacrifice at the Templo Mayor," 350.

77. Klein, "The Ideology of Autosacrifice at the Templo Mayor," 297.

78. See Bray, *The Everyday Life of the Aztecs*, 152–185; Weaver, *The Aztecs, Maya, and their Predecessors*, 446–451; George C. Vaillant, *La civilización azteca: Origen, grandeza y decadencia* (México: Fondo de Cultura Económica, 1995), 142–156.

79. See Munro Edmonson, *The Book of the Year: Middle American Calendrical Systems* (Salt Lake City: University of Utah Press, 1988); Wayne Elzey, "Some Remarks on the Space and Time of the 'Center' in Aztec Religion," *Estudios de Cultura Náhuatl* 12 (1976): 315–334; Keen, *The Aztec Image in Western Thought*, 30–48; León-Portilla, *Ritos, sacerdotes y atavíos de los dioses*; León-Portilla, *Aztec Thought and Culture*, 1966; Alberto Lhuillier, "El pensamiento náhuatl respecto de la muerte," *Estudios de Cultura Náhuatl* 4 (1963): 251–261.

80. See Miguel León-Portilla, *Toltecáyotl: Aspectos de la cultura náhuatl* (México: Fondo de Cultura Económica, 1995), 192–193.

81. León-Portilla, *Aztec Thought and Culture*, 135.

82. Quoted in Markus, "Estudio comparativo entre la educación nahuatl y la griega," 292; see also Miguel León-Portilla, *The Aztec Image of Self and Society: An Introduction to Nahua Culture* (Salt Lake City: University of Utah Press, 1992), 189–196.

83. Rudolf van Zantwijk, *The Aztec Arrangement: The Social History of Pre-Spanish Mexico* (Norman: University of Oklahoma Press, 1985), 170–171.

84. Quoted in Davies, *The Ancient Kingdoms of Mexico*, 240.

85. Davíd Carrasco, with Scott Sessions, *Daily Life of the Aztecs: People of the Sun and Earth* (Westport, CT: Greenwood Press, 1998), 103.

86. See Thelma Sullivan, "Nahuatl Proverbs, Conundrums and Metaphors Collected by Sahagun," *Estudios de Cultura Náhuatl* 4 (1963): 93–178.

87. Sullivan, "Nahuatl Proverbs, Conundrums and Metaphors Collected by Sahagun," 97.

88. Sullivan, "Nahuatl Proverbs, Conundrums and Metaphors Collected by Sahagun," 99.

89. Sullivan, "Nahuatl Proverbs, Conundrums and Metaphors Collected by Sahagun," 121.

90. Sullivan, "Nahuatl Proverbs, Conundrums and Metaphors Collected by Sahagun," 95.

91. Sullivan, "Nahuatl Proverbs, Conundrums and Metaphors Collected by Sahagun," 131.

92. Sullivan, "Nahuatl Proverbs, Conundrums and Metaphors Collected by Sahagun," 133.

93. Sullivan, "Nahuatl Proverbs, Conundrums and Metaphors Collected by Sahagun," 133.

94. Sullivan, "Nahuatl Proverbs, Conundrums and Metaphors Collected by Sahagun," 135.

95. See Infante, *La educación de los Aztecas*; León-Portilla, *Toltecáyotl: Aspectos de la cultura náhuatl*, 190–204.

96. Quoted in León-Portilla, *Aztec Thought and Culture*, 135.

97. Fagan, *The Aztecs*, 149–150.

98. See León-Portilla, *Aztec Thought and Culture*, 136.

99. Bray, *The Everyday Life of the Aztecs*, 58–59.

100. Fagan, *The Aztecs*, 151.

101. León-Portilla, *Aztec Thought and Culture*, 136.

102. See Campos, *La producción literaria de los Aztecas*, 65–66. Also of interest here is Miguel León-Portilla, *Literaturas indígenas de México* (México: Fondo de Cultura Económica, 1992).

103. Diego Durán, *Book of the Gods and Rites and the Ancient Calendar* (Norman: University of Oklahoma Press, 1971), 294.

104. See Frances F. Berdan and Patricia R. Anawalt, *The Essential Codex Mendoza* (Berkeley: University of California Press, 1997).

105. Day, *Aztec*, 23; Fagan, *The Aztecs*, 151–153; Joyce Marcus, *Mesoamerican Writing Systems: Propaganda, Myth, and History in Four Ancient Civilizations* (Princeton, NJ: Princeton University Press, 1992), 50; Elizabeth Boone and Walter Mignolo (eds.), *Writing Without Words: Alternative Literacies in Mesoamerica and the Andes* (Durham, NC: Duke University Press, 1994); Bernardino Sahagun, *El Mexico antiguo: Selección y reordenación de la historia general de las cosas de Nueva España* (Caracas: Biblioteca Ayachucho, 1981), 165–166; Remi Siméon, *Dictionnaire de la langue Nahuatl ou Mexicaine* (Graz, Germany: Akademische Druck U. Verlagsanstalt, 1963), 120; Richard Townsend, *The Aztecs* (London: Thames and Hudson, 1992), 158.

106. Townsend, *The Aztecs*, 158.

107. Fagan, *The Aztecs*, 153.

108. Durán, *Book of the Gods and Rites and the Ancient Calendar*, 290.

109. Bray, *The Everyday Life of the Aztecs*, 63; Day, *Aztec*, 23; Infante, *La educación de los Aztecas*, 57–63; Marcus, *Mesoamerican Writing Systems*, 51; Townsend, *The Aztecs*, 158–159.

110. See Hassig, *Aztec Warfare*, 30–37.

111. Hassig, *War and Society in Ancient Mesoamerica*, 142.

112. Bray, *The Everyday Life of the Aztecs*, 62–63; Fagan, *The Aztecs*, 154; Sahagun, *El Mexico antiguo*, 163–166; van Zantwijk, *The Aztec Arrangement*, 144.

113. Bray, *The Everyday Life of the Aztecs*, 63; E. Calnek, "The *Calmécac* and *Telpochcalli* in Pre-Conquest Tenochtitlán," in J. Jorge Klor de Alva, H. Nicholson, and Eloise Caber (eds.), *The Work of Bernardino de Sahagun: Pioneer Ethnographer of*

Sixteenth-Century Aztec Mexico (Albany: Institute for Mesoamerican Studies, State University of New York, 1988), 169–177.

114. See Bray, *The Everyday Life of the Aztecs,* 64; Infante, *La educación de los Aztecas,* 63–71; Marcus, *Mesoamerican Writing Systems,* 50–51; Townsend, *The Aztecs.* The study and practice of medicine were also well developed in Aztec society; see Bernard Ortiz de Montellano, *Aztec Medicine, Health, and Nutrition* (New Brunswick, NJ: Rutgers University Press, 1990).

115. León-Portilla, *Aztec Thought and Culture,* 140.

116. Fagan, *The Aztecs,* 198; see also Miguel León-Portilla, *Quince poetas del mundo náhuatl* (México: Editorial Diana, 1994), 11–24.

117. See Marcus, *Mesoamerican Writing Systems,* 50–51; Nelly Gutiérrez Solana, *Códices de México: Historia e interpretación de los grandes libros pintados prehispánicos* (México: Panorama Editorial, 1985).

118. John Cornyn, *The Song of Quetzalcoatl* (Yellow Springs, OH: Antioch Press, 1930), 9–10.

119. Bray, *The Everyday Life of the Aztecs,* 64.

120. Geoffrey Conrad and Arthur Demarest, *Religion and Empire: The Dynamics of Aztec and Inca Expansionism* (Cambridge, England: Cambridge University Press, 1984), 43.

121. Fagan, *The Aztecs,* 244.

122. Calnek, "The *Calmécac* and *Telpochcalli* in Pre-Conquest Tenochtitlán."

123. See Calnek, "The *Calmécac* and *Telpochcalli* in Pre-Conquest Tenochtitlán"; Hassig, *Aztec Warfare,* 34: León-Portilla, *Aztec Thought and Culture,* 137–138.

124. León-Portilla, *Aztec Thought and Culture,* 138.

125. See Bray, *The Everyday Life of the Aztecs,* 64; Day, *Aztec,* 33; Infante, *La educación de los Aztecas,* 71–74; Marcus, *Mesoamerican Writing Systems,* 51–52.

126. Durán, *Book of the Gods and Rites and the Ancient Calendar,* 83–85.

127. Frances Karttunen and James Lockhard (eds.), *The Art of Nahuatl Speech: The Bancroft Dialogues* (Los Angeles: UCLA Latin American Center Publications, 1987), 153–155.

128. See José Luis de Rojas, *México Tenochtitlan: Economía y sociedad en el siglo XVI* (México: El Colegio de Michoacán, Fondo de Cultura Económica, 1988), 22, 24.

129. León-Portilla, *Aztec Thought and Culture,* 134–135.

5

"Finding the True Meaning of Life": Indigenous Education in North America

> In 1992, the West . . . celebrated the quincentenary of Columbus's first voyage from an "old" world to a "new." Conventional history, written by the winners, has always taught us that this "discovery" was one of mankind's finest hours. . . . The inhabitants of America saw it differently. . . . By 1492 there were approximately 100 million Native Americans—a fifth, more or less, of the human race. . . . Within decades of Columbus's landfall, most of these people were dead and their world barbarously sacked by Europeans. The plunderers settled in America, and it was they, not the original people, who became known as Americans.
>
> —Wright (1992, pp. 3–4)

There is an extensive literature concerned with the education of Native American children,[1] and it includes a significant body of excellent historical works.[2] With very few exceptions, however, this historical literature deals with the education of Indian children after the arrival of European settlers. In other words, the focus of scholarship has been not so much on Native American education as it has been on the formal, Western schooling processes to which Indian children have been exposed (or, some would say, subjected). The history of the treatment of the indigenous peoples of North America is an important, and largely shameful, part of our history, and the historical studies of Indian education constitute a significant and potent piece of the broader history of American education. Our concern in this chapter, however, is not with the history of the interaction of Indians and others in North America, but rather, with the educational ideas and practices that existed before that interaction began, many of which continue to play roles in Native American cultural and childrearing practices even today.

In discussing Native American educational ideas and practices, we are faced with a problem very similar to that discussed in chapter 3 with respect to traditional African education. North America is geographically large, and the indigenous peoples of North America were and are very diverse culturally and linguistically. Some 250 distinct languages were spoken in North America when Europeans first arrived and, although many of these languages are now extinct, a significant number still survive.[3] American Indians, both in the past and the present, live in a wide variety of very different physical settings, and as a consequence have developed very different cultural patterns, norms, social structures, and behaviors. Indeed, even the separation of the peoples of Mesoamerica from those of North America is problematic not only geographically, but also culturally. There are clear similarities of thought and practice among all of the indigenous peoples of the Americas, although there are also significant differences. As Joseph Oxendine commented, "The great diversity among traditional Indian cultures makes it impossible to discuss Indian customs . . . as a cohesive entity. Differences in languages, means of livelihood, social structures, and traditions inhibit attempts to generalize absolutely about . . . cultural phenomena."[4] In fact, Carol Locust argued that it is the diversity of both beliefs and practices among different Indian peoples that contributes to a general lack of understanding of Indians in our society. As she explained, "One of the reasons many non-Indian people do not understand much about Indian belief systems is that they vary from tribe to tribe and from clan to clan. For example, Apaches believe that supernatural spirits seek out an individual to become a medicine person. The Tohono O'odham, on the other hand, believe that one must be born into a lineage of medicine persons or must be a twin in order to become a medicine person."[5]

Nevertheless, just as in the case of sub-Saharan Africa, it is possible to discuss a common, core unity in the midst of diversity, so too is this possible in the case of Native Americans. There are, in fact, a common core of beliefs, and of remarkably similar practices, that are common to most (although by no means all) American Indians. This is true not only with respect to their belief systems, as Locust argued, but also with respect to traditional ideas about education and childrearing. This having been said, it is important to keep in mind that variation and diversity will nonetheless characterize the reality of American Indian thought and practice, and the general claims offered here are just that—generalizations rather than absolutes. Furthermore, it is important to remember that even within a particular tribe, there may well be differences of opinion and practice related to clan distinctions, as well as differences related to the degree and amount of contact with other groups.[6]

Added to this complexity has been the tendency of historians to view American Indian history as synonymous with the history of contact with Europeans. As Calvin Martin noted:

"There are two Indians of history," recently mused an eminent anthropologist: "one is the Indian of ethnology; the other, the Indian of recent history. The first is the Indian of cultural elements: the snowshoe, puberty ceremonies, kinship organization, and the potlatch. The second is the Indian of the mines, the *encomiendas*, the missions, and the fur trade."[7]

In order to understand traditional educational thought and practice, it is with the former, more anthropologically based, view of the Native American that we are concerned here. We turn now to a brief discussion of the underlying, core belief system of Native Americans.

THE CORE BELIEF SYSTEM OF INDIGENOUS AMERICANS

Carol Locust identified ten core beliefs that she believes are common to most Indian tribes in the United States, and are probably valid for North American Indians in general. At the outset, of course, we need to recognize that any such list of "core beliefs" associated with a culture will be highly problematic. At best, a list of this sort can only provide us with a framework (and a limited framework at that) for making sense of the incredibly complex nexus of social, cultural, economic, political, and ideological factors that influence both individual and group identity and behavior. Although any articulation of cultural beliefs and practices runs the risk of distortion and misrepresentation, such efforts can, if taken with a grain of salt, be nonetheless useful. The following are the ten core beliefs identified by Locust, which are basically an attempt to summarize the key elements of what many Indians would call the "Old Teachings," that fall into this "problematic but useful" category:

- American Indians believe in a Supreme Creator. In this belief system, there are lesser beings also.
- Humans are threefold beings made up of a spirit, mind, and body.
- Plants and animals, like humans, are part of the spirit world. The spirit world exists side by side with, and intermingles with, the physical world.
- The spirit existed before it came into a physical body, and will exist after the body dies.
- Illness affects the mind and spirit as well as the body.
- Wellness is harmony in spirit, mind, and body.
- Unwellness is disharmony in spirit, mind, and body.
- Natural unwellness is caused by the violation of a sacred or tribal taboo.
- Unnatural unwellness is caused by witchcraft.
- Each of us is responsible for his or her own wellness.[8]

The overall focus of this set of core beliefs is on health, which may initially seem to be related to educational beliefs at best only tangentially. And yet this is, in fact, far from the case, because for Native Americans one's health is not only a physical condition, but a spiritual one as well. Furthermore, the separation of the spiritual from other aspects of culture not only does not exist in traditional Indian thought, it does not make sense *conceptually*. In other words, if we want to understand traditional Native American ideas about education and childrearing, then we must begin with traditional Native Americans' ideas of good health and illness.[9]

Central to Native American educational thought and practice is the view of the human being as a threefold being, consisting of a spirit, a mind, and a physical body. Each of these parts has a role to play, but the roles are distinctive and are by no means of the same relative importance. Locust explained that "of the three elements—spirit, mind, and body—the spirit is the most important, for it is the essence of the being. The instrument by which the spirit may express itself is the body. It can learn spiritual lessons and may progress toward the ultimate goal of being united with the Supreme Creator. The mind is the link between the spirit and the body and functions as an interpreter between the two."[10] Education, understood in this context, should then involve all three of the elements of which each of us is composed and, furthermore, should aid in helping the individual to achieve the goal of *harmony*. Harmony has a somewhat distinctive meaning here, referring to "the peaceful, tranquil state of knowing all is well with one's spirit, mind, and body. To be in harmony is to be at 'oneness' with life, eternity, the Supreme Creator, and oneself. . . . But harmony is not found within the environment, nor does it come from others; it comes from within and from the Supreme Creator."[11]

Although harmony is indeed associated with wellness, it is wellness of a spiritual sort.[12] Thus, learning to cope with various physical ailments may well be part of achieving harmony.[13] Just as harmony is the proper goal for education, the alternative—disharmony—is precisely what education ought to be concerned with preventing. Disharmony is the root cause for physical and psychological unwellness: "One cannot be in a state of disharmony caused by suppressed anger, frustration, heartache, or fear without sooner or later developing unwellness in the physical body from that disharmony. Disharmony may be a vague feeling of things 'not being right' in one's life, and a time of meditation may be needed in which to discover what is not right."[14]

Perhaps the most clearly articulated expression of this conception of harmony and disharmony can be found in the "pattern of the sacred circle." The sacred circle—which is also known as the "medicine wheel," the "sacred hoop," and the "peace symbol"—is common to many North American Indian tribes, and is fundamentally concerned with representing and advocating balance and harmony in all aspects of life.[15] As Robert Regnier noted, the sacred circle "is a mirror which serves as a system of meaning reflecting the essential interconnectedness, harmony, and balance among all beings."[16] Although the exact nature of the manifestation of the sacred circle, as well as elements of its interpretation, do vary from group to group, there are nonetheless strong commonalities across tribes, specifically:

- As a closed formation, the circle symbolizes the totality, interconnectedness and unity of all things.
- Divided in four equal quadrants by a line drawn from top to bottom and another one across the middle, the circle symbolizes harmony in the differences among entities, equality among the differences, and the unity of difference in one reality.
- The solid circumference on which all points are equidistant from the centre differentiates this particular geometric representation from others that display symmetrical characteristics. Indeed, the equidistance of all points on the circumference of the medicine wheel reflects a notion of balance that is unhesitatingly equal and uncompromisingly symmetrical.[17]

The sacred wheel, then, is a visual and metaphorical reminder of the need to maintain balance and harmony in one's life and in the world. This need has been explained exceptionally clearly in the case of the Cree Indians by Fiddler and Sanderson:

> The concept of the sacred circle or way of life is supported by an underlying belief that the Creator created the world in balance and harmony and gave a purpose and power to all living things. All powers are eventually traced back to the Creator. It becomes the responsibility of mankind for keeping the world in order and following the sacred laws and way of life that was given to them by the Creator. Mankind was responsible to maintain this balance and harmony, defined in the Cree language as "Wanuskewin," by correctly carrying out the obligations that went with it. These obligations are passed on, and are reinforced through stories "acimowina" that told of events of long ago in which individuals restored harmony and balance to this world.[18]

The responsibility of individuals for their own wellness extends back beyond birth, because it is believed that each spirit chooses the body that it will inhabit. Thus, as Locust explained, "In the case of a handicapped body, the spirit chooses the body knowing its limitations but choosing to use it for some purpose determined by that spirit and the Supreme Creator. Furthermore, tribal members envision the spirit inside a handicapped body as being whole and perfect and capable of understanding everything that goes on in the environment, even when it appears that the physical body cannot comprehend anything."[19]

Typical of this approach to education, and to individual differences, is the following quote from the Crow leader Plenty Crops: "My people were wise. . . . They never neglected the young. Our teachers were willing and thorough. They were our grandfathers, our fathers, or uncles. All were quick to praise excellence without speaking a word that might break the spirit of a boy who might be less capable than others. The boy who failed at any lesson got only more lessons, more care, until he was as far as he could go."[20] Such a view also has important implications for differences among learners, because such differences are not viewed normatively. Rather, they are simply taken to be part of nature and are dealt with accordingly. No sanction applies to the child who is less bright, nor does any particular reward accrue to those who are exceptionally bright. With this point in mind, we turn now to a discussion of the traditional educational beliefs and practices of the American Indians.

INDIGENOUS AMERICAN EDUCATIONAL BELIEFS AND PRACTICES

Traditional education among Native Americans was, for the most part, informal in nature, taking place as an undemarcated part of social life in general.[21] Children learned the skills and knowledge necessary for successful survival as adults through observation and imitation as well as from direct instruction from parents and other adults.[22] Included among the skills and knowledge that children learned were gender-specific skills, attitudes, values, beliefs, and content knowledge that encompassed vocational skills (hunting, fishing, trapping, agricultural skills, etc., as appropriate to the tribe), social skills and behaviors, and religious knowledge (including rituals, ceremonies, etc.).[23] All of this took place in a broadly spiritual context, which emphasized the need to live in balance with nature. As Jean Barman, Yvonne Hébert, and Don McCaskill noted, "An emphasis was placed on maintaining reciprocal relationships between the individual and the natural environment in order to ensure the provision of the subsistence required to live."[24]

The ultimate purpose of traditional Indian education, however, was spiritual in nature, as our earlier discussion of the place of harmony and wellness would lead one to expect. Indeed, among the Nisga'a, for instance, there is a saying, "*Ts'im gan wilaak'il's wil luu sisgihl gandidils*," which translates as "within the pursuit of knowledge, therein one will find the true meaning of life."[25] In other words, education comes to be seen as a "total way of life." As Jack Forbes commented in his discussion of traditional Native American philosophy:

> What is the purpose of education? . . . [I]t is not primarily the acquisition of specific skills or factual knowledge. Rather it is learning how to be a human being. That is, how to live a life of the utmost spiritual quality. A person who has

developed his character to its highest degree, and who is on that path, will also be able to master specific skills. But if they don't have that spiritual core, they will use those skills to hurt other people. . . . So knowledge without the spiritual core is a very dangerous thing.[26]

A central feature of traditional Indian education is its communal nature. Traditional educational practices were not separate from daily life, and teaching was an activity engaged in by all adults, as well as older children, in the community. As one Canadian elder noted, "In the old days not only your own elders would discipline you, but also an outsider would come in and lecture the young. This could happen anytime, just happen naturally."[27]

The responsibility for the education of the young, although a community one in the broadest sense, rested primarily on parents, relatives (in particular, on maternal uncles in many tribes),[28] and on tribal elders. The role played by tribal elders is especially important in this regard, because it is the elders who function as both the repositories and transmitters of the cultural traditions of the community.[29] Elders are elders by virtue not only of age, but also as recognition by other members of the community; their role in the community has been a significant one: "The elders, comprising the accumulation of tribal wisdom and experience, have always been a vital group in opinion-making, if not in actual decision-making. Many, if not all, of the political leaders depend on "their elders" for advice in decision-making. Some . . . perform the role of adding the cultural perceptions to the decision-making process."[30]

Although the "entire question of the status, configuration, and function of elders in educational contexts is extremely nebulous and imprecise,"[31] it is nevertheless clear that their role historically was an incredibly important one with respect to the proper upbringing of children. As one contemporary elder recalled, "As children we learned from the very beginning, by teaching and discipline, and later on through lecturing, and also by example. You saw how your elders lived, how respectful they were of one another, and how they loved each other. . . . The training went on as a child grew older, became more severe, harder, tougher. . . . It became a habit to live in a sane, sensible way, and intelligent way."[32]

One facet of the educational role of the elder in traditional Native American education was in the passing on of ritual and ceremonial knowledge. Rituals and ceremonies of various sorts played and continue to play a very important role in most Native American cultures. As Gary Witherspoon noted with respect to the Navajo:

The Navajo term *nahaghá* ("ritual") labels a large and significant category of Navajo behavior which non-Navajos least understand, and thus constitutes a major dimension of the estrangement that divides Navajos and non-Navajos. Navajos possess and perform over sixty major rites and numerous minor ones. They perform rituals for blessing, for curing, and for purification. They bless (make immune to illness and tragedy) their land, their livestock, their crops, their homes, their property, their relatives, and themselves.[33]

Oratory often played an important role in ritual and ceremony, and was integrated in speeches, myths, legends, folktales, chants, and so on, in virtually all aspects of traditional Indian social life.[34] As Oscar Kawagley noted, "Myths are the Alaska Native's tool for teaching. The human values that make me uniquely Yup'ik in cadence with the circadian and life rhythms of the universe are all slowly unfolded as my grandmother, and other elders, teach me through myths and legends."[35] In a similar vein, Joel Sherzer pointed out with respect to the Iroquois that "there was an ancient oratorical tradition which entered into all facets of traditional religious and political life, including death, curing, and agricultural ceremonies. Most Iroquois ceremonies involved many speakers, representing families, clans, or whole nations, making formal speeches. . . . This oratory was a central feature of ritual and kept the Iroquois world spiritually alive and well."[36] Indeed, the ability to use language creatively and effectively was among the key characteristics sought by many tribes in their leaders, and often such ability was at least as important as one's skills as a warrior or hunter.[37] A related point here is that traditionally Native American societies were oral ones, and so, as was the case with Africa, so too in North America was there an emphasis on the oral transmission and maintenance of knowledge. As Rik Yellow Bird explained, "Our system of learning was based on oral tradition although syllabics were used later. The nomadic lifestyle determined and strengthened the use of orally transmitted information."[38]

Although by no means a universal phenomenon, various initiation processes and ceremonies were quite common in traditional Indian societies, and such initiation ceremonies are often maintained today, although not uncommonly in modified ways. As Donald Miller wrote with respect to the Hopi:

At about the age eight or nine, when children become involved in mischief, they are initiated into one of the ritual societies. This occasion arrives annually, usually during February, at the time of the Powamu ceremony. . . . Initiation marks the beginning of attaining adult social status. A child is sponsored by a set of ceremonial parents who guide him through the ritual and perform various functions at appropriate times as described below. This new relationship sets up future "ceremonial kinship ties" with subsequent rights, duties, and reciprocal obligations attached to them, thus adding an additional significant dimension to social cohesion. . . . During the initiation a child has his head washed in yucca suds by his ceremonial mother, after which he is given a new name. It is at this time that formal instruction is given about the gods. . . . During the day, those to be initiated are taken by their ceremonial fathers into one of the village kivas where instruction begins. Each child is brought forth before the whipper Kachinas [gods] who ritually purify by literally whipping the child's backside. . . . The ceremonial father may take some or all of the lashes for him, but if the child has been particularly naughty, the father will not interfere. The whipper Kachinas are believed to have ritual power to cleanse and to heal. Later, after an evening of ritual dancing, all non-initiates and women are dismissed from the kiva, after which the Kachinas remove their large masks to reveal themselves as fathers and "uncles" of the village. Initiation marks a turning point in Hopi life. It is not unlike a graduation ceremony—a rite of passage which ritually removes childhood and admits one to the greater responsibilities of an adult world.[39]

An important aspect of traditional Indian educational practice is that of children's play and games played by both children and adults.[40] Joseph Oxendine argued that the traditional play of Indian children can be organized into three broad, if overlapping, categories: games that functioned as preparation for adult activity, games in which toys were the focus of attention, and more formal games that were played by older children and adults.[41] We explore each of these types of play briefly here.

American Indian children, like children in all societies, often engaged in play that was imitative of adult activities. Such play was largely gender-specific in nature, with boys engaging in role playing related to such traditionally male roles as hunter, warrior, and athlete, and girls playing "games that closely paralleled child-rearing, household chores, farming, or pastimes of their mothers."[42] As Ohiyesa commented with respect to play activities found among the Sioux, such play was "molded by the life and customs of our people; indeed, we practiced only what we expected to do when grown. Our games were feats with the bow and arrow, and foot and pony races, wrestling, swimming, and imitation of the customs and habits of our fathers. We had sham fights with mud balls and willow wands; we played lacrosse, made war upon bees, and coasted upon the ribs of animals and buffalo robes."[43]

Although imitation and role playing certainly comes naturally to children, this is not to say that it occurred independent of either adult supervision or input. Indeed, as George Pettitt observed more than fifty years ago, "that these activities were recreational is beyond question, but that they were carried on as spontaneous uncontrolled imitations, either of adults or of slightly older juveniles, is hardly supported by the facts. . . . It is clear that desired imitative activities are effectively fostered and undesired imitative activities neglected or discouraged."[44]

The second broad category of traditional play identified by Oxendine is play that involved the use of toys. Toys were both made by adults for children and by the children themselves. A wide variety of toys was made by adults for infants, including mobiles to be suspended over beds, colorful and noisy toys, feathers, and, at least in some tribes, rattles.[45] Typical toys for older children included bows and arrows, tops, noisemakers, and dolls. Very often such toys played roles in imitative activities, of course, and adults would engage in direct instruction (as in the case of archery) to help children learn how to use their toys properly.[46]

Finally, there were games played by both children and adults, generally of a "self-testing" nature. Among the more common games of this sort were tobogganing, playing string games (including "Cat's Cradle"), stilt walking, "battledoor" (also called "shuttlecock"), skin or blanket tossing, ring and pin, ball juggling, and hot ball.[47] These kinds of games involved challenging oneself, often both physically and intellectually, and so played an important educational as well as social role in traditional society.

TOWARD A PHILOSOPHY OF INDIGENOUS AMERICAN EDUCATION

One might think that it would have made more sense in this chapter for us to begin with a discussion of the philosophy of Native American education, but in fact this would have been anachronistic. Although the indigenous peoples of North America obviously engaged in extensive educational and child-rearing practice (as indeed do all human societies), at no point did they seek deliberately to articulate what might be termed an "educational philosophy." Rather, their educational practices were guided by commonly shared assumptions about the nature of knowledge, the nature and purpose of human beings, and child development and learning theory—all of which overlapped and paralleled the core beliefs discussed earlier in this chapter.[48]

This does not mean, however, that it is not possible to discuss a Native American conception of philosophy of education in a useful and meaningful way. In recent years, for instance, Gregory Cajete, who is himself a member of the Pueblo tribe and a gifted educational scholar, has attempted to do just this by linking a model of indigenous Native American educational philosophy to contemporary educational practice in our society.[49] Cajete's work in this regard has been truly groundbreaking and challenges us to critically reexamine many of our fundamental assumptions about both the means and the ends of education, teaching, and learning. Cajete argued, in essence, that:

> a primary orientation of Indigenous education is that each person is their own teacher and that learning is connected to each individual's life process. Meaning is looked for in everything, especially in the workings of the natural world. All things comprising Nature are teachers of mankind; what is required is a cultivated and practiced openness to the lessons that the world has to teach. Ritual, mythology, and the art of storytelling—combined with the cultivation of relationship to one's inner self, family, community, and natural environment—are utilized to help individuals realize their potential for learning and living a complete life. Individuals are enabled to reach completeness by learning how to trust their natural instincts, to listen, to look, to create, to reflect

and see things deeply, to understand and apply their intuitive intelligence, and to recognize and honor the teacher of spirit within themselves and the natural world. This is the educational legacy of Indigenous people.[50]

Embedded in such a description of Native American educational philosophy is an implicit and powerful critique of much contemporary educational practice in our society. Cajete made this critique, which is in fact a call for an ecological conception of educational thought and practice,[51] explicit elsewhere in his work:

The education that we experience today has been stripped of its former dimensions and soulful meaning and deep ecological understanding in favor of the methodological application of skill development and cognitive training. The honoring of soul, creativity, spontaneity, and play have given way to an almost complete monopoly of practical skill-based knowledge designed to weed out the dreamers and to ensure the perpetuation of the modern technologically oriented world. The goal of most of modern education is to define all aspects of human teaching and learning to such a precise degree and with such technical proficiency that education can be totally controlled from entrance to exit by the vested interests of the modern industrial-technocratic-political complex. This conceptual orientation has become so much the orientation of modern education that the only real opportunity for deep holistic learning is when one exits the system intentionally or by accident or through failure.[52]

The alternative, on Cajete's account, is an approach to education that must be guided by the following key assumptions about appropriate and ecological educational practice:

- The environmental, social, and cultural crises that we face today cannot and will not be solved by the same education process that helped to create them.
- Ecological sustainability implies the recovery of civic and cultural wisdom.
- Sustainability has to be a focus for the content and process of postmodern education, as well as a defining element of knowledge.
- We must teach for cultural and ecological literacy and transactional competence in working with various dimensions of the crises.
- Students must be acquainted with the deeper levels of the environmental crisis.
- We must rekindle the innate reflection of our inborn feeling of connectedness to the natural world.
- We must begin to teach for a contemporary expression of the indigenous and ecologically possible human.[53]

In a nutshell, Cajete is suggesting that "learning is always a creative act. We are continuously engaged in the art of making meaning and creating our world through the unique processes of human learning. Learning for humans is instinctual, continuous, and the most complex of our natural traits. Learning is also a key to our ability to survive in the environments that we create and that create us."[54]

CONCLUSIONS

The spiritual nature of traditional Indian educational thought and practice permeates virtually all aspects of its educational practice. This can be seen most clearly, perhaps, in the way that the child is viewed and treated, and the respect that is to be accorded to each individual.[55] Beyond this, however, is the sense of kinship with not only other members of one's own community, but with the larger human community, and, indeed, with everything around us. As Jack Forbes wrote:

> So everything is like a big family. We are children of the Great Spirit, children of Mother Earth, children of the sky, and so on. We have that relationship, that kinship that is part of our identity. That is knowing who we are. . . . We live in a world of many circles and these circles constitute our identity and they go out to encompass every thing that there is in this Universe. That is our kinship. Those are our relatives. The Universe is a family and we have to deal with other things in that Universe with that in mind.[56]

Although the context in which traditional Native American educational thought and practice emerged and prospered for centuries has undergone dramatic change in the last few centuries, there is nevertheless much to be learned and even emulated not only in educational activities and programs for Indians themselves, but for all of us, as the previous Forbes passage makes clear. Indeed, some scholars have argued that the very contemporary goal of sustainable development requires that we *re-learn* much of the indigenous educational tradition.[57] For educators, the implications of Native American educational thought and practice are in fact immense—not only in terms of curricula, evaluation, teaching methodologies, and even teacher assessment,[58] but also for the epistemological assumptions that guide our practice. For instance, Gloria Snively compellingly suggested:

> If schools are to do justice to Native students they must not represent a culture that ignores and denigrates the indigenous culture. Oral traditions must be respected and viewed by the teacher as a distinctive intellectual tradition, not simply as myths and legends. If the traditional beliefs, values, and ideas that have been taught to the children by their parents and grandparents are not im-

portant in the school curriculum, the message is obvious. Hence a textbook approach with emphasis on the scientifically accepted concepts only will not work. Textbooks make fine resources for the teacher, but no textbook can comprise a viable science program for culturally different students. The spiritual stories and heritage of the Native community should become part of the school science experience. . . . The current research suggests that the two traditions—Native oral tradition and western scientific thought—in combination provide a broader perspective on the natural environment than either by itself.[59]

In other words, as Oscar Kawagley argued, it is a serious mistake to suggest that indigenous knowledge and "scientific" knowledge are incompatible in the pedagogical setting. As he suggested,

I propose that it is possible to teach Native youth mathematics and, more particularly, the natural and physical sciences by capitalizing on the Native knowledge and skills that already exist in their culture. The natural sciences are nothing more than observation and mystical understanding of the interplay between Nature and man. The Native has perspicacious knowledge of Nature. The teacher must realize that these Native students entering school are not empty computer disks or sponges to be filled with facts and knowledge by the teacher. . . . Their culture provides a basis to progress in acquiring new knowledge, new skills, and introducing new ideas on how to increase the quality of life.[60]

Such, then, is the challenge before us as we, as educators, learn to "look to the mountain"!

QUESTIONS FOR REFLECTION AND DISCUSSION

1. Based on your reading, how do you believe that Native Americans would traditionally have defined an *educated person* in their societies? How does this view of an *educated person* differ from our contemporary view?

2. The American Indian view of the role of *elders* in both social life in general and in education in particular is arguably very different from that found in contemporary American society. What are the advantages of the Native American view of the role of the elder? What are its disadvantages?

3. Using the discussion of play activities as a component of traditional Native American education that was presented in this chapter as a guide, try to develop a similar classification system for play in contemporary American society. What differences do you find? How might these differences be explained?

4. The Indian concept of kinship, as expounded in the conclusion of this chapter, is potentially a very powerful one. What are its educational implications, both in terms of the aims of education and the content of education?

5. Reflect on the Native American concept of *disharmony*. What are the implications of this concept for society in general, and for the education of children in particular? Is the concept a pedagogically useful one in your view?

6. How might the concept of the sacred wheel be used to describe and change a classroom environment? What specific aspects of the classroom environment might be affected? What does this tell you about the nature and purposes of formal education in our society?

7. Explain the concept of an "ecology of education" in your own words, giving examples from classroom settings as well as from the perspective of the larger community. What are the implications of such an "ecology of education" for the classroom teacher? For the school principal? For the board of education member?

8. Oscar Kawagley is quoted in the chapter as arguing that "the natural sciences are nothing more than observation and mystical understanding of the interplay between Nature and man." Do you agree? Why or why not?

9. In the chapter, Gloria Snively suggested that a combination of Native oral tradition and Western scientific thought can be effectively utilized in the teaching of science. What other school subjects and disciplines might also benefit from combinations of this sort? Are there subjects that could not involve such combinations?

10. Based on your readings, how do you think that the Western conception of "nature" differs from that of indigenous peoples in North America? What are the implications of these differences?

RECOMMENDED FURTHER READINGS

There are a number of excellent works that present a Native American view on both American history and contemporary American society. Especially valuable are Ronald Wright, *Stolen Continents: The "New World" Through Indian Eyes* (Boston: Houghton Mifflin, 1992); Alvin Josephy, Jr.'s *500 Nations: An Illustrated History of North American Indians* (New York: Knopf, 1994), as well as the recent revision of his 1968 work *The Indian Heritage of America* (Boston: Houghton Mifflin, 1991); Alvin Josephy, Jr. (ed.), *America in 1492: The World of the Indian Peoples Before the Arrival of Columbus* (New York: Vintage, 1991); and Dee Brown, *Bury My Heart at Wounded Knee: An Indian History of the American West* (New York: Bantam, 1971). For a detailed and explicit discussion of Native American educational thought and practice and its significance for contemporary education, see Gregory Cajete, *Look to the*

Mountain: An Ecology of Indigenous Education (Durango, CO: Kivakí Press, 1994).

NOTES

1. There is a terminological problem with respect to the proper term for the indigenous peoples of North America. In this chapter, I have chosen to use both *Indian* and *Native American* interchangeably, as is a fairly common practice by such people themselves in the United States. In the Canadian setting, the term "First Nations" is now well-established as the appropriate term for the indigenous peoples of North America (and, indeed, of all indigenous peoples); see, e.g., Robert Regnier, "Bridging Western and First Nations Thought: Balanced Education in Whitehead's Philosophy of Organism and the Sacred Circle," *Interchange* 26, 4 (1995): 383–415; Celia Haig-Brown and Jo-Ann Archibald, "Transforming First Nations Research with Respect and Power," *International Journal of Qualitative Studies in Education* 9, 3 (1996): 245–267. It should also be noted that the term *North America* is being used here in a common, but nonetheless inaccurate, way to refer to what is today the United States and Canada. Thus, the civilizations of Mesoamerica (which were geographically in North America) are excluded from our focus here.

2. See, e.g., Margaret Szasz, *Education and the American Indian: The Road to Self-Determination, 1928–1973* (Albuquerque: University of New Mexico Press, 1974); Guy Senese, *Self-Determination and the Social Education of Native Americans* (New York: Praeger, 1991); K. Tsianina Lomawaima, *They Called It Prairie Light: The Story of Chilocco Indian School* (Lincoln: University of Nebraska Press, 1994); Ruth McDonald Boyer and Narcissus Gayton, *Apache Mothers and Daughters: Four Generations of a Family* (Norman: University of Oklahoma Press, 1992); Michael Coleman, *American Indian Children at School, 1850–1930* (Jackson: University Press of Mississippi, 1993).

3. See Joel Sherzer, "A Richness of Voices," in Alvin Josephy, Jr. (ed.), *America in 1492: The World of the Indian Peoples Before the Arrival of Columbus* (New York: Vintage, 1991), 251–275.

4. Joseph Oxendine, *American Indian Sports Heritage* (Champaign, IL: Human Kinetics Books, 1988), xiii.

5. Carol Locust, "Wounding the Spirit: Discrimination and Traditional American Indian Belief Systems," *Harvard Educational Review* 58, 3 (1988): 317.

6. Locust, "Wounding the Spirit," 317.

7. Calvin Martin, "Ethnohistory: A Better Way to Write Indian History," in Albert Hurtado and Peter Iverson (eds.), *Major Problems in American Indian History: Documents and Essays* (Lexington, MA: Heath, 1994), 23.

8. Locust, "Wounding the Spirit," 317–318.

9. There are also, of course, important implications here for health care and other service professions serving Native American communities; see, e.g., Madeleine McIvor, "Research into Traditional First Nations Healing Practices: A Beginning," *Canadian Journal of Native Education* 17, 2 (1990): 89–95.

10. Locust, "Wounding the Spirit," 318.

11. Locust, "Wounding the Spirit," 321–322.

12. Native American approaches to education are, in fact, profoundly spiritual in nature. See Gloria Snively, "Traditional Native Indian Beliefs, Cultural Values, and Science Instruction," *Canadian Journal of Native Education* 17, 1 (1990): 44–59. Also of interest here are Mary Atwood, *Spirit Healing: North American Magic and Medicine* (New York: Sterling, 1991); and Steve Wall, *Shadowcatchers: A Journey in Search of the Teachings of Native American Healers* (New York: HarperCollins, 1994).

13. See John Coulehan, "Navajo Indian Medicine: Implications for Healing," *Journal of Family Practice* 10 (1980): 55–61.

14. Locust, "Wounding the Spirit," 322.

15. Regnier, "Bridging Western and First Nations Thought," 387.

16. Regnier, "Bridging Western and First Nations Thought," 387.

17. Regnier, "Bridging Western and First Nations Thought," 387–388.

18. Quoted in Regnier, "Bridging Western and First Nations Thought," 388.

19. Locust, "Wounding the Spirit," 325.

20. Quoted in Jack Forbes, "Traditional Native American Philosophy and Multicultural Education," in *Multicultural Education and the American Indian* (Los Angeles: American Indian Studies Center, University of California, 1979), 10.

21. Jean Barman, Yvonne Hébert, and Don McCaskill, "The Challenge of Indian Education: An Overview," in Jean Barman, Yvonne Hébert, and Don McCaskill (eds.), *Indian Education in Canada, volume 2: The Challenge* (Vancouver: University of British Columbia Press, 1987), 3.

22. See Donald Miller, "Hopi Education: Before Schools and Teachers," *Tennessee Education* 18, 2 (1988), 28–32.

23. Barman, Hébert, and McCaskill, "The Challenge of Indian Education: An Overview," 3.

24. Jean Barman, Yvonne Hébert, and Don McCaskill, "The Challenge of Indian Education," 3.

25. Alvin McKay and Bert McKay, "Education as a Total Way of Life: The Nisga'a Experience," in Jean Barman, Yvonne Hébert, and Don McCaskill (eds.), *Indian Education in Canada, volume 2: The Challenge* (Vancouver: University of British Columbia Press, 1987), 64.

26. Forbes, "Traditional Native American Philosophy and Multicultural Education," 11.

27. Quoted in Beatrice Medicine, "My Elders Tell Me," in Jean Barman, Yvonne Hébert, and Don McCaskill (eds.), *Indian Education in Canada, volume 2: The Challenge* (Vancouver: University of British Columbia Press, 1987), 146.

28. For an extensive discussion of the role of relatives in traditional American Indian education, see George Pettitt, *Primitive Education in North America* (Berkeley: University of California Press, 1946), 15–24. Published as part of the University of California "Publications in American Archaeology and Ethnology" series, this monograph is invaluable despite its dated and highly ethnocentric bias (and title).

29. Medicine, "My Elders Tell Me," 142–152; see also Rik Yellow Bird, "Position Paper on Native Education," *Humanity & Society* 14, 3 (1990), 298–299; Teresa Scott

Kincheloe, "The Wisdom of the Elders: Cross-Cultural Perspectives," *Journal of Thought* 19, 3 (1984), 121–127.

30. Quoted in Medicine, "My Elders Tell Me," 147.

31. Medicine, "My Elders Tell Me," 143; see also Miller, "Hopi Education: Before Schools and Teachers," 28–32.

32. Quoted in Medicine, "My Elders Tell Me," 145–146.

33. Gary Witherspoon, *Language and Art in the Navajo Universe* (Ann Arbor: University of Michigan Press, 1977), 13.

34. Sherzer, "A Richness of Voices," 271. See also Karl Kroeber, "The Art of Traditional American Indian Narration," in Karl Kroeber (ed.), *Traditional Literatures of the American Indian: Texts and Interpretations* (Lincoln: University of Nebraska Press, 1981), 1–24.

35. Oscar Kawagley, "Yup'ik Ways of Knowing," *Canadian Journal of Native Education* 17, 2 (1990): 10.

36. Sherzer, "A Richness of Voices," 265.

37. Sherzer, "A Richness of Voices," 265.

38. Yellow Bird, "Position Paper on Native Education," 297.

39. Miller, "Hopi Education," 30–31.

40. See Steward Culin, *Games of the North American Indians* (New York: Dover, 1975).

41. Oxendine, *American Indian Sports Heritage*, 121.

42. Oxendine, *American Indian Sports Heritage*, 122.

43. Quoted in Oxendine, *American Indian Sports Heritage*, 123.

44. Pettitt, *Primitive Education in North America*, 41, 58.

45. Oxendine, *American Indian Sports Heritage*, 124. In some Native American cultures, rattles are viewed as sacred objects, and are used only in specific religious ceremonies. Thus, in these groups they would obviously be seen as inappropriate as children's toys.

46. See Pettitt, *Primitive Education in North America*, 41–44.

47. For detailed discussions of these games, see Oxendine, *American Indian Sports Heritage*, 131–137. An even more extensive examination of such games is provided in Culin, *Games of North American Indians*.

48. In fairness, I should note here that in my experience the same is in fact true of many educators today in our own society as well; very often discussions of "philosophy of education" among practitioners tend to be *post hoc* rather than actually guiding practice. This is not, of course, to say that this is the ideal. Philosophy of education, properly conceived and executed, can and should be an immensely valuable and important tool for the classroom teacher. See, e.g., Timothy Reagan, "Educating the 'Reflective Practitioner': The Contribution of Philosophy of Education," *Journal of Research and Development in Education* 26, 4 (1993): 189–196.

49. See Gregory Cajete, "The Making of an Indigenous Teacher: Insights into the Ecology of Teaching" in Jeffrey Kane (ed.), *Education, Information and Transformation: Essays on Learning and Thinking* (Upper Saddle River, NJ: Merrill, 1999), 161–183; Gregory Cajete, *Look to the Mountain: An Ecology of Indigenous Education* (Durango, CO: Kivakí, 1994).

50. Cajete, *Look to the Mountain*, 227.

51. See David Orr, *Ecological Literacy: Education and the Transition to a Postmodern World* (Albany: State University of New York Press, 1992).

52. Cajete, "The Making of an Indigenous Teacher," 175.

53. Cajete, "The Making of an Indigenous Teacher," 181.

54. Cajete, *Look to the Mountain*, 25.

55. See Forbes, "Traditional Native American Philosophy and Multicultural Education."

56. Forbes, "Traditional Native American Philosophy and Multicultural Education," 5–6.

57. See Orr, *Ecological Literacy*; Daniel Morales-Gómez, "Knowledge, Change and the Preservation of Progress," *IDRC Reports* 21, 1 (1993): 4–5; Neale MacMillan, "Indigenous Peoples Test the Waters," *IDRC Reports* 21, 1 (1993): 6–8; Deborah Carter, "Recognizing Traditional Environmental Knowledge," *IDRC Reports* 21, 1 (1993): 10–13; Paul Icamina, "Threads of Common Knowledge," *IDRC Reports* 21, 1 (1993): 14–16.

58. See Cajete, *Look to the Mountain*, 29–31 and 222–227; see also Sharon Nelson-Barber, "Considerations for the Inclusion of Multiple Cultural Competencies in Teacher Assessment: A Yup'ik Eskimo Case," *Canadian Journal of Native Education* 17, 2 (1990): 33–42.

59. Snively, "Traditional Native Indian Beliefs, Cultural Values, and Science Instruction," 56.

60. Kawagley, "Yup'ik Ways of Knowing," 13–14.

6

Developing the Chün-tzu: Confucius and the Chinese Educational Heritage

The importance of China is not confined to the number of its inhabitants and to the power, still largely untapped, of this nation of nearly a thousand million people. It is of a more general nature and proceeds quite as much from the past as from the present: Chinese civilization was the guiding spirit of a very large section of humanity, giving it its writing, its technology, its conception of man and of the world, its religions and its political institutions. . . . The West, which has borrowed from China right down to our day without realizing it, is far from recognizing its sizable debt to her, but for which we ourselves would not be what we are.
—Gernet (1982, pp. 1, 3)

Elements of Chinese civilization can be traced back at least as far as 6,000 years, and perhaps considerably further.[1] By the time of the Shang dynasty (roughly 1700 B.C.E. to 1100 B.C.E.; see Fig. 6.1), schools and other social institutions of a complex culture had developed, as had the foundations for the examination system that would serve throughout the history of imperial China to select government officials.[2] Although Chinese civilization evolved, developed, and changed throughout its history, it nevertheless retained a core set of features that characterize it as a single cultural tradition. Although much of the Chinese cultural heritage has been rejected in contemporary China, much remains as well. In other words, much of the culture of China that still thrives has a direct link to the civilization that emerged nearly as long ago as those of ancient Egypt and Mesopotamia.[3] The difference, of course, is that although the civilizations of Egypt and Mesopotamia may be fascinating for us to study, the ties that bind modern people to them are, at best, very distant indeed, whereas the ties that bind modern Chinese people to their past

Chinese Dynasties

Hsia Dynasty	21st to 16th centuries B.C.E.
Shang Dynasty	16th to 11th centuries B.C.E.
Western Chou Dynasty	11th century to 771 B.C.E.
Spring and Autumn Period	770 to 476 B.C.E.
Warring States Period	475 to 221 B.C.E.

First Unification
Ch'in Dynasty	221 to 207 B.C.E.
Western Han Dynasty	206 B.C.E. to 24 C.E.
Eastern Han Dynasty	25 C.E. to 220 C.E.

First Partition
Three Kingdoms Period	220 C.E. to 265 C.E.
Shu Dynasty	
Wei Dynasty	
Wu Dynasty	

Second Unification
Western Chin Dynasty	265 C.E. to 316 C.E.
Eastern Chin Dynasty	317 C.E. to 420 C.E.
Sung Dynasty	420 C.E. to 479 C.E.

Second Partition
Northern and Southern Dynasties	479 C.E. to 581 C.E.
Ch'i Dynasty	
Liang Dynasty	
Ch'en Dynasty	
Northern Wei Dynasty	
Western Wei Dynasty	
Eastern Wei Dynasty	
Northern Ch'i Dynasty	
Northern Chou Dynasty	

Third Unification
Sui Dynasty	581 C.E. to 618 C.E.
T'ang Dynasty	618 C.E. to 907 C.E.

Third Partition
Five Dynasties Period	907 C.E. to 960 C.E.
Later Liang Dynasty	
Later T'ang Dynasty	
Latin Chin Dynasty	
Later Han Dynasty	
Later Chou Dynasty	

Fourth Unification
Northern Sung Dynasty	960 C.E. to 1127 C.E.
Southern Sung Dynasty	127 C.E. to 1279 C.E.
Liao Dynasty	916 C.E. to 1125 C.E.
Chin Dynasty	1115 C.E. to 1234 C.E.
Yuan Dynasty	1271 C.E. to 1368 C.E.
Ming Dynasty	1368 C.E. to 1644 C.E.
Ch'ing Dynasty	1644 C.E. to 1911 C.E.
Establishment of the Republic	1912 C.E.

FIG. 6.1.   Chinese Dynasties.

remain powerful. Furthermore, as Michael Loewe wrote in his book *The Pride That Was China*, the impact of traditional Chinese civilization went far beyond the borders of China itself: "China's achievements have been unique. Just as the glory that was Greece and the grandeur that was Rome have left their indelible mark on Europe, so have the features of China's traditional way of life nurtured the cultural growth of East Asia; for it was largely the ideas, beliefs and ideals of China that shaped the humanities of the east, with their counterparts to the spirit and grace of Greece and the dignity and organization of Rome."[4]

If traditional Chinese culture had such a significant impact on the historical development of Asia, it was able to do so in large part because of the values and institutions that underlie its educational system. This system had to address problems related to the size of the country (China has been, and remains, one of the largest countries in the world), its geographical diversity, the ethnic and linguistic diversity of its population,[5] and the tensions in an overwhelmingly agrarian society with large urban centers competing for resources. The traditional Chinese educational system was able to meet these challenges remarkably effectively for millennia. The endurance of Chinese civilization, as well as its intellectual, cultural, and artistic contributions to world civilization, in short, make it well worth an examination of the educational thought and practice that played a key role in its maintenance, transmission, and development.

The study of the history of Chinese educational thought and practice is in many ways somewhat easier to understand than that of many other non-Western societies. Not only are many facets of traditional Chinese education still maintained in Chinese communities around the world, but even more, there is a wealth of material related to the history of the Chinese educational tradition available. As Will Durant noted in *The Story of Civilization*, "China has been called 'the paradise of historians.' For centuries and millenniums, it has had official historiographers who recorded everything that happened, and much besides. We cannot trust them further back than 776 B.C.; but if we lend them a ready ear they will explain in detail the history of China from 3000 B.C."[6]

This abundance of sources means that the challenge in discussing traditional Chinese educational thought and practice is not one of trying to reconstruct the past from limited information, but rather trying to sort through an incredibly complex and monumental historical record to identify the key issues that we need to address. In this chapter, we begin with a discussion of traditional Chinese educational thought, focusing on the special role of Confucian thought in that tradition. We then turn to the ways in which Confucian thought was manifested in practice in educational institutions and, even more, in the imperial examination system.

THE ROLE OF CONFUCIAN THOUGHT
IN TRADITIONAL CHINESE EDUCATION

It would be impossible to discuss traditional Chinese educational thought without repeated reference to Confucian thought; indeed, to a considerable extent one could argue that traditional Chinese educational thought in large part *is* Confucian educational thought.[7] Tu Wei-Ming argued that "Confucianism is still an integral part of the 'psycho-cultural construct' of the contemporary Chinese intellectual as well as the Chinese peasant; it remains a defining characteristic of the Chinese mentality,"[8] and, in a similar vein, Cheng Tien-Hsi commented that "the whole Chinese social system, or rather what may be called Chinese civilization and culture . . . is saturated with the teachings of Confucius and those of Mencius, the sage next to him and the most brilliant exponent of his doctrines."[9] As Cheng Tien-Hsi implied, however, it is important that we distinguish between the body of teaching that can be reliably ascribed to Confucius himself, and the far broader body of theories and doctrines that developed after his death and are today identified as *Confucian*.[10]

Confucius (whose real name was K'ung Ch'iu) was, according to tradition, born in the town of Ch'ü-fu, in the state of Lu, in the year 551 B.C.E., and died in the year 479 B.C.E.[11] Of relatively humble background, Confucius seems to have been largely self-educated, as well as both ambitious and relatively successful in his own time.[12] Living in a time of considerable social, political, and economic unrest and uncertainty, Confucius advocated a conception of the *good man (chün-tzu)*[13] that emphasized the twin qualities of benevolence (*ren*) and propriety (*li*). There is, in Confucian texts, an emphasis on the writings of Chinese antiquity, and his philosophy is often identified as a conservative one seeking a return to a more moral and just past.[14] This is especially interesting because, as Jacques Gernet observed about Confucius' work, "a body of teaching which aimed primarily at being faithful to tradition in fact threw up ideas that were new."[15]

The core of Confucian thought is found in a short text produced by Confucius' disciples after his death, called the *Lun-yü* or, more commonly in English, the *Analects*.[16] One interesting aspect of the *Analects* is the extent to which it continues to be generally accepted as authentic: Although some parts of the *Analects* are almost certainly not genuinely original, there is a widespread agreement among scholars about the overall authenticity of the work.[17] It would be difficult to underestimate the significance of the *Analects* in the history of Chinese thought. As Patricia Ebrey wrote:

> Confucius' ideas are known to us primarily through the sayings recorded by his disciples in the *Analects*. This book does not provide carefully organized or argued philosophical discourses, and the sayings seem to have been haphazardly arranged. Yet this short text became a sacred book, memorized by beginning

students and known to all educated people. As such it influenced the values and habits of thought of Chinese for centuries. Many of its passages became proverbial sayings, unknowingly cited by illiterate peasants.[18]

The closest analogy that one could draw to the role of the *Analects* in the Western tradition would probably be the role of the Bible. For us, regardless of our personal religious beliefs, the Bible provides a virtually limitless source of proverbs, folk wisdom, and references to people and events that color our language and fill our speech, as well as offering a framework within which much of our everyday experience is, both knowingly and unknowingly, organized. It would be inconceivable to be an educated member of Western civilization and not recognize reference to the burning bush, to Noah and the ark, to Lot's wife, or to the miracle of the loaves and fishes. The *Analects*, in short, have played a comparable role in traditional Chinese culture.

The notion of *li*, mentioned earlier, is a very important one in understanding Confucian thought.[19] Originally, the term referred merely to proper conduct in general, and in religious and ritualistic settings in particular, but for Confucius it came to encompass far more than simply ceremonial correctness. Although ritual and its proper performance was an important aspect of Confucian thought,[20] *li* entailed both a knowledge of traditional practice and behavior, and a sensitivity that would allow their modification as required by contemporary circumstances.[21] In short, "*Li* was in fact a kind of balance wheel of conduct, tending to prevent either deficiency or excess, guiding toward the middle path of socially beneficial conduct. Confucius stated it thus: 'Courtesy, if not regulated by *li*, becomes labored effort; caution, if not regulated by *li*, becomes mere timidity; courage, if not regulated by *li*, becomes mere unruliness; frankness, if not regulated by *li*, becomes mere effrontery.' "[22]

It is important to keep in mind, however, that *li* is not just a Chinese version of the ancient Greek dictum, "Moderation in all things." Moderation, to be sure, is an important part of *li*, but the concept goes well beyond this. The goal of *li* is both a social and individual one, grounded in the proper expression of social and cultural tradition. Education is the means by which the individual learns what *li* will require in a particular situation; *li* is not so much character as the means by which character is manifested.

If *li* is the way in which character is manifested, then the cultivation of character itself—defined in terms of virtues—is a significant component of education.[23] For Confucius, the *chün-tzu* will seek to develop what are called the "Five Constant Virtues": right attitude, right procedure, right knowledge, right moral courage, and right persistence.[24] Taken together, the practice of these virtues would lead to a new society based on justice and wisdom.[25] The nature of the *chün-tzu*, as described in the *Analects*, included the following characteristics:

The Master said, (the good man) does not grieve that other people do not recognize his merits. His only anxiety is lest he should fail to recognize theirs. (Book I: 16)

The Master said, In the presence of a good man, think all the time how you may learn to equal him. In the presence of a bad man, turn your gaze within! (Book IV: 17)

The Master said, A gentleman is ashamed to let his words outrun his deeds. (Book XIV: 29)

Furthermore, Confucian moral thought is grounded in the concept of the five basic human relationships: ruler and subject, father and son, husband and wife, older brother and younger brother, and between friends.[26] Each of these relationships is hierarchical, with each individual tied and obligated to the other in keeping with his or her station. Thus, children are bound to their parents by filial piety, wives to husbands, subjects to rulers, and so on. However, it is important to understand that each of these relationships, as envisaged by Confucius, was to be one of mutual responsibility. As Ron-Guey Chu explained, "Filiality originates from one's sense of obligation or gratitude. It is a natural response to the parents' love and care for one—a consequence of their initial parental solicitude. Indeed, this kind of reciprocity underlies all human relationships."[27]

This reciprocity, although very much affecting both parties in the relationship, was nonetheless in no way intended to be one of equality. Wang Gungwu, for instance, commented: "In talking about reciprocity and reciprocal rights, I am talking about unequal reciprocity in a hierarchical structure. In short, duties and implicit rights were between unequals not between equals, and therefore the shares of both duties and rights were also necessarily unequal and this was implicit in the very concept of reciprocity."[28]

The analogy drawn by Confucius of the family to the state was built on precisely this same notion of the reciprocity of the ruled and the ruler. In essence, "Confucianism thus built a new moral interpretation of the world upon the oldest and soundest foundation, the family system. It could be fitted to the political system, thus ensuring that monarchy, as an apotheosis of paternalism, would be the only conceivable form of government. The government must, however, be restrained and guided by ethical teaching and exercised in conformity with high moral principles."[29]

In summary, Confucian theory, especially as it was articulated and expanded by latter Chinese philosophers (most notably Mencius[30] and Chu Hsi[31]), provided what was taken by its proponents to be a powerful and compelling justification for a highly stratified social order that proved to be remarkably conservative and resistant to change. Confucius himself often distinguished between the *chün-tzu* (here best translated as *gentleman*) and the common people, always to the detriment of the latter, and there can be little doubt that Confucian thought did indeed have a profoundly conservative effect on Chinese society—precisely, of course, as Confucius would have wished.

And yet, there is another side to Confucian theory and practice as it relates to the role of education in the social order. Education was the key to Confucius' view of how the ideal social order could be achieved, and he was far from naive about the intellectual and moral qualities of many of those born into positions of power and influence. In essence, Confucius believed that "a good education would change men for the better, and that this should be available to those capable of benefitting from it. His remark that 'by nature men are nearly alike; but through experience they grow wide apart' supported the efficacy of schooling, and he was famed for his meritocratic outlook."[32]

Among Confucius' own pupils were individuals from virtually all social and class backgrounds, and he emphasized that wealth and honor were just "fleeting clouds."[33] Education should identify those of talent, and help them to become men fit to rule over others.[34] In other words, education for Confucius served a very pragmatic purpose—the creation of individuals who would be able to ensure better government. Indeed, Confucian philosophy in general has often been described by Western scholars as "this-worldly," in contrast to the "other-worldly" focus of much Western philosophical thought.[35] However, at the same time, the purpose of education:

> was by no means narrowly practical. Although the end of education was to bring about good government, this did not mean that the end product of education should be an efficient administrator and nothing more. Far from it, he should, in fact, be as nearly as possible the ideal man, from every point of view. He definitely should not be a mere specialist in some particular technique. . . . Confucius' object was not successful careers but good government, and this he believed to be possible only when government was administered by men who, in addition to being educated in the ordinary sense, were also endowed with integrity and poise.[36]

This brings us to one of the more criticized aspects of Confucian educational thought, which is its negative view of manual labor in general, and of agricultural pursuits in particular. Confucius himself once rebuked a student who had asked him about growing crops as a "little-minded man."[37] Thus, although education for Confucius had a practical focus, there were limits on how this practicality was to be manifested.

Although it is true that, to a considerable extent, the Confucian system in practice "reinforced the rigidly hierarchical social class structure" of imperial China,[38] it nevertheless did permit limited social class mobility based on talent, and was not incompatible with certain characteristics of a democratic social order. As H. G. Creel argued, Confucius appears to have believed, among other things, the following:

- The proper aim of government is the welfare and happiness of the whole people.
- This aim can be achieved only when the state is administered by those most capable of government.
- Capacity to govern has no necessary connection with birth, wealth, or position; it depends solely on character and knowledge.
- Character and education are produced by proper education.
- In order that the best talents may become available, education should be widely diffused.
- It follows that the government should be administered by those persons, chosen from the whole population, who prove themselves to have profited most by the proper kind of education.[39]

Such a perspective is not only reminiscent of the view of the role of education in Plato's *Republic*, but is also very close to the view of education found in Thomas Jefferson's "Bill for the More General Diffusion of Knowledge,"[40] which proposed a system of tax-supported public education for the state of Virginia long before such schooling was in fact achieved.

Finally, it should be noted that although Confucianism has indeed played a central role in the development and evolution of Chinese culture, it has not been alone in providing a conceptual and philosophical context for Chinese educational thought and practice. Challenges to Confucianism, especially those of the "Legalists" in the years preceding the rise of the Han dynasty,[41] as well as the impact of Taoism, most clearly identified with Lao-tzu's *Tao Te Ching*,[42] also impacted Chinese educational thought in important ways. Nor, as suggested earlier, was Confucian thought static; rather, it evolved and changed over time, and the articulation of Confucian thought that we know today undoubtedly has at least as much to do with the later formulations of Mencius and Chu Hsi as with Confucius himself.[43] With this in mind, we turn now to a discussion of traditional Chinese educational practice.

TRADITIONAL CHINESE EDUCATIONAL PRACTICE

Traditional Chinese educational practice, as well as traditional views about the proper upbringing of children, focused on social adaptation and a deep-seated sense of politeness. As Jacques Gernet explained:

Children were brought up to be affable, gentle and obedient. They were taught to prize self-restraint above everything else, and had to learn to be content with their lot and to live on good terms with relations, friends and strangers. The rules of politeness, widespread even among the lower classes, had no other aims but these. . . . Thus the rules of the art of living taught to children awakened in them a feeling of respect for elders and betters. They were taught not to answer back when their parents spoke to them, not to sit down if a superior—father, mother, a friend of the parents or someone senior to themselves—remained standing.[44]

Although this may sound strict and repressive to some readers, in fact it would appear that early childhood in imperial China "was one of the happiest times of life"[45]—a time during which children had a great deal of personal freedom, and were far more likely to be spoiled than beaten or punished.[46] This relatively carefree existence ended as the child reached age seven, when formal schooling and expectations of other responsibilities began in earnest.

Schooling in imperial China reflected social class background to a very great extent. Although private schools existed for the children of merchants and artisans, as did private tutors, the focus of most schooling in China was on the preparation of the sons of the elite for the imperial civil service examinations.[47] It was this latter type of school that was actively supported by the government, largely out of self-interest, because it was from the ranks of successful examinees that government officials would come. Thus, it is not surprising to find that during the early years of the Ming dynasty, as China was recovering from a century of Mongol rule and civil strife, the government invested heavily in schooling: "To provide for the nation's needs, radical steps were taken to improve the means of training; no less than 1,200 local schools were established in the prefectures and counties, at the expense of the central government and with officially appointed teachers."[48]

Raymond Dawson argued in *The Chinese Experience* that "throughout imperial Chinese history emperors were regarded as the grand patrons of education, frequently paying formal visits to the national university, issuing edicts for the establishment of schools, and paying honour to Confucius as the 'first teacher.'"[49] Nonetheless, it is important not to overemphasize the role of the government in supporting education; elementary schooling remained primarily the province and responsibility of parents,[50] which inevitably meant that such institutions were generally neighborhood-based and somewhat informal in terms of their status. As the Reverend Justus Doolittle described the system in 1865, "There is no village tax nor any aid from government received for the support of schools. Each parent must pay the teacher for the instruction of his children."[51]

Furthermore, although the emperors were indeed presented in many Chinese historical records as patrons of educational institutions, the reality is somewhat more complex. Yuan Zheng explained:

There is a wealth of historical data about Chinese education, but some of them are misleading. Almost all official historiographers in imperial China were Confucianists. To enhance the emperor's reputation and encourage rulers to devote attention to education, they would try hard to find activities of the emperor that could be described as support for education. They exaggerated the significance of these activities in the official history, hiding the fact that the emperor was indifferent to education.[52]

Rather, Yuan Zheng argued, the real test of commitment to education is to be found in financial support, and using this criteria, the support for education in imperial China would seem to have been more rhetorical than real much of the time.[53] In short, schooling in imperial China was available to those most able to pay for it, and the quality of basic education was to a significant degree reflected in one's social class background, and to one's geographic location as well, because "the closer government schools were to high-level authorities, the better their economic condition was."[54]

Preparation for the civil service examinations actually began well before the birth of a boy. Detailed advice was given to pregnant women to help them ensure the birth of a gifted son; the advice included sitting erect, avoiding strange food, and having poetry and classical literature read to her.[55]

The more formal education of the child began a bit later, around age three, when the boy began learning to read his first characters.[56] Because of the complexity of written Chinese, the acquisition of literacy played an important and time-consuming role in the educational process. From the time he was able to hold a brush, the boy would copy characters from various books intended for use with children, among which were the *Three Character Classic* and the *Thousand Character Essay*. The former "is the world's longest surviving and best selling textbook and is still in print in China."[57] These books served two distinct kinds of educational purposes: First, they provided the child with the basic lexicon he would need to become literate, and second, they provided extensive moral education in keeping with the Confucian ethic.

Schooling as such began for the boy around age seven or eight, after he had mastered the basic elements of literacy. Working with a tutor or teacher in a small group, he began an educational process that relied extensively on the memorization of the Four Books (which included both the *Analects* and the *Mencius*, as well as two shorter works, the *Great Learning* and the *Just Mean*) and the Five Classics (which included the *Book of Changes, Book of Records, Book of Odes, Book of Rites*, and the *Spring and Autumn Record*).[58]

By the time he was twelve, a boy would have memorized texts consisting of more than 400,000 characters[59]—and these texts were the same ones learned by every student preparing for the civil service examinations, assuring a broad and deep common intellectual base for each generation of Chinese officials. Once he had mastered the basic texts, the student would progress to the commentaries written about the texts, and finally, to learning the proper form for writing essays for the civil service examinations. This latter point is an important one; essay themes were set in the examinations, and examinees were required to produce what was called the "eight-legged essay"—a highly formal and rule-governed kind of writing that has been criticized for stressing technique over creativity. As Dawson commented, "This type of essay . . . required technical expertise rather than intellectual distinction for its composition, so it has been a byword in modern times for the sterility and formalism of the classical tradition."[60]

Institutions of higher education provided additional schooling for small numbers of students in imperial China. Among the institutions of higher education were the National University, the Military Academy, the Imperial Academy, and a School of Medicine.[61] These state establishments were financially supported by revenues from lands that they owned (with which they had been endowed), and were impressive complexes:

> These great colleges were surrounded by vast grounds, and consisted of numerous buildings and single pavilions used for libraries, classrooms or temples for religious ceremonies. In the National University, which recruited the largest number of students . . . there were twenty classrooms, a staff of fifteen, and nearly 2,000 students who lived in. The number of students, coming from all over China, had been fixed at 300 in the middle of the twelfth century; it was later increased to 1,000 and had reached 1,716 by 1270.[62]

Students were recruited for these institutions through competitive examinations, and their principle *raison d'être* was to prepare students for the imperial examinations.

While some boys and young men were engaged in this intensive educational undertaking, their sisters were educationally (and in a variety of other ways) less fortunate in traditional Chinese society. As John Cleverley wrote, "The world for many women was one of segregation and seclusion, often crippled by bound feet, and subject to child marriages arranged by parents."[63] Although there are a number of well-educated and politically powerful women in the long history of China, such women were clearly the exception rather than the rule.[64] For the most part, the role of the woman in traditional China was limited to the duties and obligations of being a wife and a mother, and her education was oriented toward these goals.

We turn now to an exploration of the nature and purposes of the imperial civil service examination, the focal point of traditional Chinese education and the feature of that education for which it is best known today.

THE IMPERIAL EXAMINATION SYSTEM

Written examinations to aid in the selection of government officials were used as early as the Han period (206 B.C.E. through 220 C.E.),[65] although it was only during the T'ang dynasty (618 C.E. to 907 C.E.) that they came to play a key role in the selection of such officials.[66] The purpose of the examination system was to ensure the quality of the civil service by making it more meritocratic, as well as to provide civil servants (as well as all educated people) with a common body of knowledge and experience on which they could draw.[67] Initially, the system coexisted with one of aristocratic privilege, in which recruitment to the civil service was based largely on heredity and recommendation. Under the usurper Empress Wu, however, this changed as the examination system was utilized as a political tool to challenge the power of the aristocracy, and by the 8th century the system operated as a highly effective, meritocratic means of providing a reasonably fair and objective means by which officials could be chosen.[68] As John Cleverley argued:

> The imperial civil service examination made it possible for a man from humble origin to move into a position of political power, and it also enabled districts to gain national prominence through their native sons. Because it served the cause of social mobility, it had an integrating and stabilising effect on Chinese life generally. Further, the infusion of new blood, which the examining process permitted, reduced the political power of the hereditary aristocracy and clans, and strengthened the throne.[69]

Although the examination system was not static over the long course of its existence, of course, it is nevertheless possible to present a general overview of how it operated, especially under the Ming and Ch'ing periods of Chinese history. Basically, the examination system consisted of tests at three distinct levels: the district examinations, the provincial examinations, and the metropolitan examinations.[70] The examinations were of increasing difficulty, and each required the candidate to have passed the preceding level (see Fig. 6.2). The first examination level, which was conducted in local cities by provincial education officials, granted successful examinees the title *hsiu-ts'ai* ("Flow-

---

Stage I: Preliminary Examinations

    District-level (*hsien-k'ao*)
    Prefecture-level (*fu-k'ao*)
    Examination for the *sheng-yüng* degree

Stage II: Provincial Examinations

    Examination for the *chü-jen* degree

Stage III: Metropolitan Examinations

    Major examination (known as *hui-shih*) for the *chin-shih* degree
    Palace examination (*tien-shih*)

FIG. 6.2.   An overview of the Chinese Imperial Examination System.

Lines of Cells

Inside of the Cells

FIG. 6.3.   The Chinese Imperial Examination System: Examination cells.

ering Talent"). Passing this first examination allowed one to wear special, distinctive clothing, as well as granting one's family a tax exemption, but more important, it allowed one to progress to the next level of the examination system.[71]

The second level of the examination system consisted of a test given every three years in the various provincial capitals of the empire. The examination took place in a special complex, consisting of individual cells in which the candidates spent nine days writing their answers to the set questions.[72] The cells, which contained only three boards to function as a shelf, desk, and chair, were too small to allow the individual to comfortably sleep at night (see Fig. 6.3). Successful candidates, who were generally a tiny fraction of those taking the examination, gained the title *chü-jen* ("Recommended Man"), and were now eligible for lower level government appointments.

Next, metropolitan examinations were held in order to identify those scholars who would be suitable for higher posts in the government. Only one of twenty or thirty candidates at this level could hope to become a *chin-shih* ("Presented Scholar").[73] Finally (also at the metropolitan level), the pinnacle of the examination system, the palace examination, was, in theory if not in practice, presided over by the Emperor himself. At this final level, candidates did not fail, but rather were ranked in order of merit.[74] Success at this level, although not ensuring career advancement, was nonetheless a necessary condition for it. As Dawson explained, "Success in this rigorous competition did not, however, bring automatic appointment. It merely made one a member of a social and intellectual elite from among whom appointments were made. The top palace graduates would . . . expect high office after a period in the imperial secretariat; but there were not enough jobs to go round for those who were qualified."[75]

The examinations were open to most men in Chinese society; those excluded were members of certain occupations and, hardly surprising given the patriarchal nature of traditional Chinese society, women. Furthermore, there was no restriction on the number of times an individual might try to pass, so some men spent their entire lives attempting to pass the difficult examinations. Although the rewards for success in the examination system were great, so too were the challenges and expenses, and in practice few individuals from poor backgrounds could hope to succeed.[76]

If originally a creative and thoughtful solution to the complex and difficult challenge of providing the empire with the best possible civil servants and officials, over the course of the centuries the imperial examination system gradually declined as it "failed to preserve the freshness and ingenuity of earlier days."[77] To some extent, such an outcome was understandable. As Jacques Gernet explained, "As the sole means of access to political honours and responsibilities, the examinations served to inculcate in those who sat for them the virtues of devotion and submission indispensable to the autocratic empire. At the same time they also drained the energies of generations of the literati."[78]

Furthermore, the system was increasingly plagued by problems with cheating,[79] as well as by the narrowness of view encouraged by both the content of the examination (which excluded virtually all knowledge not related to the Classics) and its form (especially the "eight-legged essay" discussed earlier).[80] In any event, by the end of the 19th century, the examination system had come into widespread disrepute, and its abolition in 1905 came as a surprise to few.

SCIENCE, TECHNOLOGY, AND DISCOVERY
IN THE CHINESE TRADITION

Given our discussion thus far, one might be led to believe that the intellectual heritage of China had been focused exclusively on literary pursuits. Although not an uncommon assumption, this view is in fact demonstrably erroneous. In fact, the scientific and technological heritage of Chinese civilization is immense, and is, in its own way, every bit as impressive and significant as

China's contributions in other areas.[81] Although modern science as we generally understand it essentially emerged in the Western European context during the Renaissance and the "scientific revolution," scientific studies, discoveries, and applications date back to the dawn of human history, and do so in virtually all human civilizations.[82] When compared with the scientific discoveries of the ancient Greeks, for instance, those of China often took place earlier and were more elaborately articulated and practically applied. In studying the history of science in the West, we are often guilty of dealing with scientific "discoveries" in much the same way that we have dealt with the "discovery" of the Americas by Christopher Columbus—which is to say, ignoring the fact that the "discovery" was such only to Europeans. For example, "the triangle called by the name of Blaise Pascal was already old in China in 1300 [C.E.]. . . . The system of linked and pivoted rings which we know as the Cardan suspension, after Jerome Cardan, really ought to be called Ting Huan's suspension because it had been used in China a whole thousand years before the time of Cardan. . . . Contrary to the usual ideas, mechanical clockwork began, not in early Renaissance Europe, but in T'ang China."[83]

This tendency remained true throughout the medieval period and into the modern period; it is only in the last few centuries, in fact, that Western science has come to significantly outpace (and, indeed, to dominate and even replace) that of traditional Chinese science. The truly fascinating aspect of China's contributions in the scientific arena, then, in the words of one of the great historians of Chinese science, is that of how "the Chinese civilisation had been much more effective than the European in finding out about Nature and using natural knowledge for the benefit of mankind for fourteen centuries or so before the scientific revolution."[84] Nor was this Chinese intellectual and scientific heritage undervalued in China itself:

> Beijing was not only the world's greatest city [in the 15th century] but its intellectual capital, with encyclopedias and libraries covering every subject known to man. In December 1404, [the Emperor] Zhu Di had appointed two longtime advisors . . . assisted by 2,180 scholars, to take charge of a project, the Yong-le-Dadian, to preserve all known literature and knowledge. It was the largest scholarly enterprise ever undertaken. The result, a massive encyclopedia of four thousand volumes containing some fifty million characters, was completed just before the Forbidden City was inaugurated [in 1421 C.E.].[85]

Without a doubt, the most thorough and comprehensive study of traditional scientific thought and practice in China, in any language, is the landmark multivolumed work of the British scholar Joseph Needham and his collaborators, *Science and Civilisation in China*.[86] Although it would be neither possible nor desirable to fully document the wide range of traditional Chinese scientific, mathematical, and technical discoveries and contributions here,

Fig. 6.4 provides at least something of an idea of the variety and significance of such discoveries and contributions.[87]

Further, although China tended to be relatively inward-looking for much of its history, there were also periods of active exploration and discovery. In *1421: The Year China Discovered the World*, Gavin Menzies offered a powerful argument for the contention that in the early 15th century, the Chinese undertook a massive exploration program, significantly ahead of the Europeans and their "age of discovery."[88] Menzies argued:

> On the 8th of March, 1421, the largest fleet the world had ever seen sailed from its base in China. The ships, huge junks nearly five hundred feet long and built from the finest teak, were under the command of Emperor Zhu Di's loyal eunich admirals. Their mission was "to proceed all the way to the end of the earth to collect tribute from the barbarians beyond the seas" and unite the whole world in Confucian harmony. The journey would last over two years and circle the globe. . . . When they returned Zhu Di lost control and China was beginning its long, self-imposed isolation from the world it had so recently embraced. The great ships rotted at their moorings and the records of their journeys were destroyed. Lost was the knowledge that Chinese ships had reached America seventy years before Columbus and circumnavigated the globe a century before Magellan. They had also discovered Antarctica, reached Australia three hundred and fifty years before Cook and solved the problem of longitude three hundred years before the Europeans.[89]

Not only did the Chinese fleet explore, according to Menzies, but it also left colonies of settlers and, even more important, plants and animals in a variety of settings around the world.[90] The argument is a careful and well-documented one, but it is also one that, if generally accepted, will certainly require a significant rethinking of world history.

CONCLUSIONS

Traditional Chinese educational thought and practice both reflected and helped to reproduce traditional Chinese society, as do all educational systems to some extent, and this was both its strength and weakness. Because traditional Chinese society was highly patriarchal and involved the oppression of girls and women in a number of ways, educational thought tended to pay little attention to the education of girls, and this meant that in practice girls were likely to receive little education beyond those things deemed necessary for wives and mothers to know. The social class organization of Chinese society was both hierarchical and fairly rigid, and again, both educational thought and practice reflected the social class structure of the society. If imperial Chi-

Agriculture
Row cultivation
Intensive hoeing
Iron plow
Efficient horse harnesses
Rotary winnowing fan
Multi-tube seed drill

Astronomy and Cartography
Recognition of sunspots as solar phenomena
Quantitative cartography
Discovery of solar wind
Mercator map-projection
Equatorial astronomical instruments

Engineering
Cast iron
Double-action piston bellows
Crank handle
"Cardan Suspension"
Manufacture of steel
Deep-drilling for natural gas
Belt-drive
Water power
Chain pump
Suspension of bridge
Essentials of steam engine
"Siemens" steel process
Segmental arch bridge
Chain-drive
Underwater salvage operations

Domestic and Industrial Technology
Lacquer (the first plastic)
Strong beer
Use of petroleum and natural gas as fuel
Paper
Wheelbarrow
Sliding calipers
Fishing reel
Stirrup
Porcelain
Biological pest control
Umbrella
Matches
Chess
Brandy
Whiskey
Mechanical clock
Printing
Playing cards
Paper money
Spinning wheel

FIG. 6.4.   *(Continued)*

Medicine
Circulation of blood
Circadian rhythms in the human body
Endocrinology
Deficiency diseases
Diabetes
Use of thyroid hormone
Immunology

Mathematics
Decimal system
Zero
Negative numbers
Extraction of higher roots and solutions of higher numerical equations
Decimal fractions
Use of algebra in geometry
Refine value of pi
"Pascal's" triangle

Magnetism
First compasses
Magnetic declination of the Earth's magnetic field
Magnetic remanence and induction

Military Inventions
Chemical warfare
Poison gas
Smoke bombs
Tear gas
Crossbow
Gunpowder
Flame-thrower
Grenades
Land mines
Sea mines
Rocket
Mortar
Guns
Repeating guns

Physical Sciences
Geobotanical prospecting
First Law of Motion
Hexagonal structure of snowflakes
Seismograph
Geology
Phosphorescent paint

FIG. 6.4. *(Continued)*

Transportation
  Kite
  Manned flight (using fites)
  Relief maps
  Contour transport canal
  Parachute
  Hot-air balloon
  Rudder
  Masts and sailing
  Watertight compartments in ships
  Helicopter rotor
  Propeller
  Paddle-wheel boat
  Canal pound-lock

FIG. 6.4.   Selected Chinese scientific and mathematical discoveries and inventions.

nese society as a whole invested huge resources in education—and it did so throughout its history—then these resources were far from equitably distributed. For some, educational endeavors would dominate their lives, whereas for the vast majority of the population, illiteracy was the norm.

At the same time, the system did in fact work well for most of its history to produce what was, in essence, an aristocracy of intellect. The system, although by no means truly meritocratic, did have features of meritocracy, and there were noteworthy instances of social class mobility based on intellectual skill and talent. China was well ahead of its time in terms of the development of a professional civil service based on talent rather than on birth. Finally, if traditional educational thought and practice in China was, as Gerald Gutek noted somewhat critically, "used for highly conservative maintenance purposes [and] not intended to promote social change,"[91] this was precisely what it was designed to do. The idea that the schools can, and should, contribute to social change flies in the face of Confucian teaching about the nature and purposes of the "good society." The point of traditional Chinese educational thought and practice was to ensure stability, and it did so effectively for most of its history.

QUESTIONS FOR REFLECTION AND DISCUSSION

1. An important theme in American education, since the time of the Common School Movement, has been on the role of the school in promoting social change. Traditional Chinese education, as we have seen, placed its emphasis instead on social stability. To what extent is contemporary schooling in

our society concerned with social maintenance, and to what extent is it concerned with promoting social change? How are each of these concerns manifested in practice?

2. The imperial civil service examination system ensured that all educated people in China would share a common educational background, based on knowing the same body of literature and having the same types of skills. What are the advantages of such a common educational background? What are the disadvantages?

3. How are national standards of the sorts that have been, and continue to be, developed in the United States similar to the Chinese notion of a common core of knowledge for all educated people? How do national standards in the U.S. context differ from the traditional Chinese model?

4. "Imperial China addressed the challenges posed by the presence of ethnic and linguistic diversity in a way that seems to share characteristics with both assimilationism and cultural pluralism." Respond to this claim, paying special attention to the role of social class and education.

5. The "eight-legged" essay consisted of a set format for responding to an examination question, and has been widely criticized for promoting an emphasis on form over content. To what extent do you believe that teaching students a particular form or format for the presentation of their ideas is a legitimate goal for education? Does the requirement of a particular form necessarily conflict with the educational goal of creativity?

6. Do you believe that a formal, institutionalized examination system such as that found in imperial China can be successfully utilized to promote meritocracy in a society? What are the constraints on such a system? In your view, is the goal of a meritocratic social order worth pursuing?

7. The concept of *li* is a very important aspect of traditional Confucian thought. In your own words, explain the basic concept of *li*, and then discuss how this concept would be manifested in practice in different kinds of societies.

8. In this chapter, it is noted that Confucius once rebuked a student as a "little-minded man" for asking about the growing of crops. Why do you think that Confucius responded in this manner? How does his response reflect important elements of traditional Chinese society?

9. In order to be admitted to a college or a university, an American student generally has to take either the SAT or ACT examination. In what ways is this requirement similar to the imperial examination system, and in what ways is it different?

10. What do you believe is the single most important lesson traditional Chinese educational thought and practice has for contemporary American education? Why?

RECOMMENDED FURTHER READINGS

There are several good general introductory works on Chinese history, including John Fairbank and Merle Goldman, *China: A New History*, enlarged ed. (Cambridge, MA: Harvard University Press, 1998); J. A. G. Roberts, *A Concise History of China* (Cambridge, MA: Harvard University Press, 1999); W. Scott Morton, *China: Its History and Culture* (New York: McGraw-Hill, 1995); Jacques Gernet, *A History of Chinese Civilization* (Cambridge, England: Cambridge University Press, 1982); and Immanuel C. Y. Hsü, *The Rise of Modern China* (New York: Oxford University Press, 1990). The best general introduction to Chinese education, both traditional and modern, is John Cleverley, *The Schooling of China: Tradition and Modernity in Chinese Education* (Sydney: Allen & Unwin, 1985). Among primary sources, D. C. Lau's excellent translations of *The Analects* (Harmondsworth: Penguin, 1979) and *Mencius* (Harmondsworth, England: Penguin, 1970) are very much worth reading.

NOTES

1. Jacques Gernet, *A History of Chinese Civilization* (Cambridge, England: Cambridge University Press, 1982), 37–38; Marcel Granet, *La civilisation chinoise: La vie publique et la vie privée* (Paris: Éditions Albin Michel, 1968); John Cleverley, *The Schooling of China: Tradition and Modernity in Chinese Education* (Sydney: Allen & Unwin, 1985), 1; Wolfgang Bauer, *China and the Search for Happiness: Recurring Themes in Four Thousand Years of Chinese History* (New York: Seabury, 1976); Henri Cordier, *Histoire général de la Chine*, 4 vols. (Paris: Geuthner, 1921).

2. Cleverley, *The Schooling of China*.

3. Gerald Gutek, *American Education in a Global Society* (New York: Longman, 1993), 178. See also Derk Bodde, *China's First Unifier: A Study of the Ch'in Dynasty as Seen in the Life of Li Ssu* (Hong Kong: Hong Kong University Press, 1967); Derk Bodde, *Essays on Chinese Civilization* (Princeton, NJ: Princeton University Press, 1981); Wolfram Eberhard, *A History of China* (Berkeley: University of California Press, 1977); Werner Eichhorn, *Chinese Civilization: An Introduction* (New York: Praeger, 1969); Mark Elvin, *The Pattern of the Chinese Past* (Stanford, CA: Stanford University Press, 1973); Ray Huang, *China: A Macro History* (London: Sharpe, 1988); Charles Hucker, *China's Imperial Past: An Introduction to Chinese History and Culture* (Stanford, CA: Stanford University Press, 1975); Michael Loewe, *Imperial China: The Historical Background to the Modern Age* (New York: Praeger, 1965); Henri Maspero and Jean Escarra, *Les institutions de la Chine: Essai historique* (Paris: Presses Universitaires de France, 1952); John Meskill, with J. Mason Gentzler (eds.), *An Introduction to Chinese Civilization* (New York: Columbia University Press, 1973).

4. Michael Loewe, *The Pride that Was China* (New York: St. Martin's Press, 1990), xix.

5. See Gernet, *A History of Chinese Civilization*, 3–13; Jerry Norman, *Chinese* (Cambridge, England: Cambridge University Press, 1988).

6. Will Durant, *The Story of Civilization: Our Oriental Heritage* (New York: Simon and Schuster, 1963), 642. See, e.g., Burton Watson, trans., *Records of the Great Historian of China*, 2 vols. (New York: Columbia University Press, 1961); Endymion Wilkinson, *Chinese History: A Manual* (Cambridge, MA: Harvard University Press, 2000).

7. See Xinzhong Yao, *An Introduction to Confucianism* (Cambridge, England: Cambridge University Press, 2000); David McMullen, *State and Scholars in T'ang China* (Cambridge, England: Cambridge University Press, 1988); Tadao Sakai, "Confucianism and Popular Educational Works," in William de Bary (ed.), *Self and Society in Ming Thought* (New York: Columbia University Press, 1970), 331–366; Don Wyatt, "A Language of Continuity in Confucian Thought," in Paul Cohen and Merle Goldman (eds.), *Ideas Across Cultures* (Cambridge, MA: Harvard University Press, 1990), 33–34; James Ball, *Things Chinese, or, Notes Connected with China*, 5th ed. (rev. by E. C. Werner) (Shanghai: Kelly and Walsh, 1925); Chen Li-Fu, *Why Confucius Has Been Reverenced as the Model Teacher of All Ages* (New York: Center of Asian Studies, St. John's University, and the Institute of Chinese Culture, 1976); Cheng Hanbang, "Confucian Ethics and Moral Education of Contemporary Students," in Silke Krieger and Rolf Trauzettel (eds.), *Confucianism and the Modernization of China* (Mainz, Germany: Hase & Koehler, 1991), 193–202; William de Bary, *Neo-Confucian Orthodoxy and the Learning of the Mind-and-Heart* (New York: Columbia University Press, 1981); William de Bary, *The Liberal Tradition in China* (Hong Kong: Chinese University Press, 1983); Fu Shufang, "A Brief Account of the Positive Factors in Confucius' Thinking," in Silke Krieger and Rolf Trauzettel (eds.), *Confucianism and the Modernization of China* (Mainz, Germany: Hase & Koehler, 1991), 175–192; Kuang Yaming, "Modern Values of the Positive Elements in Confucius' Ideas Concerning the Study of Man," in Silke Krieger and Rolf Trauzettel (eds.), *Confucianism and the Modernization of China* (Mainz, Germany: Hase & Koehler, 1991), 7–17; I. Llasera, "Confucian Education Through European Eyes," in Ruth Hayhoe and Marianne Bastid (eds.), *China's Education and the Industrialized World* (London: Sharpe, 1987), 21–32; Vitalii Rubin, *Individual and State in Ancient China: Essays on Four Chinese Philosophers* (New York: Columbia University Press, 1976); B. Staiger, "The Image of Confucius in China," in Silke Krieger and Rolf Trauzettel (eds.), *Confucianism and the Modernization of China* (Mainz, Germany: Hase & Koehler, 1991), 116–125; H. Stumpfeldt, "Confucius and Confucianism: On Their History and Status and on Their Present Theoretical and Practical Potential," in Silke Krieger and Rolf Trauzettel (eds.), *Confucianism and the Modernization of China* (Mainz, Germany: Hase & Koehler, 1991), 18–28; L. Walton, "The Institutional Context of Neo-Confucianism: Scholars, Schools, and Shu-yüan in Sung- Yüan China," in William de Bary and John Chaffee (eds.), *Neo-Confucian Education: The Formative Stage* (Berkeley: University of California Press, 1989), 457–492; Benjamin Schwartz, *The World of Thought in Ancient China* (Cambridge, MA: Harvard University Press, 1985).

8. Tu Wei-Ming, "The Confucian Tradition in Chinese History," in Paul Ropp (ed.), *Heritage of China* (Berkeley: University of California Press, 1990), 136. See also Michael Bond and Kwang-Kuo Hwang, "The Social Psychology of the Chinese People," in Michael Bond (ed.), *The Psychology of the Chinese People* (Hong Kong: Ox-

ford University Press, 1986), 213–266; Benjamin Schwartz, *The World of Thought in Ancient China* (Cambridge, MA: Harvard University Press, 1985); A. Sprenger, "Confucius and Modernization in China: An Educational Perspective," in Silke Krieger and Rolf Trauzettel (eds.), *Confucianism and the Modernization of China* (Mainz, Germany: Hase & Koehler, 1991), 454–472.

9. Cheng Tien-Hsi, *China Moulded by Confucius* (London: Stevens & Sons, 1947), 23.

10. Gernet, *A History of Chinese Civilization*, 88. See also Patricia Ebrey, *Confucianism and Family Rituals in Imperial China* (Princeton, NJ: Princeton University Press, 1991).

11. Herrlee G. Creel, *Confucius and the Chinese Way* (New York: Harper & Row, 1949), 25–26; Tu Wei-Ming, "The Confucian Tradition in Chinese History," 113–114.

12. Creel, *Confucius and the Chinese Way*, 25–26; Tu Wei-Ming, "The Confucian Tradition in Chinese History," 113–114.

13. The term *chün-tzu* literally means "son of a ruler," but is used in the more general sense of "gentleman." Even this translation is somewhat problematic, however, because it refers not so much to an assumed superiority of birth as to a superiority of character and behavior. See Arthur Waley, *The Analects of Confucius* (New York: Vintage, 1938), 34–38; Fung Yu-Lan, *A Short History of Chinese Philosophy* (New York: The Free Press, 1948), 38–48.

It should be noted that the use of male pronouns here is deliberate and meaningful; the role of women in Confucian thought is restricted, in large part, to their roles as wives and mothers. Traditional Chinese society was very much patriarchal, and this was reflected in the place of women in the social order. See Patricia Ebrey, "Women, Marriage, and the Family in Chinese History," in Paul Ropp (ed.), *Heritage of China: Contemporary Perspectives on Chinese Civilization* (Berkeley: University of California Press, 1990), 197–223; Patricia Ebrey, "Education through Ritual: Efforts to Formulate Family Rituals During the Sung Period," in William de Bary and John Chaffee (eds.), *Neo-Confucian Education: The Formative Stage* (Berkeley: University of California Press, 1989), 277–306; Patricia Ebrey, *Confucianism and Family Rituals in Imperial China*.

14. See Creel, *Confucius and the Chinese Way*, 142–144; Ebrey, *Confucianism and Family Rituals in Imperial China*.

15. Gernet, *A History of Chinese Civilization*, 88.

16. D. C. Lau, trans., *The Analects* (Harmondsworth, England: Penguin, 1979).

17. Creel, *Confucius and the Chinese Way*, 291–294.

18. Patricia Ebrey (ed.), *Chinese Civilization* (New York: The Free Press, 1993), 17.

19. See Cheng Tien-Hsi, *China Moulded by Confucius*, 30–36.

20. See Ebrey, *Confucianism and Family Rituals in Imperial China*, 3–13.

21. Creel, *Confucius and the Chinese Way*, 85.

22. Creel, *Confucius and the Chinese Way*, 86.

23. Creel, *Confucius and the Chinese Way*, 129.

24. Howard Ozmon and Samuel Craver, *Philosophical Foundations of Education*, 5th ed. (Englewood Cliffs, NJ: Prentice-Hall, 1995), 93.

25. Ozmon and Craver, *Philosophical Foundations of Education*, 93.

26. Charles Commeaux, *La vie quotidienne en Chine sous les Mandchous* (Paris: Librairie Hachette, 1970), 162–194.

27. Ron-Guey Chu, "Chu Hsi and Public Instruction," in William de Bary and John Chaffee (eds.), *Neo-Confucian Education: The Formative Stage* (Berkeley: University of California Press, 1989), 272.

28. Wang Gungwu, *The Chineseness of China* (Hong Kong: Oxford University Press, 1991), 171.

29. Louis Heren, C. P. Fitzgerald, Michael Freeberne, Brian Hook, and David Bonavia, *China's Three Thousand Years* (New York: Collier Books, 1973), 23–24.

30. See D. C. Lau, trans., *Mencius* (Harmondsworth, England: Penguin, 1970); also useful is Tu Wei-Ming, "The Confucian Tradition in Chinese History."

31. See Peter Bol, "Chu Hsi's Redefinition of Literati Learning," in William de Bary and John Chaffee (eds.), *Neo-Confucian Education: The Formative Stage* (Berkeley: University of California Press, 1989), 151–185; William de Bary, "Chu Hsi's Aims as an Educator," in William de Bary and John Chaffee (eds.), *Neo-Confucian Education: The Formative Stage* (Berkeley: University of California Press, 1989), 186–218; M. Theresa Kelleher, "Back to Basics: Chu Hsi's *Elementary Learning (Hsiao-hsüeh)*," in William de Bary and John Chaffee (eds.), *Neo-Confucian Education: The Formative Stage* (Berkeley: University of California Press, 1989), 219–251; Ron-Guey Chu, "Chu Hsi and Public Instruction."

32. Cleverley, *The Schooling of China*, 4.

33. Cleverley, *The Schooling of China*, 4.

34. Creel, *Confucius and the Chinese Way*, 77.

35. See Wyatt, "A Language of Continuity in Confucian Thought," 33–34.

36. Creel, *Confucius and the Chinese Way*, 76.

37. Cleverley, *The Schooling of China*, 7.

38. Gutek, *American Education in a Global Society*, 179.

39. Creel, *Confucius and the Chinese Way*, 165–166.

40. See Steven Tozer, Paul Violas, and Guy Senese, *School and Society: Historical and Contemporary Perspectives*, 3rd ed. (New York: McGraw-Hill, 1998), 27–39; Gordon Lee, *Crusade Against Ignorance: Thomas Jefferson on Education* (New York: Teachers College Press, 1967).

41. Raymond Dawson, *The Chinese Experience* (London: Weidenfeld and Nicolson, 1978), 108–115; Gernet, *A History of Chinese Civilization*, 90–93.

42. See T. H. Barrett, "Religious Traditions in Chinese Civilization: Buddhism and Taoism," in Paul Ropp (ed.), *Heritage of China: Contemporary Perspectives on Chinese Civilization* (Berkeley: University of California Press, 1990), 138–163; Phyllis Chew, "The Great Tao," *Journal of Bahá'í Studies*, 4, 2 (1991): 11–39; Liu Ts'un-Yan, "Taoist Self-Cultivation in Ming Thought," in William de Bary (ed.), *Self and Society in Ming Thought* (New York: Columbia University Press, 1970), 291–330; Chad Hansen, *A Daoist Theory of Chinese Thought: A Philosophical Interpretation* (New York: Oxford University Press, 1992); Gernet, *A History of Chinese Civilization*, 93–95.

43. See de Bary and Chaffee, *Neo-Confucian Education*.

44. Jacques Gernet, *Daily Life in China on the Eve of the Mongol Invasion, 1250–1276* (Stanford, CA: Stanford University Press, 1962), 151–152.

45. Gernet, *Daily Life in China*, 153.

46. Gernet, *Daily Life in China*, 153.

47. See Édouard Biot, *Essai sur l'histoire de l'instruction publique en chine et de la corporation des lettrés* (Paris: Benjamin Duprat, 1847); H. Galt, *A History of Chinese Educational Institutions*, vol. 1 (London: Arthur Probsthain, 1951); McMullen, *State and Scholars in T'ang China*; Cleverley, *The Schooling of China*, 15; William Ayers, *Chang Chih-tung and Educational Reform in China* (Cambridge, MA: Harvard University Press, 1971); James Liu (ed.), *Political Institutions in Traditional China: Major Issues* (New York: Wiley, 1974); Pei-yi Wu, "Education of Children in the Sung," in William de Bary and John Chaffee (eds.), *Neo-Confucian Education: The Formative Stage* (Berkeley: University of California Press, 1989), 307–324; Evelyn Rawski, *Education and Popular Literacy in Ch'ing China* (Ann Arbor: University of Michigan Press, 1979).

48. Loewe, *The Pride that Was China*, 145.

49. Dawson, *The Chinese Experience*, 20.

50. See Richard Smith, *China's Cultural Heritage: The Ch'ing Dynasty, 1644–1912* (Boulder, CO: Westview, 1983), 250.

51. Justus Doolittle, *Social Life of the Chinese*, vol. 1 (1865; Taipei: Ch'eng-Wen, 1966), 376–377; see also Isaac Headland, *Home Life in China* (London: Methuen & Co., 1914).

52. Yuan Zheng, "Local Government Schools in Sung China: A Reassessment," *History of Education Quarterly*, 34, 2 (1994): 213.

53. Yuan Zheng, "Local Government Schools in Sung China," 193–213.

54. Yuan Zheng, "Local Government Schools in Sung China," 212.

55. Cleverley, *The Schooling of China*, 16.

56. A few words about the nature of written Chinese are in order here. The Chinese writing system is not phonetic in the same way as Western, alphabetically based systems. Rather, each Chinese character represents a single morpheme, and contains two elements, one of which carries semantic information and the other phonological information, which is used for sound value alone. Thus, the character for the word *liáng* ("wolf") contains the graph for "dog" on the left and a graph for the word *liáng* (literally meaning "good") on the right. Thus, the combination gives the reader an idea of the semantic content, coupled with the appropriate sound. Although far more complicated to learn than an alphabetically based system, the Chinese system has the advantage that it can be used to represent different spoken languages, which is in essence what has taken place historically, because China is in fact very diverse linguistically. An orthographic system such as that used by Chinese basically functions as a sort of written *lingua franca*, serving as an additional unifying force where spoken language would tend to work against unity. See Norman, *Chinese*, 58–63; S. Robert Ramsey, *The Languages of China* (Princeton, NJ: Princeton University Press, 1987), 134–137.

57. Cleverley, *The Schooling of China*, 17.

58. See Kiang Kang-Hu, *On Chinese Studies* (Shanghai: Commercial Press, 1934); S. Wells Williams, *The Middle Kingdom*, vol. 1 (New York: Scribner's, 1907), 627–673.

59. Smith, *China's Cultural Heritage*, 47.

60. Dawson, *The Chinese Experience*, 34.

61. Gernet, *Daily Life in China*, 154–155.

62. Gernet, *Daily Life in China*, 154.

63. Cleverley, *The Schooling of China*, 27.

64. See Bettine Birge, "Chu Hsi and Women's Education," in William de Bary and John Chaffee (eds.), *Neo-Confucian Education: The Formative Stage* (Berkeley: University of California Press, 1989), 325–367; Ebrey, "Women, Marriage, and the Family in Chinese History."

65. Dawson, *The Chinese Experience*, 33.

66. Ebrey, *Chinese Civilization*, 128; see also Peter Bol, *"This Culture of Ours": Intellectual Transitions in T'ang and Sung China* (Stanford, CA: Stanford University Press, 1992), 36–48.

67. See Thomas H. C. Lee, *Government Education and Examinations in Sung China* (Hong Kong: Chinese University Press, 1985); Ping-Ti Ho, *The Ladder of Success in Imperial China* (New York: Columbia University Press, 1962); John Chaffee, *Education and Examinations in Sung Society* (Ph.D. dissertation, University of Chicago, 1979); Irene Bloom, *Knowledge Painfully Acquired: The K'un-chih chi by Lo Ch'in-shun* (New York: Columbia University Press, 1987); Joseph Needham, *Science in Traditional China: A Comparative Perspective* (Cambridge, MA: Harvard University Press, 1981), 23–24.

68. Dawson, *The Chinese Experience*, 33–34; see also Hsiung-Huei Lee, *Education in Taiwan During the Ch'ing Dynasty, 1683–1895* (Ph.D. dissertation, University of Connecticut, 1995), 193–272.

69. Cleverley, *The Schooling of China*, 19.

70. See Immanuel C. Y. Hsü, *The Rise of Modern China* (New York: Oxford University Press, 1990), 75. For a detailed discussion of the examination system, see Smith, *China's Cultural Heritage*, 47–51; also interesting is Doolittle, *Social Life of the Chinese*, chaps. 15, 16, and 17.

71. Dawson, *The Chinese Experience*, 34.

72. Hsiung-Huei Lee, *Education in Taiwan During the Ch'ing Dynasty*, 217–222.

73. Dawson, *The Chinese Experience*, 36.

74. Dawson, *The Chinese Experience*, 36.

75. Dawson, *The Chinese Experience*, 36.

76. Hsiung-Huei Lee, *Education in Taiwan During the Ch'ing Dynasty*, chap. 5. See also Leon Stover, *The Cultural Ecology of Chinese Civilization: Peasants and Elites in the Last of the Agrarian Societies* (New York: Pica, 1974).

77. Dawson, *The Chinese Experience*, 34.

78. Gernet, *A History of Chinese Civilization*, 505. This is not to suggest, however, that the system was entirely unchanging or static; see, e.g., Joanna Handlin, *Action in Late Ming Thought: The Reorientation of Lü K'un and Other Scholar-Officials* (Berkeley: University of California Press, 1983).

79. Cleverley, *The Schooling of China*, 20; Hsiung-Huei Lee, *Education in Taiwan During the Ch'ing Dynasty*, 212–216.

80. Cleverley, *The Schooling of China*, 20–21.

81. See Ho Peng Yoke, *Li, Qi and Shu: An Introduction to Science and Civilization in China* (Hong Kong: Hong Kong University Press, 1985). I am deeply indebted to the late Philip Steedman for bringing the work of Joseph Needham to my attention.

82. This is not, however, to suggest that science, even when passed from one cultural setting to another, in earlier times was in any meaningful way conceptually or epistemologically "universal." As Needham pointed out,

> The sciences of the mediaeval world were in fact tied closely to their ethnic environment, and it was difficult if not impossible for people of those different environments to find any common basis of discourse. For example, if Chang Heng had tried to talk to Vitruvius about the Tin and the Yang or the Five Elements, he would not have got very far, even if they could have understood each other at all. But that did not mean that it was impossible for inventions of great sociological importance to pass from one civilisation to another, and that they did, right through the Middle Ages. (see Needham, *Science in Traditional China*, 9)

This leaves open the question, of course, of the extent to which modern science, can be said to be "universal"; see, e.g., the work of the radical philosopher of science Paul Feyerabend, including his *Against Method*, 3rd ed. (London: Verso, 1993), *Farewell to Reason* (London: Verso, 1987), and *Three Dialogues on Knowledge* (Oxford, England: Basil Blackwell, 1989); as well as Alan Sokal and Jean Bricmont's powerful critique of postmodern philosophy of science, *Fashionable Nonsense: Posmodern Intellectuals' Abuse of Science* (New York: Picador, 1998).

83. Needham, *Science in Traditional China*, 10–12.

84. Needham, *Science in Traditional China*, 3.

85. Gavin Menzies, *1421: The Year China Discovered America* (New York: William Morrow, 2003), 35.

86. *Science and Civilisation in China* is, by any definition, a monumental work, and can be overwhelming for the nonspecialist. An extremely useful abridged version of the work has now been produced; see Colin Ronan, *The Shorter Science and Civilisation in China, An Abridgement of Joseph Needham's Original Text*, 4 vols. (Cambridge, England: Cambridge University Press, 1978–1994).

87. See Robert Temple, *The Genius of China: 3,000 Years of Science, Discovery, and Invention* (New York: Simon and Schuster, 1986).

88. Tellingly, when published in the United States, the title of the book was changed to *1421: The Year China Discovered America*.

89. Taken from the Web site www.1421.tv, which is devoted to Menzies' book and the upcoming television documentary based on the book.

90. Menzies, *1421: The Year China Discovered America*, 394–399.

91. Gutek, *American Education in a Global Society*, 179; see also, however, Marianne Bastid, "Servitude or Liberation? The Introduction of Foreign Educational Practices and Systems to China," in Ruth Hayhoe and Marianne Bastid (eds.), *China's Education and the Industrialized World* (London: Sharpe, 1987), 3–20.

7

"An Intelligent Man Attends on a Wise Person": Traditional Hindu and Buddhist Educational Thought and Practice

> *The study of Indian philosophy is important historically, philosophi-*
> *cally, and even politically. The Indian philosophical tradition is man's*
> *oldest as well as the longest continuous development of speculation about*
> *the nature of reality and man's place therein. It began with the ancient*
> *Vedas, which are probably the earliest documents of the human mind*
> *that have come down to us, and has continued age after age in progres-*
> *sive philosophical advance in the effort to understand life and reality.*
> *But it is not as a piece of antiquarian investigation that we of today*
> *should study Indian philosophy. Despite the tendency to respect and re-*
> *vere the greatness of the past, Indian thinkers of all ages have been deeply*
> *and profoundly concerned with the ultimate truth which is timeless. . . .*
> *India's concentrated study of the inner nature of man is, in the end, a*
> *study of man universal.*
> —Kadhakrishnan & Moore (1957, p. xxx)

The Indian subcontinent is the home of three important, and related, cultural and religious traditions: Hinduism, Buddhism, and Jainism, each of which has educational traditions no doubt meriting a book of its own.[1] In this book, we examine the traditional educational thought and practices associated with two of these three religions. Specifically, in this chapter we explore selected aspects of the Hindu and Buddhist educational traditions.

THE ORIGINS OF HINDUISM

It is difficult both to identify the origins of Hinduism and to provide a suc-cinct, clear summation describing the essence of Hinduism. To some extent, these problems are related, because Hinduism is incredibly ancient and has been open to diversity and the assimilation of new ideas and practices throughout its long history.[2] According to Hindu tradition, the *Vedas* (or "body of knowledge") that constitute the sacred literature of Hinduism date back as far as 6000 B.C.E. in their oral form, but most historians would argue that the written literature, although not nearly as old as the tradition would suggest, nonetheless dates to around 1500 to 1000 B.C.E.[3] In fact, we know relatively little about the early history of Hinduism, and what today is called *Hinduism*[4] is actually the product of the blending of four distinct religious traditions. These four traditions are presented in chronological order of their impact of the development of Hinduism:

- The religious and spiritual traditions of the original, indigenous people of the subcontinent, whose stone-age culture dates back some half million years
- The religious and spiritual traditions of the Indus civilization, which encompassed much of Northern and Northwestern India
- The religious and spiritual traditions of the Dravidian culture
- The Vedic religion, which was brought to the subcontinent by Aryan invaders roughly between 200 B.C.E. and 900 B.C.E.[5]

Later contacts with Jews, Christians, and Muslims, as well as with Buddhists whose religious tradition is related to and in part derived from that of Hinduism, have also impacted Hinduism in various ways, as have both Jainism and Sikhism. This openness to other religious traditions has not, however, meant that the fundamental essence of Hinduism has differed significantly through its long history. As Klaus Klostermaier noted in *A Survey of Hinduism*, "Despite its openness to many influences and the considerable changes that it has undergone throughout the ages, there is a distinct character, an unbroken tradition, and a unifying principle that allows Hinduism to be faithful to itself while inviting others to share whatever treasures they may possess."[6]

Hindus themselves call their religion *sanatana dharma*, which is generally translated as "eternal religion," although it might just as well be translated as "eternal truth." However, the term implies far more than the English translation.[7] *Sanatana* means "eternal" or "ageless" in the sense that the religion is believed by its practitioners to have always existed, and to be *the* religion.[8] *Dharma*, often translated simply as "religion," actually encompasses such concepts as "duty," "righteousness," and "natural law," thus suggesting a much broader understanding than that generally accorded the term "religion" in the West.[9] In fact, as Troy Organ argued in *The Hindu Quest for the Perfection of Man*, underlying the notion of *dharma* is a far more encompassing conception of the duties of the individual, involving "the total disciplinary methods of training the will, rather than to the moral rightness or wrongness of single acts as measured by a fixed law."[10]

Not only is the translation of *sanatana dharma* problematic, but the actual nature of the religion itself is somewhat difficult to define. Indeed, as Stephen Cross commented, "One of the ways in which Hinduism differs strikingly from those religions that we in the West are most used to is that it has no fixed minimum doctrine. There is no Hindu creed and no central authority. . . . Hinduism is not a tightly defined religion but rather the way of thought of an entire ancient and populous civilization."[11] As David Kinsley explained, "One cannot find the equivalent of a Hindu pope or an authoritative Hindu council. . . . Historically, Hinduism has never insisted on the necessity of a supreme figure in religious matters and has never agreed on certain articles of belief as essential for all Hindus. Throughout its long history, Hinduism has been highly decentralized."[12]

Further complicating this situation have been the close ties between Hinduism as a religious tradition and Indian nationalism in recent times.[13] Although certainly not all Indians are Hindu, and although there are of course non-Indian Hindus, for the most part there is a commonly assumed connection between Hinduism and Indian cultural identity. To assume such a connection is hardly unreasonable because, as Arvind Sharma explained, "95 percent of the Hindus in the world live in India, over 80 percent of whose population is Hindu."[14] The contemporary reality of the situation is that Hinduism actually exists (or, perhaps more accurately, coexists) both as an ethnic religion and as a universal religion.[15] This has led to a degree of conceptual tension within Hinduism, as Sharma noted: "The ethnic and universal aspects of Hinduism thus together constitute the paradoxical axes of Hindu pluralism, keeping the map of Hinduism, as it were, forever on the drawing board of history."[16]

Identification of oneself as Hindu, then, inevitably depends less on doctrinal agreement than on self-definition and acceptance by the Hindu community, to a far greater extent than would be the case with most other religious traditions, especially those with which we in the West tend to be most familiar. This having been said, however, one common way of distinguishing Hindus from non-Hindus is that the former accept the authority of the *Vedas* in spiritual matters.[17] The centrality of the *Vedas* to Hinduism provides a valuable entry point for us as we try to understand Hinduism and the traditional educational thought and practice associated with Hinduism.

THE VEDIC TRADITION

The body of sacred writings in Hinduism is extensive, and includes a number of different kinds of literature. As Klostermaier pointed out, "No other living tradition can claim scriptures as numerous or as ancient as Hinduism; none can boast an unbroken tradition preserved as faithfully as the Hindu tradition. The sources of Hinduism are not only historical materials to be studied by the scholar of antiquity, they have been recited and studied by the faithful throughout the ages."[18] The two most significant of the elements in the sacred literature of Hinduism's "living tradition" are *shruti* and *smrti*,[19] each of which is now briefly discussed. We also consider the unique role of Sanskrit in the Hindu literary tradition.

Shruti

Shruti means "that which is heard," and is commonly associated primarily with the *Vedas*. The *Vedas* are believed to constitute divine revelation. As Fisher explained, "According to orthodox Hindus, the *Vedas* are not the work of any humans. They are believed to be the breath of the eternal, as 'heard' by the ancient sages, or *rishis*. The scriptures are thought to transcend human time and are thus as relevant today as they were thousands of years ago."[20]

Although the *Vedas* have been written down, they are first and foremost oral texts,[21] and there is a strong view in the Hindu tradition that they are best transmitted orally.[22] There are actually four distinct bodies of work that together make up the *Vedas*; specifically, there are the *Rig Veda*, the *Yajur Veda*, the *Sama Veda*, and the *Atharva Veda*.[23] Each of these *Vedas* is, in turn, divided into four parts, including devotional hymns (*Samhita* or *Mantra*), priestly texts (*Brahmanas*), forest treatises (*Aranyakas*), and philosophic texts (the *Upanishads*), which were actually produced later and are more correctly called *Vendantic* texts.[24]

The *Vedas* play a role in Hinduism that is in some ways similar to that of texts believed to be divinely inspired in other religions, but that is also different in important ways. As Sharma noted:

> The *Vedas*, by virtue of their historical priority and canonical primacy, play a very significant role in Hinduism but in unsuspecting ways. . . . The *Vedas*, for the tradition as a whole then, functioned as a symbol of the tradition and as the ultimate rather than the proximate basis of its beliefs and practices, for anything not inconsistent with the *Vedas* was considered admissible as Hindu. This negative criterion for orthodox inclusion once again attests to Hinduism's reluctance to limit itself.[25]

Smrti

Smrti is the body of religious literature in Hinduism that seeks to explain how the timeless spiritual truths of the *Vedas* are to be understood and applied in one's daily life.[26] In practice, the term s*mrti*, which means "that which has been remembered," can be used either to refer to works that are basically codes of conduct, or "extended to embrace virtually all forms of sacred writings of human origin."[27] *Smrti,* at least in the former sense, consists of a variety of different books that seek to provide guidance for virtually all aspects of human life, the most widely accepted of which is the *Manusmrti* (the "Laws of Manu"). They tend to be highly prescriptive, complex, and analytic in nature but, as Sharma explained, there is an underlying reason for this: "Their passion for classification baffles modern readers. A 'method' may, however, underlie the 'madness.' Marriage is classified as being of eight kinds. A deep compassion perhaps underlies this classification, which is so exhaustive that it is virtually impossible for anyone to be born out of wedlock!"[28]

Although recognized by Hindus as being of human origin, s*mrti* is arguably of considerably greater immediate importance than are the *Vedas* themselves for most Hindus, because it regulates daily life in a way that *shruti* does not.[29] Finally, it is worth noting that although Hindus accept *shruti* as divine scripture, Hinduism as it is generally recognized has, since the Classical Hindu Period (roughly 300 C.E. to 1200 C.E.), been characterized to a far greater extent by compliance with *smrti* than *shruti.*[30]

The Role of Sanskrit in the Vedic Tradition

Sanskrit, a language brought to India by the Aryan invaders of the subcontinent between 1500 B.C.E. and 1200 B.C.E., has played and continues to play an important role in Hinduism. The *Vedas* are written in Sanskrit, as are many other important religious writings. Although there is also an extensive religious literature in the various vernacular languages of India, Sanskrit remains very much the "sacred tongue *par excellence*" of Hinduism.[31] Furthermore, having ceased to function as a spoken language in daily life more than 2,000 years ago, Sanskrit was maintained for much of its history not merely as a sacred language, but as a sacred language of which knowledge was reserved for a small elite in Indian society who maintained both their religious and social status in part through their knowledge of it.[32]

Sanskrit, incidentally, is also important in another, far different, context. European scholars gained access to both the language and the texts written in Sanskrit only in the 18th century—an undertaking that had been quite difficult, because the Brahmins were hesitant to let foreigners (*mlecchas*) learn the sacred language. In 1786, Sir William Jones delivered a paper on Sanskrit in which he argued that the language bore striking similarities to Latin and Greek.[33] Jones noted:

> The Sanskrit language, whatever may be its antiquity, is of a wonderful structure; more perfect than the Greek, more copious than the Latin, and more exquisitely refined than either, yet bearing to both of them a stronger affinity, both in the roots of the verbs and in the forms of grammar, than could possibly have been produced by accident; so strong indeed that no philologer could ex-

amine them all three, without believing them to have sprung from some common source, which, perhaps no longer exists.[34]

The similarities identified by Jones were later explored in considerable detail and led to the discovery that Sanskrit, and many other languages as well, were indeed related. In fact, it proved to be the beginning of the discovery of the Indo-European language family, to which not only Sanskrit, but also English and the other Germanic languages, the Celtic languages, the Romance languages, the Slavic languages, the Hellenic languages, the Baltic languages, and the Indo-Iranian languages, all belong.

HINDU BELIEFS AND PRACTICES

As we have already seen, it is very difficult indeed to identify the core beliefs of Hinduism. However, keeping in mind that there is, and probably could be, no "creed" to which all Hindus subscribe, it is nevertheless possible to summarize some of the key beliefs that are most prevalent and common among Hindus. A good start in this effort has been made by the Himalayan Academy, an American Hindu organization, which identified the following "Nine Beliefs of Hinduism":

- That there is "one, all-pervasive Supreme Being";
- That there are "endless cycles of creation, preservation and dissolution" (that is, a cyclical view of time and history);
- That "all souls are evolving" toward or seeking "*Moksha*" or "liberation";
- That there is a "law of cause and effect" known as Karma;
- That there is "reincarnation";
- That there are "divine beings and forces" that require "temple worship" and "personal worship," or Puja, in the home;
- That there is a need for "an awakened Master of Sat Guru" (that is, a reliable, personal teacher) for one's personal and ethical life;
- That "all life is sacred" and that one should pursue "*ahimsa* or non-violence"; and
- That "no particular religion teaches the only way to salvation about all others, but that all genuine religious paths are . . . deserving (of) tolerance and understanding."[35]

Although this list is useful, it has also been carefully, and understandably, constructed to avoid, for the most part, issues that Americans might find problematic. It is not, however, universally accepted by Hindus—the need for a "guru," for instance, is by no means generally accepted as a core belief of Hinduism. One additional feature of classical Hinduism that must be explicitly addressed here in order to help make sense of traditional Hindu educational thought and practice is that of the caste system that is so closely associated with Hinduism.

The Hindu caste system had its origins in the culture brought to India by the Aryan invaders, who, like other Indo-European peoples, divided their society into three classes of people: a priesthood, a class of warriors and rulers, and a class concerned with meeting the economic needs of the society (farmers, merchants, craftsmen, etc.). In addition, the Aryans developed a fourth class, who functioned as servants for the members of the other three classes. These four classes of people, called *varnas*, were called *Brahmins, Kshatriyas, Vaishyas*, and *Shudras*, respectively.[36] To this division of society, the Aryans added a fifth group, consisting of the indigenous people of India whom they had conquered, to whom were delegated various socially necessary but "impure" activities. This group was the "untouchables," because it came to be believed that even contact with them could pollute others. The social divisions among these five classes of people, which were established in the *Vedas*, were in practice replaced with an hereditary system based on *jati* (birth) in traditional Hindu society.[37] Thus, the divisions, which had always been hierarchical, came to be religiously sanctioned and, for the most part, permanent and binding in nature. Thus, what had begun as social classes gradually became castes. Over time, the caste system further developed so that today there are actually more than 3,000 different castes, reflecting different trades, professions, backgrounds, and so on.[38] Although an understanding of traditional Hinduism certainly requires a familiarity with the caste system, especially in terms of traditional Hindu educational thought and practice, it is important to note that the caste system is not in fact part of the religion itself. As Cross noted, "The whole system has thus become attached in the popular mind, and in that of many foreign observers, to Hinduism, but in reality it has little to do with it. The caste system is a social phenomenon masquerading as religion."[39]

It is also possible for us to talk about Hinduism in terms of the legitimate goals for human life. Specifically, an important component of Hinduism has been what is termed the *doctrine of the four goals of life*, or *purusharthas*.[40] These four goals are:

- *Dharma* (the leading of a moral life)
- *Artha* (the earning of wealth)
- *Kama* (the enjoyment of the pleasures of the senses)
- *Moksha* (the seeking of liberation)[41]

Ideally, these four goals are to be reflected chronologically in one's life as distinct "stages of life," with *dharma* as the goal for one's first twenty-five years, followed by each of the other goals in its turn, although in practice most Hindus only progress through the first two.[42] The ultimate goal for the individual that underlies all of these four goals is, of course, the "quest for perfection,"[43] but the focus of this goal in Hinduism is on the process rather than on the product. As Organ argued in *The Hindu Quest for the Perfection of Man*, "Hinduism is a pursuit, an endeavor, a striving. According to the *Mahabharata* it is the 'pursuit of Brahman or self-knowledge' that is immortality. This continuous endeavor toward fulfillment is a promise, and, like all ideals, a forever falling short of the goal."[44]

We now turn to an examination of how individuals were educated for this pursuit in traditional Hindu society.

HINDU EDUCATIONAL THOUGHT

At the base of traditional Hindu educational thought is a deep concern with epistemology, or the theory of knowledge. Human beings are believed to be held captive by our ignorance, and thus, ways of knowing (*pramana*) become very important in Hinduism.[45] Hindu theologians and philosophers have identified six different methods of knowing: sense perception (*pratyaksha*), inference (*anumana*), authority (*shabda*), analogy (*upamana*), hypothetical supposition (*arthapatti*), and negation (*anupalabdhi*).[46] Although the ultimate purpose of epistemology in Hinduism is spiritual in nature, it is important to keep in mind that none of these six methods of knowing is intended to provide direct knowledge of the Absolute; rather, each is useful in assisting us to "discern the realities which are assumed to be manifestations of the Reality, and hence are instrumental in the quest for Absolute Reality."[47] Each of these methods of knowing is briefly discussed here:

1. *Pratyaksha*, or sense perception, is arguably the most important source of knowledge. It refers to those things that we learn by means of our senses (which, in Hinduism, are taken to include the five external senses—touch, taste, sight, sound, and smell—as well as an internal sense, mind [*manas*]).[48]
2. *Anumana*, or inference, refers to what might be called logical argument, and includes both inductive and deductive reasoning. Typical of *anumana* is the five-part syllogism characteristic of Hindu philosophy, which precedes the development of syllogistic reasoning in the West. The five-part syllogism includes the following steps:
   a. The thesis that is to be established.
   b. The reason for maintaining the thesis.
   c. The example of the reason.

d. The application of the reason and example.

e. The conclusion (i.e., the thesis established).[49]

3. *Shabda*, or authority, is concerned primarily with scriptural authority, whether *shruti* or *smrti*. The study and analysis of the scripture plays an important role in Hinduism, and the concern with *shabda* led early on to extensive Hindu scholarship on the nature and structure of language. Religious knowledge is derived primarily from *shabda*.[50]

4. Analogical reasoning, or *upamana*, has a higher status in Hindu philosophical thought than it does in the West. Analogies are, in essence, comparisons of two things that share certain common characteristics, and suggest that because they share those characteristics, they are likely to share other characteristics as well. Basically, analogy in the West is used as a possible source for hypotheses, whereas in Hindu thought it is considered a possible source of knowledge.[51]

5. *Arthapatti*, or hypothetical supposition, is also sometimes called the "method of implication." It involves identifying a missing premise in a dilemma or argument. Thus, if a person is fasting during the day, but nonetheless is gaining weight, one would be led to suspect that he is eating at night.[52]

6. The last of the six methods of knowing is called *abhava*, or negation, and is, in a way, a sort of extension of *pratyaksha*, or sense perception. The idea here is that "non-existence . . . can be known by non-cognition."[53] In other words, the fact that I do not sense x around me can be taken to be evidence for the nonexistence of x in my immediate vicinity.

Beyond its epistemological concerns, traditional Hindu educational thought emphasizes the need to think of individuals apart from their social context. As Radha Mookerji explained in *Ancient Indian Education*:

Hindu thought takes up the position that the individual as conceived in the context of social life, and the laws of the State, is essentially a psychological and biological fact. But the individual, in order that his ultimate datum of personality may be understood, must be viewed from other perspectives, those of his elemental nature, his potentiality for growth and transformation, his self-sufficiency, his capacity for effecting harmony between conflicting trends of impulses. Such a view of the self will necessarily take it out of its usual habitat. It means that the normal functions in terms of which the biological self ties itself to its material home must be checked so as to lay bare the core and kernel of one's being, the true self, the naked personality, stripped of the envelope with which it is shrouded by the accretions of passing impulses and emotions.[54]

In other words, the focus and purpose of education is on the spiritual growth and development of the individual, rather than on any particular instrumental goal or objective. However, the purpose of emphasizing the individual is in fact to move the learner beyond individuation, and toward emancipation. This involves moving away from the physical, material world around us, as well as beyond the limits of our own individual minds:

> When the mind is withdrawn from the world of matter, and does not engage in individuation, Omniscience, the Knowledge of the Whole, dawns on it. Individuation shuts out omniscience. Individuation is concretion of the Mind. The Mind takes the form of the object in knowing it. It limits itself to the object, like the water rained down from the clouds limiting itself in a tank. Thus Individuation is Bondage. It limits vision, knowledge, omniscience.[55]

The goal of the traditional Hindu educational endeavor, then, will not be on the acquisition of bits of knowledge or on "objective knowledge," but rather on the knowledge of the totality of the universe. In short, rather than looking for the components of knowledge, the point of education is to help us to find the source of knowledge. We turn now to a discussion of how this search for knowledge took place in traditional Hindu educational practice.

TRADITIONAL HINDU EDUCATIONAL PRACTICE

Given the very long history of Hinduism, it is hardly surprising that traditional Hindu educational thought has been manifested in practice in a variety of ways. Mookerji, for example, distinguished among the educational practices of the Rigvedic era, later Vedic educational practices, educational practices described in the Sutra literature, education in the time of Panini, and so on.[56] Although traditional Hindu education has, indeed, taken a variety of forms, there has also been an underlying unity that holds these different sets of practices together, and it is that underlying unity that is our focus here.

Hindu educational practice has focused on three distinct steps, discussed in detail in the *Upanishads*. Specifically, education is concerned with *shravana, manana,* and *nididhyasana.*[57] *Shravana* refers to the process of listening to one's teacher, and learning the oral tradition on which the Hindu religious tradition is largely based. It is *shravana* that provides the content base necessary for a person to become educated. *Shravana* is followed by *manana*, which involves reflection on that which is contained in the *shravana*. *Manana* is best understood as the process by which one begins to think about and reflect on the meaning of what one has learned, and is essentially an intellectual rather than a spiritual process. *Manana* is followed by *nididhyasana*, or "meditation," in which the goal is the realization of truth and the "consciousness of the One." Each in its own way, all of the different traditional

Hindu educational practices follow this same general process of increasing spirituality.

Formal education in traditional Indian society was almost exclusively the domain of males, and of Brahmin males at that.[58] To be sure, exceptions did exist, and one can make a case from the extensive Hindu literature that learning was intended, at least in principle, to be a far more general endeavor. Sures Banerji, for instance, argued that "in matters of education, the narrow barriers of the caste-system appeared to have crumbled down."[59] In terms of typical practice, however, this does not, in fact, seem to have been the case for much of Hindu history, when non-Brahmins and girls were generally excluded from the educational sphere.[60]

Brahmin education began when the boy was about five years old, with a ritual called *vidyarambha* (which means "knowledge beginning"). This involved learning the Sanskrit alphabet in a ceremonial way, and generally lasted about an hour.[61] The boy would then commence studying at home, reading and writing, practicing on simple texts, as well as learning basic arithmetic. At around age eight, the boy would undergo what is called the "sacred thread ceremony" (*upanayana*), which involved his new teacher whispering his *gayatri mantra* to him and beginning the more formal part of his education.[62]

Formal education then commenced, with the boy living in the home of his teacher. A teacher, or *guru*, would accept only a small number of students, thus ensuring that education remained the highly individualized undertaking that Hinduism required. The student, in this system:

> lived with the [teacher] as a member of his family, ministered to his needs, obeyed his *guru's* commands implicitly and treated him with divine reverence. He wore his hair long, dressed simply, practised penances, and studied under the direction of the *guru*. He had to collect fuel and tend the sacred fires, look after the cattle, help in agriculture and attend to the running of the household. If the need arose he had to go begging on behalf of his master.[63]

At age ten, the boys would begin their study of the *Vedas* themselves, memorizing many texts and learning to perform the *samdhya* ("daily devotions") appropriately.[64] A boy's education was also characterized by a commitment to sexual chastity, an important aspect of the vow of *brahmacharya* that the student had to take.[65] Adolescence, marked by a special ceremony called *keshanta* ("the first shaving of the beard"), marked the end of formal education for many Brahmins.[66] For those who continued, study expanded and intensified, and could last for as long as an additional fifteen years.

Much traditional Hindu education took place as described earlier, in *ashramas* run by individual teachers. As Mookerji noted, "The vital principle of ancient Indian education was that of individual and intimate relationship between pupils and their teachers, as members of the same family, living in a common home, the home of the teacher functioning as the school."[67] However, there were also notable educational institutions of a more formal, institution type in traditional Hindu society, often tied to temples and monasteries.[68] Still, even in these more institutional settings, the focus of traditional Hindu education was always on the individual and his personal spiritual growth.

THE CASE OF VEDIC MATHEMATICS

In recent years, there have been significant and in some instances quite controversial efforts by some Indian scholars and academics to articulate the relations between Western approaches to knowledge and indigenous Hindu approaches to knowledge. One area in which such efforts are both fascinating and informative has been in the area of mathematics, in particular with the growing interest in what is called "Vedic Mathematics." In essence, Vedic mathematics is mathematics grounded in the *Vedas*, and, more specifically, in sixteen sutras from the appendix of the *Atharva Veda*.[69] In actuality, Vedic mathematics can be conceptualized in three fairly distinct ways: as the historical study of mathematics in the Vedas,[70] as a specific approach to the teaching and learning of mathematics,[71] and from the perspective of contemporary mathematics.[72] Each of these ways of thinking about Vedic mathematics has its advocates and its benefits, but it is nonetheless important to understand that these different conceptualizations also entail some fundamentally different sets of starting assumptions.

The historical approach to Vedic mathematics focuses on the very real and significant contributions of Indian philosophers and mathematicians to the development of mathematics writ large. As H. C. Khare noted:

> The Hindu contributions in mathematics are significant. Their greatest achievement is the principle of place value which of all the mathematical inventions has contributed most. Their skill in handling problems and equations of more than one variable was unique. Their method of solution of quadratic equations should find a place in modern textbooks. The solution of cubic and quartic led to the modern development in the treatment of these equations. The Hindus unhesitatingly accepted irrational numbers as the solution. The immensely important concept of absolute negative is due to the Hindus. The most outstanding contribution was the study of indeterminate equation. . . . The concept of zero is India's contribution to mathematics.[73]

Perhaps the most common approach to Vedic mathematics in recent years has been concerned with the conceptualization of Vedic mathematics as a metaphysically based approach to the teaching and learning of mathematics. As Narendra Puri argued:

> The Vedas are the source of all knowledge and of all sciences. They are not only the oldest but also the best. The Vedas have guided millions of aspirants on the path of knowledge. With the passage of time most of the Vedic knowledge has been scattered. Vedic Mathematics is no exception to it. . . . Vedic Mathematics originated from the Vedas, which manifest divine knowledge. Any knowledge derived from the Vedas is bound to have a touch of the divine bliss. Therefore, the very natural, easy and superfast algorithms of Vedic Mathematics bring an upsurge of joy and bliss. Owing to its very special and universal features, the Vedic maths system converts the dry and tedious maths into a playful and joyful subject, which children learn with a smile. Therefore, Vedic maths is the gift of the Veda to solve the problem of "Maths anxiety" faced in maths education all over the world.[74]

In this approach to Vedic mathematics, the concern is primarily focused on the relative ease of teaching and learning mathematics when placed in a Vedic context.

Finally, contemporary Western-trained mathematicians have, in some instances, attempted to explore Vedic mathematics in light of modern mathematical knowledge. To be sure, such efforts are unusual, and it is far more common to find modern mathematicians and advocates of Vedic mathematics engaged in mutual renunciation. What is needed, as S. N. Pandey suggested, is better two-way communication: "But one thing is demanded from both of the sides. The traditional Sanskrit scholars and pandits should realize the fact that the contribution of the West to knowledge is as 'pious' as the Vedas and the western-minded scholars and mathematicians should realize that the knowledge hidden in the Vedas and the sastras is not 'trash.' It is as scientific and systematic as any knowledge can be."[75]

HINDUISM: TYING IT TOGETHER

The Hindu educational tradition is both one of the oldest and one of the richest in the world. It has functioned for millennia, in different forms, providing an education that emphasized the individual and his spiritual needs, even as it taught that only by renouncing the self could one achieve unity with the whole of the universe. Although sharing common roots with the West in the very distant past (as reflected in the ties of the Sanskrit language to other Indo-European languages), Hinduism presents us with a very different view of both the *educated person* and of the purposes of education than those with which most of us in the West are most familiar and comfortable.[76] Furthermore, as we see in the next part of this chapter, Hinduism also provides the

foundation on which Buddhism and, indeed, several other religious traditions, are based. In short, it is undoubtedly a good idea for us to reflect on the
lessons that we can learn from the wisdom of Hinduism and its educational
tradition.

THE BUDDHIST TRADITION

Buddhism emerged in India during the period between the 7th and 5th centuries B.C.E., which was a time of intense intellectual ferment in the subcontinent.[77] Developing in the context of classical Hinduism, Buddhism shared
many common ideas and themes with Hinduism, even as it seems to have di-
verged from the Hindu tradition in significant ways.[78] Nonetheless, the distinction between Hinduism and Buddhism is often a difficult one to articulate in practice. As Ananda Coomaraswamy wrote in his comparative study of
the two religions:

> The more superficially one studies Buddhism, the more it seems to differ from
> the Brahmanism in which it originated; the more profound our study, the
> more difficult it becomes to distinguish Buddhism from Brahmanism, or to say
> in what respects, if any, Buddhism is really unorthodox. The outstanding dis-
> tinction lies in the fact that Buddhist doctrine is propounded by an apparently
> historical founder. . . . Beyond this there are only broad distinctions of empha-
> sis.[79]

As this passage suggests, the obvious starting point in trying to understand
Buddhism is with its founder, the Buddha ("the Awakened One"). As Noble
Ross Reat wrote in *Buddhism: A History*:

> Given his enormous historical significance, remarkably few Westerners are
> even vaguely acquainted with the Buddha or the religion he founded. . . . In
> terms of influence upon human history, the Buddha can be compared with
> only two historical individuals: Jesus and Muhammad, the founders of Chris-
> tianity and Islam. As with Jesus and Muhammad, little is known of the early life
> of the Buddha, but in his later years as a teacher he stands out as one of the first
> figures ever to be recorded in history as a real, recognizable human personality
> rather than as a two-dimensional character in a mythologized narrative. In this
> sense, he is comparable to the Greek philosopher Socrates (fifth century
> B.C.E.) and to some of the figures in the *Hebrew Bible* or *Old Testament*.[80]

The man who became the Buddha was born in the village of Lumbini, in
what is today southern Nepal, and the most common dates for his life are from
563 to 483 B.C.E. (although Chinese sources give the significantly later dates of
roughly from 445 to 365 B.C.E.).[81] His name was Siddhartha Gotama (also

commonly written Gautama) and, as a prince, he was born into a life of privilege and comfort. He was a sensitive youth, concerned about human suffering around him, and so gave up his privileged life to become a wandering "seeker of truth." He studied meditation, and ultimately, at age thirty-five, achieved what is known in Buddhism as the "Great Enlightenment" one night while sitting under the Bodhi tree (the "tree of enlightenment").[82] The "awakening" achieved by the Buddha, which can be achieved by others as well, is both difficult to attain and to describe. As Reat noted, "Buddhist doctrine emphasizes that the specific content of the Buddha's experience on the night of enlightenment—or the equivalent experience of an *arahat* [one who has achieved the awakening]—can never be conveyed by mere words."[83] In general terms, however, the Buddha is said to have experienced what are called the "three knowledges": "remembrance of his past rebirths in detail, ability to discern the past and future rebirths of other beings, and knowledge that he himself was free of all faults and illusions and would therefore never be reborn again. The 'third knowledge' is synonymous with the realization of nirvana."[84]

Although originating in India, Buddhism spread through Asia and has come to be identified more with other countries than with India itself. Buddhism remains the dominant religious tradition in Tibet, Sri Lanka, and Thailand, and has had a powerful impact both culturally and religiously in a number of other societies, including those of China, Korea, and Japan.[85] There are, as a consequence, many varieties and forms of Buddhism that co-exist, both with each other and with other religious traditions.[86] As Malcolm Eckel noted:

> If you have never thought of religion without thinking of God, or if you think that a religion has to have clear boundaries that separate insiders from outsiders, you will be intrigued and challenged by your encounter with Buddhism. For over two thousand years in Asia, and more recently in Europe and North America, the Buddhist tradition has brought joy, consolation, and meaning to human life without affirming the existence of a personal God, and it has found ways to exist side by side with other religious traditions without many of the great conflicts that have plagued religious life in the West.[87]

We turn now to an exploration of this intriguing and challenging religious tradition, focusing on the two major streams of Buddhism, *Theravada* and *Mahayana Buddhism*, and then moving on to a discussion of traditional Buddhist educational thought and practice.

AN OVERVIEW OF BUDDHISM

The core of Buddhism is expressed in what is called the *Triple Refuge* (*trisharana*), which is the basic "profession of faith" for the Buddhist. Every Buddhist recites the Triple Refuge (which is also sometimes called the *Three*

Jewels or the *Three Treasures*) daily, and one becomes a Buddhist by reciting it three times. The Triple Refuge is as follows: "I go to refuge to the Buddha; I go for refuge to the Doctrine (*Dharma*); I go for refuge to the community (*Sangha*)."[88] Included in the Triple Refuge, then, are the place of the Buddha himself, the place of his teachings, and the role of the Buddhist community. We have already briefly discussed the Buddha, and so we now turn to the teachings of Buddhism.

Buddhism is, at its core, arguably less concerned with metaphysical and theological matters than with psychological ones.[89] The teachings of the Buddha are all basically concerned with human suffering and achieving freedom from that suffering.[90] Summarized in the Four Noble Truths, which are common to all of the different types of Buddhism, the teachings of the Buddha include the following ideas:

- Human life inevitably involves suffering (*dukkha*).
- Suffering arises from our desires (*samudaya*).
- There is a state of being in which there is no suffering (*nirodha*).
- There is a way to achieve this state of being (*marga*).[91]

The way to achieve this state of being free from suffering is a systematic approach taught by the Buddha called the *Eightfold Path of Liberation*. As Mary Pat Fisher explained, "The Eightfold Path offers ways to burn up all past demerits, avoid accumulating new demerits, and build up merit for a favorable rebirth. Perfection of the path means final escape from the cycle of death and rebirth, into the peace of Nirvana."[92] The eight factors that comprise the Eightfold Path can be divided into three broad categories (known as *khandha*, or *pillars*), dealing respectively with wisdom (*panna*), ethics (*sila*), and meditation (*samadhi*).[93] The particular factors included in each of these three broad categories are discussed briefly next.

Wisdom

The factors included in this category include right understanding (*sammaditthi*) and right intention (*samma-sankappa*). Right understanding refers to making sense of the world and questioning one's assumptions, within the framework provided by the Four Noble Truths. Right intention in essence involves the application of right understanding in one's life, and constitutes the core of Buddhist morality. Specifically, right intention includes renunciation (*nekkhama*), benevolence (*avyapada*), and nonviolence (*avihimsa*).[94]

Ethics

This category is concerned with conduct and the rules that underlie appropriate conduct. Taken as a whole, they seek to ensure that one's conduct is harmful neither to oneself nor to others. Specifically, the factors included here are right speech (*samma-vacha*), right action (*samma-kammanta*), and right livelihood (*samma-ajiva*). Right speech focuses on the need to avoid gossip, lying, slander, and other kinds of idle or hurtful language. Right action involves what are known as the Five Precepts (*sikkha-pada*) in Buddhism, which include the avoidance of violence toward any living thing, stealing, harmful speech, sexual misconduct, and abuse of drugs and alcohol.[95] Right livelihood refers to the need to ensure that one's way of earning a living in no way violates any of the Five Precepts.[96]

Meditation

The final three factors in the Eightfold Path are right effort (*samma-yayama*), right self-possession or mindfulness (*samma-sati*), and right meditation (*samma-samadhi*). These three factors are all very closely related, and basically involved "the cultivation of the wholesome (*kusala*) and rejection of the unwholesome (*akusala*)." They involve continuous striving to reject unwholesome states of mind, and to develop the mental quietness that leads to liberation.[97]

The ultimate goal of the Eightfold Path, as suggested here, is to avoid the ongoing cycle of death and rebirth, and to achieve Nirvana. This is done by leading a passion-free existence that has no karmic consequences, as is suggested by the term *Nirvana* itself, which actually refers to "the extinguishing of a flame from lack of fuel."[98]

For Westerners, one of the more puzzling aspects of Buddhism is its lack of concern for or interest in a personal God. Melford Spiro, for example, in his book *Buddhism and Society*, commented that "Buddhism is a religion without a God. Just as the body has no soul which guides and directs its action, so the universe has no Creator who brought it into being, who guides its course, or who presides over the destiny of man. More important, there is no Being—no savior God—to whom man can turn for salvation. Each man, as it were, must save himself."[99]

It is important to note that the Buddha did not actually deny the existence of God. Rather, the Buddha argued that "curiosity about such matters was like a man who, upon being wounded by a poisoned arrow, refused to have it pulled out until he was told the caste and origin of his assailant, his name, his height, the color of his skin, and all details about the bow and arrow. In the meantime, he died."[100] In other words, for Buddhism "speculations concerning the origin of the Universe are held to be immaterial. . . . They are not merely a waste of time but they may also postpone deliverance from suffering by engendering ill-will in oneself and in others."[101] In short, Buddhism is best understood simply as a "nontheistic" religion that does not, like other religions, presuppose the existence of a personal God.[102] Furthermore, although the monotheistic religions with which most of us are most familiar identify God with supreme good, for Buddhism it is emptiness (i.e., the absence of both good and evil) that is the ultimate goal.[103] As Masao Abe explained:

> [Buddhism] overcomes all duality completely and attains a nondualistic position. This means that both ends of duality, for instance good and evil, are equally overcome through the double negation of the two ends—i.e., good and evil. This double negation of both ends of duality does not entail the supreme good, but that which is neither good nor evil. This is the reason why in Buddhism ultimate reality is not God as the supreme good, but Emptiness, which is neither good nor evil. . . . Buddhism *completely* overcomes the duality of value judgment in the axiological dimension through the negation of negation, and thus reaches the religious dimension, which is entirely free from even the notion of absolute good.[104]

For the most part, the beliefs discussed thus far are common to all Buddhists. Within Buddhism, however, there coexist a number of different schools of thought. The two most important of these schools of thought are those of Theravada Buddhism and Mahayana Buddhism. The distinction between Theravada Buddhism and Mahayana Buddhism is one of both geography and emphasis. *Theravada Buddhism*, which emphasizes the original Buddhist scriptural tradition (hence its name, which means "Teaching of the Elders"), is sometimes called the Southern School because it is found primarily in the south Asian countries (Sri Lanka, Myanmar, Thailand, Kampuchea, and Laos). *Mahayana Buddhism* is, on the other hand, known as the Northern School, and is the kind of Buddhism found in Nepal, Tibet, China, Korea, Mongolia, and Japan. Theravada Buddhism is a somewhat more austere kind of Buddhism and involves an emphasis not only on the early Buddhist scriptures, but also on the monastic life, whereas Mahayana Buddhism accepts a wider variety of scriptural traditions and gives greater freedom in terms of devotional and metaphysical beliefs and practices than does Theravada Buddhism, which tends to be more uniform.[105] At heart, however, there is an essential unity in Buddhism, as Edward Conze explained:

> Throughout its history, Buddhism has the unity of an *organism*, in that each new development takes place in continuity from the previous one. Nothing could look more different from a tadpole than a frog, and yet they are stages of the same animal, and evolve continuously from each other. The Buddhist ca-

pacity for metamorphosis must astound those who only see the end-products separated by long intervals of time, as different as chrysalis and butterfly. In fact they are connected by many gradations, which lead from one to the other, and which only close study can detect. There is in Buddhism really no innovation, but what seems so is in fact a subtle adaptation of pre-existing ideas.[106]

This essential unity includes not only Theravada Buddhism and Mahayana Buddhism, but also Tibetan Buddhism (which is actually a distinctive branch of Mahayana Buddhism) and Zen Buddhism, as well as the many different varieties of each that have developed in different social and cultural contexts.[107] With this brief introduction to Buddhism in mind, we turn now to a discussion of the educational thought and practice associated with Buddhism.

HISTORICAL BUDDHIST EDUCATIONAL THOUGHT AND PRACTICE

Education in traditional Buddhism, at least in a formal sense, existed almost exclusively within the context of the monastery, both in terms of secular and religious education. As Radha Mookerji noted in *Ancient Indian Education*:

> The history of the Buddhist system of education is practically that of the Buddhist Order or *Sangha*. Buddhist education and learning centred round monasteries. . . . The Buddhist world did not offer any educational opportunities apart from or independently of its monasteries. All education, sacred as well as secular, was in the hands of the monks. They had the monopoly of learning and the leisure to impart it.[108]

In other words, our discussion of traditional Buddhist educational thought and practice brings us back to the final element of the Triple Refuge: the religious (i.e., monastic) community. Heinrich Dumoulin observed, "Taking refuge in the *sangha* is an essential co-condition of the other two refuges. From its beginnings, the Buddhist religion confronts us as a communal, and specifically as a monastic formation. . . . Though Buddhism has not yet developed a theology of community, it is clear that Buddhist faith has an essential communal dimension."[109]

The fact that traditional education was controlled by the *sangha*, however, in no way means that it was jealously guarded or hidden; indeed, quite the reverse is the case. Buddhist monasteries are not separate from the surrounding world. Rather, they are closely tied to the surrounding community in a sort of symbiotic relationship, and monasteries are commonly the center of village life.[110] Furthermore, at least in Theravadin societies, it is quite common for young men to take what are essentially temporary vows of monkhood (during, e.g., the rainy season when they are not required for agricultural work).[111]

A number of general themes characterized traditional Buddhist educational practice. Traditional Buddhist education was based on the close, intimate relationship that existed between the student and his teacher, whom he was to serve in much the same way as was expected in Vedic education. The relationship between student and teacher was a reciprocal one, however, and although the obligations of the student to the teacher were substantial, so too were the obligations of the teacher to the student.[112] All students observed the two fundamental principles that demarcate monastic life from that of the laity: celibacy and poverty.[113] Instruction was primarily oral, and was based on a knowledge of the Buddhist scriptural tradition, although an introduction to basic literacy was also provided.

The focus of education was on far more than mere memorization of texts, however. Debate played a central role in the educational process in traditional Buddhism. As Mookerji argued, "Buddhist education made dialectic skill and ability in argumentation a most important part of intellectual equipment essential to leadership."[114] The importance of such skill is made clear in a number of written texts in the Buddhist tradition, one of which, composed around the year 400 C.E., contains a detailed discussion of the subject of debate, the place in which debate should take place, the means by which a debate should be conducted, the qualifications of the debaters, the points of defeat in a debate, the fitness or appropriateness of a debate, and finally, the need for self-confidence in the debater.[115] It is interesting to note here that in a comparative study of traditional and contemporary education in Tibet, David Eckel observed:

> In the traditional monastery, even with its emphasis on memorization and rote learning, students were required from an early age to defend what they had learned in formal debate. The debating hall was a lonely place, where rank and authority were no help. A student or teacher had to be able to defend his understanding before the whole assembly. It is hard to picture a 12-year-old monk standing up in a doctoral examination to question a scholar more than twice his age and still think of the traditional system as fostering only the values of dependence and submission. The irony of the Tibetan transition to modern styles of education is that it endangers not only the sense of dependence and respect for tradition, but the formal means for developing a sense of self-reliance and autonomy.[116]

Traditional Buddhist education, in short, involved what would today be called basic schooling for young boys, as well as more advanced education for monks (including a noteworthy university level educational system, as we shall see).[117] For the most part, it did not concern itself with the educational needs of girls and women and, although there were notable exceptions (including female monasteries where women were indeed well educated), traditional Buddhism paid relatively little attention to females' education.[118]

HIGHER EDUCATION IN ANCIENT INDIA

What we would today call university education, or at least something roughly equivalent to our understanding of higher education, existed in ancient India at least as early as the 7th century B.C.E. and probably much earlier. Indeed, by the 7th century B.C.E., Taxila (Takshasila) had already achieved considerable fame as a center of advanced learning. It drew scholars and students from throughout India, and was familiar to Greeks from the time of Alexander the Great.[119] Taxila never existed as a single institution in the way a modern university does; rather, it was an educational center where scholars and students met, studied, and interacted. Individuals could study a wide range of disciplines, among them medicine (and surgery), archery and the military arts, the Vedas and Vendanta philosophy, grammar, astronomy and astrology, accounting, commerce, agriculture, music, dancing, painting, magic, snake-charming, and even elephant-lore.[120]

Another well-known center of higher education in ancient India was Banaras, a seat of both Hindu and Buddhist learning that, like Taxila, consisted not of a single institution but rather functioned as an informal collection of masters, each teaching his own students. Banaras was described by one European visitor as the "Athens of India," which gives one some sense of its intellectual vitality. Unlike Taxila, which ceased functioning as an educational center around the 3rd century C.E., Banaras continued to be a significant intellectual center, and was in fact the center of the 16th- and 17th-century Hindu intellectual revival in northern India.[121]

Although there was extensive overlap between Hindu and Buddhist higher education and a great deal of intellectual and scholarly interaction that enriched both traditions, particular settings tended to be dominated by one or the other religion.[122] The most famous of the Buddhist centers of higher education in ancient India was Nalanda, which was founded at some point in mid-5th century C.E. Nalanda was, unlike Taxila and Banaras, a single complex institution that consisted of a large campus, including large public halls for lectures, smaller classrooms, and a number of monasteries that functioned as dormitories for the students studying at Nalanda. The university also possessed three large libraries and an astronomical observatory. An intellectual stronghold for Mahayana Buddhism, the university curriculum included the Vedas, the Upanishads, Jainism, grammar, logic, metaphysics, and literature, and drew students and teachers from throughout southeast Asia. At its peak, the university had some 8,500 students and 1,500 teachers, and, perhaps most interestingly, "out of the income derived from its estates the

University provided all its students with clothes, food, bedding and medi-cines."[123]

CONCLUSIONS

Given the highly decentralized nature of Buddhist institutions, as well as the tolerance for diversity within the Buddhist tradition, it is hardly surprising that traditional Buddhist education took somewhat different forms in differ-ent Buddhist societies. What is remarkable is the degree of uniformity that in fact seems to have existed on a number of important points. Perhaps most in-teresting in this regard is the role of the monastery as the sole educational in-stitution in Buddhist societies and the reliance on the monasteries for both secular and religious education.[124] Also of significance here has been the em-phasis on the individual teacher and the relationship between the teacher and the student—an emphasis that is to some extent indicated in the *Dham-mapada*, in which we read the prescription that, "An intelligent man attends on a wise person."[125] Furthermore, it is clear that traditional Buddhist educa-tional thought and practice had a powerful impact on the societies in which they existed, in many instances providing a cultural and intellectual base for the society concerned. This was, for instance, the case in Japan, as B. H. Chamberlain noted: "All education was for centuries in Buddhist hands, Bud-dhism introduced art, introduced medicine, moulded the folklore of the country, created its dramatic poetry, deeply influenced politics and every sphere of social and intellectual activity. In a word, Buddhism was the teacher under whose instruction the nation grew up."[126]

In short, traditional Buddhist educational thought and practice served a wide array of social, cultural, and spiritual functions as well as educational ones successfully, and did so in ways generally accepted in various Buddhist societies for centuries. This alone would merit our attention.

QUESTIONS FOR REFLECTION AND DISCUSSION

1. Given your understanding of the difference between *schooling* and *edu-cation*, do you think the traditional Hindu educational practice of placing stu-dents in the homes of their teachers, where they become essentially part of the teacher's household, is an example of *schooling* or *education*? Why?

2. To a very great extent, the whole point of Hindu education is spiritual. What are the advantages of such a focus in education? What are the disadvan-tages? How does this emphasis on spirituality differ from the approaches to education found in contemporary American society?

3. It was suggested in this chapter that an oral tradition played an important role in traditional Hindu educational thought and practice, and yet, the Hindu tradition is very much text based. How can this seeming contradiction be reconciled?

4. The six "methods of knowing" discussed in this chapter provide us with an understanding of Hindu epistemology. In what ways, and to what extent, do these "methods of knowing" differ from the "scientific method"?

5. Traditional Hindu education is based on the student's progress through three stages: *shravana*, *manana*, and *nididhyasana*. Are these stages reflected at all in contemporary American public schooling? What lessons can be learned by considering these stages as we examine public schooling in our society?

6. The role of the *sangha* in traditional Buddhist education presents an interesting parallel to that of the monastery in medieval Europe. In what ways are the educational undertakings of these two kinds of religious communities similar, and in what ways do they differ? How can the similarities, and the differences, be explained?

7. Explain the educational significance of each of the three components of the Triple Refuge. How do these three components relate to one another, and what are the social and educational implications of these relations?

8. If the spiritual goal of Buddhism is "emptiness," then what purpose does education serve? Why is education needed in the quest for Nirvana?

9. Given your own understanding of *religion*, was traditional Buddhist education a religious education? Was it a spiritual education? What, in your view, is the difference between these two kinds of education?

10. What, in your view, were the strengths of traditional Buddhist education? What were its weaknesses? Can you identify any lessons from the study of traditional Buddhist education for contemporary schooling in our own society?

RECOMMENDED FURTHER READINGS

In terms of general introductions to Hinduism, some of the better works currently available are Gavin Flood, *An Introduction to Hinduism* (Cambridge, England: Cambridge University Press, 1996); Stephen Cross, *The Elements of Hinduism* (Shaftsbury, England: Element, 1994); A. L. Herman, *A Brief Introduction to Hinduism: Religion, Philosophy, and Ways of Liberation* (Boulder, CO: Westview, 1991); and Ed Viswanathan, *Am I a Hindu? The Hinduism Primer* (San Francisco: Halo Books, 1992). Among the Hindu texts available in translation are Juan Mascaró, trans., *The Upanishads* (Harmondsworth,

England: Penguin, 1965); Wendy Doniger O'Flaherty, trans., *The Rig Veda: An Anthology* (Harmondsworth, England: Penguin, 1981); and S. Radhkrishnan (ed.), *The Principal Upanishads* (New Delhi: Indus, 1994). In addition, the *Bhagavad Gita*, which is considered to be one of the more accessible and readable Hindu texts, is widely available in a number of translations. Also very useful is Arvind Sharma, *Classical Hindu Thought: An Introduction* (New Delhi: Oxford University Press, 2000). A very readable collection of short essays on contemporary Hinduism is provided in Eleanor Zelliot and Maxine Bernsten (eds.), *The Experience of Hinduism* (Albany: State University of New York Press, 1988).

Among the better general introductions to Buddhism that are readily available are Huston Smith and Philip Novak, *Buddhism: A Concise Introduction* (New York: HarperSanFrancisco, 2003); Steven Heine and Chalres Prebish (eds.), *Buddhism in the Modern World: Adaptation of an Ancient Tradition* (Oxford, England: Oxford University Press, 2002); Thich Nhat Hanh, *The Heart of the Buddha's Teaching* (New York: Broadway Books, 1998); Malcoln Eckel, *Buddhism* (Oxford, England: Oxford University Press, 2002); Heinrich Dumoulin, *Understanding Buddhism: Key Themes* (New York: Weatherhill, 1994); Nolan Pliny Jacobson, *Understanding Buddhism* (Carbondale: Southern Illinois University Press, 1986); and Nancy Wilson Ross, *Buddhism: A Way of Life and Thought* (New York: Vintage, 1980). An especially powerful contemporary work is Thich Nhat Hanh's *Old Path White Clouds: Walking in the Footsteps of the Buddah* (Berkeley, CA: Parallax, 1991). Also of considerable value is Eric Cheetham, *Fundamentals of Mainstream Buddhism* (Boston: Charles E. Tuttle, 1994). For an interesting and insightful personal account, see Tenzin Gyatso, *Freedom in Exile: The Autobiography of the Dalai Lama* (New York: Harper Perennial, 1990). Finally, there is a plethora of works readily available that deal explicitly with Zen Buddhism. Good basic introductions to Zen Buddhism include Kazuaki Tanahashi and Tensho David Schneider, *Essential Zen* (San Francisco: HarperCollins, 1994); David Scott and Tony Doubleday, *The Elements of Zen* (Shaftesbury, England: Element, 1992); and Thich Thien-An, *Zen Philosophy, Zen Practice* (Berkeley, CA: Dharma Publishing, 1975).

NOTES

1. See Harold G. Coward (ed.), *Modern Indian Responses to Religious Pluralism* (Albany: State University of New York Press, 1987); Friedhelm Hardy, *The Religious Culture of India: Power, Love and Wisdom* (Cambridge, England: Cambridge University Press, 1994); Donald Lopez (ed.), *Religions of India in Practice* (Princeton, NJ: Princeton University Press, 1995). Although Jainism is not discussed in this book, it is a fascinating religious tradition well worth examination. See Subramania Gopalan,

Outlines of Jainism (New York: Halsted, 1973); Paul Dundas, *The Jains* (London: Routledge, 1992); Caroline Humphrey and James Laidlaw, *The Archetypal Actions of Ritual: A Theory of Ritual Illustrated by the Jain Rite of Worshop* (Oxford, England: Clarendon, 1994).

2. Klaus Klostermaier, *A Survey of Hinduism* (Albany: State University of New York Press, 1989), 30–31; Madeleine Biardeau, *L'Hindouisme: Anthropologie d'une civilization* (Paris: Flammarion, 1981).

3. Mary Pat Fisher, *Living Religions,* 2nd ed. (Englewood Cliffs, NJ: Prentice-Hall, 1994), 64–66.

4. Klostermaier noted that "the very name *Hinduism* owes its origin to chance; foreigners . . . extended the name of the province of Sindh to the whole country lying across the Indus river and simply called all its inhabitants *Hindus* and their religion *Hinduism.*" See Klostermaier, *A Survey of Hinduism,* 31.

5. Klostermaier, *A Survey of Hinduism,* 31; see also Arvind Sharma, "Hinduism," in Arvind Sharma (ed.), *Our Religions: The Seven World Religions Introduced by Pre-eminent Scholars from Each Tradition* (San Francisco: Harper, 1993), 36–38; Robert C. Zaehner, *Hinduism* (London: Oxford University Press, 1962), 19–22; David Knipe, *Hinduism* (San Francisco: Harper, 1991), 17–25; K. M. Sen, *Hinduism* (Harmondsworth: Penguin, 1961), 17–21; David Kinsley, *Hinduism: A Cultural Perspective,* 2nd ed. (Englewood Cliffs, NJ: Prentice-Hall, 1993), 11–25.

6. Klostermaier, *A Survey of Hinduism,* 45.

7. Fisher, *Living Religions,* 62; Zaehner, *Hinduism,* 2–4. Especially useful here is Gavin Flood, *An Introduction to Hinduism* (Cambridge, England: Cambridge University Press, 1996), 51–74.

8. Klostermaier, *A Survey of Hinduism,* 31.

9. Fisher, *Living Religions,* 62.

10. Troy Organ, *The Hindu Quest for the Perfection of Man* (Athens, OH: Ohio University Press, 1970), 4.

11. Stephen Cross, *The Elements of Hinduism* (Shaftesbury, Dorset: Element, 1994), 3. See also A. K. Banerjee, *Discourses on Hindu Spiritual Culture* (Delhi: S. Chand & Co., 1967), 3–4.

12. David Kinsley, *Hinduism: A Cultural Perspective,* 2nd ed. (Englewood Cliffs, NJ: Prentice-Hall, 1993), 6.

13. Klostermaier, *A Survey of Hinduism,* 40–41.

14. Sharma, "Hinduism," 6.

15. Sharma, "Hinduism," 7–11.

16. Sharma, "Hinduism," 11.

17. Cross, *The Elements of Hinduism,* 3–4; see also Sharma, "Hinduism," 26–27.

18. Klostermaier, *A Survey of Hinduism,* 61.

19. Zaehner, *Hinduism,* 11–13.

20. Fisher, *Living Religions,* 66.

21. Colin Renfrew, *Archaeology and Language: The Puzzle of Indo-European Origins* (Cambridge, England: Cambridge University Press, 1987), 178–183.

22. Klostermaier, *A Survey of Hinduism,* 26; Cross, *The Elements of Hinduism,* 16–17.

23. Klostermaier, *A Survey of Hinduism*, 26; Cross, *The Elements of Hinduism*, 17.

24. Klostermaier, *A Survey of Hinduism*, 27; Sharma, "Hinduism," 26–27.

25. Sharma, "Hinduism," 27.

26. There is actually a third level of Hindu scripture as well, called *Itihasas*, which is essentially histories of individuals who, by virtue of the sanctity of their lives, have come to be seen as incarnations of God. Two works in particular are generally classified as *Itihasas*: the *Ramayana* ("The Deeds of Rama") and the *Mahabharata*, of which the *Bhagavadgita* is a part. See Sharma, "Hinduism," 29–30.

27. Sharma, "Hinduism," 27.

28. Sharma, "Hinduism," 27.

29. Klostermaier, *A Survey of Hinduism*, 67.

30. Gerald Larson, "Hinduism in India and in America," in Jacob Neusner (ed.), *World Religions in America* (Louisville, KY: Westminster/John Knox Press, 1994), 185–186.

31. Zaehner, *Hinduism*, 15–16.

32. Cross, *The Elements of Hinduism*, 12.

33. Victoria Fromkin and Robert Rodman, *An Introduction to Language*, 2nd ed. (New York: Holt, Rinehart and Winston, 1978), 295–296; Leonard Bloomfield, "Language," in Oscar L. Chavarria-Aguilar (ed.), *Traditional India* (Englewood Cliffs, NJ: Prentice-Hall, 1964), 112–113; Robert H. Robins, *A Short History of Linguistics*, 2nd ed. (London: Longman, 1979), 134–135. Also of interest here is Winfred Lehmann, *Theoretical Bases of Indo-European Linguistics* (London: Routledge, 1993).

34. Quoted in Renfrew, *Archaeology and Language*, 9.

35. Quoted in Larson, "Hinduism in India and in America," 197. For an extensive presentation of contemporary Hindu beliefs, see Satguru Sivaya Subramuniyaswami, *Dancing with Siva: Hinduism's Contemporary Catechism* (Concord, CA: Himalayan Academy, 1993); also of interest here is Bansi Pandit, *The Hindu Mind: Fundamentals of Hindu Religion and Philosophy for All Ages*, 2nd ed. (Glen Ellyn, IL: B & V Enterprises, 1993).

36. Fisher, *Living Religions*, 68; Cross, *The Elements of Hinduism*, 15–16; Biardeau, *L'Hindouisme*.

37. Cross, *The Elements of Hinduism*, 16; see also Sen, *Hinduism*, 27–31.

38. Cross, *The Elements of Hinduism*, 16; see also Sen, *Hinduism*, 27–31.

39. Cross, *The Elements of Hinduism*, 16; see also Sen, *Hinduism*, 27–31.

40. Larson, "Hinduism in India and in America," 189; Sharma, "Hinduism," 24; Biardeau, *L'Hindouisme*.

41. Larson, "Hinduism in India and in America," 189; Sharma, "Hinduism," 24; Biardeau, *L'Hindouisme*; Kinsley, *Hinduism: A Cultural Perspective*, 84–96.

42. Larson, "Hinduism in India and in America," 189. See also Patrick Olivelle, *The Ashrama System: The History and Heurmeneutics of a Religious Institution* (New York: Oxford University Press, 1993).

43. See Organ, *The Hindu Quest for the Perfection of Man*.

44. Organ, *The Hindu Quest for the Perfection of Man*, 173.

45. Organ, *The Hindu Quest for the Perfection of Man*, 47.

46. Klostermaier, *A Survey of Hinduism*, 69–70.

47. Organ, *The Hindu Quest for the Perfection of Man*, 47.

48. Organ, *The Hindu Quest for the Perfection of Man*, 48.

49. Organ, *The Hindu Quest for the Perfection of Man*, 48–49.

50. Klostermaier, *A Survey of Hinduism*, 69–70.

51. Organ, *The Hindu Quest for the Perfection of Man*, 49.

52. Organ, *The Hindu Quest for the Perfection of Man*, 49.

53. Organ, *The Hindu Quest for the Perfection of Man*, 50.

54. Radha Mookerji, *Ancient Indian Education* (Delhi: Motilal Banarsidass, 1969), xxiii; see also Suresh Chandra Ghosh, *The History of Education in Ancient India, c. 3000 B.C. to A.D. 1192* (New Delhi: Munshiram Manoharlal Publishers, 2001).

55. Mookerji, *Ancient Indian Education*, xxiii–xxiv.

56. Mookerji, *Ancient Indian Education*, xxiii–xxiv.

57. Mookerji, *Ancient Indian Education*, xxxi–xxxiii.

58. Benjamin Walker, *The Hindu World: An Encyclopedic Survey of Hinduism*, vol. 1 (New York: Praeger, 1968), 320.

59. Sures Banerji, *Society in Ancient India: Evolution Since the Vedic Times Based on Sanskrit, Pali, Prakrit and Other Classical Sources* (New Delhi: D. K. Printworld, 1993), 228–229.

60. For discussions of the role and place of women in Hindu society, see Julia Leslie (ed.), *Roles and Rituals for Hindu Women* (Rutherford, NJ: Fairleigh Dickinson University Press, 1991). Also of interest here are Christopher J. Fuller, *The Camphor Flame: Popular Hinduism and Society in India* (Princeton, NJ: Princeton University Press, 1992), 182–203; Arthur L. Basham, *The Origins and Development of Classical Hinduism* (Boston: Beacon Press, 1989), 104–106.

61. Walker, *The Hindu World*, 320; Mookerji, *Ancient Indian Education*, 173.

62. Mookerji, *Ancient Indian Education*, 174–175, see also David Miller and Dorothy Wertz, *Hindu Monastic Life and the Monks and Monasteries of Bhubaneswar* (Montréal: McGill-Queen's University Press, 1976), 3.

63. Walker, *The Hindu World*, 320–321.

64. Walker, *The Hindu World*, 321.

65. Walker, *The Hindu World*, 321.

66. Walker, *The Hindu World*, 321.

67. Mookerji, *Ancient Indian Education*, 366.

68. See Mookerji, *Ancient Indian Education*, 366–373; Walker, *The Hindu World*, 322.

69. H. C. Khare, "Vedic Mathematics," in H. C. Khare (ed.), *Issues in Vedic Mathematics* (Delhi: Motilal Banarsidass Publishers, 1991), 13.

70. See J. L. Bansal, "Leading Mathematicians of Ancient India," in H. C. Khare (ed.), *Issues in Vedic Mathematics* (Delhi: Motilal Banarsidass Publishers, 1991), 79–81; S. A. Paramhans, "Glimpse of Mathematical Heritage of Ancient India and Its Transmission to Other Countries," in H. C. Khare (ed.), *Issues in Vedic Mathematics* (Delhi: Motilal Banarsidass Publishers, 1991), 105–116.

71. See Narendra Puri, "An Overview of Vedic Mathematics," in H. C. Khare (ed.), *Issues in Vedic Mathematics* (Delhi: Motilal Banarsidass Publishers, 1991),

41–59; Narinder Puri, *Higher Applications of Vedic Mathematics* (Bareilly, India: Prakash Book Depot, 1992).

72. See S. N. Pandey, "Vedic Mathematics: An Appraisal from the Perspective of Modern Mathematics," in H. C. Khare (ed.), *Issues in Vedic Mathematics* (Delhi: Motilal Banarsidass Publishers, 1991), 103–104.

73. Khare, "Vedic Mathematics," 16.

74. Puri, "An Overview of Vedic Mathematics," 41.

75. Pandey, "Vedic Mathematics," 104.

76. See Sushila Raval, *Basic Education in Modern India: A Critique of Gandhian Educational Philosophy* (M.A. thesis, The American University, Washington, D.C., 1958), 2–8.

77. William T. de Bary (ed.), *The Buddhist Tradition in India, China and Japan* (New York: Modern Library, 1969), 3; see also Donald Lopez, *The Story of Buddhism: A Concise Guide to Its History and Future* (New York: HarperSanFrancisco, 2001); Donald Mitchell, *Buddhism: Introducing the Buddhist Experience* (Oxford, England: Oxford University Press, 2002).

78. See, e.g., Amamda Coomaraswamy, *Hinduism and Buddhism* (Westport, CT: Greenwood, 1971); Roderick Hindery, *Comparative Ethics in Hindu and Buddhist Traditions* (Delhi: Motilal Banarsidass, 1978); Pandit, *The Hindu Mind*, 85–86.

79. Coomaraswamy, *Hinduism and Buddhism*, 45.

80. Noble Ross Reat, *Buddhism: A History* (Berkeley, CA: Asian Humanities Press, 1994), 1.

81. Reat, *Buddhism*, 1–2; see also Fisher, *Living Religions*, 113.

82. See David Kalupahana, *A History of Buddhist Philosophy: Continuities and Discontinuities* (Honolulu: University of Hawaii Press, 1992), 22–29; Fisher, *Living Religions*, 114.

83. Reat, *Buddhism*, 12.

84. Reat, *Buddhism*, 12.

85. Malcolm Eckel, "Buddhism in the World and in America," in Jacob Neusner (ed.), *World Religions in America: An Introduction* (Louisville, KY: Westminster/John Knox Press, 1994), 203; see also Richard Seager, *Buddhism in America* (New York: Columbia University Press, 1999).

86. See John Snelling, *The Buddhist Handbook: A Complete Guide to Buddhist Schools, Teaching, Practice, and History* (Rochester, VT: Inner Traditions, 1991), 103–189; Masao Abe, "Buddhism," in Arvind Sharma (ed.), *Our Religions* (San Francisco: Harper, 1993), 85–100.

87. Eckel, "Buddhism in the World and in America," 203.

88. Abe, "Buddhism," 73–74.

89. De Bary, *The Buddhist Tradition in India, China and Japan*, 9.

90. Melford Spiro, *Buddhism and Society* (New York: Harper & Row, 1970), 38–39; see also Hindery, *Comparative Ethics in Hindu and Buddhist Traditions*, 226–228; Mary Tucker and Duncan Williams (eds.), *Buddhism and Ecology: The Interconnection of Dharma and Deeds* (Cambridge, MA: Harvard University Press, 1977).

91. Fisher, *Living Religions*, 116; Abe, "Buddhism," 86; Heinrich Dumoulin, *Understanding Buddhism: Key Themes* (New York: Weatherhill, 1994), 21–24; Snelling, *The Buddhist Handbook*, 43–46.

92. Fisher, *Living Religions*, ; Hardy, *The Religious Culture of India*, 179.

93. Reat, *Buddhism*, 40; see also Anthony K. Warder, *Indian Buddhism* (Delhi: Motilal Banarsidass, 1970), 100–106.

94. Reat, *Buddhism*, 40–41; Fisher, *Living Religions*, 117–118.

95. See Edward Conze, trans., *Buddhist Scriptures* (Harmondsworth, England: Penguin, 1959), 69–73.

96. Reat, *Buddhism*, 41–42; Fisher, *Living Religions*, 117.

97. Reat, *Buddhism*, 42; Fisher, *Living Religions*, 118–119.

98. Fisher, *Living Religions*, 120.

99. Spiro, *Buddhism and Society*, 7.

100. Fisher, *Living Religions*, 115.

101. Edward Conze, *Buddhism: Its Essence and Development* (New York: Harper & Row, 1975), 39.

102. Eckel, "Buddhism in the World and in America," 212.

103. The doctrine of emptiness (*sunyata*) is a very important one in Buddhist thought. In actuality, there are two distinct theories of emptiness in Buddhism, a moderate view and a more extreme view. See Kalupahana, *A History of Buddhist Philosophy*, 130–131; Reat, *Buddhism*, 56–58; Conze, *Buddhism*, 130–135.

104. Abe, "Buddhism," 119.

105. For discussions of the distinctions between Theravada Buddhism and Mahayana Buddhism, see de Bary, *The Buddhist Tradition in India, China and Japan*; Christmas Humphreys, *Buddhism: An Introduction and Guide* (Harmondsworth, England: Penguin, 1951).

106. Edward Conze, *A Short History of Buddhism* (Bombay: Chetana, 1960), xi–xii.

107. For Tibetan Buddhism, see Emil Schlagintweit, *Buddhism in Tibet*, 2nd ed. (London: Susil Gupta, 1968). For works that deal with Zen Buddhism, see David Scott and Tony Doubleday, *The Elements of Zen* (Shaftesbury, England: Element, 1992); Daisetz Teitaro Suzuki, *An Introduction to Zen Buddhism* (New York: Philosophical Library, 1949); Trevor Leggett (ed.), *Zen and the Ways* (London: Routledge & Kegan Paul, 1978); Kenneth Kraft (ed.), *Zen: Tradition and Transition* (New York: Grove, 1988); Christopher Ives, *Zen Awakening and Society* (Honolulu: University of Hawaii Press, 1992).

108. Mookerji, *Ancient Indian Education*, 394.

109. Dumoulin, *Understanding Buddhism*, 56–57.

110. Abe, "Buddhism," 110.

111. Fisher, *Living Religions*, 123.

112. Mookerji, *Ancient Indian Education*, 403–405.

113. Mookerji, *Ancient Indian Education*, 409–412.

114. Mookerji, *Ancient Indian Education*, 454.

115. Mookerji, *Ancient Indian Education*, 454.

116. Quoted in Susan Pollak, *Ancient Buddhist Education (Papers from the Bernard Van Leer Foundation Project on Human Potential)* (Cambridge, MA: Harvard Graduate School of Education, 1983), 18. This publication, available through ERIC, is taken directly from Mookerji's earlier work.

117. Mookerji, *Ancient Indian Education*, 557–610.

118. Mookerji, *Ancient Indian Education*, 462–464. See also Diane Y. Paul, *Women in Buddhism: Images of the Feminine in the Mahayana Tradition* (Berkeley: University of California Press, 1985); Rita Gross, *Buddhism After Patriarchy: A Feminist History, Analysis and Reconstruction of Buddhism* (Albany: State University Press of New York, 1993); Lenore Friedman and Susan Moon (eds.), *Being Bodies: Buddhist Women on the Paradox of Embodiment* (Boston: Shambhala, 1997).

119. See Sunderrao R. Dongerkery, *University Education in India* (Bombay: Manaktalas, 1967), 2.

120. Dongerkery, *University Education in India*, 2.

121. Dongerkery, *University Education in India*, 2–3.

122. Dongerkery, *University Education in India*, 3.

123. Dongerkery, *University Education in India*, 4.

124. Pollak, *Ancient Buddhist Education*, 17.

125. Jaroslav Pelikan (ed.), *Sacred Writings, volume 6: Buddhism, The Dhammapada* (New York: Quality Paperback Book Club, 1987), 23.

126. Quoted in Pollak, *Ancient Buddhist Education*, 16–17; see also Alicia Matsunaga, *The Buddhist Philosophy of Assimilation: The Historical Development of the Honji-Suijaku Theory* (Tokyo: Sophia University, 1969).

8

"Familiar Strangers": The Case of the Rom

Gypsies are a part of our world and yet are distinct from the rest of us. They live in the world we know, yet they seem to offer an alternative way to be in our world. The Gypsy woman who appears on your doorstep sell-ing clothespins may be poor and dressed in threadbare clothes, but most likely she will have a style, a panache, and a charm denied to most of the rest of us. It is no accident that the question everyone wants answered about the Gypsies concerns their origins, since we have difficulty in plac-ing these outside-insiders, understanding where they come from. . . . There is always an ambivalence in our feelings toward the Gypsies. By their difference, they remind us of our ordinariness, and though their unruliness may lift us out of ourselves, at other times we resent it. Alter-nately, we find them attractive and threatening.

—Stewart (1997, p. 12)

Gypsies have, throughout modern history, been synonymous in many peo-ples' minds with colorfully painted caravans, exotic music and dance, trained animals, fortune-telling, and perhaps an enviably free "life on the road." They have also been the ultimate "Other," maintaining their own language, cus-toms, values, social norms, and ethnic identity in virtually every setting in which they have found themselves, and have all too commonly been seen as dishonest, immoral, criminal, and as a threat to society and "decent folk." As the "Other" in every society in which they live, they have often suffered, and continue to experience, persecution and oppression. Although there are ele-ments of truth in the popular characterizations and stereotypes of Gypsies, there are also serious distortions that mask the complexity and diversity of a fascinating and resilient people. In this chapter, an overview of the history and complexity of the Gypsy world is presented, its core cultural values ex-plored, and the way in which children in the community are raised and edu-cated is discussed.

A WORD ABOUT LABELS

Terminology presents some incredible challenges in this chapter. The people and communities with whom we are concerned share a common, distant origin in India. Their ancestors arrived in Europe around the 14th century C.E. and dispersed throughout the continent.[1] For the most part (although with some notable exceptions), they share a number of characteristics, including speaking varieties of a common language (Romani)[2] and, at least traditionally, often maintaining a nomadic lifestyle. They are also, importantly, not only distinct from but unrelated to other groups of nomadic peoples in Europe, such as the Tinkers in Ireland and Scotland and the Taters in Norway.[3]

The most common term to describe these people and communities historically has been "Gypsy" in English (roughly comparable to the use of *Tsigane* in French, *Ziguener* in German, *gitano* in Spanish, etc.). Although etymologically based on the mistaken notion that the Gypsies originated in Egypt, this term (which is also sometimes perceived to be pejorative) does have the advantage of emphasizing the commonality of an internally very diverse group and is widely used not only in the scholarly literature but also among many Gypsies themselves to refer to the generic communal group (indeed, there is no equivalent term in Romani itself for the entire Gypsy population, but rather only terminology for specific subgroups). However, some contemporary scholars and political activists have strongly argued for the use of the term *Rom*, or *Roma*, to describe all of the diverse communities that make up the Gypsy world. The problem here is that Rom can refer either to all Gypsies or only to a particular subset (those whose ethnonym is *Rom*). In fact, some groups within the Gypsy world have explicitly rejected the use of the common label *Rom*.[4] Further complicating the situation are debates among the Gypsies themselves about who constitute the "true Rom" or "true Gypsies."[5] Given the complexity of this situation, Matt Salo, in a study of Gypsy ethnicity, suggested:

> It may be helpful to scholars to continue to use the term "Gypsy" only as a cover term for the totality of groups considered by scholarly tradition to be historically and/or linguistically related. The familiar designation is thus retained tentatively, but restricted to a single connotation. This is roughly analogous to the way the term "Slav" is used. . . . Since the term "Gypsy" does not denote any single group, we avoid the vicariously ethnocentric point of view. . . . "Gypsy" does not refer to an ethnic group, but to a set of groups tentatively considered related.[6]

There is, however, still the problem of the pejorative overtones of the term *Gypsy*. And, given this problem, coupled with what I take to be the general preference among most of the people concerned, I have decided to use the term *Rom* here, with the understanding that it is being employed in its most general sense to refer to the overarching characteristics of the various communities that might be deemed to be Gypsy regardless of whether they would accept the term *Rom* to describe themselves. It is also, of course, very important to keep in mind that the people whom we are discussing are incredibly diverse in many ways and that any general claims made about Rom will be true of some, and untrue of others.

THE ORIGINS OF THE ROM

The historical origins of the Rom were very much clouded in mystery until the mid–18th and 19th centuries.[7] Indeed, the Rom themselves made use of a variety of fictitious origin stories to facilitate their travels and acceptance in different settings. In the 15th and early 16th centuries, Rom throughout Europe, capitalizing on European fears of the expansion of the Ottoman Empire, sought and received letters of protection and safe passage, and even economic support in the form of alms from various European Christian rulers and communities,[8] by claiming that "their ancestors in Lesser Egypt [*in minori Aegypto*] had formerly abandoned for some years the Christian religion and turned to the error of the pagans and that, after their repentance, a penance had been imposed upon them that, for as many years, some members of their families should wander about the world and expiate in exile the guilt of their sin."[9] This tale, which Angus Fraser called "the Great Trick,"[10] was in fact merely an expedient ruse and was never believed by the Rom themselves.

Among the Rom, historical knowledge, passed on in their oral traditions, was quite limited and provided no real clues about their origin. Judith Okely noted that "the Gypsies . . . have scarcely written their own history. Theirs is a non-literate tradition, so their history is found fragmented in the documents of the dominant non-Gypsy . . . society."[11] Not only is the historical record incomplete and written by outsiders, but it has been written by outsiders who all too often sought "to exoticise, disperse, control, assimilate or destroy" the Rom.[12] It was their language, Romani, that provided the necessary basis for tracing the history of the Rom, although more recently physical anthropology and genetics have provided additional support for hypotheses developed based on linguistic evidence.[13] As Alexandre Paspati commented in his book *Études sur les Tchinghianés* in 1870, "The true history of the Gypsy race is in the study of their language."[14] Romani is an Indo-Aryan language, historically related to Sanskrit, whose closest modern relative is Hindi.[15] This discovery, supported by other kinds of material evidence, provides the foundation for our contemporary understanding of the early history of the Rom. Thomas Acton summarized this understanding as follows:

The ancestors of the Romani-speaking peoples left India some one thousand years ago, moving along trade routes trodden over the centuries by countless other migratory nations. Some two or three hundred years later, contemporary documents attest their arrival in eastern Europe; before the end of the fifteenth century their presence is recorded in the British Isles. They brought with them a language whose Indian construction was in the eighteenth century to betray their history to the learned world; but with the Indian base came loan words from every country on their path; and hybridisation and creolisation with other languages has fragmented the Romani language into hundreds of dialects. Today, like the Jews, they live throughout the world, sometimes intermarrying, sometimes not, disunited politically, heterogeneous culturally, and with the most diverse aspirations.[16]

Although it is probable that the Rom originally left northern India around 1000 C.E., we know very little about what motivated their exodus, or even whether they left as a single group or over time in smaller groups (although the latter appears to be more likely). Similarly, we do not know much about the role and place of the ancestors of the Rom in India before they left, although a number of possible scenarios have been proposed. Many scholars believe that the Rom began as a relatively low caste group, in Sanskrit called the *domba* (from which the modern term *Rom* may be derived), who are known to have been musicians as early as the 6th century C.E.[17] Others, however, have suggested that the ancestors of today's Rom were more likely higher caste *kshatriyas*, or warriors.[18] In any event, after leaving India, the Rom entered Persia, and gradually moved through Armenia and on to the heart of the Byzantine Empire. They then traveled (and many remained and settled) in the Balkans and, between the 14th through 16th centuries, throughout Europe.[19]

THE CHALLENGE OF STUDYING THE ROM

If the origins and early history of the Rom are difficult to identify and understand, the same can be said, perhaps paradoxically, to be even more true of any effort to understand contemporary Rom life, values, behaviors, and so on. The world of the Rom is very much a secret one, neither particularly visible nor welcoming to outsiders.[20] The Rom have historically faced (and in many places continue to face) prejudice, discrimination, and persecution of incredible proportions, and so it is hardly surprising that they have developed not only suspicions of *gadje* (non-Rom), but very effective means of avoidance and deception to resist efforts to learn about them. Although the Rom necessarily live in the midst of *gadje* and rely on contacts with *gadje* to survive, they nonetheless (and for good reason) "like being familiar strangers . . . their status as strangers protects them in a number of ways. The less we know about them, the less we can harass them."[21] As William Kephart noted, "The boundaries between Rom and *gadje* are sharp, and the Rom have every intention of maintaining the sharpness. Deception, avoidance, misrepresentation, and lying are part of the Gypsies' arsenal, and they have had hundreds of years to perfect and embellish their defenses."[22] And yet, even given these barriers, there is a substantial and growing body of anthropological, sociological, and linguistic research about the Rom, some of it conducted by Rom scholars, which is opening a window into the world of the Rom.[23]

CULTURAL AND SOCIAL VALUES AND NORMS

Rom culture and society is fundamentally oppositional in nature, in the sense that the most basic distinction made is that between Rom and *gadje*. Regardless of the diversity present *within* the Rom world, this insider–outsider distinction is virtually universal among all Rom.[24] The distinction is not merely a social one; it is a *moral* one, grounded in Rom beliefs about ritual purity. Sutherland, for instance, noted that "the Rom and *gadje* are moral opposites and constitute the most important social boundary in terms of behaviour. Relations with *gadje* are restricted to economic exploitation and political manipulation. Social relations in the sense of friendship, mutual aid, and equality are not appropriate with them."[25] Such distinctions are not, of course, unique to the Rom; indeed, to some extent such oppositional identity is common to most groups that have been subjected to discrimination and prejudice.[26] Nevertheless, the extent to which both group and individual identity in the case of the Rom is oppositional is both unusual and significant.

Wuzho and Marimé: Concepts of Ritual Purity and Impurity

At the heart of Rom culture is the concept of ritual purity, or *wuzho*. *Wuzho* suggests not merely ritual or ceremonial purity, however, but also "purity of a physical and moral nature."[27] It is contrasted with *marimé* that, in a superficial literal sense, refers to defilement or pollution.[28] *Marimé*, however, is a far more powerful concept than this definition might suggest. Carol Miller, in her discussion of what she termed the "ideology of defilement" among American Rom, commented that *marimé*:

> is pervasive to Rom categories of belief and thought, and extends to all areas of Rom life in some way, underwriting a hygienic attitude towards the world, themselves, and others. Pollution ideas work on the life of Rom society, especially in the sense of symbolizing certain dangers and expressing a general view of the social order. Lines are drawn between the Gypsy and the non-Gypsy, the

clean and the unclean, health and disease, the good and the bad, which are made obvious and visible through the offices of ritual avoidance.[29]

In its most basic sense, the distinction between *wuzho* and *marimé* refers to the division of the human body into two parts: above the waist and below the waist. The area above the waist, and in particular the head and mouth, are considered *wuzho*, whereas the parts of the body below the waist (especially anal and genital areas) are *marimé*.[30] This distinction is seen as fundamental, and any contact between the two parts must be avoided, as must be any contact between any items and surfaces that are in any way associated with one or the other part of the body.[31] Thus, "items that come into contact with these areas are separately maintained, washed in running water or special basins and stored apart from ordinary items; items like soaps, towels, razors and combs, clothes, pillows, furniture like the backs of chairs, the tops of tables, tablecloths, aprons, sinks, food utensils and, of course, food itself, which is prepared, served, and eaten with the greatest consideration for ritual quality."[32] In practice, this means, for instance, that clothing worn above the waist and below the waist must be washed and kept separately. Otherwise, what was *wuzho* becomes *marimé*. As Ronald Lee, himself a Rom, explained, "You can't wash clothes, dishes, and babies in the same pan, and every Gypsy has his own eating utensils, towels, and soap. Other dishes and utensils are set aside for guests, and still others for pregnant women. Certain towels are for the face, and others for the nether regions—and there are different colored soaps in the sink, each with an allotted function."[33] The concept of *marimé* applies not only to objects, but to people as well. *Gadje* are, by definition, *marimé*:

> The major offence of the *gadje*, the one offence that the Rom can never forgive, is their propensity to defilement. *Gadje* confuse the critical distinction between the pure and the impure. They are observed in various situations which the Rom regard as compromising; forgetting to wash in public bathrooms; eating with the fork they rescued from the floor of the restaurant; washing face towels and tablecloths with underwear at the local self-service laundry; relaxing with their feet resting upon the top surface of the table.[34]

Beyond these are common practices of *gadje* that strike the Rom as further evidence, should any be needed, of the impure practices and lifestyles of *gadje*: "For their part, Gypsies can easily be stunned by examples of *gadjo* squalor that the *gadje* aren't even aware of. For example, keeping dogs as pets in the house, and, worse, tolerating cats, and indeed upholding them as unusually clean animals. Among Gypsies, the cat is *marimé* because it licks its fur and genitals and so brings dirt inside itself."[35]

It is important to understand that *marimé* does not mean merely "dirty"; something can be dirty (*melaló*) without being impure (*marimé*).[36] Rom believe that they are in constant danger of being polluted so long as they are in the midst of *gadje*, because not only the *gadje* themselves but anything they touch becomes *marimé*. This not only helps to explain the social barriers between Rom and *gadje*, but also demonstrates the incredible social control such a concept has for maintaining group boundaries.[37] As Salo observed:

> The separation of Gypsies from non-Gypsies is marked by differences of both values and other cultural traits. There seems to be a high degree of agreement among the Gypsies as to what the most basic and general values are. The most important values of family and group solidarity are exhibited by a host of symbolic objects and behaviors which so permeate all aspects of Gypsy life as to make contrast with outsiders constant and inevitable. The criteria for the ideal Gypsy man or woman are markedly lacking in most *gadje*, a fact that can be confirmed daily to the disgust and scorn of the Gypsy. Only the loosening of the Gypsy moral code could allow closer relationships to develop with the gadje.[38]

Family and Kinship Patterns

If the contrast of Rom and *gadje* is the most basic for the Rom, internal divisions among different groups of Rom are nonetheless significant as well. Every individual Rom has a complex personal identity tied to an intricate pattern of family relationships.[39] At the core of this set of relationships is membership in the *familia*, or extended family, which functions both as an economic unit and as a support network. As Kephart noted:

> The *familia* is particularly effective as a *supportive institution*. Whether the problem is economic, social, political, or medical, the various family members unite in their efforts to provide aid. Should a police official, social worker, inspector, tax collector, or any other unwelcome *gadjo* appear on the scene, the intruder will be met with formidable—and generally effective—opposition. Should a family member fall ill, the *familia* will spare no expense in obtaining professional help, especially if it is a serious illness.[40]

Beyond the level of the *familia* is the *vitsa*, which is a collection of related *familiyi*. Although sometimes called "clans," the ties that hold members of a *vitsa* together are stronger than this would suggest. Membership in a *vitsa* is used by Rom as a "unit of identity" in determining their place in the broader Rom community, and certain obligations are owed to the other members of one's *vitsa*.[41] Finally, each *vitsa* is tied to one of the thirteen or more *natsiyi*, or "tribes," of the Rom world.[42] Different in kind from the kinship-based *familia*, each individual household is also a member of a *kumpania*, which is essentially an economically based unit that also serves as "the basic political unit and its members can make decisions on moral, social, political and eco-

nomic questions which are considered to be public rather than family matters."[43]

Gender Roles and Expectations

Within the Rom community, gender roles and expectations are both clearly
defined and highly significant. As Sutherland noted, "The male–female division is the most fundamental in Rom society. Men and women between puberty and old age are given entirely different status and rule within a relationship category. Actual physical separation of the sexes is very great, and this
both exemplifies as well as reinforces the difference in treatment of men and
women."[44] The separation of men and women, at least traditionally,[45] includes social functions of various types, daily activities, duties and responsibilities, and occupational roles. For the Rom, the world of men and the world
of women may overlap and interconnect, but they nonetheless remain very
much separate. Kephart described these different worlds as follows: "Women
cook and take care of the household chores. Men are responsible for the acquisition and maintenance of transportation facilities. In many areas, the
women bring in more money than the men. . . . The women's income seems
to be steadier and more reliable than the men's. It is the men, nevertheless,
who normally hold positions of power in the *familia*, the *vitsa*, and the
kumpania."[46]

One way to conceptualize the differing roles of men and women in Rom
society is in terms of the need for the community to concern itself with both
biological and cultural/political survival. As Rena Cotten explained, "The
woman is most active in those facets of life necessary for biological survival,
but cultural survival is in male hands since the men are the initiators and major participants of group institutions. To phrase it another way: the focal
point of interest for the men is the *vitsa* and its component extended families;
the center of concern for the woman is her own conjugal biological family."[47]

The point at which gender roles most clearly intersect, of course, is in the
context of marriage. Marriage is, for the Rom as for others, very important; in
fact, for the Rom, marriage is a prerequisite for full participation in the life of
the community.[48] The traditional view of the nature and purposes of marriage
among the Rom, however, differs dramatically from that of most contemporary societies. As Rena Gropper explained in *Gypsies in the City*, the husband–wife dimension of marriage is among its *least* important facets:

> Aside from having a sex partner and someone besides his mother to fulfill his
> needs and give him money, the groom experiences little change in his lifestyle
> when he marries. His age-peers may joke about his sexual activities, and his
> mother and sisters may tell him to ask his wife for something because they are
> too busy. Gypsy marriage is not predicated on romantic love, and the Rom

frown against any display of affection between husband and wife. The husband wants his wife to perform services for him, but he continues to spend much of his time with brothers and cousins. Husband and wife rarely go out together.[49]

Marriages are arranged only partly in terms of the *individuals* involved; although the husband and wife must be compatible, the marriage is a union not only of a man and a woman, but also a union of *families*. Thus, as Sutherland and others observed, there is a strong preference for marriages between cousins, which is to say with "a person of one's own *vitsa*, or of the *vitsa* of one's female progenitors, that is, the mother, mother's mother, or father's mother."[50] Although marriages of first cousins are not considered the ideal, they do take place and are not restricted. In fact, with the exception of certain illegitimate *marimé* unions,[51] any marriage within the community is potentially possible and acceptable.[52] Marriage with *gadje*, however, is not acceptable, although on occasion a non-Rom woman will be allowed to marry into the community.[53] The business nature of the marriage is reinforced and made clear by the role of the *daro*, or "bride price," in the negotiations between the bride and groom's families.[54]

Earning a Living

Throughout their history, the Rom have survived by functioning as what some scholars call a "middleman minority."[55] There have been, and continue to be, a wide array of such "middleman minorities" in the world, including, in various contexts, the Chinese, the Indians, the Jews, and the Rom. These groups, whose position in any particular society is often tenuous at best because they remain "outsiders" in important senses, have—although they have been faced with considerable adversity—been "able to develop and perpetuate a cultural heritage involving a high degree of ethnocentrism and adaptive skills which enabled them to improve or maintain their competitive resources."[56] In the case of the Rom, vocational and occupational skills necessary for survival have developed over time in response to both changing social situations and needs. Judith Okely identified the following skills that have served the Rom well in adapting to different host environments:

- Knowing the local economy and its potential where demand and supply are irregular
- Knowing the local people, an alien population, and recognizing their psychological needs and weaknesses
- Opportunism and ingenuity in choice of occupation in the local context
- Flexibility in occupation at a given time and over a period of time
- Salesmanship
- Flexibility in role-playing

- Manual dexterity and mechanical ingenuity
- Bargaining skills
- Highly developed memory
- Physical strength and stamina[57]

These skills are manifested in practice in a number of ways, but are perhaps most visible in the multioccupational approach to life taken by the Rom. As Sway commented:

> It has become a business principle among the Gypsies never to depend on one occupation. Since so many of the Gypsies' occupations are seasonal, tempo-rary, marginal, and even precarious, they engage in a number of endeavors si-multaneously. . . . The practice of being multioccupational affords the Gypsies a peculiar form of job security. Since the Gypsies never rely on one mode of work, they are never without a means to earn a living. If a particular market closes to them because it has been exhausted or they have been harassed by the police, they can quickly turn to other methods of earning a living. This occupa-tional flexibility and pluralism should be viewed as a result of years of eco-nomic adaptation to unfriendly and unreliable market situations. The Gypsy practice of diversity enables them to survive the harshest of economic circum-stances.[58]

In contemporary American society, there are a number of occupations pursued (often simultaneously) by Rom. For males, dealing in used cars and fender and body work have become major sources of income, supplemented by work as coppersmiths, farm labor, entertainers, junk dealers, and a host of other "free professions"[59]—but not, for the most part, as part of the normal wage-labor system in place in modern industrialized societies.[60] For women, fortune-telling remains the most common and respected occupation, if not necessarily a terribly lucrative one.[61] In fact, fortune-telling often provides the most consistent and reliable source of income for the Rom, and this is consis-tent with the economic role of the woman in Rom society:

> In all Gypsy societies, the woman functions as the family treasurer, and the Ro-many definition of the role differs considerably from ours. In Gypsy terms, part of the treasurer's responsibility is to ensure that there is always something in the treasury. It is the woman who is expected to bring in the daily money for routine expenses. . . . The woman is the one required to furnish daily food pro-visions and even pocket money for the men whenever they need it.[62]

Fortune-telling is more, however, than merely an essential economic activity. As Carol Silverman observed:

Fortune-telling is the most widespread and traditional occupation of Rom women. It is not only their primary means of earning money, but also it is the way of being a Gypsy woman and of acquiring prestigious skills. As one Gypsy put it, "For a woman not to be able to read a palm is an insult." Every major American city hosts fortune-tellers. They are called "readers and advisers" because predicting the future for money is illegal. In New York City alone, there are hundreds of fortune-telling parlors. Customers are drawn exclusively from the non-Gypsy population. Since fortune-telling seems to strike a responsive chord in diverse cultures, it continues to be in demand in urban as well as rural settings among many ethnic groups.[63]

The Rom function in a perpetual symbiotic economic relationship with the surrounding *gadje* community; as Gropper noted, "No Gypsy group makes its living from other Gypsies."[64] A good example of this symbiosis can be found in Rom attitudes toward welfare benefits where they are available. As Marlene Sway commented:

The Gypsies' historical willingness to undertake work that no one else wanted has led them to develop the attitude that earning money even under the most humiliating circumstances is still honorable and productive. As a result of this attitude, the Gypsies . . . actively seek out and exploit welfare benefits in societies where they are obtainable. . . . The Gypsies do not view welfare as charity or aid; rather it is just one more method of outsmarting the non-Gypsy. Since collecting welfare is time-consuming in terms of hours required in agency offices, the Gypsies feel justified in being compensated for the income they lose while waiting. Additionally, since welfare agencies put restrictions on the Gypsies and the Gypsies have to "earn" their money by playing the role of a welfare recipient in a believable fashion, they feel they are justified in accepting the welfare benefits.[65]

Although it would be both misleading and dishonest to suggest that all, or even most, Rom engage in such practices, there is nevertheless something of an underside to Rom economic life. Working from the assumption that all *gadje* are fools who are asking to be cheated, many Rom do in fact engage in what Anne Sutherland called "less legitimate ways of making a living." Such ways include the *xoxano baro*, or "Big Lie," of the fortune-tellers in its many forms (all of which involve, in some way, confidence games of some sort), as well as theft, pick-pocketing, and so on.[66] In addition, Sutherland pointed out that it is still common for "some groups of men [to] travel around in trucks and camp in parking lots. They tar roofs or spray asphalt on driveways. Some of them have developed quite a racket from this by diluting the tar so much that it never dries, but it costs less to them and therefore their profits are higher. By the time the home-owners discover their dilemma, the men have packed up their trucks and moved to another city."[67]

For the most part, however, the Rom have been remarkably successful economically without resorting to such tricks. This is an especially impressive accomplishment when one considers that, "unlike . . . other middleman minorities, Gypsies are largely illiterate. As a consequence of their illiteracy, the educated and professional classes including attorneys, historians, sociologists, and politicians lack Gypsies who could represent their interests as an ethnic group on various levels. Yet despite this obvious liability, the Gypsies have managed to exploit one middleman niche after another and endure as a commercially successful ethnic group."[68]

Religious Belief and "Protective Coloration"

One of the ways in which the Rom are very different from most other "middleman minorities" is with respect to religion, religious belief, and religious practice. Religion often plays a central role in in-group identification for such groups and helps to maintain the boundaries between the group and the surrounding host society. This is not really the case with the Rom, who have tended, throughout their history, to adopt the dominant religion of whatever society they are in: "Traditionally tolerant and respectful toward all religions, the Rom readily have absorbed practices around them. So, in Spain, Italy, and France, they became Roman Catholic; in England, usually Protestant; and in southeast Europe (occupied for so long by Muslim conquerors) they are either Muslim or Greek Orthodox."[69]

The outward adoption of the dominant faith of the surrounding community has functioned as "protective coloration" for the Rom, without seriously challenging or altering the core folk religious beliefs of their community.[70] Writing about Rom in Albania, for instance, Isabel Fonseca noted:

> It is commonly said that Gypsies are irreligious, adopting the going faith as it suits them, in the hopes of avoiding persecution and possibly of reaping whatever benefits group membership might bring. This is true. For one thing, they have often been made to listen to sermons from outside the church. But the deeper reason is that among themselves they have no need of the religions of other nations. It was hard to say exactly what it meant to the Gypsies of Kinostudio to be Muslims, as they claimed. Their women were chaste and wore long skirts, but this was the code of "decent" Gypsies everywhere.[71]

To be sure, elements of adopted religions often permeate Rom life, but these elements (e.g., holidays, naming patterns, etc.) are little more than outward trappings rather than evidence of deep conviction. As Marlene Sway compellingly argued, "The Gypsies are not Christian and never have been, although they have successfully convinced outsiders that they are."[72] This is not to suggest, however, that the Rom are insincere in their religious beliefs.

Rather, their indigenous religious belief system simply allows for a wide range of formal religious commitment and rejects the common Western assumption that membership in a religious community must be exclusive in nature.[73]

Performance and "Impression Management"

One of the most intriguing and insightful studies of the Rom to appear in the scholarly literature in recent years is Carol Silverman's study of "impression management."[74] Silverman argued:

> When Gypsies interact with non-Gypsies, they have various motives for influencing the impression received. To lawyers, they may be interested in demonstrating their credibility as American citizens; to welfare workers, their victimization as an afflicted minority; to fortune-telling customers, their spirituality. By controlling the communicative situation, they control what is perceived by the "audience." Gypsies are highly skillful in performance. . . . Different performances are required for fortune-telling customers, for landlords, for truant officers, for welfare workers, etc. Various "impressions," "Faces," or "identities" are managed by communicating highly selective information. Furthermore, Gypsies are highly skilled in face-shifting. Of course, this occurs in all groups and individuals, but the Gypsies have developed this process to an art, are quite conscious and reflexive about it . . . and have used it as a tactic for survival in hostile environments.[75]

Such behavior is interesting on a number of levels and can give us considerable insight not only into the way in which the Rom view the *gadje* world in general, but also into the kinds of skills and knowledge that will be of greatest value within the Rom community. Given the history of the Rom, it is hardly surprising that the ability to hide one's identity as a Rom has proven to be both necessary and expedient:

> An important and frequent Gypsy performance is "passing" as a non-Gypsy. Gypsies deliberately conceal their ethnicity to avoid confrontations with and harassment by truant officers, landlords, the police, and the welfare department; they pass as Puerto Ricans, Mexicans, Armenians, Greeks, Arabs, and other local ethnics in order to obtain jobs, housing, and welfare. Gypsies usually report themselves as members of other groups to census takers, causing Gypsy census statistics to be extremely unreliable. Gypsies have developed the skills of passing so well that many Americans are unaware that there are any Gypsies in America.[76]

"Passing," however, is but one of the many performances employed by the Rom. Another related phenomenon is that of "naming." In the American context, for instance, not only have many Rom adopted Americanized names (as have members of many other groups, of course), but further:

Gypsies use a multiplicity of names to avoid visibility. One Gypsy family may list their apartment under one name, the telephone under another, and the fortune-telling business under yet another. The argument may be extended to addresses: because many urban Rom are semi-nomadic, addresses change continuously. The multiplicity makes Gypsies hard to identify and trace, producing precisely the effects the Gypsy seeks. In Western society, a name is an indelible mark which rarely changes. For Gypsies, on the other hand, changeable American names are a strategy they use to remain invisible, concealed, and untraceable.[77]

Yet another aspect of "impression management" that has been very effectively utilized by the Rom is attracting different clientele with group-specific advertising. For example, in discussing bilingual (Spanish-English) handbills used in California by one fortune-teller, Silverman reported, "This handbill . . . presents two sets of ascribed problems fitting two separate customer populations."[78] In other words, the appeal that is made to the middle-class English-speaking population differs dramatically from that made to the working-class *chicano* population. The handbill, in short, is really two separate documents, distinguished not only by language but also by target audience.

THE FEARS AND REALITIES OF PERSECUTION:
"EVEN PARANOIDS HAVE ENEMIES"

The complexities of "impression management" discussed earlier reflect, among other things, serious concerns about the risk of persecution. It is only reasonable to ask how realistic such concerns and fears are; certainly in the contemporary American context, I suspect that many people would be astonished to discover such worries and would likely see them as evidence of group paranoia. Yet, not only the history of the Rom, but recent events, especially in Eastern Europe, would seem to strongly support such fears and worries. Gabrielle Tyrnauer, for example, powerfully reminded us that:

> the upheaval in Europe has had a strong impact on the Gypsies of the continent. Those from Eastern Europe are becoming refugees in unprecedented numbers, knocking on the gates of Western European countries, often afraid to acknowledge their ethnic identities, even as refugees. . . . Gypsies who remain in the East, like Jews, are once more becoming strangers in their own lands, targets of diffuse hostility, scapegoats for the frustrations of societies in the convulsions of rapid change. . . . Hatred of the Gypsy minority is often all that unites the warring ethnic groups of ex-communist nations of eastern and central Europe.[79]

The Rom have been easy scapegoats and targets of persecution throughout their long history. Victims of prejudice, discrimination, disenfranchisement, forced migrations and expulsions, and even slavery and murder, the survival of the Rom can be attributed in no small measure to their (often quite legitimate) suspicions of *gadje*.[80]

Without a doubt, the most horrendous example of anti-Rom persecution in recent history has been the Holocaust. Although many individuals and groups suffered horribly at the hands of the Nazis, only two groups—the Jews and the Rom—were specifically "targeted for annihilation by National Socialist ideology and its state apparatus."[81] Although accurate figures are, as always with the Rom, difficult to determine, somewhere between at least a quarter and a half million Rom were murdered by the Nazis[82]—and the number could well be double this estimate according to some scholars.[83] In other words, as much as half the total Rom population in Europe may have been killed during the Holocaust. This aspect of the Holocaust, however, is relatively unknown, leading some to talk about the murder of the Rom as "the forgotten Holocaust."[84] In recent years, there has been considerable debate in Germany both about the persecution of the Rom during the Nazi era and the status of the Rom in contemporary German society, and this debate has made clear that there remain on-going issues with respect to the toleration (and lack thereof) for the Rom.[85]

CHILDREARING AND EDUCATION

In 1967, a report entitled *Children and Their Primary Schools* was issued by the Central Advisory Council for Education in London. The report, commonly called "The Plowden Report," asserted that Rom children "are probably the most severely deprived children in the country. Most of them do not even go to school and the potential abilities of those who do are stunted."[86] Such critical views are far from uncommon; a somewhat more recent publication of the Council of Europe makes clear the educational challenge facing those concerned with the schooling of Rom children:

> It is safe to assume that over one-half of Gypsies . . . of school age in Europe are not attending school. Of those that are, many receive inappropriate instruction which is frequently trying for them as well as their families. Depending on the country, the attendance rate for children and young people below the statutory school-leaving age varies between 20% and 60% to 70%. . . . The illiteracy rate among those over the school-leaving age varies between 65% and 95%.[87]

The same general pattern has been historically true in the United States as well, but has been changing in recent years:

> Within the past decade, there has been a revolutionary trend among Gypsies of all countries to send their children to public school. While Gypsy parents

would like their children to learn how to read, write, and perform basic arithmetic, education is not the primary reason they send their children to school. In recent years, welfare workers have moved to tie welfare benefits to the children's attendance at public school. . . . Children help the Gypsies make money for the family through welfare benefits, and, additionally, the public school is a free babysitter.[88]

Such a description of contemporary Rom practice might lead one to agree with the conclusions of the "Plowden Report"—but if so, one would be very much mistaken. Such views, however common, are a serious distortion of both the Rom view of children and childrearing and do an important disservice to the nature of Rom family life.

The Rom value, love, and respect their children. Their response to public education is a reflection not of indifference or of a lack of concern, but rather of serious (and well-founded) reservations about the nature and purposes of such education. There is also a basic difference in the way in which the Rom and the dominant society view children and childhood. For the Rom, children are born as distinct individuals:

> Children are considered miniature versions of adults, lacking only the motor strength and skill of adults and, of course, lacking experience in life. But willpower and desires, emotions and potential intelligence are all inborn and are functional immediately. It follows, therefore, that their rights are also the same as those of adults. Their wishes should be respected to the same extent as the wishes of other human beings.[89]

Such a view of children has important implications for education broadly conceived. Ultimately, because they are in no significant way different from adults, children "should have the right to participate in all the affairs of the adults; in such manner they can learn the ways of their forefathers."[90] In other words, within the Rom community children are prepared for adult life by observation and participation in that life, as well as through ongoing exposure to the oral tradition of the community.[91] As Okely explained, traditionally:

> The Gypsy child learnt by direct participation. . . . Most Gypsy children spent the major part of the day with a parent or substitute parent, and at times were in the charge of older siblings. The skills required for earning a living were learnt when "calling" at houses or factories with parents or relatives, from the age of a toddler. . . . Children were encouraged to handle and earn money from an early age. . . . Children were also socialized into Gypsy life and values by long hours of observing and listening to adults' conversations and exchanges. . . . The children were generally treated as "little adults," being entrusted with secrets and given early responsibilities.[92]

Childcare is viewed as a responsibility of the entire family; interestingly, because of the relative economic importance of women (especially as fortune-tellers), "childcare often becomes a male responsibility. Since children are considered a nuisance at a fortune-telling parlor, they spend long hours with their fathers, uncles, and grandfathers. Typically the children accompany the men wherever they go—on body and fender jobs, shopping, and visiting other Gypsies. When a Gypsy child is ill, often the father acts as nurturer, tending the child's needs and chauffeuring him or her to doctor and dental appointments."[93]

As for public education, from a Rom perspective the fundamental problem is that children should be separated as much as possible from the *gadje* world. Public education is, by its very nature, a means by which community ties are weakened—in essence, a door through which young Rom could go and not return. The lessons of public education go far beyond reading, writing, and basic arithmetic; public schools socialize children into the dominant, mainstream culture. Children are likely to form friendships with *gadje*; they are also unwittingly exposed to all sorts of *marimé*.[94] Ultimately, then, schools pose a very real threat to the continuity of the Rom community itself. It is with this aspect of public education that the Rom have their greatest problems. The solution most commonly adopted in Rom communities is to allow children to attend public schools until they are 10 or 11 years old. As one Swedish informant suggested, "It's no use telling children below the age of ten years, they don't understand anything till then."[95] After that point, however, public education becomes too great a threat to be tolerated. As Jean-Pierre Liégeois commented, "As an external element affecting the education of their children, the school is *a priori* disturbing, because it impinges on their upbringing within the group."[96] It is interesting to note that, despite the relatively limited involvement in public schooling experienced by many Rom children, recent research has suggested, among other things, that such children are able to produce incredibly rich examples of narrative discourse—clearly a benefit of traditional Rom childrearing practices.[97]

CONCLUSIONS

The Rom present us with a fascinating example of a remarkably successful, highly adaptive cultural community in our midst, many of whose core values, among them beliefs about education, are radically different from those of the dominant society. The conception of education that motivates the Rom is one oriented to survival: economic and vocational survival, to be sure, but also physical and cultural survival. The bureaucratic institutions that modern governments have created and on which they rely (including, of course, schools) in some sense depend on the acquiescence and acceptance of their legitimacy by the population that they serve. It is this very legitimacy that is denied by the Rom, whose own core group identity outweighs any other social obligation, commitment, or identity. All that the Rom really want, of course, is to be allowed to be Rom, but this is the challenge for the societies in which they live because being Rom necessarily means *not* being something else.

QUESTIONS FOR REFLECTION AND DISCUSSION

1. Write an essay in which you respond to the idea that children are just "miniature adults." Is this a reasonable conception of childhood in your view? How does this view differ from that offered by Rousseau? By Dewey? What educational advantages would such a notion have? What disadvantages?

2. What are the major challenges that would face the classroom teacher of Rom children in the United States today? How could teachers be better prepared to meet the needs of these children?

3. In the literature on the Rom, some writers have noted a number of common themes that would seem to make the Rom and the Jews (at least in traditional settings) somewhat analogous cases. To what extent, and in what ways, do you think that this is a credible comparison? How do the two groups differ? What are the social and educational implications of these similarities and differences?

4. The concept of *marimé* is a key one in understanding Rom cultural beliefs and practices. In this chapter, it is suggested that in public schools, Rom children are exposed to all sorts of *marimé*. Can you think of examples of *marimé* in the context of the typical elementary school classroom? What (if anything) might the classroom teacher do to address this problem?

5. Which of the ten general skills identified by Judith Okely are taught in the context of the public school? What does this tell you about the nature of public schooling? About the nature of Rom life?

6. "The educational practices of the Rom are in fact more sound than those of the typical public school classroom. Children learn by doing; they construct their own knowledge." Respond to this claim. To what extent is it true? In what ways is it misleading?

7. One of the core issues raised in this chapter concerns deciding on the purposes of public schooling. With respect to culturally different groups in our society, what do you believe that the purposes of public schooling should be? To what extent do you believe that the school should seek to provide a common cultural experience for all children in our society?

8. What, in your view, is the greatest strength of the traditional Rom approach to childrearing and education? What is its greatest weakness?

9. The discussion of performance and "impression management" in this chapter raises a number of questions about education. How do *all* children

engage in performance and "impression management" in the classroom? How do *teachers* engage in performance and "impression management"? Can you think of ways to make use of these behaviors in pedagogically useful ways?

10. In this chapter, it is argued that "Rom society and culture are fundamentally oppositional in nature." What does this mean, and what are its implications for educational practice in the school setting?

RECOMMENDED FURTHER READINGS

The best general introduction to Rom life and culture, especially in the United States, remains Anne Sutherland, *Gypsies: The Hidden Americans* (Prospect Heights, IL: Waveland, 1975). Two exceptionally powerful works that sympathetically, if not always entirely accurately, present views of the world of the Rom are Isabel Fonseca, *Bury Me Standing: The Gypsies and Their Journey* (New York: Vintage, 1995); and Michael Stewart, *The Time of the Gypsies* (Boulder, CO: Westview, 1997). An outstanding recent publication on the Gypsies is Patrick Williams' *Gypsy World: The Silence of the Living and the Voices of the Dead* (Chicago: University of Chicago Press, 2003).

NOTES

1. See Francois de Vaux de Foletier, *Mille ans d'historie des Tsiganes* (Paris: Fayard, 1970); Angus Fraser, *The Gypsies*, 2nd ed. (Oxford, England: Blackwell, 1995); Rena Gropper, *Gypsies in the City: Cultural Patterns and Survival* (Princeton, NJ: Darwin Press, 1975).

2. The spelling of terms in Romani (and, in fact, even the name of the language itself, which is also commonly written "Romany" and "Romanes") varies considerably, as a result both of the lack of a standardized written norm and the considerable diversity of dialects within Romani. See, e.g., Ian Hancock, *A Handbook of Vlax Romani* (Columbus, OH: Slavica, 1995); Ian Hancock, "Romani and Angloromani," in Peter Trudgill (ed.), *Language in the British Isles* (Cambridge, England: Cambridge University Press, 1984), 367–383; Yaron Matras (ed.), *Romani in Contact: The History, Structure, and Sociology of a Language* (Amsterdam: John Benjamins, 1995); George Campbell, *Concise Compendium of the World's Languages* (London: Routledge, 1995), 419–424.

3. The Irish Tinkers, e.g., are Celtic in origin and speak Shelta, a Celtic language that is rapidly undergoing the process of lexical replacement and has already become largely grammatically English; see Ian Hancock, "Shelta and Polari" in Peter Trudgill (ed.), *Language in the British Isles* (Cambridge, England: Cambridge University Press, 1984), 384–403; William Kephart, *Extraordinary Groups: The Sociology of Unconven-*

tional Lifestyles, 2nd ed. (New York: St. Martin's Press, 1982), 8. For more detailed information about these groups, see Bettina Barnes, "Irish Travelling People," in Farnham Rehfisch (ed.), *Gypsies, Tinkers, and Other Travellers* (London: Academic Press, 1975), 231–256; A. and Farnham Rehfisch, "Scottish Travellers or Tinkers," in Farnham Rehfisch (ed.), *Gypsies, Tinkers, and Other Travellers* (London: Academic Press, 1975), 271–283; Fredrik Barth, "The Social Organization of a Pariah Group in Norway," in Farnham Rehfisch (ed.), *Gypsies, Tinkers, and Other Travellers* (London: Academic Press, 1975), 285–299.

4. For example, a number of Gypsy groups use the term *Roma* to describe other Gypsy groups, but do not accept the term for themselves. This is the case for the Romanichal, Gitanos, Kalé, Sinti, and Manush. See Anne Sutherland, *Gypsies: The Hidden Americans* (Prospect Heights, IL: Waveland, 1975), 14–18.

5. See Sutherland, *Gypsies: The Hidden Americans*, 14–18; Thomas Acton, *Gypsy Politics and Social Change* (London: Routledge & Kegan Paul, 1974), 53–93.

6. Matt Salo, "Gypsy Ethnicity: Implications of Native Categories and Interaction for Ethnic Classification," *Ethnicity* 6 (1979): 94–95.

7. De Vaux de Foletier, *Mille ans d'historie des Tsiganes*, 13.

8. Fraser, *The Gypsies*, 63–78.

9. Quoted in Fraser, *The Gypsies*, 65.

10. Fraser, *The Gypsies*, 60–83.

11. Judith Okely, *The Traveller-Gypsies* (Cambridge, England: Cambridge University Press, 1983), 1.

12. Okely, *The Traveller-Gypsies*, 1.

13. Fraser, *The Gypsies*, 25; Gropper, *Gypsies in the City*, 2.

14. Quoted in Fraser, *The Gypsies*, 12.

15. Matt Salo and Sheila Salo, *The Kalderas in Eastern Canada* (Ottawa: National Museums of Canada, 1977), 1.

16. Acton, *Gypsy Politics and Social Change*, 1.

17. Fraser, *The Gypsies*, 25; see also Marlene Sway, *Familiar Strangers: Gypsy Life in America* (Urbana: University of Illinois Press, 1988), 31–33.

18. Fraser, *The Gypsies*, 25–26.

19. Gropper, *Gypsies in the City*, 6–12; see also David Crowe, *A History of the Gypsies of Eastern Europe and Russia* (New York: St. Martin's Griffin, 1996); David Crowe and John Kolsti (eds.), *The Gypsies of Eastern Europe* (London: M. E. Sharpe, 1991).

20. Kephart, *Extraordinary Groups: The Sociology of Unconventional Life-Styles*, 12–14; see also Saga Weckman, "Researching Finnish Gypsies: Advice from a Gypsy," in Diane Tong (ed.), *Gypsies: An Interdisciplinary Reader* (New York: Garland, 1998), 3–10. The more general problem with respect to insider–outsider status in research is discussed quite clearly in John Elliott, "Educational Research and Outsider–Insider Relations," *International Journal of Qualitative Studies in Education* 1, 2 (1988): 155–166.

21. Sway, *Familiar Strangers: Gypsy Life in America*, 6.

22. Kephart, *Extraordinary Groups: The Sociology of Unconventional Life-Styles*, 12.

23. See, e.g., Diane Tong (ed.), *Gypsies: An Interdisciplinary Reader* (New York: Garland, 1998).

24. Salo, "Gypsy Ethnicity," 81–82; Kephart, *Extraordinary Groups: The Sociology of Unconventional Life-Styles*, 17; de Vaux de Foletier, *Mille ans d'histoire des Tsiganes*, 213–224.

25. Sutherland, *Gypsies: The Hidden Americans*, 258; see also Kephart, *Extraordinary Groups: The Sociology of Unconventional Life-Styles*, 17–18.

26. See Karen Ross, Deniz Derman, and Nevena Dakovic (eds.), *Mediated Identities* (Istanbul: Istanbul Bilgi University Press, 2001).

27. Sutherland, *The Hidden Americans*, 258; Salo and Salo, *The Kalderas in Eastern Canada*, 115–129.

28. The term *marimé* actually has a double meaning in Rom culture. In addition to the meaning discussed in the chapter, it is also the word used to describe the most serious sanctions issued by a *kris*, a Rom judicial body. See Sway, *Familiar Strangers*, 76–94; Sutherland, *Gypsies: The Hidden Americans*, 262–263.

29. Carol Miller, "American Rom and the Ideology of Defilement," in Farnham Rehfisch (ed.), *Gypsies, Tinkers, and Other Travellers* (London: Academic Press, 1975), 41.

30. Miller, "American Rom and the Ideology of Defilement."

31. Miller, "American Rom and the Ideology of Defilement"; see also Gropper, *Gypsies in the City*, 91–96.

32. Miller, "American Rom and the Ideology of Defilement," 42.

33. Quoted in Kephart, *Extraordinary Groups: The Sociology of Unconventional Life-Styles*, 15.

34. Miller, "American Rom and the Ideology of Defilement," 45.

35. Isabel Fonseca, *Bury Me Standing: The Gypsies and Their Journey* (New York: Vintage, 1995), 104.

36. Sutherland, *Gypsies: The Hidden Americans*, 268–270.

37. Kephart, *Extraordinary Groups: The Sociology of Unconventional Life-Styles*, 14. The comparison to *kashrut* in Judaism is obvious here; see Sway, *Familiar Strangers: Gypsy Life in America*, 24–26.

38. Salo, "Gypsy Ethnicity," 82.

39. Fraser, *The Gypsies*, 238.

40. Kephart, *Extraordinary Groups: The Sociology of Unconventional Life-Styles*, 21.

41. Fraser, *The Gypsies*, 238–239; Sutherland, *Gypsies: The Hidden Americans*, 181–184.

42. Fraser, *The Gypsies*, 238–239; Sutherland, *Gypsies: The Hidden Americans*, 185–188.

43. Fraser, *The Gypsies*, 239.

44. Sutherland, *Gypsies: The Hidden Americans*, 149.

45. For a discussion of recent changes with respect to gender roles and expectations among the Rom, see Rena Cotten, "Sex Dichotomy Among the American Kalderas Gypsies," in Diane Tong (ed.), *Gypsies: An Interdisciplinary Reader* (New York: Garland, 1998), 228–230.

46. Kephart, *Extraordinary Groups: The Sociology of Unconventional Life-Styles*, 38.

47. Cotten, "Sex Dichotomy Among the American Kalderas Gypsies," 223.

48. Sutherland, *Gypsies: The Hidden Americans*, 206.

49. Gropper, *Gypsies in the City*, 88.

50. Sutherland, *Gypsies: The Hidden Americans*, 206–207.

51. Sutherland, *Gypsies: The Hidden Americans*, 241–247. For example, marriages between individuals who are more closely related than first cousins, as well as between a man and his brother's wife or son's wife, would be *marimé*.

52. Sutherland, *Gypsies: The Hidden Americans*, 206–208.

53. Gropper, *Gypsies in the City*, 141. However, Matt Salo noted that in fact in the American context marriages between male Rom and female non-Rom were actually more common than intergroup marriages within the Rom communities (i.e., between Rom, Ludari, and Romnièel). He noted that "The reason for this apparent contradiction is simple enough. The gažia (feminine plural) were viewed as practically without culture and thus could be removed from their families and remodeled to fit into Gypsy life. This was considered much more difficult to do with members of other Gypsy groups. The Romnièel view was that it would involve the confrontation of 'two stubbornnesses.' As one Romani phrased it, 'You can't take the Gypsy out of a Gypsy and put in another Gypsy!' " (Salo, "Gypsy Ethnicity," 92).

54. For detailed discussions of the *daro*, see Sutherland, *Gypsies: The Hidden Americans*, 220–223; Sway, *Familiar Strangers: Gypsy Life in America*, 67–69; Kephart, *Extraordinary Groups: The Sociology of Unconventional Life-Styles*, 24–26.

55. Sway, *Familiar Strangers: Gypsy Life in America*, 16–30.

56. Sway, *Familiar Strangers: Gypsy Life in America*, 17.

57. Okely, *The Traveller-Gypsies*, 58–60.

58. Sway, *Familiar Strangers: Gypsy Life in America*, 110–111.

59. Sway, *Familiar Strangers: Gypsy Life in America*, 110–111.

60. Okely, *The Traveller-Gypsies*, 53–56.

61. Sutherland, *Gypsies: The Hidden Americans*, 87.

62. Gropper, *Gypsies in the City*, 38–39.

63. Carol Silverman, "Everyday Drama: Impression Management of Urban Gypsies," *Urban Anthropology* 11, 3/4 (1982): 386.

64. Gropper, *Gypsies in the City*, 30.

65. Sway, *Familiar Strangers: Gypsy Life in America*, 96.

66. Sutherland, *Gypsies: The Hidden Americans*, 93–95; Gropper, *Gypsies in the City*, 41–43.

67. Sutherland, *Gypsies: The Hidden Americans*, 93.

68. Sway, *Familiar Strangers: Gypsy Life in America*, 95.

69. Gropper, *Gypsies in the City*, 109.

70. Sway, *Familiar Strangers: Gypsy Life in America*, 57–59; see also Silverman, "Everyday Drama: Impression Management of Urban Gypsies," 383.

71. Fonseca, *Bury Me Standing: The Gypsies and Their Journey*, 48.

72. Sway, *Familiar Strangers: Gypsy Life in America*, 59.

73. See, e.g., Salo and Salo, *The Kalderas in Eastern Canada*, 94–114; Elwood Trigg, *Gypsy Demons and Divinities: The Magic and Religion of the Gypsies* (Secaucus, NJ: Citadel Press, 1973).

74. Silverman, "Everyday Drama: Impression Management of Urban Gypsies," 377–398.

75. Silverman, "Everyday Drama: Impression Management of Urban Gypsies," 378.

76. Silverman, "Everyday Drama: Impression Management of Urban Gypsies," 382.

77. Silverman, "Everyday Drama: Impression Management of Urban Gypsies," 383.

78. Silverman, "Everyday Drama: Impression Management of Urban Gypsies," 391.

79. Gabrielle Tyrnauer, *Gypsies and the Holocaust: A Bibliography and Introductory Essay*, 2nd ed. (Montréal: Montréal Institute for Genocide Studies, Concordia University, 1991), iii.

80. See, e.g., Susan Tebbutt (ed.), *Sinti and Roma: Gypsies in German-Speaking Society and Literature* (New York: Berghahn, 1998); Rachel Tritt, *Struggling for Ethnic Identity: Czechoslovakia's Endangered Gypsies* (New York: Human Rights Watch, 1992); Ignacy-Marek Kaminski, *The State of Ambiguity: Studies of Gypsy Refugees* (Gothenburg, Sweden: Mobilis, 1980); Crowe, *A History of the Gypsies of Eastern Europe and Russia*; Crowe and Kolsti, *The Gypsies of Eastern Europe*; Fonseca, *Bury Me Standing: The Gypsies and Their Journey*; Stewart, *The Time of the Gypsies*. Although only tangentially concerned with the Rom, a work of considerable value in terms of recent developments in Eastern Europe is Christina Bratt Paulston and Donald Peckham (eds.), *Linguistic Minorities in Central and Eastern Europe* (Clevedon, England: Multilingual Matters, 1998). For a fascinating historical study of the interactions between the Rom and the Inquisition in Spain, see Maria Helena Sánchez Ortega, *La inquisición y los gitanos* (Madrid: Taurus Ediciones, 1988).

81. Tyrnauer, *Gypsies and the Holocaust*, vii. Actually, the Rom presented the Nazi race theory with a difficult challenge. As Tyrnauer explained:

> The Nazi's ideological dilemma, stemming from the presumed "Aryan" origin of the Gypsies, was nowhere more clearly seen than in the conflicting recommendations made by "racial scientists" and those in authority. While [some racial theorists] recommended sparing the more assimilated, those with "less than half Gypsy blood," others . . . showed a marked preference for the nomadic "pure" Gypsies, and proposed special reserves where they could roam freely, speak their own language, preserve ancient "Aryan" customs and multiply for the study of future German "scientists." (1991, xiv)

Despite this "academic" debate, however, in 1942 Himmler signed the "Auschwitz Decree," which sent nearly all of Germany's Rom to Auschwitz and their deaths. For an even more complex treatment of this issue, and one that raises some important questions about the extent to which the Jewish and Gypsy persecutions by the Nazis were really parallel, see Michael Zimmermann, *Rassenutopie und Genozid: Die nationalsozialistische "Lösung der Zigeunerfrage"* (Hamburg, Germany: Christians, 1996).

82. Tyrnauer, *Gypsies and the Holocaust,* vii.

83. See, e.g., Ian Hancock, *The Pariah Syndrome: An Account of Gypsy Slavery and Persecution* (Ann Arbor, MI: Karoma, 1987).

84. Christian Bernadac, *L'Holocauste oblié: Le massacre des Tsiganes* (Paris: France-Empire, 1979); see also Sybil Milton, "Gypsies and the Holocaust," *The History Teacher* 24, 4 (1991): 375–387.

85. See Gilad Margalit, *Germany and its Gypsies: A Post-Auschwitz Ordeal* (Madison: University of Wisconsin Press, 2002), 180–220.

86. Quoted in Okely, *The Traveller-Gypsies,* 160.

87. Jean-Pierre Liégeois, *Gypsies and Travellers: Socio-cultural data, socio-political data* (Strasbourg, Germany: Council for Cultural Co-operation, 1987), 140.

88. Sway, *Familiar Strangers: Gypsy Life in America,* 72.

89. Gropper, *Gypsies in the City,* 130.

90. Gropper, *Gypsies in the City,* 32.

91. See, e.g., Zita Réger and Jean Berko Gleason, "Romani child-directed speech and children's language among Gypsies in Hungary," *Language in Society* 20 (1991): 601–617; Zita Réger, "A Preliminary Typology of Genres in the Oral Culture of Children Living in a Traditional Gypsy Community," paper presented at the Fourth International Conference on Romani Linguistics held at the University of Manchester, England, September 2–5, 1998.

92. Okely, *The Traveller-Gypsies,* 77–78.

93. Sway, *Familiar Strangers: Gypsy Life in America,* 104.

94. See Albert Vogel and Nan Elsasser, "Rom (Gypsy), Merimé, and the Schools," *Theory into Practice* 20, 1 (1981): 70–72.

95. Quoted in Sway, *Familiar Strangers: Gypsy Life in America,* 72.

96. Liégeois, *Gypsies and Travellers,* 59.

97. See Beatriz Martín del Campo and David Poveda, "Las narraciones de los niños y las niñas gitanas: Un análisis de géneros discursivos," *Discurso y Sociedad* 4 (2002): 53–80.

9

"No Gift Is Better than Education": The Islamic Educational Enterprise

The twenty-first century will be the century of Islam. Muslim civiliza-
tion will be central to understanding where we will be moving in the fu-
ture. Consider the facts: a population of 1.3 billion and growing; 55
states—and one of them nuclear; about 25 million living permanently in
the West and many of them now making an impact on social, political,
and economic life; and a religion that comes with commitment and pas-
sion. . . . Understanding Islam is therefore imperative to anyone want-
ing to make sense of living in the twenty-first century. . . . Islam has
much to contribute to this century. Islam's ideas of justice, compassion,
and tolerance can contribute to a world desperately in need of these. It is
here where Islam joins with those who desire a world based on these
rules. However, for this vision to be fulfilled, Muslims and non-Muslims
must work together in a spirit of mutual understanding. The first step is
to begin to understand Islam.

—Ahmed (2002, pp. 1, 4)

When the first edition of *Non-Western Educational Traditions* was being written in the mid–1990s, I noted that "it is, in an important sense, inappropriate
for a book concerned with non-Western educational traditions to include a
chapter on Islam and the Islamic educational heritage." I observed that, after
all, Islam is one of the world's three great monotheistic religions, along with
Judaism and Christianity, and approximately one-fifth of the world's population is Muslim.[1] More important, I suggested that Islam as a religion is not independent of the religions of the West in the same way as Buddhism and Hinduism. Rather, I pointed out that Islam is part of what can be termed the
Judeo-Christian-Islamic tradition, sharing with Judaism and Christianity
many core beliefs, ideas, and values.[2] To be sure, the idea that all three religions are part of a single, unified tradition is for some people a problematic
one, because just as they share many elements, so too do they disagree about
key issues.[3] Nevertheless, historically the three faiths are closely related in

ways quite different from their relations with most other religions. This suggests, of course, that Islam is not really "non-Western" in the same way as the other societies and religions examined in this book. Indeed, much of what we consider to be the basis for the Western tradition from the period of classical antiquity was preserved for us not in the West, but rather by Islamic scholars in the Middle Ages.[4]

I then went on to explain why the inclusion in the book nevertheless seemed to me to make a certain amount of sense, using arguments that I still believe to be both valid and relevant. My basic argument was—and remains—a pragmatic and straightforward one. While Islam may well be closely connected with Judaism and Christianity, it has, throughout Western history, been perceived to be alien and different.[5] This view of Islam as an "Other" in our own culture is in many ways as powerful today as ever before, encouraged by the resurgence of what has been called "militant Islam" and other events in the post–9/11 world in which we now live.[6] For many in the West, a lack of knowledge about and understanding of Islam is coupled quite closely with a fear and, in some cases, an active dislike for both the faith and its practitioners. In short, although Islam ought not be seen as non-Western, it nevertheless *is* seen in this light, and so should be treated here if for no other reason than to encourage a more accurate understanding of both Islam and the place of Islam in our own heritage. As John Esposito argued, "A basic knowledge of Islam is becoming essential for every American today. There are five million Muslims living in America. In fact, Islam is the third largest U.S. religion, and by the year 2010 it is expected to be second largest. . . . Islam, like Judaism and Christianity, is an American religion."[7]

Furthermore, given the historical relationship between the West and the Islamic world, one can offer an even stronger case for including the study of Islamic education in a book of this type. As Carolyn Fluehr-Lobban suggested in *Islamic Society in Practice*:

> Perhaps if the recent history of the world were different and Western society did not have the imperial advantage that it has inherited from the legacy of colonialism and economic domination, we might have studies of our culture by non-western people. A chapter entitled "Western Values and Social Practice" in such a study might include sections on individualism, self-sufficiency, entrepreneurial spirit, male supremacy, or optimism. The treatise, written in Arabic, might be read in translation by some "natives" who think it is reductionist and a simplification of their complex, multifaceted social reality.[8]

Just as such a chapter might have been written had recent history been different, then, so must a chapter such as this one be included in a book on non-Western educational traditions. Indeed, I would go so far as to suggest that in terms of its potential relevance for classroom teachers in the U.S. setting, this chapter may well be the most important in the book. Even as the Muslim population in the world, and in our own nation (and, indeed, in many nations throughout the West), continues to increase, our relations with and understanding of the Islamic world continue to be, at best, problematic. Not only is this of concern for us globally; it is also of direct significance for the growing numbers of Muslim students in U.S. schools. In recent years, we have witnessed a number of attacks on Islam and Muslims from religious conservatives in the United States. Rev. Jerry Vines, a past president of the Southern Baptist Convention, incited a public tempest of sorts when he said, "They would have us believe that Islam is just as good as Christianity. Christianity was founded by the virgin-born son of God, Jesus Christ. Islam was founded by Muhammad, a demon-possessed pedophile who had 12 wives, the last one of which was a 9-year-old girl. . . . And I will tell you Allah is not Jehovah, either. Jehovah's not going to turn you into a terrorist."[9] Nor has Vines been alone in attacking Islam: Rev. Jerry Fallwell called Muhammad a terrorist on national television, Rev. Franklin Graham described Islam as a "very evil and wicked religion" and claimed that the *Qur'an* "preaches violence," and Rev. Pat Robertson claimed that Islam is a "monumental scam" and that Muhammed was "an absolutely wild-eyed fanatic . . . a robber and a brigand . . . a killer."[10] Indeed, even an effort simply to expose incoming students to the study of the *Qur'an* as part of a summer reading assignment at the University of North Carolina at Chapel Hill[11] resulted in a lawsuit (ultimately unsuccessful) from a conservative Christian group (the Virginia-based Family Policy Network). In short, Islam is both a timely and controversial topic in U.S. society, and one with which teachers and other educators desperately need to be familiar.

In this chapter, we begin by exploring the basic tenets of Islam as a religion, and then discuss the implications of these tenets for an understanding of what can be called an "Islamic philosophy of education." Next, we examine the ways in which this Islamic philosophy of education has been manifested in traditional Islam education practice.

ISLAM: AN OVERVIEW

There is an unfortunate tendency in the West to attempt to deal with Islam and the Islamic world as if the two were both synonymous and monolithic. Karim H. Karim, in a study of the treatment of Islam by Western media, argued that "the terms 'Muslim world' or 'Islamic world' . . . reinforce the false impression of a monolithic global Muslim entity, the self-image of a unified Muslim *ummah* (community) notwithstanding."[12] This is a significant point that has been made repeatedly by any number of informed writers about Islam, and yet it is also one that has often failed to be understood. As Bruce Lawrence suggested:

Islam is . . . Islam is . . . Islam is . . . Islam is many things. Just as there is no single America or Europe or the West, a seamless caption etching diverse groups and persons with the same values and meanings, so there is no single place or uniform culture called Islam. There is no monolithic Islam. There is a Muslim world spanning Africa and Asia. It is as pluralistic as the West, outstripping both Europe and America in the numerous regions, races, languages, and cultures that it encompasses. The Afro-Asian Muslim world is also internally pluralistic, containing multiple groups who might be said to represent Islamic norms in each Muslim country.[13]

Islam is not monolithic, any more than Christianity is monolithic. Just as the views about Islam quoted previously from the Revs. Vines, Fallwell, Graham, and Robertson do not represent the views of all (or even of most) Christians, so intemperate comments and even extremist actions by some Muslims cannot be taken to represent the Muslim community, Islam itself, or the Islamic world as a whole. As Akbar Ahmed noted in the quote with which this chapter begins, Islam constitutes a faith community of some 1.3 billion human beings, spread throughout not only some fifty-five nations that are predominantly Muslim, but also throughout the West. Such a community must inevitably be highly diverse, and so indeed it is. However, just as Christians share certain common beliefs and practices, despite their differences, so too are Muslims united both with respect to core beliefs and common religious practices, as we shall see. What is essential in this regard is to understand both the diversity and the unity that are present in the Islamic world, and among individual Muslims.

Muhammed: The Prophet of Islam

Discussions of Islam intended for non-Muslims often begin with Muhammad, but this is perhaps misleading. The word *Islam* actually means "submission," as in "submission to the will of God," and the real focus of Islam is not Muhammad, but rather Allah (God).[14] Muhammad is important in his role as God's Prophet, as God's messenger bringing the word of God to humanity, and as a perfect example of how a Muslim should seek to lead his life. As Mary Pat Fisher explained, "Muhammad's life story is important to Muslims, for his example is considered a key that opens the door to the Divine Presence."[15] Nevertheless, Muhammad was a man, the last prophet (*nabi*) in a long series of prophets sent by God to reveal His will—a series of prophets that included Adam, Abraham, Noah, Moses, and Jesus, among others.[16] Islam, however, is far more than its messenger. With this in mind, we turn now to a brief account of the life of Muhammad.

Muhammad was born in 569 or 570 C.E. in the Arabian city of Mecca. His father had died before his birth, and his mother died when he was still quite young. He was initially cared for by his impoverished grandfather, but his grandfather died when Muhammad was only eight years old. The boy was then raised by an uncle, Abu Talib, working first as a shepherd and later accompanying his uncle on caravan trade missions. As a young adult, Muhammad was well known in Mecca for his spirituality and his honesty. He was hired by a wealthy widow, Khadijah, who eventually married him.[17]

From age thirty-five on, Muhammad often spent time alone in spiritual retreats in order to engage in prayer and meditation.[18] At age forty, during one of these retreats, the angel Gabriel appeared to him and told him that God had chosen him to be His messenger to all mankind. The angel insisted that Muhammad recite what he was told, and it was in this way that what we now know as the Qur'an was transmitted from Gabriel through Muhammad to humanity. Three years later, after a pause during which Muhammad continued to pray and meditate, Gabriel appeared again to Muhammad and commanded him to begin publicly proclaiming God's revelation. His message was simple and clear: "the belief in One Transcendent God, in Resurrection and the Last Judgment."[19] His message was a profoundly moral one, grounded in the revelations he was receiving from God—revelations that continued throughout his life, and that his followers were expected to learn by heart. It was also a message that contained hope for the oppressed, which helps to explain both the historical and contemporary power of Islam in many parts of the world.

Muhammad and his followers were persecuted by the Meccan leaders, who saw Muhammad as a social and political revolutionary, threatening the status quo, much as Jesus had been seen in his time. This led, in the year 622 C.E., to Muhammad's departure from Mecca to the more welcoming town of Yathrib (now Medina), where he established the first Muslim community.[20] This event, called the hijrah ("migration"), was a crucial one in the development of Islam, and it is from the date of the hijrah—not that of Muhammad's birth, or even of the first appearance of Gabriel to Muhammad—that the Muslim calendar begins. Ultimately, in 630 C.E., Muhammad and his followers returned triumphantly to Mecca, and then onward to northern Africa, the Persian states, and beyond.

Muhammad's active ministry lasted about twenty-three years, and was a period of immense, indeed of radical, social, and moral change. As one Muslim writer noted, "The most outstanding characteristic of the life of the Prophet is the amazing success which he achieved. The transformation wrought within the space of less than a quarter of a century is in fact unparalleled in the history of the world. There is not a single reformer who brought about such an entire change in the lives of a whole nation inhabiting such a vast country."[21] Not only was Muhammad responsible for a number of far-reaching changes in the values and lifestyles of his followers, but he was also a remarkable individual whose life both inspired and provided a model for others. Muhammad's personal life and character are impressive in their own right, as Caesar Farah explained:

> What kind of person was Muhammad to cause such a deep and lasting stir in the wastes of Arabia? What kind of personality did he have? . . . From what we know, he appears to have been a humble and unpretentious being, if not outrightly austere in his habits and manner of living. He dwelt in a very simple abode in unaffected surroundings. . . . Muhammad possessed a gentle disposition, and his temperament rarely gave way to anger. He was endowed with high moral standards and qualities of trustworthiness to such a degree that his contemporaries were prompted to call him *al-Amin* (the trusted one) long before he embarked on his mission. . . . The dignity of his personal habits, his stately and commanding stature, tact, equilibrium, and self-control made of Muhammad a natural leader of men. . . . He exuded joy to those who were happy and tender sympathy to the afflicted and bereaved. Generous and magnanimous, Muhammad shared his food with the hungry and when he died he left all his modest belongings to the faithful.[22]

It is somewhat difficult to reconcile this image of Muhammad with that offered by Rev. Jerry Vines earlier in this chapter—how could the Muhammad described here be the same man as the "demon-possessed pedophile who had 12 wives, the last one of which was a 9-year-old girl"? The answer is that the latter description is simply wrong, based on ignorance and a misunderstanding of the historical facts of the life and times of Muhammad. Perhaps among the most widely misunderstood aspects of Muhammad's life in the West has been the fact that Muhammad did indeed have a total of twelve wives. This fact has been distorted, and is often used to present Muhammad as a lascivious and even sex-crazed cult leader. The truth, however, is a far different matter. As Akbar Ahmed commented, "The Prophet's marriages have led to colourful innuendoes by critics of Islam. They were often cited in the Middle Ages to prove the voluptuous sensuality of the Prophet. In medieval Europe they helped to create a powerful image which contrasted with the spiritual and ascetic Jesus who never married. But even a cursory examination of the marriages will dispel the charge."[23]

For the first twenty-five years of his life, Muhammad, by all of the accounts available to us, led a celibate and modest life.[24] During this time, he developed a reputation as a thoughtful, fair, and exceedingly moral young man. At the age of twenty-five, he married Khadijah, a woman several years his senior (she was about forty when they were married). Despite the fact that the society in which they lived both sanctioned and encouraged polygamy, Muhammad and Khadijah maintained a monogamous marriage throughout Khadijah's life.[25] After Khadijah's death, which occurred when Muhammad was fifty-four years old, Muhammad did contract a total of eleven additional marriages. However, these marriages were contracted primarily to ensure the protection of women themselves. The women Muhammad married during this period were "between forty and fifty, divorced, often more than once, and had offspring by previous spouses when the Prophet married them. In the harsh terrain of Arabia, and in the difficult circumstances of those days, people aged rapidly, and these women would have been elderly."[26] As Farah explained:

> Muhammad's marriages after Khadijah's [death], yielding about eleven wives in all, were due partly to political reasons and partly to his concern for the wives of his Companions who had fallen in battle defending the nascent Islamic community. In spite of the calumnies heaped upon him by his detractors who, among other things described him as a voluptuary and wife-hungry, a study of Muhammad's marital inclinations reveals that . . . pity and elementary concern prompted him in later years to take on wives who were neither beautiful nor rich, but mostly old widows. The wives of companions fallen in battle had to be looked after, and Muhammad married them in order to offer them shelter and care.[27]

The one noteworthy exception during this period was Muhammad's marriage to A'ishah, the daughter of his most trusted companion Abu Bakr. Although betrothed around age ten, A'ishah was probably about fifteen at the time of her marriage to Muhammad.[28] It is clear that A'ishah and Muhammad had an especially loving relationship, with a great deal of mutual respect and admiration. Whereas today fifteen seems very young to be married, in Muhammad's time and place this was in no way unusual or inappropriate.

The Central Beliefs of Islam

For Islam, there is a close interrelation between belief and practice, and the distinction between being a believer (*mu'min*) and an unbeliever (*kafir*) is to a significant extent based on one's practice.[29] This is so because the basic beliefs of Islam in large part presume certain practices, as we see later in this chapter. This having been said, it is nonetheless possible for us to delineate the beliefs at the core of the Islamic worldview. These core beliefs of Islam are identified clearly in the *Qur'an* itself: "The Prophet believes in what has been revealed to him from his Lord, and so do the Believers. They all believe in God, His angels, His scriptures and His messengers, making no distinction among His prophets. And they say, 'We hear and we obey. Grant us Thy forgiveness, our Lord, and unto Thee is the journeying'" (Sura 2: 285).

As these core beliefs are discussed, it is important to keep in mind the following warning from Suzanne Haneef: "The principles on which the Islamic systems are based are constant, unalterable and universal ones originating in Divine revelation. However, the details of their application may certainly be adjusted as necessary within the Islamic framework to fit existing needs and circumstances."[30] In other words, although the core beliefs may be the same, the ways in which they will be manifested in practice may differ in various social and cultural contexts.[31]

The most fundamental belief of Islam is in the unity and Oneness of God. From a Muslim point of view, "the Oneness of God is the primordial religion taught by all prophets of all faiths. Muhammad merely served to remind people of it."[32] In Arabic, the concept of the unity of God is expressed in the term *tawhid*, which Khurshid Ahmad explained as follows: "*Tawhid* is a revolutionary concept and constitutes the essence of the teachings of Islam. It means that there is only One Supreme Lord of the universe. He is Omnipotent, Omnipresent and the Sustainer of the world and of mankind."[33]

Islam, as noted earlier, teaches that God has sent a series of prophets to mankind—in fact, according to a saying of Muhammad, there have been some 124,000 prophets, beginning with Adam.[34] Before Muhammad, each prophet was sent to renew the message of God's Oneness and unity to a particular people.[35] Only Muhammad, however, "was entrusted with the final and complete statement of God's guidance for the whole of humanity for all time to come."[36] Because of his special role, Muhammad is called the "Seal of the Prophets" in the *Qur'an*, and is believed by Muslims to be the last and final authority in this prophetic tradition.[37]

Two Islamic beliefs that are closely related to the role of the prophetic tradition are the belief in angels and the role of revealed Scriptures. It was the angel Gabriel who appeared to Muhammad, and this was necessary, as Haneef explained:

> Because the glory and majesty of the Creator is so awesome and overwhelming that a limited, flesh-and-blood human being is unable to bear direct contact with Him, God chose to convey His revelation to the prophets, including Muhammad . . . through the agency of an angel. . . . It is because of this vital role of angels as bringers of the Divine revelation to the prophets that belief in them is so important as to form a fundamental article of faith in Islam.[38]

Many of the prophets were also messengers (*rasul*), which is to say that the revelation they left was in written form. Thus, Islam accepts both the Hebrew Torah and the Christian Gospels as revealed Scripture, and Jews and Christians are both recognized in Islam as "people of the Book" (*ahl al-kitab*).[39] The status of the *Qur'an*, however, is somewhat different than that of other Scripture, as we see later in this chapter. For now, it is sufficient to note that for a Muslim, the "*Qur'an* is the only divinely-revealed scripture in the history of mankind which has been preserved to the present time in its exact original form."[40]

Finally, Muslims believe in both an afterlife and in a "Last Judgment" at which people will have to answer for their sins. As stipulated in the *Qur'an*,

"The works of each person We have bound about his neck. On the Day of Resurrection, We shall confront him with a book spread wide open, saying, 'Read your book. Enough for you this day that your own soul should call you to account' " (Sura 17: 13–14).

Islam teaches that there will be a physical, bodily resurrection, followed by either eternal paradise or eternal punishment, depending on God's judgment. Much has been made by writers about the descriptions of paradise found in the *Qur'an*, which emphasize physical and material pleasures. As John Esposito, using the *Qur'an* as his source, described it, the "Garden of Paradise is a heavenly mansion of perpetual peace and bliss with flowing rivers, beautiful gardens, and the enjoyment of one's spouses and beautiful, dark-eyed female companions."[41] Granting that such descriptions are indeed to be found in the *Qur'an*, Hamidullah compellingly pointed out, however, that "all this is easily explained when one thinks of the vast majority of men, of the common masses, to whom the Divine message is addressed. It is necessary to speak to every one according to his capacity of understanding and of intelligence. . . . The *Qur'an* speaks of Paradise and Hell simply as a means of persuading the average man to lead a just life and to march in the path of truth; it attaches no importance to details whether they describe a place or a state of things."[42]

We turn now to a discussion of how these different core beliefs of Islam are manifested in practice in the lives of Muslims.

The Five Pillars of Islam

Although there is a great deal of diversity in the Islamic world with respect to religious practice, there is a core of practices shared by all Muslims. Specifically, there are five essential practices, commonly called the *pillars of Islam*, which are universally accepted throughout the Islamic world.[43] These five pillars of Islam are the profession of faith (*shahadah*), prayer (*salah*), almsgiving (*zakah*), fasting (*sawm*), and the pilgrimage to Mecca (*hajj*).[44]

The *profession of faith* (or *shahadah*, literally "witness" or "testimony") refers to the obligation of Muslims to declare their faith that "there is no god but Allah, and Muhammad is His Prophet" ("*La ilaha illa Allah, Muhammadu Rasul Allah*" in Arabic)[45] (see Fig. 9.1). In other words, the believer accepts the absolute monotheism of Islam, the oneness and unity (*tawhid*) of God, and accepts Muhammad as God's final messenger to humanity. Furthermore, this implies that one accepts the obligation to inform others of the faith, although the *Qur'an* explicitly rejects the use of coercion in such efforts: "Let there be no compulsion in religion; truth stands out clear from error: whoever rejects evil and believes in God has grasped the most trustworthy handle, that never breaks" (Sura 2: 256).

The second pillar of Islam is prayer (*salah*). Muslims pray five times a day, at daybreak, noon, midafternoon, sunset, and evening.[46] Prayer is preceded

FIG. 9.1. A calligraphic presentation of the *Shadadah*.

by ritual ablutions (*wudu'*), normally done with water, which help to prepare the individual for worship. The Muslim then faces Mecca and recites a series of prayers and *Qur'anic* passages. On Fridays, the noon prayer is a congregational one, led by a religious leader (called an *imam*). Prayer is thus both an individual and a communal obligation for the Muslim. As Jane Smith commented:

> For the Muslim, prayer is not simply a mental or spiritual attitude or even just a matter of thanksgiving of the mind and heart. It involves a total bodily response, not simply sitting but putting oneself through a series of complete prostrations. For that reason, mosques do not have chairs or pews. Each of the five daily prayers consists of a series of ritual bowings and bendings (each called a *raka'*) accompanied by the appropriate prayers and invocations. Standing shoulder to shoulder, feet to feet, the worshippers are lined in rows facing the imam, or leader, of the payer. . . . Together they perform several sets of prayer prostrations, which include standing, bowing at the waist with hands placed near the knees, and kneeling and placing one's forehead on the carpet in full supplication. "When you are in that position of complete vulnerability," explains the imam, "you really get a feel for what it means to submit yourself fully to God."[47]

Almsgiving (*zakah*) "is an act both of worship or thanksgiving to God and of service to the community."[48] Although the basic goal of almsgiving is to redress economic inequities and to support the poor, it is not charity, in that it is obligatory rather than voluntary.[49] Muslims are required to donate at least 2.5% of their income in this manner,[50] and the funds are used both for the poor (including widows and orphans) and for the spread of the faith (which includes support for religious and educational institutions). This emphasis on the obligation to help those in need is one that occurs repeatedly in the *Qur'an*: "Who denies religion? It is the person who repulses the orphan and does not promote feeding the poor. Woe to those who worship but are neglectful, those who want to be noticed but who withhold assistance from those in need" (Sura 107: 1–7).

Once each year, during the entire month of Ramadan, all adult Muslims who are able are required to fast (*sawm*) from sunrise to sunset.[51] During the fast, Muslims must abstain from food, drink, smoking, and sexual activity. This is a time for reflection and self-discipline, and "a time to thank God for His blessings, repent and atone for one's sins, discipline the body and strengthen moral character, remember one's ultimate dependence upon God, and respond to the needs of the poor and hungry."[52]

The fifth pillar of Islam is the pilgrimage (*hajj*) to Mecca.[53] All Muslims who can possibly do so are expected to make the pilgrimage at least once in their lifetime. The *hajj* "constitutes a form of worship with the totality of the Muslim's being: with his body, mind and soul, with his time, possessions and the temporary sacrifice of all ordinary comforts, conveniences and tokens of status and individuality which human beings normally enjoy, to assume for a few days the condition of a pilgrim totally at God's service and disposal, His slave who seeks only His pleasure."[54]

Underlying all five of the pillars of Islam is the unity of belief and practice, as well as the idea that Islam is not simply a body of religious beliefs, but is rather a unified and consistent way of life for both the individual and the community.[55] *Shari'a*, or Islamic religious law, provides the framework within which Islamic communities should exist, thus ensuring consistency with the mandates of the *Qur'an*.[56] As Ghulam Sarwar explained, "Islam is a complete way of life. It is the guidance provided by Allah, the Creator of the Universe, for all mankind. It covers all the things people do in their lifetime. Islam tells us the purpose of our creation, our final destiny and our place among other creatures. It shows us the best way to conduct our private, social, political, economic, moral and spiritual affairs."[57]

One of the more controversial aspects of Islam has been the role and place of women in society, and this is an area about which there is considerable debate both in the West and in many contemporary Islamic societies.[58] There can be little doubt that in the time of the Prophet the status of women was improved markedly by Islam, and women are indeed accorded important rights and privileges by *shari'a*.[59] Islamic law grants women the right to enter into contracts, to earn money, and to possess goods in their own right, as well as ensuring their right to inherit.[60] Even more important for our concerns here, women are "equal to [men] in the pursuit of education and knowledge. When Islam enjoins the seeking of knowledge upon Muslims, it makes no distinction between man and woman. Almost fourteen centuries ago, Muhammad declared that the pursuit of knowledge is incumbent on every Muslim male and female."[61]

There are, however, significant distinctions in the rights, duties, and responsibilities of men and women. The distinctions in treatment between them are argued to be manifestations of the different natures of the two genders, and it is commonly asserted that men and women are indeed *equal* in Islam, but they are not the *same*, and Islam therefore accords them appropriately different social positions and responsibilities.[62] As David Waines explained the "Islamic feminist" view:

> Women have the right to education, to religious instruction, to honor and respect, to the vote, and to employment. There are, however, restrictions sanctioned by the religious law for the welfare and stability of society as a whole. A woman can be neither a political leader nor a judge; she must only appear in public modestly dressed, and her natural and sacred task is to keep the household smoothly functioning and to raise and instruct her children to be good Muslims. Men, for their part, must shoulder the burden of providing for the family in material ways. Liberation for a woman does not mean being like a male, or taking up male tasks, but rather being herself and fulfilling the destiny Allah created for her.[63]

In short, both with respect to the role of women and in terms of other aspects of social organization, Islam provides far more than a framework for social organization; it is a total, comprehensive way of life[64] in which religion is integral to economics,[65] politics,[66] law, and society.[67] Indeed, one of the areas in which great deal of philosophical and theological work is being done by contemporary Muslim scholars is that of the "Islamicization of knowledge."[68] The objectives of such an "Islamicization of knowledge," according to Ismail Raji al-Faruqi, include:

- To master the modern disciplines.
- To master the Islamic legacy.
- To establish the specific relevance of Islam to each area of modern knowledge.
- To seek ways for a creative synthesis between the legacy and modern knowledge.
- To launch Islamic thought on the trajectory that leads it to fulfillment of the divine patterns of Allah . . .[69]

These objectives, as we shall see, have important implications for both the philosophy and practice of Islamic education.

The Role of the Qur'an

An understanding of Islam is possible only with an understanding of the *Qur'an*, which holds a unique place in Islam. Whereas both Judaism and Christianity have scriptural traditions that include sacred texts (and are, therefore, as we have already noted, *ahl al-kitab*—i.e., "people of the Book"— from an Islamic perspective), these texts are viewed by most believers in a way quite different from the view of the *Qur'an* in Islamic thought. The *Qur'an* is not the "inspired" Word of God, nor is it a record of what was reported to have been told to Muhammad. Rather, for the Muslim, the *Qur'an* is the exact, literal transcription of the words of God Himself, precisely as they were given to Muhammad.[70] In other words, the *Qur'an* is "the unadulterated word of God, which has become audible through Muhammad."[71] As Suzanne Haneef, writing as a Muslim herself, commented, "The Holy *Qur'an* is the only divinely-revealed scripture in the history of mankind which has been preserved to the present time in its exact original form."[72] This means, of course, that because the *Qur'an* was revealed in Arabic, it was spoken by God (through the angel Gabriel) in Arabic, and should therefore only be read and recited in that language: "To recite the *Qur'an* is the most sublime and edifying occupation for the Muslim, even when he or she does not intellectually understand its words, as is the case with most non-Arab believers. Because the *Qur'an* is the Divine Word *par excellence*, Muslims consider it inconceivable to 'translate' it into any language."[73]

Nor is the *Qur'an* merely written in Arabic; the Arabic in which it is composed is believed by Muslims to be "inimitable and of superhuman beauty and power."[74] Not only do Muslims believe that it is not possible to match the beauty of the style of the *Qur'an*, but they use this style as compelling evidence for its divine origin.[75] Because Muhammad was illiterate, and because the records we have in the *Hadith* (the "Traditions of the Prophet")[76] of his speech make clear that he spoke in a language quite different from that of the *Qur'an*, it follows that he was, as he claimed, only the means of transmission for the *Qur'an*.[77] Therefore, it makes no sense to talk meaningfully about an English-language *Qur'an*, nor can one really talk about a translation into English of the *Qur'an*. Instead, for Muslims, English-language translations are best discussed as "interpretations" of the *Qur'an*. As Haneef explained:

> Because of its extremely distinctive style and language, it is impossible for a translation to do more than convey its bare meaning. The great nobility of its form of expression, the earnest, moving, eloquent style which is its outstanding characteristic, cannot be translated, and hence any translation must be regarded (as all translators themselves confirm) as a mere approximation to the sense of the words.[78]

Finally, unlike both Jewish and Christian scriptures, which were in large part created as written texts, the *Qur'an* is, in essence, an oral text preserved in written form—in fact, the word itself is often translated, "the Recitation." The oral nature of the *Qur'an* is reinforced by the inclusion of *Qur'anic* passages in daily prayers and by the emphasis placed on its recitation by Muslims.[79]

This understanding of the nature of the *Qur'an*, of course, has important educational implications for the Muslim.[80] First, literacy becomes an important religious obligation. Indeed, the name of the *Qur'an* itself, which can also be translated as "that which is to be read," entails a challenge to become literate. Muslims the world over not only read the *Qur'an* but, regardless of their native language, memorize the *Qur'an* in Arabic. Thus, the role of Arabic, as the language not only of the *Qur'an* but also of Islamic prayer, takes on a great significance for the believer as well.

The description of the nature and role of the *Qur'an* in Islam that has been presented thus far in this chapter would, I believe, be seen as reasonably accurate and acceptable by the vast majority of Muslims throughout the world. Although *Qur'anic* exegesis (technically, *al-Tafsir*) has always played an important role in Islamic scholarship, such exegesis has not been informed by the same sorts of scholarly and disciplinary perspectives and methodologies found in much contemporary Jewish and Christian biblical scholarship. Ibn Warraq, in a powerful attempt to advocate for the utilization of such methodologies in the study of Islam, argued that "while modern biblical studies has made great progress building on the works of such pioneers as Wellhausen and Graf, Koranic studies is still lying contentedly, self-satisfied in the procrustean bed prepared by Muslim tradition more than a thousand years ago."[81] Although Warraq's position is certainly outside of the mainstream of Islamic thought and scholarship, his recent edited book *What the Koran Really Says: Language, Text, and Commentary*[82] does offer a fascinating glimpse of what such scholarship might look like. This having been said, it is nevertheless the case that critical historical approaches to the study of Islam and of the *Qur'an* and *Hadith* are neither typical nor accepted within mainstream Islamic intellectual circles.

ISLAMIC PHILOSOPHY OF EDUCATION

Education has, since the time of the Prophet, played a key role in Islam. As A. L. Tibawi commented, "The mosques, became the first schools in Islam [and] it would be equally true to say that the *Qur'an* was the first textbook."[83] In fact, *education* from an Islamic point of view makes little sense if one removes it from a religious context, and it is in the *Qur'an* that educational thought should be grounded.[84] As Abdul-Rahman Salih Abdullah explained:

> Since the *Qur'an* provides the Muslim with an outlook towards life, its principles must guide Islamic education. One cannot talk about Islamic education

without taking the *Qur'an* as one's starting point. . . . The *Qur'an* lays down the foundation for education aims and methods. Moreover, the Muslim educator will find in the *Qur'an* the guiding principles which help in selecting the content of the curriculum.[85]

Given the view of the nature of the *Qur'an* discussed earlier in this chapter, such a view of its centrality for educational thought is hardly surprising. Islamic educational thought, although based on the *Qur'an* and the *Hadith*, has nevertheless been further developed and articulated by Muslim scholars and educators. Among the best examples of such educational philosophers in the Islamic tradition is the theologian, mystic, and teacher al-Ghazali, about whom Tibawi wrote, "Classical Arabic literature contains no theory of education more authoritative, systematic and comprehensive than had been bequeathed by al-Ghazali."[86] Al-Ghazali's philosophy of education provided the bedrock for Islamic educational thought for generations, and "practically all educational literature down to the beginning of modernization in the nineteenth century is either inspired by his writings or directly derived from them."[87]

Al-Ghazali's view of education is characterized by a deep spirituality coupled with both a good deal of common sense and an obvious concern and affection for children. In essence, al-Ghazali believed that there were two ways in which knowledge might be acquired: through human reason and from "light from God." In a good educational setting, a balance will be achieved between these two, albeit one in which the latter is viewed as of greater significance than the former—a resolution of the faith/reason problem reminiscent of that of St. Thomas Aquinas. Furthermore, al-Ghazali believed that all children have the capacity to learn: "Knowledge exists potentially in the human soul like a seed in the soil; by learning the potential becomes actual."[88] The focus of education for al-Ghazali is largely on what might today be called *moral education* rather than on academic learning alone. As Tibawi explained:

> "The child," [al-Ghazali] wrote, "is a trust [placed by God] in the hands of his parents, and his innocent heart is a precious element capable of taking impressions." If the parents, and later on the teachers, brought him up in righteousness he would live happily in this world and the next and they would be rewarded by God for their good deed. If they neglected the child's upbringing and education he would lead a life of unhappiness in both worlds and they would bear the burden of the sin of neglect.[89]

It is worth noting here that within an Islamic framework, unlike in Christianity with its doctrine of "original sin," children are believed to have a basically good nature (*fitrah*),[90] and thus the purpose of education is not viewed as one of "correcting" or "remediating" a sinful nature but rather one of guidance—precisely the same goal as of the *Qur'an* itself.[91]

Another Islamic scholar who contributed important insights to the development of an Islamic philosophy of education was the historian Ibn Khaldun. Ibn Khaldun believed that education could only take place in a civilized social order, and, like the American philosopher of education John Dewey centuries later, he focused on the social nature of education: "Ibn Khaldun starts from first principles: education is a social phenomenon and teaching is one of the social crafts; man is a social animal and his prosecution of learning is conditioned by the nature of the material, intellectual and spiritual forces of the civilization in which he lives."[92]

Ibn Khaldun, like al-Ghazali before him, also addressed the role of reason in the learning process. It is reason that provides the base for education, on Ibn Khaldun's account. As he himself wrote, "Man is distinguished from animals by a capacity to reason. His reason guides him to make a living, to cooperate with other members of his society and to accept what God has revealed through His prophets for man's welfare in this world and the next. Man is therefore a reasoning animal, and reasoning is the foundation of all learning."[93] The ability to reason is not, however, given equally to all people, and there are innate intellectual differences among people. Furthermore, all learning ultimately rests on divine guidance—Ibn Khaldun recommended that learners "seek God's guidance which had illuminated the way of learners before you and taught them that which they knew not."[94] This is an important facet of Islamic educational thought, because it makes clear that any Islamic educational philosophy *must* be value-laden—in the words of Yusuf Waghid, "a theory of Islamic education cannot be epistemologically 'neutral.' "[95]

It is possible for us to identify some of the broad outlines of an Islamic philosophy of education. Abdul-Rahman Salih Abdullah articulated some of the key elements in such a philosophy of education (although he preferred the term *hikmah*) as follows:

The Islamic theory of education is fundamentally based upon the *Qur'anic* concepts. In this theory the door is left open for concepts which come from different fields of knowledge provided that they fit the *Qur'anic* perspective. All elements which cannot be reconciled with Islamic principles should be excluded. It has been pointed out that traditional philosophy which gives excessive weight to reason cannot offer any help to our theory.[96]

Islamic philosophy of education recognizes three distinct kinds of educational aims. Specifically, there are physical aims (*ahdaf jismiyyah*), spiritual aims (*ahdaf ruhiyyah*), and mental aims (*ahdaf 'aqliyyah*).[97] In essence, these aims taken together are concerned with ensuring that education results not merely in the Platonic goal of "a sound mind in a sound body," but rather in a thoroughly integrated personality grounded in the *Qur'an* and in *Qur'anic* morality, because "a person who truly accepts the message of Islam should accept all the ideals embodied in the *Qur'an*."[98] Underlying these different kinds of educational aims in Islamic philosophy of education are the following common, unifying characteristics:

- Islamic education should be concerned with developing the unique characteristics of the individual human beings in such a way as to allow them to adapt to the standards of their society (which should share the ideals of Islam).
- Islamic educational aims should be both realistic and idealistic. In other words, Islamic education must take into account biological needs, while at the same time not accepting an individual's yielding to temptation.
- Because the *Qur'an* and its ideals are timeless and unchangeable, so too must educational ideals grounded in the *Qur'an* be seen as timeless and unchanging. The aims of Islamic philosophy of education are thus universal in nature.
- Islamic education should be concerned both with preparation for this life and with preparation for the Hereafter.
- Islamic educational aims and objectives should be translated into observable behavior.[99]

Having briefly discussed Islamic educational thought, we now turn to an examination of the ways in which this Islamic philosophy of education has been manifested in practice in traditional Islamic schools.

TRADITIONAL ISLAMIC EDUCATIONAL PRACTICE

The traditional Islamic educational system has varied from time to time and from place to place in a number of ways, but underlying the diversity in terms of curricula, teaching methods, and so on, there has been a common core that allows us to talk about a general approach to *Qur'anic* education in the Islamic world.[100] It is important to keep in mind, however, that what is being discussed here is the Islamic educational tradition, rather than the Western-inspired and derived, formal educational systems that are found today in most Islamic countries. Although such modern systems may include religious instruction, they are not "Islamic" in the same sense as traditional *Qur'anic* schools and often coexist with such *Qur'anic* schools, serving very distinct and different purposes, even today.

The basis of traditional Islamic education is the *kuttab*, or *Qur'anic* school, which had developed and become widespread by the 8th century.[101] This institution bears the responsibility for providing all children with the foundations necessary for the practice of their faith. The curriculum focuses on the memorization of the *Qur'an*[102] and the ability to read Arabic, although in some societies this basic curriculum was expanded to include the study of Arabic grammar, poetry, writing, and often penmanship.[103] However, it is important to note here that by "reading Arabic" what is often meant for non-Arabic-speaking children is simply an ability to decode written Arabic for purposes of pronunciation, rather than fluent reading for meaning in what is for them a second language. As Lisbet Holtedahl and Mahmoudou Djingui noted:

> Young Muslims will begin by learning the Arabic alphabet, then go on to recognize letters and repeat them in speech, learn by heart some of the last suras (chapters) of the Quran, and conclude their studies by reciting the entire Quran without necessarily knowing its meaning. Throughout this period of study, they will learn all they need to know in order to say their prayers correctly. Having successfully recited the Quran, a young man may be called a *mallum* and may, if he wishes, establish a school for beginners.[104]

The skills taught in such basic *Qur'anic* schools are both valuable and necessary in the context of an Islamic society, and, in comparing such traditional schooling with that of other societies, it is clear that although such *Qur'anic* schooling "did not take [children] very far . . . it fulfilled the requirements of the great mass of Muslims in the Middle Ages, indeed up to quite recent times, in that it gave them basic literacy. It is worth observing . . . that the level of literacy among the masses of the people in the Islamic world during the Middle Ages, and perhaps even up to the establishment of state primary education in European countries, was probably higher than in Christendom."[105]

Beyond the level of the *kuttab* are other Islamic educational institutions that are responsible for the preparation of Islamic professionals—the scribes, theologians, magistrates, and so on, upon whom an Islamic society relies. Among these advanced institutions are mosque schools, mosque circles, bookshops, and universities (see Fig. 9.2). The most common and significant of these advanced institutions for most Islamic societies have traditionally been the *madaris* (singular, *madrasah*), which provided curricula that include the study of *tafsir* (*Qur'anic* exegesis), the *Hadith, shari'a, fiqh* (Islamic jurisprudence), and a variety of other appropriate subjects (see Fig. 9.3), often at very sophisticated levels of scholarship.[106] An important aspect of such higher education is the role of disputation or "dialectic" (*jadal*), which serves not only as an organizing framework for classroom teaching, but also gives considerable insight into the goals of Islamic higher education in general.[107] In the case of contemporary Shi'ite *madrasa* education, for instance, Roy Mottahedeh observed:

> The image of education as disputation is so powerful that in theory when a student wins a disputation with the teacher, the teacher should cede his place to

PRESCHOOL	No formal organization, home-based
BASIC SCHOOLING	Kuttab
TRANSITIONAL SCHOOLING (Secondary/College)	Palace Schools Masjid (Mosque Schools) Halqha (Mosque Circles) Madrasah
HIGHER EDUCATIONAL INSTITUTIONS	Bait-al-Hikmas (Houses of Wisdom) Bookshop Schools Literary Salons Universities Selected Mosques (e.g., Al-Azhar)

FIG. 9.2.   Traditional types of Islamic educational institutions (8th–14th centuries C.E.).

Linguistic Studies	Arabic Grammar (*al-Nahw wa'l-Sarf*) Rhetoric (*al-Balaghah*) Literature (*al-Adab*)
Qur'anic and Islamic Studies	Scriptural (*Qur'anic*) Knowledge (*al-Qira'at*) Knowledge of the Hadith Scriptural Exegesis (*al-Tafsir*) Theology (*al-Kalam*) Jurisprudence (*al-Fiqh*)
"Philosophical" Studies	Alchemy (Chemistry) Anatomy Astrology Astronomy Botony Geology History Logic Mathematics (including arithmetic, algebra, and geometry) Medicine Meterology Music Philology Philosophy (non-Islamic) Physics Zoology

FIG. 9.3.   Curricular areas of study in traditional Islamic higher education.

another teacher. While this seldom happens, and while there are limits beyond which challenges to the teacher might amount to unacceptable behavior and/ or an unacceptable denial of fundamental precepts of Islam, teachers are likely to teach only those texts over which they feel they have complete mastery. This self-selection more or less decides what level teachers achieve in the system. And, since students can shop around and find which teacher teaches the set text-books in a way most congenial to him, there is a natural selection that "re-tires" unpopular teachers to provincial seminaries or other tasks in the Shi'ite religious establishment.[108]

It is also worth noting at this point that traditional *madrasah* education has come under considerable criticism in many Islamic societies and is often per-ceived (not entirely incorrectly) to be a challenge to Western-oriented state schooling.[109] Typical of the criticisms of traditional *madrasah* education is A. H. Nayyar's claim that "present-day *madrasah* education indicates the ex-istence of an ice age of the intellect."[110] It is interesting to note that such chal-lenges, although grounded in and enunciated in Islamic societies, are in many ways similar to criticisms of some religiously based educational institutions in the West.

CONCLUSIONS

Traditional Islamic educational thought and practice are, in short, insepara-ble from the fabric of Islamic religious thought and practice. As Carolyn Fluehr-Lobban commented about Islam in general, "Islam has been a power-ful unifier because . . . its teachings blend religious, moral, and social practice into an indivisible whole for the believer-practitioner."[111] This unity of Islam is the context in which its educational thought and practice must be under-stood. To a very considerable extent, an understanding of the *Qur'an* is a nec-essary condition for a real understanding of traditional Islamic educational thought and practice. Indeed, the Islamic view of the importance of educa-tion is nowhere articulated more clearly than in the *Qur'an* itself, where we read, "And say, O Muhammad, 'My Lord, increase me in knowledge' " (Sura 20: 114). Three passages from the *Hadith* provide additional support for the importance of education in Islam:

> The Prophet prayed, "O my Lord, do not let the sun set on any day during which I did not increase in knowledge."
> No gift among all the gifts of a father to his child is better than education.[112]
> The person who goes in search of knowledge is on active service for God until he returns.

As the numbers of Muslim students increase in U.S. public schools, an understanding and awareness of Islam will become increasingly significant for classroom teachers and other educators. The challenge before all of us is to find ways to accommodate traditional Islamic beliefs and practices in a 21st-century, highly pluralistic society while at the same time ensuring that all children will receive appropriate educations in public educational institutions.

QUESTIONS FOR REFLECTION AND DISCUSSION

1. Memorization constitutes a central feature of traditional *Qur'anic* educational practice. What are the advantages of learning selected texts (e.g., in the case of Islamic education, the *Qur'an*) by heart? Are there comparable advantages, in our own society, to memorizing other kinds of literature? What, in your view, are the problems associated with the use of extensive memorization in education?

2. The author begins this chapter by suggesting that it may be the most important chapter in the book. Do you agree or disagree with this assessment? Why?

3. In this chapter, it is suggested that Muslims, when discussing the issue of gender and gender relations in Islam, commonly argue that men and women are indeed *equal* in Islam, but they are not the *same*, and Islam therefore accords them appropriately different social positions and responsibilities. What are the educational implications for this argument? How does this view differ from those generally advocated by Western educators?

4. For the Muslim educator, what is the role of moral development in the educational process? Does moral education simply "come with the territory" for the educator, or is there an even stronger relation between the two than this suggests?

5. In contemporary American society, are there other religious groups whose view of the role and purpose of education would parallel that found in Islam? What other commonalities are there between the groups you identify and Muslims? How might one explain these similarities?

6. From a Muslim perspective, the appropriate aims of education, because they are grounded in the *Qur'an*, are understood to be "timeless and unchanging." Does this view of the nature of philosophy of education differ from others with which you are familiar? What are the strengths of such a philosophy? The weaknesses?

7. Although not discussed explicitly in this chapter, an important feature of Islamic educational thought is its underlying epistemology. What generalizations can you make, from your knowledge of Islam and traditional Islamic educational thought and practice, about the epistemological beliefs of Islamic educational thought?

8. As increasing numbers of Muslim students begin attending American public schools in the years ahead, what kinds of changes and adjustments may be required of classroom teachers? What changes, if any, might be needed in the curriculum?

9. How do the three kinds of educational aims identified in this chapter (physical aims, spiritual aims, and mental aims) interrelate and overlap? What are the implications of such a view of educational aims for the curriculum? For teaching methods?

10. Do you agree with the author that there is, in fact, a "Judeo-Christian-Islamic" heritage? Why or why not? How would you describe the relation among these three religious traditions?

RECOMMENDED FURTHER READINGS

There are a number of excellent introductions to Islam. David Waines' *An Introduction to Islam* (Cambridge, England: Cambridge University Press, 1995) and Abdulkader Tayob's *Islam: A Short Introduction* (Oxford: OneWorld, 1999) are recent works of this sort; John Esposito's *Islam: The Straight Path*, expanded ed. (New York: Oxford University Press, 1991), is widely used and available. A very thorough guide to Islam is provided in Caesar Farah's *Islam: Beliefs and Observations*, 7th ed. (Hauppage, NY: Barron's Educational Series, 2003). Other good general works include Karen Armstrong, *Islam: A Short History* (New York: Modern Library, 2002); George W. Braswell, Jr., *Islam: Its Prophet, Peoples, Politics and Power* (Nashville, TN: Broadman & Holman, 1996); Thomas Lippman, *Understanding Islam: An Introduction to the Muslim World*, 2nd rev. ed. (New York: Meridan, 1995); Kenneth Cragg, *The Event of the Qur'an: Islam and Its Scripture* (Oxford, England: OneWorld, 1994); Akbar S. Ahmed's *Discovering Islam: Making Sense of Muslim History and Society* (London: Routledge, 1988), as well as his more recent edited book, *Islam Today: A Short Introduction to the Muslim World* (London: I. B. Tauris, 2001); Frederick Denny's *Islam* (San Francisco: Harper, 1987); and Malise Ruthven, *Islam in the World*, 2nd ed. (Oxford, England: Oxford University Press, 2000). Suzanne Haneef provided an outstanding introduction to Islam from the perspective of an American convert to the faith in her book, *What Everyone Should Know About Islam and Muslims* (Des Plaines, IL: Library of Islam, 1985); and Ruqaiyyah Maqsood's *Islam* (London: NTC Publishing Group, 1994) provides a useful "hands on" introduction to Islam. Finally, a fascinating and sophisticated treatment of contemporary Islam is found in Akbar S. Ahmed's *Postmodernism and Islam: Predicament and Promise* (London: Routledge, 1992).

NOTES

1. See Mary Pat Fisher, *Living Religions*, 2nd ed. (Englewood Cliffs, NJ: Prentice-Hall, 1994), 297.

2. Fisher, *Living Religions*, 297.

3. See, e.g., the fascinating discussion of the way in which the three religions view Abraham in Hans Küng, *Judaism: Between Yesterday and Tomorrow* (New York: Crossroad, 1992), 11–18. A more extended discussion of the same topic is provided in Bruce Feiler, *Abraham: A Journey to the Heart of Three Faiths* (New York: William Morrow, 2002).

4. See George Holmes (ed.), *The Oxford Illustrated History of Medieval Europe* (Oxford, England: Oxford University Press, 1988), 50–51; see also Majid Fakhry, *A History of Islamic Philosophy*, 2nd ed. (New York: Columbia University Press, 1983); Oliver Leaman, *Introduction to Classical Islamic Philosophy* (Cambridge, England: Cambridge University Press, 2002); Franz Rosenthal, *The Classical Heritage in Islam* (London: Routledge, 1992).

5. See Edward Said, *Orientalism* (New York: Vintage, 1978).

6. Godrey H. Jansen, *Militant Islam* (New York: Harper & Row, 1979). Also of interest here are Maxime Rodinson, *L'Islam: Politique et croyance* (Paris: Fayard, 1993); Gilles Kepel and Yann Richard (eds.), *Intellectuels et militants de l'Islam contemporain* (Paris: Éditions du Seuil, 1990); John Voll, *Islam: Continuity and Change in the Modern World*, 2nd ed. (Syracuse, NY: Syracuse University Press, 1994).

7. John Esposito, "Islam in the World and in America," in Jacob Neusner (ed.), *World Religions in America: An Introduction* (Louisville, KY: Westminster/John Knox, 1994), 243. Also of interest here are Jane Smith, *Islam in America* (New York: Columbia University Press, 1999); Shahid Athar, *Reflections of an American Muslim* (Chicago: Kazi, 1994); George W. Braswell, Jr., *Islam: Its Prophet, Peoples, Politics and Power* (Nashville, TN: Broadman & Holman, 1996), 207–246; Yvonne Haddad, Byron Haines, and Ellison Findly (eds.), *The Islamic Impact* (Syracuse, NY: Syracuse University Press, 1984); Jane Smith, *Islam in America* (New York: Columbia University Press, 1999); Sha'ban Muftah Ismail, "Islamic Education in North America: A Reality, a Fact and a Responsibility," *Muslim Education Quarterly* 11, 3 (1994): 63–71; Aminah McCloud, *African American Islam* (London: Routledge, 1995); Yvonne Haddad (ed.), *The Muslims of America* (New York: Oxford University Press, 1991); Michael Wolfe (ed.), *Taking Back Islam: American Muslims Reclaim Their Faith* (New York: Rodale, 2002).

8. Carolyn Fluehr-Lobban, *Islamic Society in Practice* (Gainesville: University of Florida Press, 1994), 44.

9. Quoted in A. Cooperman, "Anti-Muslim Remarks Stir Tempest," *The Washington Post* (20 June 2002), A-3.

10. Quoted in Muslim Public Affairs Council, "Action Alert: Keep Contacting President Bush Regarding Fallwell's Bigotry" (14 October 2002).

11. The assignment was to read Michael Sells, *Approaching the Qur'an: The Early Revelations* (Ashland: White Cloud, 1999).

12. Karim H. Karim, *Islamic Peril: Media and Global Violence* (Montréal: Black Rose Books, 2000), 7.

13. Bruce Lawrence, *Shattering the Myth: Islam Beyond Violence* (Princeton, NJ: Princeton University Press, 1998), 4.

14. See Hammudah Abdalati, *Islam in Focus* (Indianapolis, IN: American Trust Publications, 1975), 1. This is a very important point, and helps to explain why the term *Mohammedan*, which implies (falsely) that Muslims worship Muhammad, is deeply offensive to Muslims. See Maryam Jameelah, *Islam in Theory and Practice* (Lahore, Pakistan: Mohammad Yusuf Khan & Sons, 1986), 20–21; Fluehr-Lobban, *Islamic Society in Practice*, 6–7.

15. Fisher, *Living Religions*, 298; see also Esposito, "Islam in the World and in America," 244–245; Khurshid Ahmad (ed.), *Islam: Its Meaning and Message* (London: Islamic Foundation, 1980).

16. Esposito, "Islam in the World and in America," 244; M. Hamidullah, *Introduction to Islam* (Chicago: Kazi, 1981), 58–61.

17. A very thorough description of Muhammad's early life is provided in Muhammad Husayn Haykal, *The Life of Muhammad* (Indianapolis, IN: American Trust Publications, 1976). See also Karen Armstrong, *Muhammad: A Biography of the Prophet* (San Francisco: Harper, 1992); Clinton Bennett, *In Search of Muhammad* (London: Cassell, 1998); Yahiya Emerick, *Muhammad* (Indianapolis. IN: Alpha, 2002); Ibn Ishaq, *The Life of Muhammad* (London: Oxford University Press, 1967); Martin Lings, *Muhammad: His Life Based on the Earliest Sources* (Rochester, CT: Inner Traditions, 1983); Abdul Hameed Siddiqui, *Life of Muhammad* (Des Plaines, IL: Library of Islam, 1991); Syed Ameer Ali, *The Spirit of Islam: A History of the Evolution and Ideals of Islam with a Life of the Prophet* (Delhi: Low Price Publications, 1990); Maxime Rodinson, *Mohammed* (New York: Vintage, 1974).

18. Hamidullah, *Introduction to Islam*, 6–7; see also Fazlur Rahman, *Islam*, 2nd ed. (Chicago: University of Chicago Press, 1979), 11–29; W. Montgomery Watt, *Muhammad at Mecca* (Karachi, Pakistan: Oxford University Press, 1953).

19. Hamidullah, *Introduction to Islam*, 8.

20.Esposito, "Islam in the World and in America," 245; see also W. Montgomery Watt, *Muhammad at Medina* (Karachi, Pakistan: Oxford University Press, 1956).

21. Maulana Muhammad Ali, *The Living Thoughts of the Prophet Muhammad* (Dublin, OH: Ahmadiyya Anjuman Ishaat Islam, 1992), 4.

22. Caesar Farah, *Islam* (Hauppauge, NY: Barron's, 2003), 66–67.

23. Akbar S. Ahmed, *Islam Today: A Short Introduction to the Muslim World* (London: I. B. Tauris, 2001), 19.

24. Ali, *The Living Thoughts of the Prophet Muhammad*, 28–29.

25. Emerick, *Muhammad*, 33–46.

26. Ahmed, *Islam Today*, 19–20.

27. Farah, *Islam*, 68.

28. See Ali, *The Living Thoughts of the Prophet Muhammad*, 30.

29. John Esposito, *Islam: The Straight Path* (New York: Oxford University Press, 1988), 68–69; see also Maulana Ali, *The Religion of Islam*, 6th ed. (Columbus, OH: Ahmadiyya Anjuman Ishaat Islam, 1990); John Bowker, *What Muslims Believe* (Oxford, England: OneWorld, 1998).

30. Suzanne Haneef, *What Everyone Should Know About Islam and Muslims* (Des Plaines, IL: Library of Islam, 1985), 93.

31. See Alfred Willms, "Nordafrika," in Michael Ursinus (ed.), *Der Islam in der Gegenwart* (München, Germany: Verlag C. H. Beck, 1984), 561–569; Lode Frank Brakel, "Indonesien," in Michael Ursinus (ed.), *Der Islam in der Gegenwart* (München, Germany: Verlag C. H. Beck, 1984), 570–581; Merwyn Hiskett, *The Development of Islam in West Africa*, 2nd ed. (Edinburgh: Edinburgh University Press, 1994); R. O. Lasisi, "French Colonialism and Islamic Education in West Africa, 1900–1939," *Muslim Education Quarterly* 12, 3 (1995): 12–22; Hassan Amdouni, *La famille musulmane: Relations familiales et éducations* (Paris: Al Qalam, 1992).

32. Fisher, *Living Religions*, 308.

33. Khurshid Ahmad, "Islam: Basic Principles and Characteristics," in Khurshid Ahmad (ed.), *Islam: Its Meaning and Message* (London: The Islamic Foundation, 1980), 29; see also Ghulam Sarwar, *Islam: Beliefs and Teaching* (London: Muslim Educational Trust, 1989), 19.

34. Sarwar, *Islam*, 27. Also relevant here is Maulana M. Ali, *History of the Prophets* (Columbus, OH: Ahmadiyya Anjuman Ishaat Islam, 1996).

35. Haneef, *What Everyone Should Know About Islam and Muslims*, 20–21.

36. Haneef, *What Everyone Should Know About Islam and Muslims*, 20.

37. Fisher, *Living Religions*, 309.

38. Haneef, *What Everyone Should Know About Islam and Muslims*, 16–17; see also Fisher, *Living Religions*, 310–311; Sarwar, *Islam*, 27–28.

39. Annemaric Schimmel, *Islam: An Introduction* (Albany: State University of New York Press, 1992), 70; Hamidullah, *Introduction to Islam*, 57–58.

40. Haneef, *What Everyone Should Know About Islam and Muslims*, 18.

41. Esposito, *Islam*, 35.

42. Hamidullah, *Introduction to Islam*, 61.

43. Esposito, "Islam in the World and in America," 247; Fisher, *Living Religions*, 319; Fluehr-Lobban, *Islamic Society in Practice*, 23–37; Peter Riddell and Peter Cotterell, *Islam in Context: Past, Present and Future* (Grand Rapids, MI: Baker Academic, 2003), 45–57.

44. See Fisher, *Living Religions*, 320–323; Sarwar, *Islam*, 40–83; Shaykh Fadhlalla Haeri, *The Elements of Islam* (Shaftesbury, England: Element, 1993), 37–42.

45. See Haneef, *What Everyone Should Know About Islam and Muslims*, 11–15, 42–43; Hamidullah, *Introduction to Islam*, 51–53; Fluehr-Lobban, *Islamic Society in Practice*, 23–24.

46. See Abdalati, *Islam in Focus*, 55–86; Haneef, *What Everyone Should Know About Islam and Muslims*, 43–46; Fluehr-Lobban, *Islamic Society in Practice*, 25–28.

47. Smith, *Islam in America*, 1–2.

48. Esposito, *Islam*, 92.

49. Esposito, *Islam*, 92.

50. Fisher, *Living Religions*, 321.

51. Sarwar, *Islam*, 76–78; Haneef, *What Everyone Should Know About Islam and Muslims*, 46–48.

52. Esposito, "Islam in the World and in America," 249.

53. For a fascinating history of the *hajj*, see Francis E. Peters, *The Hajj: The Muslim Pilgrimage to Mecca and the Holy Places* (Princeton, NJ: Princeton University Press, 1994).

54. Haneef, *What Everyone Should Know About Islam and Muslims*, 51.

55. Ahmad, "Islam," 35–37; Jansen, *Militant Islam*, 17–18. Also of interest here is Christoffel van Nieuwenhuijze, *The Lifestyles of Islam: Recourse to Classicism, Need of Realism* (Leiden, The Netherlands: E. J. Brill, 1985), 93–132.

56. See Joseph Schacht, *An Introduction to Islamic Law* (Oxford, England: Clarendon, 1964); Bassam Tibi, *Islam and the Cultural Accommodation of Social Change* (Boulder, CO: Westview, 1990), 59–75; Ahmad Ibrahim, "Islam and the Law," in *Toward Islamization of Disciplines* (Herndon, VA: International Institute of Islamic Thought, 1989), 381–391; Hamidullah, *Introduction to Islam*, 122–138; Fluehr-Lobban, *Islamic Society in Practice*, 115–141; Ignaz Goldziher, *Introduction to Islamic Theology and Law* (Princeton, NJ: Princeton University Press).

57. Sarwar, *Islam*, 13.

58. See Sarwar, *Islam*, 166–170; Haneef, *What Everyone Should Know About Islam and Muslims*, 142–148; Abdalati, *Islam in Focus*, 184–191; John Esposito with Natana DeLong-Bas, *Women in Muslim Family Law*, 2nd ed. (Syracuse, NY: Syracuse University Press, 2001); Fatima Mernissi, *The Veil and the Male Elite: A Feminist Interpretation of Women's Rights in Islam* (Reading, MA: Addison-Wesley, 1987); Fatima Mernissi, *Beyond the Veil: Male–Female Dynamics in Modern Muslim Society* (Bloomington: Indiana University Press, 1987); Eleanor Doumato, *Getting God's Ear: Women, Islam, and Healing in Saudi Arabia and the Gulf* (New York: Columbia University Press, 2000).

59. Sarwar, *Islam*, 166–167; Abdalati, *Islam in Focus*, 184–185.

60. Abdalati, *Islam in Focus*, 187.

61. Abdalati, *Islam in Focus*, 186.

62. Haneef, *What Everyone Should Know About Islam and Muslims*, 145–146; Abdalati, *Islam in Focus*, 187–191; Braswell, *Islam*, 148–156.

63. David Waines, *An Introduction to Islam* (Cambridge, England: Cambridge University Press, 1995), 255.

64. See Ahmad, "Islam," 37–38; Maxime Rodinson, *Islam et capitalisme* (Paris: Éditions du Seuil, 1966).

65. For detailed discussions about the nature of Islamic economics, see Hamidullah, *Introduction to Islam*, 139–154; Muhammad Najatullah Siddiqi, "Islamizing Economics," in *Toward Islamization of Disciplines* (Herndon, VA: International Institute of Islamic Thought, 1989), 253–261; Mahmoud Abu Saud, "Toward Islamic Economics," in *Toward Islamization of Disciplines* (Herndon, VA: International Institute of Islamic Thought, 1989), 265–270; Muhammad Abdul Mannan, "The Frontiers of Islamic Economics: Some Philosophical Underpinnings," in *Toward Islamization of Disciplines* (Herndon, VA: International Institute of Islamic Thought, 1989), 295–311.

66. See Johannes Reissner, "Die innerislamische Diskussion zur modernen Wirtschafts-und Sozialordnung," in Michael Ursinus (ed.), *Der Islam in der Gegenwart* (München, Germany: Verlag C. H. Beck, 1984), 155–169; Hamidullah, *In-*

troduction to Islam, 107–121; Aziz Al-Azmeh, *Islams and Modernities* (London: Verso, 1993), 89–103.

67. See Schacht, *An Introduction to Islamic Law;* Tibi, *Islam and the Cultural Accommodation of Social Change*, 59–75; Ahmad Ibrahim, "Islam and the Law"; Hamidullah, *Introduction to Islam*, 122–138; Fluehr-Lobban, *Islamic Society in Practice*, 115–141.

68. For detailed discussions of this topic, see Masudul Alam Choudhury, "A Critical Examination of the Concept of Islamization of Knowledge in Contemporary Times," *Muslim Education Quarterly* 10, 4 (1993): 3–34; M. A. Kazi, *Islamic Thought and Modern Science* (Amman, Jordan: Islamic Academy of Sciences, 1997); Talat Sultan, "The Role of Islamic Universities in the Islamization of Education," *Muslim Education Quarterly* 14, 3 (1997): 57–63; John Esposito and François Burgat (eds.), *Modernizing Islam: Religion in the Public Sphere in Europe and the Middle East* (New Brunswick, NJ: Rutgers University Press).

69. Quoted in Mohammad Ishaq Khan, *Experiencing Islam* (Karachi, Pakistan: Oxford University Press, 1996), 99.

70. John Sahadat, "Divine Revelation and the Status of the Qur'an," *Muslim Education Quarterly* 13, 4 (1996): 4–17; see also Mohammad Kahn (ed.), *Education and Society in the Muslim World* (Jeddah, Saudi Arabia: King Abdulaziz University, 1981); Mohammad Abu-Hamdiyyah, *The Qur'an: An Introduction* (London: Routledge, 2000); Michael Cook, *The Koran: A Very Short Introduction* (Oxford, England: Oxford University Press, 2000); Maulana Ali, *Introduction to the Study of the Holy Qur'an* (Columbus, OH: Ahmadiyya Anjuman Ishaat Islam, 1992); Muhammad Haleen, *Understanding the Qur'an: Themes and Style* (London: I. B. Tauris, 2001); Farid Esack, *The Qur'an: A Short Introduction* (Oxford, England: OneWorld, 2002); Riddell and Cotterell, *Islam in Context*, 58–68.

71. Schimmel, *Islam*, 29; see also Alfred Guillaume, *Islam* (Harmondsworth, England: Penguin, 1956), 55; Mohammad Arkoun, *Rethinking Islam: Common Questions, Uncommon Answers* (Boulder, CO: Westview, 1994), 35–39.

72. Haneef, *What Everyone Should Know About Islam and Muslims*, 18; see also Sarwar, *Islam*, 32–33.

73. Haneef, *What Everyone Should Know About Islam and Muslims*, 18.

74. Schimmel, *Islam*, 30; see also W. Montgomery Watt and Richard Bell, *Introduction to the Qur'an* (Edinburgh: Edinburgh University Press, 1970).

75. See Abdalati, *Islam in Focus*, 193; Esposito, *Islam*, 22–23.

76. See Ram Swarup, *Understanding the Hadith: The Sacred Traditions of Islam* (Amherst, NY: Prometheus, 2002); Thomas Cleary, *The Wisdom of the Prophet: Says of Muhammad, Selections from the Hadith* (Boston: Shambhala, 2001).

77. Haneef, *What Everyone Should Know About Islam and Muslims*, 19.

78. Haneef, *What Everyone Should Know About Islam and Muslims*, 19.

79. See Waines, *An Introduction to Islam*, 23–24.

80. Helmut Gätje, *Koran und Koranexegese* (Zurich: Artemis Verlag, 1971); Allahbukhsh Brohi, "The *Qur'an* and Its Impact on Human History," in Khurshid Ahmad (ed.), *Islam: Its Meaning and Message* (London: The Islamic Foundation, 1980), 89–91; Charles Stanton, *Higher Learning in Islam: The Classical Period, A.D. 700–1300* (Savage, MD: Rowman & Littlefield, 1990), 1–20.

81. Ibn Warraq, "Introduction," in Ibin Warraq (ed.), *What the Koran Really Says: Language, Text, and Commentary* (Amherst, NY: Prometheus, 2002), 90.

82. See Warraq, *What the Koran Really Says: Language, Text, and Commentary*.

83. Abdul L. Tibawi, *Islamic Education: Its Traditions and Modernization into the Arab National Systems* (London: Luzac & Co., 1972), 24.

84. Seyyed Hossein Nasr, "Islamic Education and Science: A Summary Appraisal," in Yvonne Haddad, Byron Haines, and Ellison Findly (eds.), *The Islamic Impact* (Syracuse, NY: Syracuse University Press, 1984), 48; see also Seyyed Hossein Nasr, *Traditional Islam in the Modern World* (London: Routledge & Kegan Paul, 1987), 147–163; S. Waqar Ahmed Husaini, *Islamic Science and Public Policies: Lessons from the History of Science*, 2nd rev. ed. (Indianapolis, IN: Islamic Book Service, 1986), 16–24; Shmad Shalabi, *History of Muslim Education* (Beirut, Lebanon: Dar Al-Kashshaf, 1954), 15.

85. Abdul-Rahman Salih Abdullah, *Educational Theory: A Qur'anic Outlook* (Makkah, Saudi Arabia: Umm Al-Qura University, 1982), 25.

86. Tibawi, *Islamic Education*, 39.

87. Tibawi, *Islamic Education*, 41.

88. Quoted in Tibawi, *Islamic Education*, 40.

89. Tibawi, *Islamic Education*, 40.

90. Abdullah, *Educational Theory*, 31.

91. See Nasr, "Islamic Education and Science," 48.

92. Tibawi, *Islamic Education*, 42.

93. Quoted in Tibawi, *Islamic Education*, 42.

94. Quoted in Tibawi, *Islamic Education*, 43.

95. Yusuf Waghid, "Why a Theory of Islamic Education Cannot Be Epistemologically 'Neutral,'" *Muslim Education Quarterly* 13, 2 (1996): 43–54.

96. Abdullah, *Educational Theory*, 43.

97. Abdullah, *Educational Theory*, 119.

98. Abdullah, *Educational Theory*, 121.

99. Abdullah, *Educational Theory*, 129–133.

100. See, e.g., Seydon Cissé, *L'enseignement islamique en Afrique noire* (Paris: L'Harmattan, 1992); Dale Eickelman, *Knowledge and Power in Morocco: The Education of a Twentieth-Century Notable* (Princeton, NJ: Princeton University Press, 1985), 59–65; J. Berkey, *The Transmission of Knowledge in Medieval Cairo: A Social History of Islamic Education* (Princeton, NJ: Princeton University Press, 1992). The development of Islam in sub-Saharan Africa in particular has been explored in depth by a number of scholars in enlightening and useful ways. See Eva Rosander and David Westerlund (eds.), *African Islam and Islam in Africa* (Athens, OH: Ohio University Press, 1997); Hiskett, *The Course of Islam in Africa*; Roman Loimeier, *Islamic Reform and Political Change in Northern Nigeria* (Evanston, IL: Northwestern University Press, 1997); René Otayek (ed.), *Le radicalisme islamique au sud du Sahara: Da'wa, arabisation et critique de l'Occident* (Paris: Éditions Karthala, 1993); Christian Coulon, *Les musulmans et le pouvoir en Afrique noire: Religion et contre-culture* (Paris: Éditions Karthala, 1988).

101. Bayard Dodge, *Muslim Education in Medieval Times* (Washington, DC: The Middle East Institute, 1962), 3–5; Mehdi Nakosteen, *History of Islamic Origins of Western Education, A.D. 800–1350* (Boulder, CO: University of Colorado Press, 1964), 44–45.

102. See Corinne Fortier, "Mémorisation et audition: L'enseignement coranique chez les Maures de Mauritanie," *Islam et Sociétiés au Sud du Sahara* 11 (1997): 85–105.

103. See Tibawi, *Islamic Education*, 43.

104. Lisbet Holtedahl and Mahmoudou Djingui, "The Power of Knowledge," in Eva Rosander and David Westerlund (eds.), *African Islam and Islam in Africa* (Athens, OH: University of Ohio Press, 1997), 259.

105. Hiskett, *The Development of Islam in West Africa*, 55.

106. Hiskett, *The Development of Islam in West Africa*, 55; see Arkoun, *Rethinking Islam*, 35–48.

107. It is important to note here that the nature of such disputation as a means of study and understanding, although bearing some outward similarity to Talmudic study, is in fact firmly grounded in Aristotelean logic and methodology. Thus, its closest parallel in the West is probably to medieval scholastic philosophy. See Roy Mottahedeh, "Traditional Shi'ite Education in Qom," in Amelie Rorty (ed.), *Philosophers on Education: New Historical Perspectives* (London: Routledge, 1998), 451–457; Stanton, *Higher Learning in Islam*, 42–46, 53–90.

108. Mottahedeh, "Traditional Shi'ite Education in Qom," 453.

109. See, e.g., Aziz Talbani, "Pedagogy, Power, and Discourse: Transformation of Islamic Education," *Comparative Education Review* 40, 1 (1996): 66–82.

110. A. H. Nayyar, "Madrasah Education Frozen in Time," in Pervez Hoodbhoy (ed.), *Education and the State: Fifty Years of Pakistan* (Karachi, Pakistan: Oxford University Press, 1998), 215.

111. Fluehr-Lobban, *Islamic Society in Practice*, 2.

112. Quoted in Haneef, *What Everyone Should Know About Islam and Muslims*, 162.

10

Themes and Lessons in the Study of Non-Western Educational Traditions: Toward a Beginning

The first chapter of this book suggested that "it is neither idealistic nor unrealistic to suggest that we can learn much from non-Western educational traditions." We have explored and examined a number of non-Western educational traditions in *Non-Western Educational Traditions: Indigenous Approaches to Educational Thought and Practice*, and are now in a better position to evaluate this claim. In each of the traditions that we have studied, there have been similarities both to other non-Western educational traditions and to our own Western tradition, just as each of the traditions has offered unusual and even unique features. In this final chapter, we look at some of the themes that appear to be fairly common across the different traditions we have examined and try to determine what lessons might be learned from these common themes. We also briefly discuss some of the many non-Western educational traditions that have not been addressed in this book, but that might merit the attention of scholars and educators in the future.

SOME COMMON THEMES IN INDIGENOUS EDUCATIONAL TRADITIONS

Underlying the common themes that seem to be reflected in the various non-Western educational traditions that we have studied is a powerful answer to the question, "Have we lost something important and valuable in Western education?" Until recently, Western scholars tended to view non-Western educational traditions as largely irrelevant and unrelated to their concerns, and, when they have dealt with such areas at all, they all too often did so through a very potent and distorting lens. That lens was the assumption that non-Western educational traditions were in some significant way "primitive."

Thus, when George Pettitt in the mid–1940s wrote what remains the single most comprehensive study of Native American educational thought and practice, he and others saw nothing odd about naming his monograph *Primitive Education in North America*.[1] And yet, if there is any single conclusion that can be reasonably reached from the cases that we have examined in this book, it is that there is much that those of us in the West can and should learn from the traditions of the non-Western world. In short, we have indeed lost something important and valuable, and that "something" can be found in the very traditions that were wrongly labeled "primitive." As Adam Kuper forcefully argued, the very idea of a "primitive society" is a concept developed by Western scholars to delegitimize the societies and social systems of others.[2] Given the evidence now available, it is simply not credible to believe that non-Western approaches to childrearing and education are in any way inferior to those with which we are more familiar. They are different, to be sure, and they functioned to prepare children and young people for very different kinds of societies—but they did so, for the most part, effectively and humanely.

Moving beyond the rejection of the view of non-Western educational traditions as primitive, we find that there are at least seven broad themes that seem to be fairly (although not universally) common among the different traditions that we have studied in this book. Each of these themes is now briefly discussed.

A fundamental distinction between contemporary Western conceptions of education and many of the non-Western systems that we have examined is that between formal schooling and education. Formal schooling played important roles in many non-Western traditions (consider, e.g., its potency in traditional Chinese education), and it was to some extent present in most of the traditions that we studied (e.g., in initiation schools in Africa). However, it is also clear that the common tendency in our own society to conflate and confuse "formal schooling" with "education"—a tendency reflected in our concern with formal certification and degrees rather than with competence per se—has been far less common in non-Western traditions. To be sure, this may well be explained in large part by the nature and needs of different kinds of social organization. Our concerns with formal schooling no doubt reflect the nature of modern society, and in earlier times our tradition was far less concerned with formal schooling. The difference between formal schooling and education is, nonetheless, an important one for us to keep in mind, and the study of non-Western educational traditions certainly functions effectively to bring it to the forefront of our attention.

A second common theme in the non-Western educational traditions that we have studied is that education has tended to be community-based and communal in nature to a very great extent. Not only have adults and older children in the community tended to play important educational roles in the society, but with relatively few exceptions there has been relatively little focus on identifying educational specialists in non-Western societies. Education and childrearing have commonly been seen as a social responsibility shared by all of the members of the community. Although individuals may play greater or lesser roles in this undertaking, it is significantly seen as the province of everyone. Thus, the concept of some adults being *teachers* and others (presumably) being *non-teachers* is a somewhat alien one to many traditions. Furthermore, it is interesting to note that in none of the cases examined here—even those with the most fully articulated formal educational systems—was there any explicit, formal training for those who would play teaching roles. The idea of teachers engaging in a profession, with specialized knowledge and expertise not held by others, appears to be a Western, and indeed relatively recent, innovation.

Related to the community-based focus of many non-Western educational traditions is the broadly shared concern with what might be called *civic education*. In every case we have studied, there is a concern with helping children grow into the kind of adults who will function effectively and appropriately in their society. In many of the non-Western traditions that we have examined, this focus has clear political overtones, whereas in others a more spiritual concern is at issue. Furthermore, although there is a common concern with preparing the children for life in their society, this is not to say that there is a blind acceptance of the *status quo*. Indeed, just the opposite seems to be true—even in the more conservative instances, there is always room for individuals to challenge their society, albeit often at considerable personal cost. Thus, for instance, in the African tradition we find the role of the *imbongi*, whereas in the Chinese case we learn that in all relationships the rights and privileges of the educated person are seen in reciprocal terms; and in Aztec society, the higher one's rank, the greater the punishment for violating social norms.

Not only do non-Western educational traditions stress what can be called civic education, but they also emphasize the need for all children to be prepared to function economically in their society. Thus, what would today be called *vocational education* can be found in every case that we have studied. In some cases, occupations can be chosen by the child or the child's family, whereas in others special skills and aptitudes are required. Still other occupations are open only to selected individuals, often on the basis of birth. Finally, it is in the area of preparation to function economically that one finds the greatest degree of gender stratification. In most non-Western societies, the roles of men and women are different, and the differences are clearly demarcated. Thus, girls learn the skills they will need from the mothers (and, often, from other female relatives), whereas boys learn the skills that they will need from their fathers, uncles, and other adult male role models. It is also important in this context to note that although all of the traditions examined in this book pay attention to the vocational needs of the individual, this focus is different from that found in contemporary American society in a significant way. In modern capitalist societies in general, and in American society in particular, educational institutions are often expected to serve the needs of the economy (or, more accurately, of employers) rather than the needs of individual workers. To be sure, one could suggest that these two sets of needs ought to be, at least in the ideal, very similar, but they are by no means the same. In the cases examined in this book, the emphasis placed on vocational preparation is largely an empowering one, with the greater emphasis normally placed on the needs and aptitudes of the individual rather than on the needs of the employer.

The role of the family is, in every case we have examined, the central facet of education. Other social institutions may well play important and valuable roles, and nonfamily members may also perform important educational roles, but it is the family that is the key to the child's education. To be sure, different societies define the family in different ways, but what is common is the idea that it is the family as a unit that bears the ultimate responsibility for the children and for their education and upbringing. At the same time, in the cases examined here (and, in fact, in non-Western traditions generally), it is clear that the final say in decisions about childrearing and education almost always rests with the family rather than with the society at large.

The role of language plays a surprisingly important part in almost all non-Western educational traditions. Although many non-Western traditions do indeed have rich written traditions, others have been entirely oral. This has meant that the way in which language skills are taught and used may vary among different non-Western societies, but the concern with the *proper* use of language, knowledge of the spoken traditions of the community, and the ability to sue language creatively to reason and to argue are all powerful components of language use, and they are virtually universal in the cases we have examined. Perhaps most interesting in this regard is the explicit Rom recognition of the role of performance and "impression management"—activities in which we all participate, but that are not generally discussed in our own society and culture.

Last, we come to the issue of values, morality, and spirituality in education. In every educational tradition that we have studied in *Non-Western Educational Traditions: Indigenous Approaches to Educational Thought and Practice*, the principal goal of education seems to be the development of a *good person*. Although there may be differences of opinion about selective aspects of the nature of this good person, there are also a number of core features (such as honesty) that are agreed on in every case we have studied. As Jack Forbes, writing about Native American education, argued:

> The main thing I want to emphasize is that there can be no education that is multicultural involving the Native American tradition unless it gets into this area of the meaning of life, unless it gets into the area of values. . . . I don't have

the answer as to how you bring a spiritual path into schools in a society which is going in the opposite direction. I don't have the answer as to how you do that, except that we must try.[3]

Each of these common themes that have been identified and briefly discussed here have much to teach us about not only what others have done and believed about education, but about what we ourselves seem to assume and believe about education. There are many valuable lessons that could be learned from the wisdom of others, and such insights should not be lightly put aside. We turn now to a discussion of the challenges, both epistemological and conceptual, presented by various indigenous knowledge systems and traditions, and will then move on to briefly explore some of the non-Western educational traditions that we have not examined in this book.

THE EPISTEMOLOGY AND EPISTEMOLOGICAL CHALLENGE OF INDIGENOUS KNOWLEDGES

Knowledge, as we saw in chapter 1, is always constructed in a particular social context. When we speak of "indigenous knowledges," what we are concerned with are non-Western approaches to understanding reality. Such indigenous knowledges continue to coexist with Western constructions of knowledge in many parts of the world, even as they continue to be denigrated and rejected as "unscientific" and even "primitive" and "backward" by many. In fact, indigenous knowledges are bodies of knowledge and understanding that have developed and evolved over time, and therefore contain significant quantities of information and connections about the world in which we live. To be sure, not all indigenous knowledge is correct, but then neither is much of the knowledge that is believed as part of the Western intellectual and scholarly tradition. More to the point, much indigenous knowledge—especially knowledge about the physical world in which people have lived often for centuries and even millennia—may in fact be far ahead of Western knowledge of the same physical areas. In recent years we have witnessed a growing interest among Western scientists in the pharmacological properties and potential of various traditional remedies for different illnesses and medical conditions. Furthermore, as Semali and Kincheloe argued, "The dilemma we face in defining indigenous knowledge and what it means in the context of millions of indigenous peoples of the world is central to the postmodern and post-colonial debates on the origins of knowledge and the manner in which it is produced, retrieved and distributed throughout the academy."[4] As this passage suggests, the value of indigenous knowledges is not only practical and pragmatic, as some would suggest, but is rather profoundly *epistemological* in nature. Ultimately, what we are concerned with is "the transformative power of indigenous knowledge, the ways that such knowledge can be used to foster empowerment and justice in a variety of cultural contexts. A key aspect of this transformative power involves the exploration of human consciousness, the nature of its production, and the process of its engagement with cultural difference. . . . Indigenous knowledge is a rich social resource for any justice-related attempt to bring about social change."[5]

Indigenous knowledges are important not just because of the potential value of what is known, but also because they can provide us with alternative ways of coming to know. As Marcel Viergever noted:

> Most strategies for the preservation of indigenous knowledge concentrate on documentation and *ex-situ* storage. This is a direct consequence of the fact that most scientists do not acknowledge that indigenous knowledge is the product of a dynamic and creative system to resolve perceived problems. . . . If, however, we accept . . . that the generation of knowledge is a dynamic process embedded in the physical and social environment of communities, storage of specific knowledge is insufficient, or even detrimental to the continuation of the processes responsible for knowledge generation.[6]

In other words, it is both the process and products of indigenous knowledges with which we need to be concerned, and there is a growing scholarly literature addressing both of these aspects of indigenous knowledges.[7] What needs to be understood, in short, is what is essentially the intellectual colonialism of narrow Western conceptions of science:

> We see various ways that Western science is deployed as a tool of oppression. While understanding progressive uses of Western science and the complexity of its socio-political role, we emphasize in this context the problematic nature of Western science and its power saturated relationship with indigenous knowledge. Western modernism has often understood the experience of various "others," including the indigenous other, from a narrow Eurocentric perspective.[8]

This does not, of course, mean the rejection of Western science; it merely calls on us to be a bit more open to alternative ways of knowing, and alternative constructions of reality.

AREAS FOR FUTURE RESEARCH

In *Non-Western Educational Traditions: Indigenous Approaches to Educational Thought and Practice* we have examined a number of different non-Western educational traditions, but there are, of course, far more non-Western educational traditions that have not even been mentioned thus far. It is certainly not the point of this chapter to cover all of the ground that remains; indeed, even if we wished to do so, it would not be possible. What we can do, however, is to simply identify other non-Western educational traditions that merit further, careful study. The following are among those traditions that have much to teach us, and that provide both interesting counterpoints to some of the cases discussed in this book and often strong support for the common themes that we have identified:

- The traditional educational thought and practice of the different peoples in Oceania, including certainly the fascinating case of the Maori civilization.
- The traditional educational thought and practice of different groups of the Australian Aborigines (the indigenous peoples of Australia).
- A detailed study of both childrearing and formal education in the Inca empire before the Conquest.
- Detailed, focused examinations of particular groups in Africa, the Americas, and so on.
- The traditional educational thought and practice of various societies in Asia (and, in particular, those of Japan and Korea), especially with respect to how indigenous practices have interacted with those imported from China.

Another related area for future study is that of the interaction between traditional forms of educational thought and practice and imposed Western ones. There are relatively few instances today where formal schooling is anything but Western in structure; government schooling is virtually always fundamentally Western in orientation. As Levinson and Holland observed:

Around the world, modern schools are central to the social and cultural shaping of the young. Relatively new to history, especially for those people situated on the margins of industrialization, institutions of mass schooling often remove children from their families and local communities, encouraging mastery of knowledges and disciplines that have currency and ideological grounding in wider spheres. . . . These schools have served to inculcate the skills, subjectivities, and disciplines that undergird the modern nation-state. No matter how the knowledgeable person is locally defined, regardless of the skills and sensibilities that count as indicators of "wisdom" and intelligence in the home and immediate locale, schools interject an educational mission of extra-local proportions.[9]

Finally, the issues surrounding indigenous knowledges, discussed earlier in this chapter, are clearly of significance, and this is an area of research in which scholars are only now beginning to explore. Needless to say, these topics and areas for future study are far from an exhaustive list. This book is intended to be at most a first step in our study of non-Western educational traditions, and it is a first step on a very long road. This having been said, it should also be kept in mind that every trip, no matter how long, must begin with a first step.

CONCLUSIONS

The first chapter of this book ended with an intriguing quote from Ali Mazrui. Mazrui, a noted African scholar, argued: "I cannot help feeling that it is about time Africa sent missionaries to Europe and America, as well as teachers, engineers, doctors, and ordinary workers. . . . It is indeed time that Africa counter-penetrated the western world."[10]

If Mazrui was correct, then perhaps not only Africa, but the rest of the non-Western world as well needs to send us missionaries, for they do indeed have much to teach us. At the same time, we need not reject everything in our own tradition. In the operetta *The Mikado*, Gilbert and Sullivan spoke disparagingly about "the man who loves every century but this and every country but his own." Other societies and traditions have many strengths, as does our own, just as they have many weaknesses, as does our own. The fundamental point of this book has been that there is much in *every* society that is worthwhile and valuable, and we need to learn to do a better job of learning from one another.

QUESTIONS FOR REFLECTION AND DISCUSSION

1. What are the implications of the concept of "indigenous knowledges" for educators, both in the Western world and elsewhere? Do you believe that indigenous knowledges and Western, "scientific" knowledge are compatible or incompatible? Why?

2. It is pointed out in this chapter that "the idea of teachers engaging in a profession, with specialized knowledge and expertise not held by others, appears to be a Western, and indeed relatively recent, innovation." What are the benefits of viewing teachers as a specialized profession? What problems do you see with this development in our society?

3. One of the common themes identified in this chapter is that of the role of spirituality in education. In your view, should spirituality play a significant role in a secular, public education? What limits, if any, need to be observed in "spiritual education"?

4. How are the common themes found in the non-Western educational traditions discussed in this chapter reflected or manifested in contemporary American education? What lessons can we learn from these themes?

5. In your view, what is the single most important idea that has emerged in our study of non-Western educational traditions and practices? How do you see that idea affecting your practice as an educator?

RECOMMENDED FURTHER READINGS

Although works that deal explicitly with non-Western educational thought and practice continue to be rare, a number of outstanding works have appeared in recent years. Among the best are Ladislaus Semali and Joe Kincheloe's edited collection, *What Is Indigenous Knowledge? Voices from the Academy* (New York: Falmer Press, 1999); Seanna McGovern's *Education, Modern Development and Indigenous Knowledge: An Analysis of Academic Knowledge Production* (New York: Garland: 1999); and Maenette Benham and Joanne Cooper's edited work, *Indigenous Educational Models for Contemporary Practice: In Our Mother's Voice* (Hillsdale, NJ: Lawrence Erlbaum Associates, 2000). Works dealing with specific non-Western traditions are cited in the bibliography.

NOTES

1. George Pettitt, *Primitive Education in North America* (Berkeley: University of California Press, 1946).

2. See Adam Kuper, *The Invention of Primitive Society: Transformations of an Illusion* (London: Routledge, 1988).

3. Jack Forbes, "Traditional Native American Philosophy and Multicultural Education," in *Multicultural Education and the American Indian* (Los Angeles: American Indian Studies Center, University of California, 1979), 11.

4. Ladislaus Semali and Joe Kincheloe, "Introduction: What Is Indigenous Knowledge and Why Should We Study It?" in L. Semali and J. Kincheloe (eds.), *What Is Indigenous Knowledge? Voices from the Academy* (London: Falmer Press, 1999), 4.

5. Semali and Kincheloe, "Introduction," 15.

6. Marcel Viergever, "Indigenous Knowledge: An Interpretation of Views from Indigenous Peoples," in L. Semali and J. Kincheloe (eds.), *What Is Indigenous Knowledge? Voices from the Academy* (London: Falmer Press, 1999), 338.

7. See, e.g., D. Brokensha and O. Warren (eds.), *Indigenous Knowledge Systems and Development* (Lanham, MD: University Press of America, 1980); A. Agrawal, "Indigenous Knowledge and Scientific Knowledge: Some Critical Comments," *Indigenous Knowledge and Development Monitor* 3 (1995): 3–6; D. Shankar, "The Epistemology of the Indigenous Medical Knowledge Systems in India," *Indigenous Knowledge and Development Monitor* 4 (1996): 13–14; R. Barnhardt, "Higher Education in the Fourth World: Indigenous People Taking Control," *Canadian Journal of*

Native Education 18 (1990): 199–231; James Handawela, "Towards a Methodology to Test Indigenous Knowledge," *Compass* (March 2001): 44–46; D. Warren, L. Slikker-veer, and D. Brokensha (eds.), *The Cultural Dimension of Development: Indigenous Knowledge Systems* (London: Intermediate Technology Publications, 1995).

8. Semali and Kincheloe, "Introduction," 25.

9. B. Levinson and D. Holland, "The Cultural Production of the Educated Person: An Introduction," in B. Levinson, D. Foley, and D. Holland (eds.), *The Cultural Production of the Educated Person: Critical Ethnographies of Schooling and Local Practice* (Albany: State University of New York Press, 1996), 1.

10. Ali Mazrui, *The African Condition: The Reith Lectures* (London: Heinemann, 1980), 16.

Bibliography

Abdalati, H. (1975). *Islam in focus.* Indianapolis, IN: American Trust Publications.

Abdullah, A. R. S. (1982). *Educational theory: A Qur'anic outlook.* Makkah, Saudi Arabia: Umm Al-Qura University.

Abe, M. (1993). Buddhism. In A. Sharma (Ed.), *Our religions* (pp. 69–137). San Francisco: Harper.

Abu-Hamdiyyah, M. (2000). *The Qur'an: An introduction.* London: Routledge.

Achebe, C. (1958). *Things fall apart.* London: Heinemann.

Achebe, C. (1960). *No longer at ease.* London: Heinemann.

Achebe, C. (1966). *A man of the people.* London: Heinemann.

Achebe, C. (1974). *Arrow of God* (2nd ed.). London: Heinemann.

Acton, T. (1974). *Gypsy politics and social change.* London: Routledge & Kegan Paul.

Adams, R. (1991). *Prehistoric Mesoamerica* (Rev. ed.). Norman: University of Oklahoma Press.

Adegbola, E. (Ed.). (1983). *Traditional religion in west Africa.* Nairobi, Kenya: Uzima.

Agrawal, A. (1995). Indigenous knowledge and scientific knowledge: Some critical comments. *Indigenous Knowledge and Development Monitor* 3: 3–6.

Ahmad, K. (1980). Islam: Basic principles and characteristics. In K. Ahmad (Ed.), *Islam: Its meaning and message* (pp. 27–44). London: Islamic Foundation.

Ahmad, K. (Ed.). (1980). *Islam: Its meaning and message.* London: Islamic Foundation.

Ahmed, A. S. (1988). *Discovering Islam: Making sense of Muslim history and society.* London: Routledge.

Ahmed, A. S. (1992). *Postmodernism and Islam: Predicament and promise.* London: Routledge.

Ahmed, A. S. (2001). *Islam today: A short introduction to the Muslim world.* London: I. B. Tauris.

Ahmed, A. S. (Ed.). (2002). *Inside Islam: The faith, the people, and the conflicts of the world's fastest growing religion.* New York: Marlowe.

Aiello, A. P., & Aiella, M. (2001). Cochlear implants and deaf identity. In L. Bragg (Ed.), *DEAF-WORLD: A historical reader and primary sourcebook* (pp. 406–407). New York: New York University Press.

Aizpuro, P. (1990). *Historia de la educación en la época colonial: El mundo indígena.* México: Colegio de México.

Al-Azmeh, A. (1993). *Islams and modernities.* London: Verso.

Ali, M. M. (1990). *The religion of Islam* (6th ed.). Columbus, OH: Ahmadiyya Anjuman Ishaat Islam.

Ali, M. M. (1992a). *Introduction to the study of the holy Qur'an*. Columbus, OH: Ahmadiyya Anjuman Ishaat Islam.

Ali, M. M. (1992b). *The living thoughts of the Prophet Muhammad*. Dublin, OH: Ahmadiyya Anjuman Ishaat Islam.

Ali, M. M. (1996). *History of the Prophets*. Columbus, OH: Ahmadiyya Anjuman Ishaat Islam.

Ali, S. A. (1990). *The spirit of Islam: A history of the evolution and ideals of Islam with a life of the Prophet*. Delhi: Low Price Publications.

Alonzo, G. Z. (1995). *An overview of the Mayan world* (11th ed.). Mérida, Yucatán, México: Author.

Amdouni, H. (1992). *La famille musulmane: Relations familiales et éducations*. Paris: Al Qalam.

Andersson, Y. (1990). The deaf world as a linguistic minority. In S. Prillwitz & T. Vollhaver (Eds.), *Sign language research and application* (pp. 155–161). Hamburg, Germany: Signum.

Andersson, Y. (1994). Deaf people as a linguistic minority. In I. Ahlgren & K. Hyltenstan (Eds.), *Bilingualism in deaf education* (pp. 9–13). Hamburg, Germany: Signum.

Andrews, J. (1975). *An introduction to classical Nahuatl*. Austin: University of Texas Press.

Ani, M. (1994). *Yurugu: An African-centered critique of European cultural thought and behavior*. Trenton, NJ: Africa World Press.

Appiah, K. (1989). *In my father's house: Africa in the politics of culture*. Oxford, England: Oxford University Press.

Apple, M. (1996). *Cultural politics and education*. New York: Teachers College Press.

Apple, M. (2000). *Official knowledge: Democratic education in a conservative age* (2nd ed.). New York: Routledge.

Apple, M. (2001). *Educating the "right" way: Markets, standards, God, and inequality*. New York: RoutledgeFalmer.

Archibald, J. (1990). Coyote's story about orality and literacy. *Canadian Journal of Native Education* 17, 2: 66–81.

Arens, W. (1979). *The man-eating myth: Anthropology and anthropophagy*. New York: Oxford University Press.

Argüelles, J. (1987). *The Mayan factor: Path beyond technology*. Sante Fe, NM: Bear & Co.

Arkoun, M. (1994). *Rethinking Islam: Common questions, uncommon answers*. Boulder, CO: Westview.

Armstrong, K. (1992). *Muhammad: A biography of the Prophet*. San Francisco: Harper.

Armstrong, K. (2002). *Islam: A short history*. New York: Modern Library.

Asad, T. (Ed.). (1973). *Anthropology and the colonial encounter*. London: Ithaca.

Asante, M. (1988). *Afrocentricity* (Rev. ed.). Trenton, NJ: Africa World Press.

Asante, M. (1990). *Kemet, Afrocentricity and knowledge*. Trenton, NJ: Africa World Press.

Asante, M., & Asante, K. (Eds.). (1990). *African culture: Rhythms of unity*. Trenton, NJ: Africa World Press.

Athar, S. (1994). *Reflections of an American Muslim*. Chicago: Kazi.

Atwood, M. (1991). *Spirit healing: Native American magic and medicine*. New York: Sterling.

Austin, A. (1976). El fundamento mágico-religioso del poder. *Estudios de Cultura Náhuatl* 12: 197–240.

Austin, A. L. (1985). *La educacíon de los antiguos nahuas*, 2 vols. México: Secretaría de Educacíon Pública—Caballito.

Aveni, A. (Ed.). (1992). *The sky in Mayan literature*. Oxford, England: Oxford University Press.

Ayers, W. (1971). *Chang Chih-tung and educational reform in China*. Cambridge, MA: Harvard University Press.

Ayisi, E. (1979). *An introduction to the study of African culture*. London: Currey.

Ayittey, G. B. (1991). *Indigenous African institutions*. Ardsley-on-Hudson, NY: Transnational Publishers.

Baker, C. (1999). Sign language and the deaf community. In J. Fishman (Ed.), *Handbook of language and ethnic identity* (pp. 122–139). New York: Oxford University Press.

Ball, J. (1925). *Things Chinese, or, Notes connected with China* (5th ed., rev. by E. C. Werner). Shanghai: Kelly and Walsh.

Ball, S. (Ed.). (1990). *Foucault and education: Disciplines and knowledge.* London: Routledge.

Balme, M., & Lawall, G. (1990). *Athenaze: An introduction to Ancient Greek, Book I.* New York: Oxford University Press.

Banerjee, A. K. (1967). *Discourses on Hindu spiritual culture.* Delhi: S. Chand & Co.

Banerji, S. (1993). *Society in ancient India: Evolution since the Vedic times based on Sanskrit, Pali, Prakrit and other classical sources.* New Delhi: D. K. Printworld.

Bansal, J. L. (1991). Leading mathematicians of ancient India. In H. C. Khare (Ed.), *Issues in Vedic mathematics* (pp. 79–81). Delhi: Motilal Banarsidass Publishers.

Baquero, R. (1997). *Vigotsky y el aprendizaje escolar.* Buenos Aires: Aique.

Baquero, R., Camilloni, A., Carretero, M., Castorina, J., Lenzi, A., & Litwin, E. (1998). *Debates constructivistas.* Buenos Aires: Aique.

Barman, J., Hébert, Y., & McCaskill, D. (1987). The challenge of Indian education: An overview. In J. Barman, Y. Hébert, & D. McCaskill (Eds.), *Indian education in Canada, Volume 2: The challenge* (pp. 1–21). Vancouver: University of British Columbia Press.

Barman, J., Hébert, Y., & McCaskill, D. (Eds.). (1987). *Indian education in Canada, Volume 2: The challenge.* Vancouver: University of British Columbia Press.

Barnes, B. (1975). Irish traveling people. In F. Rehfisch (Ed.), *Gypsies, tinkers, and other travelers* (pp. 231–256). London: Academic Press.

Barnhardt, R. (1990). Higher education in the Fourth World: Indigenous people taking control. *Canadian Journal of Native Education* 18: 199–231.

Barrett, T. H. (1990). Religious traditions in Chinese civilization: Buddhism and Taoism. In P. Ropp (Ed.), *Heritage of China: Contemporary perspectives on Chinese civilization* (pp. 138–163). Berkeley: University of California Press.

Barth, F. (1975). The social organization of a pariah group in Norway. In F. Rehfisch (Ed.), *Gypsies, tinkers, and other travelers* (pp. 285–299). London: Academic Press.

Barton, L. (1997). Blaming the victims: The political oppression of disabled people. In R. Farnen & H. Sünker (Eds.), *The politics, sociology and economics of education: Interdisciplinary and comparative perspectives* (pp. 63–72). Houndsmills, England: Macmillan.

Bascom, W. (1975). *African dilemma tales.* The Hague: Mouton.

Basham, A. L. (1989). *The origins and development of classical Hinduism.* Boston: Beacon.

Bastid, M. (1987). Servitude or liberation? The introduction of foreign educational practices and systems to China. In R. Hayhoe & M. Bastid (Eds.), *China's education and the industrialized world* (pp. 3–20). London: Sharpe.

Bauer, W. (1976). *China and the search for happiness: Recurring themes in four thousand years of Chinese cultural history.* New York: Seabury.

Bayton, D. (1996). *Forbidden signs: American culture and the campaign against sign language.* Chicago: University of Chicago Press.

Becker, C. (1955). What are historical facts? *Western Political Quarterly* 7: 327–340.

Belenky, M. F., Clinchy, B. M., Goldberger, N. R., & Tarule, J. M. (1986). *Women's ways of knowing: The development of self, voice, and mind.* New York: Basic Books.

Bell, B. (Ed.). (1967). *Indian Mexico: Past and present.* Los Angeles: University of California at Los Angeles, Latin American Center.

Benedict, J. (2001). *Without reservation: How a controversial Indian tribe rose to power and built the world's largest casino.* New York: Perennial.

Benham, M., & Cooper, J. (Eds.). (2000). *Indigenous educational models for contemporary practice: In our mother's voice.* Hillsdale, NJ: Lawrence Erlbaum Associates.

Bennett, C. (1998). *In search of Muhammad.* London: Cassell.

Benson, S. (1981). *Ambiguous ethnicity.* Cambridge, England: Cambridge University Press.

Berdan, F. (1976). La organización del tributo en el imperio azteca. *Estudios de Cultura Náhuatl* 12: 185–195.

Berdan, F., & Anawalt, P. (1997). *The essential Codex Mendoza.* Berkeley: University of California Press.

Berkey, J. (1992). *The transmission of knowledge in medieval Cairo: A social history of Islamic education.* Princeton, NJ: Princeton University Press.

Bernadac, C. (1979). *L'Holocauste oblié: Le massacre des Tsiganes.* Paris: France-Empire.

Bernal, M. (1987). *Black Athena: The Afroasiatic roots of classical civilization, Volume 1: The fabrication of ancient Greece, 1785–1985.* New Brunswick, NJ: Rutgers University Press.

Bernal, M. (1991a). *Black Athena: The Afroasiatic roots of classical civilization, Volume 2: The archeological and documentary evidence.* New Brunswick, NJ: Rutgers University Press.

Bernal, M. (1991b). Response to Edith Hall. *Arethusa* 24, 2: 203–214.

Bernal, M. (1992). Animadversions on the origins of Western science. *Isis* 83: 596–607.

Bernal, M. (1993). Response. *Journal of Women's History* 4, 3: 119–135.

Berrelleza, J. (1987). Offering 48 of the Templo Mayor: A case of child sacrifice. In E. Boone (Ed.), *The Aztec Templo Mayor: A symposium at Dumbarton Oaks* (pp. 131–143). Washington, DC: Dumbarton Oaks Research Library and Collection.

Bertaux, P. (1997). *Africa: Desde la prehistoria hasta los estados actuales.* Madrid: Sieglo Veintiuno de España Editores.

Besmer, F. (1983). *Horses, musicians, and gods: The Hausa cult of possession-trance.* Zaria, Nigeria: Ahmadu Bello University Press.

Biardeau, M. (1981). *L'Hindouisme: Anthropologie d'une civilization.* Paris: Flammarion.

Bienvenu, M. J. (1994). Reflections of deaf culture in deaf humor. In C. Erting, R. Johnson, D. Smith, & B. Snider (Eds.), *The deaf way: Perspectives from the International Conference on Deaf Culture* (pp. 16–23). Washington, DC: Gallaudet University Press.

Biesold, H. (1999). *Crying hands: Eugenics and Deaf people in Nazi Germany.* Washington, DC: Gallaudet University Press.

Bill, M. (1991). Rhythmical patterning of Tsonga children's traditional oral poetry. *South African Journal of African Languages* 11, 4: 133–143.

Biot, E. (1847). *Essai sur l'histoire de l'instruction publique en Chine.* Paris: Benjamin Duprat.

Birge, B. (1989). Chu Hsi and women's education. In W. de Bary & J. Chaffee (Eds.), *Neo-Confucian education: The formative stage* (pp. 325–367). Berkeley: University of California Press.

Bloom, I. (1987). *Knowledge painfully acquired: The K'un-chih chi by Lo Ch'in-shun.* New York: Columbia University Press.

Bloomfield, L. (1964). Language. In O. Chavarria-Aguilar (Ed.), *Traditional India* (pp. 112–113). Englewood Cliffs, NJ: Prentice-Hall.

Boateng, F. (1990). African traditional education: A tool for intergenerational communication. In M. Asante & K. Asante (Eds.), *African culture: Rhythms of unity* (pp. 109–122). Trenton, NJ: Africa World Press.

Bodde, D. (1967). *China's first unifier: A study of the Ch'in dynasty as seen in the life of Li Ssu.* Hong Kong: Hong Kong University Press. (Original work published 1938)

Bodde, D. (1981). *Essays on Chinese civilization.* Princeton, NJ: Princeton University Press.

Boe, P. (1983). Circumcision: The rites of manhood in the Bille tribe. In E. Adegbola (Ed.), *Traditional religion in West Africa* (pp. 73–89). Nairobi, Kenya: Uzima.

Bol, P. (1989). Chu Hsi's redefinition of literati learning. In W. de Bary & J. Chaffee (Eds.), *Neo-Confucian education: The formative stage* (pp. 151–185). Berkeley: University of California Press.

Bol, P. (1992). *"This culture of ours": Intellectual transitions in T'ang and Sung China.* Stanford, CA: Stanford University Press.

Bond, M. (Ed.). (1986). *The psychology of the Chinese people.* Hong Kong: Oxford University Press.

Bond, M., & Kwang-kuo Hwang. (1986). The social psychology of the Chinese people. In M. Bond (Ed.), *The psychology of the Chinese people* (pp. 213–266). Hong Kong: Oxford University Press.

Boone, E. (Ed.). (1987). *The Aztec Templo Mayor: A symposium at Dumbarton Oaks, 8th and 9th October 1983.* Washington, DC: Dumbarton Oaks Research Library and Collection.

Boone, E., & Mignolo, W. (Eds.). (1994). *Writing without words: Alternative literacies in Mesoamerica and the Andes.* Durham, NC: Duke University Press.

Borland, C. H. (1969). The oral and written culture of the Shona. *LIMI: Bulletin of the Department of Bantu Languages, University of South Africa* 8: 1–27.

Boswell, J. (1988). *The kindness of strangers: The abandonment of children in Western Europe from late antiquity to the Renaissance.* New York: Pantheon.

Bouchauveau, G. (1994). Deaf humor and culture. In C. Erting, R. Johnson, D. Smith, & B. Snider (Eds.), *The deaf way: Perspectives from the International Conference on Deaf Culture* (pp. 24–30). Washington, DC: Gallaudet University Press.

Bowker, J. (1998). *What Muslims believe.* Oxford, England: OneWorld.

Boyer, R., & Gayton, N. (1992). *Apache mothers and daughters: Four generations of a family.* Norman: University of Oklahoma Press.

Bragg, L. (Ed.). (2001). *DEAF-WORLD: A historical reader and primary sourcebook.* New York: New York University Press.

Brakel, L. F. (1984). Indonesien. In M. Ursinus (Ed.), *Der Islam in der Gegenwart* (pp. 570–581). München, Germany: C. H. Beck.

Brandt, R. (1961). *Value and obligation.* New York: Harcourt, Brace & World.

Braswell, G., Jr. (1996). *Islam: Its Prophet, peoples, politics and power.* Nashville, TN: Broadman & Holman.

Bray, W. (1968). *The everyday life of the Aztecs.* New York: Dorset.

Brodwin, P. (1996). *Medicine and morality in Haiti: The contest for healing power.* Cambridge, England: Cambridge University Press.

Brohi, A. (1980). The *Qur'an* and its impact on human history. In K. Ahmad (Ed.), *Islam: Its meaning and message* (pp. 81–97). London: Islamic Foundation.

Brokensha, D., & Warren, O. (Eds.). (1980). *Indigenous knowledge systems and development.* Lanham, MD: University Press of America.

Brown, D. (1971). *Bury my heart at Wounded Knee: An Indian history of the American West.* New York: Bantam.

Brundage, B. (1972). *A rain of darts: The Mexica Aztecs.* Austin: University of Texas Press.

Brundage, B. (1975). *Two heavens, two earths: An essay contrasting the Aztecs and the Incas.* Albuquerque: University of New Mexico Press.

Brundage, B. (1979). *The fifth sun: Aztec gods, Aztec world.* Austin: University of Texas Press.

Buchanan, R. (1999). *Illusions of equality: Deaf Americans in school and factory, 1850–1950.* Washington, DC: Gallaudet University Press.

Bullivant, B. (1991). *The pluralist dilemma in education: Six case studies.* Sydney: Allen & Unwin.

Cajete, G. (1994). *Look to the mountain: An ecology of indigenous education.* Durango, CO: Kivakí.

Cajete, G. (1999). The making of an indigenous teacher: Insights into the ecology of teaching. In J. Kane (Ed.), *Education, information and transformation: Essays on learning and thinking* (pp. 161–183). Upper Saddle River, NJ: Merrill.

Calnek, E. (1988). The *calmécac* and *telpochcalli* in pre–Conquest Tenochtitlán. In J. Klor de Alva, H. Nicholson, & E. Keber (Eds.), *The work of Bernardino de Sahagun: Pioneer ethnographer of sixteenth-century Aztec Mexico* (pp. 169–177). Albany: Institute for Mesoamerican Studies, State University of New York.

Calvert, L.-J. (1984). *La tradition orale.* Paris: Presses Universitaires de France.

Campbell, G. (1995). *Concise compendium of the world's languages.* London: Routledge.

Campbell, S. S. (1998). *Called to heal: Traditional healing meets modern medicine in southern Africa today.* Halfway House: Zebra.

Campos, R. (1936). *La producción literaria de los Aztecas.* México: Talleres Gráficos del Museo Nacional de Arqueología, Historia y Ethnografía.

Carrasco, D. (1982). *Quetzalcoatl and the irony of empire: Myths and prophecies in the Aztec tradition.* Chicago: University of Chicago Press.

Carrasco, D. (1990). *Religions of Mesoamerica: Cosmovision and ceremonial centers.* San Francisco: HarperSanFrancisco.

Carrasco, D., with Sessions, S. (1998). *Daily life of the Aztecs: People of the sun and earth.* Westport, CT: Greenwood.

Carter, D. (1993). Recognizing traditional environmental knowledge. *IDRC Reports* 21, 1: 10–13.

Chaffee, J. (1979). *Education and examinations in Sung society.* Ph.D. dissertation, University of Chicago.

Chaffee, J. (1989). Chu Hsi in Nan-k'ang: *Tao-hsüeh* and the politics of education. In W. de Bary & J. Chaffee (Eds.), *Neo-Confucian education: The formative stage* (pp. 414–431). Berkeley: University of California Press.

Charlton, J. (1998). *Nothing about us without us: Disability oppression and empowerment.* Berkeley: University of California Press.

Chase, D., & Chase, A. (Eds.). (1992). *Mesoamerican elites: An archeological assessment.* Norman: University of Oklahoma Press.

Chavarria-Aguilar, O. L. (Ed.). (1964). *Traditional India.* Englewood Cliffs, NJ: Prentice-Hall.

Cheetham, E. (1994). *Fundamentals of mainstream Buddhism.* Boston: Tuttle.

Cheng Hanbang. (1991). Confucian ethics and moral education of contemporary students. In S. Krieger & R. Trauzettel (Eds.), *Confucianism and the modernization of China* (pp. 193–202). Mainz, Germany: Hase & Koehler.

Chen Li-Fu. (1976). *Why Confucius has been reverenced as the model teacher of all ages.* New York: Center of Asian Studies, St. John's University, and the Institute of Chinese Culture.

Cheng Tien-Hsi. (1947). *China moulded by Confucius: The Chinese way in Western light.* London: Stevens & Sons.

Chew, P. (1991). The great Tao. *Journal of Bahá'í Studies* 4, 2: 11–39.

Chisholm, J. (1983). *Navajo infancy: An ethological study of child development.* Hawthorne, NY: Aldine.

Choudhury, M. A. (1993). A critical examination of the concept of Islamization of knowledge in contemporary times. *Muslim Education Quarterly* 10, 4: 3–34.

Chu, R. (1989). Chu Hsi and public instruction. In W. de Bary & J. Chaffee (Eds.), *Neo-Confucian education: The formative stage* (pp. 252–273). Berkeley: University of California Press.

Chün-fang Yü. (1989). Ch'an education in the Sung: Ideals and procedures. In W. de Bary & J. Chaffee (Eds.), *Neo-Confucian education: The formative stage* (pp. 57–104). Berkeley: University of California Press.

Cissé, S. (1992). *L'enseignement islamique en Afrique noire.* Paris: L'Harmattan.

Clarke, J. J. (1997). *Oriental enlightenment: The encounter between Asian and Western thought.* London: Routledge.

Cleary, T. (2001). *The wisdom of the Prophet: Sayings of Muhammad, selections from the Hadith.* Boston: Shambhala.

Clendinnen, I. (1991). *Aztecs: An interpretation.* Cambridge, England: Cambridge University Press.

Cleverley, J. (1985). *The schooling of China: Tradition and modernity in Chinese education.* Sydney: Allen & Unwin.

Cobb, P. (1994). Where is the mind? Constructivist and socioculturalist perspectives on mathematical development. *Educational Researcher* 23: 13–20.

Cobb, P. (1996). Where is the mind? A coordination of sociocultural and cognitive constructionist perspectives. In C. Fosnot (Ed.), *Constructivism: Theory, perspectives, and practice* (pp.
34–52). New York: Teachers College Press.

Cobern, W. (1993). Contextual constructivism: The impact of culture on the learning and teaching of science. In K. Tobin (Ed.), *The practice of constructivism in science education* (pp. 51–69).
Hillsdale, NJ: Lawrence Erlbaum Associates.

Coe, M. (1987). *The Maya* (4th rev. ed.). London: Thames and Hudson.

Coe, M. (1992). *Breaking the Maya code.* London: Thames and Hudson.

Coertze, P. J. (1959). *Inlediding tot die Algemene Volkekunde.* Johannesburg: Voortrekkerpers.

Coertze, R. D. (1991). Aanvang can Volkekinde aan Afrikaansatalige universiteite in Suid-Afrika.
South African Journal of Ethology 14: 25–34.

Coetzee, P. H., & Roux, A. P. (Eds.). (1998). *The African philosophy reader.* London: Routledge.

Cohen, P., & Goldman, M. (Eds.). (1990). *Ideas across cultures: Essays on Chinese thought in
honor of Benjamin I. Schwartz.* Cambridge, MA: Harvard University Press.

Coleman, M. (1993). *American Indian children at school, 1850–1930.* Jackson: University Press of
Mississippi.

Collin, F. (1997). *Social reality.* London: Routledge.

Commeaux, C. (1970). *La vie quotidienne en Chine sous les Mandchous.* Paris: Librairie Hachette.

Confrey, J. (1995). How compatible are radical constructivism, sociocultural approaches, and
social constructivism? In L. Steffe & J. Gale (Eds.), *Constructivism in education* (pp. 185–225).
Hillsdale, NJ: Lawrence Erlbaum Associates.

Conrad, G., & Demarest, A. (1984). *Religion and empire: The dynamics of Aztec and Inca expansionism.* Cambridge, England: Cambridge University Press.

Conze, E. (Trans.). (1959). *Buddhist scriptures.* Harmondsworth, England: Penguin.

Conze, E. (1960). *A short history of Buddhism.* Bombay: Chetana.

Conze, E. (1975). *Buddhism: Its essence and development.* New York: Harper & Row.

Cook, M. (2000). *The Koran: A very short introduction.* Oxford, England: Oxford University
Press.

Coomaraswamy, A. (1971). *Hinduism and Buddhism.* Westport, CT: Greenwood.

Cooperman, A. (2002). Anti-Muslim remarks stir tempest. *The Washington Post* (20 June), A-3.

Cope, T. (Ed.). (1968). *Izibongo: Zulu praise poems.* Oxford, England: Oxford University Press.

Cordier, H. (1921). *Histoire générale de la Chine,* 4 vols. Paris: Geuthner.

Cornog, E. (1998). American antiquity: How DeWitt Clinton invented our past. *The American
Scholar* 67: 53–61.

Cornyn, J. (1930). *The song of Quetzalcoatl.* Yellow Springs, OH: Antioch.

Cotten, R. (1998). Sex dichotomy among the American Kalderas Gypsies. In D. Tong (Ed.),
Gypsies: An interdisciplinary reader (pp. 219–232). New York: Garland.

Cotterell, M. (1997). *The supergods: They came on a mission to save mankind.* London: Thorsons.

Coulehan, J. (1980). Navajo Indian medicine: Implications for healing. *Journal of Family Practice*
10: 55–61.

Coulon, C. (1988). *Les musulmans et le pouvoir en Afrique noire: Religion et contre-culture.* Paris:
Editions Karthala.

Coward, H. G. (Ed.). (1987). *Modern Indian responses to religious pluralism.* Albany: State University of New York Press.

Cragg, K. (1994). *The event of the Qur'an: Islam and its scripture.* Oxford, England: Oneworld.

Creel, H. (1949). *Confucius and the Chinese way.* New York: Harper & Row.

Cross, S. (1994). *The elements of Hinduism.* Shaftesbury, England: Element.

Crowe, D. (1996). *A history of the Gypsies of eastern Europe and Russia.* New York: St. Martin's
Griffin.

Crowe, D., & Kolsti, J. (Eds.). (1991). *The Gypsies of eastern Europe.* London: Sharpe.

Crystal, D. (1991). *A dictionary of linguistics and phonetics* (3rd ed.). Oxford, England: Blackwell.

Culin, S. (1975). *Games of the North American Indians.* New York: Dover.

Curtin, P., Feierman, S., Thompson, L., & Vansina, J. (1995). *African history: From earliest times to independence* (2nd ed.). London: Longman.

Darwin, C. (1871). *The origin of species and the descent of man.* New York: Random House.

Davidson, B. (1991). *Africa in history* (Rev. ed.). New York: Macmillan.

Davidson, B. (Ed.). (1991). *African civilization revisited: From antiquity to modern time.* Trenton, NJ: African World Press.

Davies, C. (1973). *Los mexicas: Primeros pasos hacia el imperio.* México: Universidad Nacional Autónoma de México, Instituto de Investigaciones Históricas.

Davies, L. (Ed.). (1997). *The disability studies reader.* New York: Routledge.

Davies, N. (1982). *The ancient kingdoms of Mexico.* New York: Penguin.

Davies, N. (1987). *The Aztec empire: The Toltec resurgence.* Norman: University of Oklahoma Press.

Davis, L. (1995). *Enforcing normalcy: Disability, deafness, and the body.* London: Verso.

Davis, L. (Ed.). (1997). *The disabilities study reader.* New York: Routledge.

Davis, L. (2000). *My sense of silence: Memoirs of a childhood with deafness.* Urbana: University of Illinois Press.

Davis-Floyd, R., & Sargent, C. (Eds.). (1997). *Childbirth and authoritative knowledge: Cross-cultural perspectives.* Berkeley: University of California Press.

Dawson, R. (1978). *The Chinese experience.* London: Weidenfeld and Nicholson.

Day, J. (1992). *Aztec: The world of Moctezuma.* Niwot, CO: Denver Museum of Natural History and Roberts Rinehart Publishers.

Debaene, S. (1997). *The number sense: How the mind creates mathematics.* New York: Oxford University Press.

de Bary, W. (1981). *Neo-Confucian orthodoxy and the learning of the mind-and-heart.* New York: Columbia University Press.

de Bary, W. (1983). *The liberal tradition in China.* Hong Kong: Chinese University Press.

de Bary, W. (1989). Chu Hsi's aims as educator. In W. de Bary & J. Chaffee (Eds.), *Neo-Confucian education: The formative stage* (pp. 186–218). Berkeley: University of California Press.

de Bary, W. (Ed.). (1969). *The Buddhist tradition in India, China and Japan.* New York: Modern Library.

de Bary, W., & Chaffee, J. (Eds.). (1989). *Neo-Confucian education: The formative stage.* Berkeley: University of California Press.

de Vaux de Foletier, F. (1970). *Mille ans d'historie des Tsiganes.* Paris: Fayard.

de Villiers, M., & Hirtle, S. (1997). *Into Africa: A journey through the ancient empires.* Johannesburg: Jonathan Ball.

de Villiers, S., & Hartshorne, S. H. (1981). Education. In A. Myburgh (Ed.), *Anthropology for Southern Africa* (pp. 145–153). Pretoria: van Schaik.

Denny, F. M. (1987). *Islam.* San Francisco: Harper.

Diamond, R. (1970). *Old English: Grammar and reader.* Detroit, MI: Wayne State University Press.

Diop, C. A. (1962). *The cultural unity of Negro Africa.* Paris: Presence Africaine.

Diop, C. A. (1989). *The cultural unity of Black Africa.* London: Karnak House.

Diop, C. A. (1991). *Civilization or barbarism: An authentic anthropology.* Chicago: Hill.

Diouf, W., Sheckley, B., & Kehrhahn, M. (2000). Adult learning in a non-Western context: The influence of culture in a Senegalese farming village. *Adult Education Quarterly* 51: 32–44.

Dodge, B. (1962). *Muslim education in medieval times.* Washington, DC: The Middle East Institute.

Dolnick, E. (1993). Deafness as culture. *The Atlantic* 272: 37–53.

Dongerkery, S. R. (1967). *University education in India.* Bombay: Manaktalas.

Donnelly, I. (1976). *Atlantis: The antediluvian world.* New York: Dover. (Original work published 1882)

Doolittle, J. (1966). *Social life of the Chinese: With some account of their religious, governmental, educational, and business customs and opinions*, 2 vols. Taipei: Ch'eng-Wen. (Original work published 1865)

Doumato, E. (2000). *Getting God's ear: Women, Islam, and healing in Saudi Arabia and the Gulf.* New York: Columbia University Press.

Driver, R., Asoko, H., Leach, J., Mortimer, E., & Scott, P. (1994). Constructing scientific knowledge in the classroom. *Educational Researcher* 23: 5–12.

Dubow, S. (1995). *Illicit union: Scientific racism in modern South Africa.* Cambridge, England: Cambridge University Press.

Duffy, T., & Jonassen, D. (Eds.). (1992). *Constructivism and the technology of instruction.* Hillsdale, NJ: Lawrence Erlbaum Associates.

Duminy, P. (1973). *African pupils and teaching them.* Pretoria: van Schaik.

Duminy, P. (Ed.). (1967). *Trends and challenges in the education of the South African Bantu.* Pretoria: van Schaik.

Dumoulin, H. (1994). *Understanding Buddhism: Key themes.* New York: Weatherhill.

Dundas, P. (1992). *The Jains.* London: Routledge.

Durán, D. (1964). *The Aztecs: The history of the Indies of New Spain.* New York: Orion.

Durán, D. (1971). *Book of the gods and rites and the ancient calendar.* Norman: University of Oklahoma Press.

Durant, W. (1963). *The story of civilization: Our Oriental heritage.* New York: Simon & Schuster.

Eberhard, W. (1977). *A history of China.* Berkeley: University of California Press.

Ebrey, P. (1989). Education through ritual: Efforts to formulate family rituals during the Sung period. In W. de Bary & J. Chaffee (Eds.), *Neo-Confucian education: The formative stage* (pp. 277–306). Berkeley: University of California Press.

Ebrey, P. (1990). Women, marriage and the family in Chinese history. In P. Ropp (Ed.), *Heritage of China: Contemporary perspectives on Chinese civilization* (pp. 197–223). Berkeley: University of California Press.

Ebrey, P. (1991). *Confucianism and family rituals in imperial China: A social history of writing about rites.* Princeton, NJ: Princeton University Press.

Ebrey, P. (Ed.). (1993). *Chinese civilization: A sourcebook* (2nd ed.). New York: The Free Press.

Eckel, M. (1994). Buddhism in the world and in America. In J. Neuser (Ed.), *World religions in America: An introduction* (pp. 203–218). Louisville, KY: Westminster/John Knox.

Eckel, M. (2002). *Buddhism.* Oxford, England: Oxford University Press.

Edmonson, M. (1988). *The book of the year: Middle American calendrical systems.* Salt Lake City: University of Utah Press.

Eichhorn, W. (1969). *Chinese civilization: An introduction.* New York: Praeger.

Eickelman, D. (1985). *Knowledge and power in Morocco: The education of a twentieth-century notable.* Princeton, NJ: Princeton University Press.

Eisler, K. (2001). *Revenge of the Pequots: How a small native American tribe created the world's most profitable casino.* New York: Simon & Shuster.

Ekei, J. C. (2001). *Justice in communalism: A foundation of ethics in African philosophy.* Lagos, Nigeria: Realm Communications.

El Fadl, K. (2002). *The place of tolerance in Islam.* Boston: Beacon.

Elliott, J. (1988). Educational research and outsider–insider relations. *International Journal of Qualitative Studies in Education* 1, 2: 155–166.

Elvin, M. (1973). *The pattern of the Chinese past.* Stanford, CA: Stanford University Press.

Elzey, W. (1976). Some remarks on the space and time of the "center" in Aztec religion. *Estudios de Cultura Náhuatl* 12: 315–334.

Emerick, Y. (2002). *Muhammad.* Indianapolis, IN: Alpha.

Ennis, R. (1969). *Logic in teaching.* Englewood Cliffs, NJ: Prentice-Hall.

Erlandson, D., Harris, E., Skipper, B., and Allen, S. (1993). *Doing naturalistic inquiry: A guide to methods.* Newbury Park, CA: Sage.

Esack, F. (2002). *The Qur'an: A short introduction.* Oxford, England: OneWorld.

Escalante, P. (1985). *Educacíon e ideologia en el México antiguo.* México: Secretaría de Educacíon Pública—Caballito.

Esposito, J. (1988). *Islam: The straight path.* New York: Oxford University Press.

Esposito, J. (1991). *Islam: The straight path* (Exp. ed.). New York: Oxford University Press.

Esposito, J. (1994). Islam in the world and in America. In J. Neuser (Ed.), *World religions in America: An introduction* (pp. 243–258). Louisville, KY: Westminster/John Knox.

Esposito, J., & Burgat, F. (Eds.). (2003). *Modernizing Islam: Religion in the public sphere in Europe and the Middle East.* New Brunswick, NJ: Rutgers University Press.

Esposito, J., with DeLong-Bas, N. (2001). *Women in Muslim family law* (2nd ed.). Syracuse, NY: Syracuse University Press.

Eze, E. C. (Ed.). (1998). *African philosophy: An anthology.* Oxford, England: Blackwell.

Fadipe, N. (1970). *The sociology of the Yoruba.* Ibadan, Nigeria: Ibadan University Press.

Fafunwa, A. B. (1974). *A history of education in Nigeria.* London: Allen & Unwin.

Fagan, B. (1984). *The Aztecs.* New York: Freeman.

Fairbank, J. (1992). *China: A new history.* Cambridge, MA: Harvard University Press.

Fairbank, J., & Goldman, M. (1988). *China: A new history* (Enlarged ed.). Cambridge, MA: Harvard University Press.

Fairbank, J., & Kwang-Ching, L. (Eds.). (1980). *The Cambridge history of China, Volume 11: Late Ch'ing, 1800–1911, Part 2.* Cambridge, England: Cambridge University Press.

Fajana, A. (1986). Traditional methods of education in Africa: The Yoruba example. In J. Okpaku, A. Opubor, & B. Oloruntimehim (Eds.), *The arts and civilization of Black and African peoples, Volume 6: Black civilization and pedagogy* (pp. 42–59). Lagos, Nigeria: Center for Black and African Arts and Civilization.

Fakhry, M. (1983). *A history of Islamic philosophy* (2nd ed.). New York: Columbia University Press.

Farah, C. (2003). *Islam: Beliefs and observances* (7th ed.). Hauppage, NY: Barron's Educational Series.

Feiler, B. (2002). *Abraham: A journey to the heart of three faiths.* New York: Morrow.

Feyerabend, P. (1987). *Farewell to reason.* London: Verso.

Feyerabend, P. (1991). *Three dialogues on knowledge.* Oxford, England: Blackwell.

Feyerabend, P. (1993). *Against method* (3rd ed.). London: Verso.

Finlayson, R. (1982). *Hlonipha:* The women's language of avoidance among the Xhosa. *South African Journal of African Languages* (Suppl. 1): 35–59.

Finlayson, R. (1986). Linguistic terms of respect among the Xhosa. In P. Raper (Ed.), *Names 1983: Proceedings of the Second South African Names Congress* (pp. 128–138). Pretoria: Human Sciences Research Council.

Finnegan, R. (1970). *Oral literature in Africa.* Nairobi, Kenya: Oxford University Press.

Finnegan, R. (1992). Reflecting back on *Oral literature in Africa:* Some reconsiderations after 21 years. *South African Journal of African Languages* 12, 2: 39–47.

Fisher, M. P. (1994). *Living religions* (2nd ed.). Englewood Cliffs, NJ: Prentice-Hall.

Flood, G. (1996). *An introduction to Hinduism.* Cambridge, England: Cambridge University Press.

Fluehr-Lobban, C. (1994). *Islamic society in practice.* Gainesville: University of Florida Press.

Fonseca, I. (1995). *Bury me standing: The Gypsies and their journey.* New York: Vintage.

Forbes, J. (1979). Traditional Native American philosophy and multicultural education. In *Multicultural education and the American Indian* (pp. 3–13). Los Angeles: American Indian Studies Center, University of California.

Fordham, S., & Ogbu, J. (1986). Black students' school success: Coping with the "burden of acting white." *The Urban Review* 18: 176–206.

Fortes, M. (1979). Foreword. In E. Ayisi, *An introduction to the study of African culture* (2nd ed., pp. vii–ix). London: Currey.

Fortier, C. (1997). Mémorisation et audition: L'enseignement coranique chez les Maures de Mauritanie. *Islam et Sociétiés au Sud du Sahara* 11: 85–105.

Fosnot, C. (Ed.). (1996). *Constructivism: Theory, perspectives, and practice.* New York: Teachers College Press.

Foucault, M. (1975). *Surveiller et punir: Naissance de la prison.* Paris: Gallimard.

Fraser, A. (1995). *The Gypsies* (2nd ed.). Oxford, England: Blackwell.

Freidel, D., Schele, L., & Parker, J. (1993). *Maya cosmos: Three thousand years on the shaman's path.* New York: Morrow.

Friedman, L., & Moon, S. (Eds.). (1997). *Being bodies: Buddhist women on the paradox of embodiment.* Boston: Shambhala.

Fromkin, V., & Rodman, R. (1978). *An introduction to language* (2nd ed.). New York: Holt, Rinehart and Winston.

Fuller, C. J. (1992). *The camphor flame: Popular Hinduism and society in India.* Princeton, NJ: Princeton University Press.

Fung Yu-lan. (1948). *A short history of Chinese philosophy.* New York: The Free Press.

Furlong, D. (1997). *The keys to the temple.* London: Piatkus.

Furniss, G., & Gunner, L. (Eds.). (1995). *Power, marginality and African oral literature.* Cambridge, England: Cambridge University Press.

Fu Shufang. (1991). A brief account of the positive factors in Confucius' thinking. In S. Krieger & R. Trauzettel (Eds.), *Confucianism and the modernization of China* (pp. 175–192). Mainz, Germany: Hase & Koehler.

Gallenkamp, C. (1985). *Maya: The riddle and rediscovery of a lost civilization* (3rd rev. ed.). New York: Penguin.

Galt, H. (1951). *A history of Chinese educational institutions, Vol. 1.* London: Probsthain.

Gannon, J. (1981). *Deaf heritage: A narrative history of deaf America.* Silver Spring, MD: National Association of the Deaf.

Gardner, K., & Lewis, D. (1996). *Anthropology, development and the post-modern challenge.* London: Pluto.

Gardner, M. (1998). Is cannibalism a myth? *Skeptical Inquirer* 22: 14–16.

Gätje, H. (1971). *Koran und Koranexegese.* Zurich: Artemis Verlag.

Gendrop, P. (1992). *Les mayas* (5th ed.). Paris: Presses Universitaires de France.

Gergen, K. (1982). *Towards transformation in social knowledge.* New York: Springer.

Gergen, K. (1995). Social construction and the educational process. In L. Steffe & J. Gale (Eds.), *Constructivism in education* (pp. 17–39). Hillsdale, NJ: Lawrence Erlbaum Associates.

Gernet, J. (1962). *Daily life in China on the eve of the Mongol invasion, 1250–1276.* Stanford, CA: Stanford University Press.

Gernet, J. (1982). *A history of Chinese civilization.* Cambridge, England: Cambridge University Press.

Geertz, C. (1973). *The interpretation of culture.* New York: Basic Books.

Geertz, C. (1983). *Local knowledge: Further essays in interpretive anthropology.* New York: Basic Books.

Ghosh, S. C. (2001). *The history of education in ancient India, c. 3000 B.C. to A.D. 1192.* New Delhi: Munshiram Manoharlal Publishers.

Gilligan, C. (1982). *In a different voice: Psychological theory and women's development.* Cambridge, MA: Harvard University Press.

Goetz, D., & Morley, S. (Trans.). (1950). *Popol Vuh: The sacred book of the ancient Quiché Maya.* Norman: University of Oklahoma Press.

Goldziher, I. (1981). *Introduction to Islamic theology and law.* Princeton, NJ: Princeton University Press.

Gomez, E. A. (1996). *Popol Vuh.* Mérida, México: Producción Editorial Dante.

Goody, J. (1987). *The interface between the written and the oral.* Cambridge, England: Cambridge University Press.

Gopalan, S. (1973). *Outlines of Jainism*. New York: Halsted.

Gordon, R. (1991). Serving the Volk with Volkekund: On the rise of South African anthropology. In J. Jansen (Ed.), *Knowledge and power in South Africa: Critical perspectives across the disciplines* (pp. 79–97). Johannesburg: Skotaville.

Gossen, G. (1974). *Chamulas in the world of the sun: Time and space in a Maya oral tradition*. Prospect Heights, IL: Waveland.

Graham, C. (1998). *Ideologies of epic: Nation, empire, and Victorian epic poetry*. Manchester, England: Manchester University Press.

Granet, M. (1968). *La civilisation chinoise: La vie publique et la vie privée*. Paris: Editions Albin Michel.

Gregory, S., & Hartley, G. (Eds.). (1991). *Constructing deafness*. London: Pinter Publishers, in association with the Open University.

Groce, N. (1985). *Everyone here spoke sign language: Hereditary deafness on Martha's Vineyard*. Cambridge, MA: Harvard University Press.

Gropper, R. (1975). *Gypsies in the city: Cultural patterns and survival*. Princeton, NJ: Darwin Press.

Gross, R. (1993). *Buddhism after patriarchy: A feminist history, analysis and reconstruction of Buddhism*. Albany: State University of New York Press.

Guillaume, A. (1956). *Islam*. Harmondsworth, England: Penguin.

Guma, S. (1977). *The form, content and technique of traditional literature in Southern Sotho* (2nd ed.). Pretoria: van Schaik.

Gunnarsson, B. (1997). On the sociohistorical construction of scientific discourse. In B. Gunnarsson, P. Linell, & B. Nordberg (Eds.), *The construction of professional discourse* (pp. 99–126). London: Longman.

Gunnarsson, B., Linell, P., & Nordberg, B. (Eds.). (1997). *The construction of professional discourse*. London: Longman.

Gunner, L., & Gwala, M. (Eds.). (1991). *Musho: Zulu popular praises*. Johannesburg: Witwatersrand University Press.

Gutek, G. (1993). *American education in a global society: Internationalizing teacher education*. New York: Longman.

Gyatso, T. (1990). *Freedom in exile: The autobiography of the Dalai Lama*. New York: Harper Perennial.

Hacking, I. (2001). *The social construction of what?* Cambridge, MA: Harvard University Press.

Haddad, Y. (Ed.). (1991). *The Muslims of America*. New York: Oxford University Press.

Haddad, Y., Haines, B., & Findly, E. (Eds.). (1984). *The Islamic impact*. Syracuse, NY: Syracuse University Press.

Haeri, S. F. (1993). *The elements of Islam*. Shaftesbury, England: Element.

Hagemeyer, A. (1992). *The red notebook*. Silver Spring, MD: National Association of the Deaf.

Haig-Brown, C., & Archibald, J. (1996). Transforming First Nations research with respect and power. *International Journal of Qualitative Studies in Education* 9, 3: 245–267.

Haleen, M. (2001). *Understanding the Qur'an: Themes and style*. London: I. B. Tauris.

Hall, R. N. (1969). *Ancient ruins of Rhodesia: Monomotapae Imperium* (2nd ed. rev. and enlarged). New York: Negro Universities Press. (Original work published 1904)

Hamer, R. (1970). *A choice of Anglo-Saxon verse*. London: Faber & Faber.

Hamidullah, M. (1981). *Introduction to Islam*. Chicago: Kazi.

Hammond, N. (1988). *Ancient Maya civilization*. New Brunswick, NJ: Rutgers University Press.

Hammond-Tooke, W. D. (Ed.). (1974). *The Bantu-speaking peoples of Southern Africa*. London: Routledge & Kegan Paul.

Hammond-Tooke, W. D. (1997). *Imperfect interpreters: South Africa's anthropologists, 1920–1990*. Johannesburg: University of the Witwatersrand Press.

Hancock, I. (1984a). Romani and Angloromani. In P. Trudgill (Ed.), *Language in the British Isles* (pp. 367–383). Cambridge, England: Cambridge University Press.

Hancock, I. (1984b). Shelta and Polari. In P. Trudgill (Ed.), *Language in the British Isles* (pp. 384–403). Cambridge, England: Cambridge University Press.

Hancock, I. (1987). *The pariah syndrome: An account of Gypsy slavery and persecution.* Ann Arbor, MI: Karoma.

Hancock, I. (1995). *A handbook of Vlax Romani.* Columbus, OH: Slavica.

Handawela, J. (2001). Towards a methodology to test indigenous knowledge. *Compass* (March): 44–46.

Handlin, J. (1983). *Action in late Ming thought: The reorientation of Lü K'un and other scholar-officials.* Berkeley: University of California Press.

Haneef, S. (1985). *What everyone should know about Islam and Muslims.* Des Plaines, IL: Library of Islam.

Hanh, T. N. (1991). *Old path white clouds: Walking in the footsteps of the Buddah.* Berkeley, CA: Parallax.

Hanh, T. N. (1998). *The heart of the Buddha's teaching.* New York: Broadway Books.

Hansen, C. (1992). *A Daoist theory of Chinese thought: A philosophical interpretation.* New York: Oxford University Press.

Hardy, F. (1994). *The religious culture of India: Power, love and wisdom.* Cambridge, England: Cambridge University Press.

Harris, J. (1992). *Against relativism: A philosophical defense of method.* LaSalle, IL: Open Court.

Harris, J. (1995). *The cultural meaning of deafness: Language, identity and power relations.* Aldershot, England: Ashgate.

Harrold, F., & Eve, R. (Eds.). (1995). *Cult archaeology and creationism: Understanding pseudoscientific beliefs about the past* (Exp. ed.). Iowa City: University of Iowa Press.

Hassig, R. (1985). *Trade, tribute, and transportation: The sixteenth century political economy of the Valley of Mexico.* Norman: University of Oklahoma Press.

Hassig, R. (1988). *Aztec warfare: Imperial expansion and political control.* Norman: University of Oklahoma Press.

Hassig, R. (1992). *War and society in ancient Mesoamerica.* Berkeley: University of California Press.

Hastrup, K. (1995). *A passage to anthropology: Between experience and theory.* London: Routledge.

Hayhoe, R., & Bastid, M. (Eds.). (1987). *China's education and the industrialized world: Studies in cultural transfer.* London: Sharpe.

Haykal, M. H. (1976). *The life of Muhammad.* Indianapolis, IN: American Trust Publications.

Headland, I. (1914). *Home life in China.* London: Methuen.

Hedberg, T. (1994). Name signs in Swedish Sign Language: Their formation and use. In C. Erting, R. Johnson, D. Smith, & B. Snider (Eds.), *The deaf way: Perspectives from the International Conference on Deaf Culture* (pp. 416–424). Washington, DC: Gallaudet University Press.

Heine, S., & Probish, C. (Eds.). (2003). *Buddhism in the modern world: Adaptation of an ancient tradition.* Oxford, England: Oxford University Press.

Hellbom, A. (1967). *La participación cultural de las mujeres: Indias y mestizas en el México precortesiano y postrevolucionario* (Monograph Series, Publication 10). Stockholm, Sweden: The Ethnographic Museum.

Heren, L., Fitzgerald, C. P., Freeberne, M., Hook, B., & Bonavia, D. (1973). *China's three thousand years: The story of a great civilisation.* New York: Collier.

Herman, A. L. (1991). *A brief introduction to Hinduism: Religion, philosophy, and ways of liberation.* Boulder, CO: Westview.

Hersh, R. (1997). *What is mathematics, really?* New York: Oxford University Press.

Hindery, R. (1978). *Comparative ethics in Hindu and Buddhist traditions.* Delhi: Motilal Banarsidass.

Hirsch, E. D. (1988). *Cultural literacy: What every American needs to know.* New York: Vintage.

Hirsch, E. D. (1996). *The schools we need and why we don't have them.* New York: Doubleday.

Hiskett, M. (1994). *The development of Islam in West Africa* (2nd ed.). Edinburgh: Edinburgh University Press.

Ho Peng Yoke. (1985). *Li, qi and shu: An introduction to science and civilization in China*. Hong Kong: Hong Kong University Press.

Hofstede, G.(1997). *Cultures and organizations: Software of the mind.* New York: McGraw-Hill.

Hofstede, G. (2001). *Culture's consequences* (2nd ed.). Thousand Oaks, CA: Sage.

Hogg, G. (1990). *Cannibalism and human sacrifice.* London: Hale.

Holmes, G. (Ed.). (1988). *The Oxford illustrated history of medieval Europe.* Oxford, England: Oxford University Press.

Holtedahl, L., & Djingui, M. (1997). The power of knowledge. In E. Rosander & D. Westerlund (Eds.), *African Islam and Islam in Africa* (pp. 254–285). Athens, OH: University of Ohio Press.

Hornung, E. (2001). *The secret lore of Egypt: Its impact on the West.* Ithaca, NY: Cornell University Press.

Horrocks, G. (1997). *Greek: A history of the language and its speakers.* London: Longman.

Horton, R. (1970). African traditional thought and Western science. In B. Wilson (Ed.), *Rationality* (pp. 131–171). New York: Harper & Row.

Howe, M. (1992). Untruths in advertising: Cochlear implants. In M. Garretson (Ed.), *Viewpoints on deafness: A Deaf American monograph, Vol. 42* (pp. 67–68). Silver Spring, MD: National Association of the Deaf.

Howe, S. (1998). *Afrocentrism: Mythical pasts and imagined homes.* London: Verso.

Hsiung-huei Lee. (1995). *Education in Taiwan during the Ch'ing dynasty, 1683–1895.* Ph. D. dissertation, University of Connecticut.

Hsü, I. C. Y. (1990). *The rise of modern China.* New York: Oxford University Press.

Huang, R. (1988). *China: A macro history.* London: Sharpe.

Hucker, C. (1975). *China's imperial past: An introduction to Chinese history and culture.* Stanford, CA: Stanford University Press.

Hulbert, J. (1935). *Bright's Anglo-Saxon reader.* New York: Holt.

Humphrey, C., & Laidlaw, J. (1994). *The archetypal actions of ritual: A theory of ritual illustrated by the Jain rite of worship.* Oxford, England: Clarendon.

Humphries, C. (1951). *Buddhism: An introduction and guide.* Harmondsworth, England: Penguin.

Hurtado, A., & Iverson, P. (Eds.). (1994). *Major problems in American Indian history: Documents and essays.* Lexington, MA: Heath.

Husaini, S. W. A. (1986). *Islamic science and public policies: Lessons from the history of science* (2nd rev. ed.). Indianapolis, IN: Islamic Book Service.

Hutton, C. (1999). *Linguistics and the Third Reich: Mother-tongue fascism, race, and the science of language.* London: Routledge.

Hymes, R. (1989). Lu Chiu-yüan, academies, and the problem of the local community. In W. de Bary & J. Chaffee (Eds.), *Neo-Confucian education: The formative stage* (pp. 432–456). Berkeley: University of California Press.

Ibrahim, A. (1989). Islam and the law. In *Toward Islamization of disciplines* (pp. 381–391). Herndon, VA: International Institute of Islamic Thought.

Icamina, P. (1993). Threads of common knowledge. *IDRC Reports* 21, 1: 14–16.

Infante, F. (1983). *La educación de los Aztecas.* México: Panorama Editorial.

Irele, A. (Ed.). (1992). *African education and identity.* Ibadan, Nigeria: Spectrum.

Ishaq, I. (1967). *The life of Muhammad.* London: Oxford University Press.

Ishumi, A. (1986). Black civilization and pedagogy: A search for modern methods. In J. Okpaku, A. Opubor, & B. Oloruntimehin (Eds.), *The arts and civilization of Black and African peoples, Volume 6: Black civilization and pedagogy* (pp. 60–79). Lagos, Nigeria: Center for Black and African Arts and Civilization.

Ismail, S. M. (1994). Islamic education in North America: A reality, a fact and a responsibility. *Muslim Education Quarterly* 11, 3: 63–71.

Ives, C. (1992). *Zen awakening and society*. Honolulu: University of Hawaii Press.

Izquierdo, A. (1983). *La educación maya en los tiempos prehispánicos*. México: Universidad Nacional Autónoma de México.

Jacobson, N. P. (1986). *Understanding Buddhism*. Carbondale: Southern Illinois University Press.

Jameelah, M. (1986). *Islam in theory and practice*. Lahore, Pakistan: Mohammad Yusuf Khan & Sons.

Janesick, V., & Moores, D. (1992). Ethnic and cultural considerations. In T. Kluwin, D. Moores, & M. Gaustad (Eds.), *Toward effective public school programs for deaf students: Context, process and outcomes* (pp. 49–65). New York: Teachers College Press.

Jankowski, K. (1997). *Deaf empowerment: Emergence, struggle, and rhetoric*. Washington, DC: Gallaudet University Press.

Jansen, G. H. (1979). *Militant Islam*. New York: Harper & Row.

Jansen, J. (Ed.). (1991). *Knowledge and power in South Africa: Critical perspectives across the disciplines*. Johannesburg: Skotaville.

Jolly, J. (1989). *Histoire de continent Africain*, 2 vols. Paris: Editions l'Harmattan.

Jones, E., Palmer, E., & Jones, M. (Eds.). (1992). *Orature in African literature today*. London: Currey.

Josephy, A. (1991). *The Indian heritage of America*. Boston: Houghton Mifflin. (Original work published 1968)

Josephy, A. (Ed.). (1991). *America in 1492: The world of the Indian peoples before the arrival of Columbus*. New York: Vintage.

Josephy, A. (1994). *500 nations: An illustrated history of North American Indians*. New York: Knopf.

Josserand, J. K., & Dakin, K. (Eds.). (1988). *Smoke and mist: Mesoamerican studies in memory of Thelma D. Sullivan, part II*. Oxford, England: B.A.R.

Kahn, M. (Ed.). (1981). *Education and society in the Muslim world*. Jeddah, Saudi Arabia: King Abdulaziz University.

Kalupahana, D. (1992). *A history of Buddhist philosophy: Continuities and discontinuities*. Honolulu: University of Hawaii Press.

Kaminski, I. (1980). *The state of ambiguity: Studies of Gypsy refugees*. Gothenburg, Sweden: Mobilis.

Karim, K. H. (2000). *Islamic peril: Media and global violence*. Montréal: Black Rose Books.

Karttunen, F., & Lockhard, J. (Eds.). (1987). *The art of Nahuatl speech: The Bancroft dialogues*. Los Angeles: UCLA Latin American Center Publications.

Kaschula, R. (1991). The role of Xhosa oral poetry in contemporary South African society. *South African Journal of African Languages* 11, 2: 47–54.

Kaschula, R. (Ed.). (1993). *Foundations in Southern African oral literature*. Johannesburg: Witwatersrand University Press.

Kaschula, R. (Ed.). (2001). *African oral literature: Functions in contemporary societies*. Cape Town: New Africa Books.

Katengo, M., & Mwale, G. (1986). Can traditional education be integrated with the modern educational system? In S. Moyo, T. Sumaili, & J. Moody (Eds.), *Oral traditions in Southern Africa, Vol. 6.* (pp. 456–481). Lusaka, Zambia: Division for Cultural Research, Institute for African Studies, University of Zambia.

Katz, F. (1966). *Situación social y económica de los Aztecas durante los siglos XV y XVI*. México: Universidad Nacional Autónoma de México, Instituto de Investigaciones Históricas.

Kawagley, O. (1990). Yup'ik ways of knowing. *Canadian Journal of Native Education* 17, 2: 5–17.

Kazi, M. A. (1997). *Islamic thought and modern science*. Amman, Jordan: Islamic Academy of Sciences.

Keen, B. (1971). *The Aztec image in Western thought*. New Brunswick, NJ: Rutgers University Press.

Kefai, Y., & Risnick, M. (Eds.). (1996). *Constructionism in practice: Designing, thinking, and learning in a digital world.* Hillsdale, NJ: Lawrence Erlbaum Associates.

Kelleher, M. T. (1989). Back to basics: Chu Hsi's *Elementary learning (Hsiao-hsüeh).* In W. de Bary & J. Chaffee (Eds.), *Neo-Confucian education: The formative stage* (pp. 219–251). Berkeley: University of California Press.

Kellogg, S. (1988). Cognatic kinship and religion: Women in Aztec society. In J. Josserand & K. Dakin (Eds.), *Smoke and mist: Mesoamerican studies in memory of Thelma D. Sullivan, Part II* (pp. 665–681). Oxford, England: B.A.R.

Kepel, G., & Richard, Y. (Eds.). (1990). *Intellectuels et militants de l'Islam contemporain.* Paris: Éditions du Seuil.

Kephart, W. (1982). *Extraordinary groups: The sociology of unconventional lifestyles* (2nd ed.). New York: St. Martin's Press.

Kersting, S. (1997). Balancing between deaf and hearing worlds: Reflections of mainstreamed college students on relationships and social interactions. *Journal of Deaf Studies and Deaf Education* 2: 252–263.

Khan, M. I. (1996). *Experiencing Islam.* Karachi, Pakistan: Oxford University Press.

Khare, H. C. (Ed.). (1991a). *Issues in Vedic mathematics.* Delhi: Motilal Banarsidass Publishers.

Khare, H. C. (1991b). Vedic mathematics. In H. C. Khare (Ed.), *Issues in Vedic mathematics* (pp. 13–17). Delhi: Motilal Banarsidass Publishers.

Kiang Kang-Hu. (1934). *On Chinese studies.* Shanghai: Commercial.

Kimmerle, H. (1991). *Philosophie in Afrika—Afrikanische Philosophie.* Frankfurt/Main, Germany: Campus Verlag.

Kincheloe, T. S. (1984). The wisdom of the elders: Cross-cultural perspectives. *Journal of Thought* 19, 3: 121–127.

Kinsley, D. (1993). *Hinduism: A cultural perspective* (2nd ed.). Englewood Cliffs, NJ: Prentice-Hall.

Klein, C. (1987). The ideology of autosacrifice at the Templo Mayor. In E. Boone (Ed.), *The Aztec Templo Mayor: A symposium at Dumbarton Oaks* (pp. 293–370). Washington, DC: Dumbarton Oaks Research Library and Collection.

Kleinman, A. (1980). *Patients and healers in the context of culture: An exploration of the borderland between anthropology, medicine, and psychiatry.* Berkeley: University of California Press.

Klor de Alva, J., Nicholas, H., & Keber, E. (Eds.). (1988). *The work of Bernardino de Sahagun: Pioneer ethnographer of sixteenth century Aztec Mexico.* Albany: Institute for Mesoamerican Studies, The University of Albany, State University of New York.

Klostermaier, K. (1989). *A survey of Hinduism.* Albany: State University of New York Press.

Kluckhohn, C., & Leighton, D. (1962). *The Navajo* (Rev. ed.). Garden City, NY: Doubleday.

Knauft, B. (1996). *Genealogies for the present in cultural anthropology.* New York: Routledge.

Knipe, D. (1991). *Hinduism.* San Francisco: Harper.

Koopman, A. (2002). *Zulu names.* Pietermaritzburg: University of Natal Press.

Kraft, K. (Ed.). (1988). *Zen: Tradition and transition.* New York: Grove.

Krieger, S., & Trauzettel, R. (Eds.). (1991). *Confucianism and the modernization of China.* Mainz, Germany: Hase & Koehler.

Kroeber, K. (1981). The art of traditional American Indian narration. In K. Kroeber (Ed.), *Traditional literatures of the American Indian: Texts and interpretations* (pp. 1–24). Lincoln: University of Nebraska Press.

Kroeber, K. (Ed.). (1981). *Traditional literatures of the American Indian: Texts and interpretations.* Lincoln: University of Nebraska Press.

Krugly-Smolska, E. (1994). An examination of some difficulties in integrating Western science into societies with an indigenous scientific tradition. *Interchange* 25, 4: 324–334.

Kuang Yaming. (1991). Modern values of the positive elements in Confucius' ideas concerning the study of man. In S. Krieger & R. Trauzettel (Eds.), *Confucianism and the modernization of China* (pp. 7–17). Mainz, Germany: Hase & Koehler.

Kubik, G. (1990). *Visimu vya mukatikati:* Dilemma tales and "arithmetical puzzles" collected among the Valuchazi. *South African Journal of African Languages* 10, 2: 59–68.

Kubik, G. (1992). A Luchazi riddle session: Analysis of recorded texts in a south-central African Bantu language. *South African Journal of African Languages* 12, 2: 51–82.

Kuhn, T. (1970). *The structure of scientific revolutions* (2nd enlarged ed.). Chicago: University of Chicago Press.

Kuhn, T. (1977). *The essential tension: Selected studies in scientific tradition and change.* Chicago: University of Chicago Press.

Kuklick, H. (1991). *The savage within: The social history of British anthropology, 1885–1945.* Cambridge, England: Cambridge University Press.

Kunene, D. (1971). *Heroic poetry of the Basotho.* Oxford, England: Oxford University Press.

Küng, H. (1992). *Judaism: Between yesterday and tomorrow.* New York: Crossroad.

Kuper, A. (1988). *The invention of primitive society: Transformations of an illusion.* London: Routledge.

Kyle, J. (1990). The deaf community: Custom, culture and tradition. In S. Prillwitz & T. Vollhaber (Eds.), *Sign language research and application* (pp. 175–185). Hamburg, Germany: Signum.

Ladd, P. (2003). *Understanding deaf culture: In search of deafhood.* Clevedon, England: Multilingual Matters.

Lanczkowski, G. (1970). *Aztekische Sprach and überlieferung.* Berlin: Springer.

Lane, H. (Ed.). (1984a). *The deaf experience: Classics in language and education.* Cambridge, MA: Harvard University Press.

Lane, H. (1984b). *When the mind hears: A history of the deaf.* New York: Random House.

Lane, H. (1992a). Cochlear implants are wrong for young deaf children. In M. Garretson (Ed.), *Viewpoints on deafness: A Deaf American monograph, Vol. 42* (pp. 89–92). Silver Spring, MD: National Association of the Deaf.

Lane, H. (1992b). *The mask of benevolence: Disabling the deaf community.* New York: Knopf.

Lane, H. (1993a). Cochlear implants: Their cultural and historical meaning. In J. Van Cleve (Ed.), *Deaf history unveiled: Interpretations from the new scholarship* (pp. 272–291). Washington, DC: Gallaudet University Press.

Lane, H. (1993b). The medicalization of cultural deafness in historical perspective. In R. Fischer & H. Lane (Eds.), *Looking back: A reader on the history of deaf communities and their sign languages* (pp. 479–493). Hamburg, Germany: Signum.

Lane, H. (1995). Reproductive control of deaf people and the deaf search for a homeland. In M. Garretson (Ed.), *Deafness: Life and culture II, A Deaf American monograph, Vol. 45* (pp. 73–78). Silver Spring, MD: National Association of the Deaf.

Lane, H., Hoffmeister, R., & Bahan, B. (1996). *A journey into the DEAF-WORLD.* San Diego, CA: DawnSign Press.

Larson, G. (1994). Hinduism in India and in America. In J. Neusner (Ed.), *World religions in America* (pp. 177–202). Louisville, KY: Westminster/John Knox.

Lasisi, R. O. (1995). French colonialism and Islamic education in West Africa, 1900–1939. *Muslim Education Quarterly* 12, 3: 12–22.

Last, M., & Chavunduka, G. L. (Eds.). (1986). *The professionalisation of African medicine.* Manchester, England: Manchester University Press, in association with the International African Institute.

Lau, D. C. (Trans.). (1970). *Mencius.* Harmondsworth, England: Penguin.

Lau, D. C. (Trans.). (1979). *The Analects.* Harmondsworth, England: Penguin.

Lawrence, B. (1998). *Shattering the myth: Islam beyond violence.* Princeton, NJ: Princeton University Press.

Leaman, O. (2002). *An introduction to classical Islamic philosophy.* Cambridge, England: Cambridge University Press.

Lee, G. (1967). *Crusade against ignorance: Thomas Jefferson on education.* New York: Teachers College Press.

Lee, T. (1989). Sung schools and education before Chu Hsi. In W. de Bary & J. Chaffee (Eds.), *Neo-Confucian education: The formative stage* (pp. 105–136). Berkeley: University of California Press.

Lee, T. H. C. (1985). *Government education and examinations in Sung China.* Hong Kong: Chinese University Press.

Lefkowitz, M. (1996). *Not out of Africa: How Afrocentrism became an excuse to teach myth as history.* New York: Basic Books.

Lefkowitz, M., & Rogers, G. M. (Eds.). (1996). *Black Athena revisited.* Chapel Hill: University of North Carolina Press.

Leggett, T. (Ed.). (1978). *Zen and the ways.* London: Routledge & Kegan Paul.

Lehmann, W. (1993). *Theoretical bases on Indo-European linguistics.* London: Longman.

León-Portilla, M. (Ed.). (1958). *Ritos, sacerdotes y atavíos de los dioses: Textos de los informantes de Sahagun, 1.* México: Universidad Nacional Autónoma de México, Instituto de Historia.

León-Portilla, M. (1963). *Aztec thought and culture.* Norman: University of Oklahoma Press.

León-Portilla, M. (1966). *La filosofía Nahuatl: Estudio en sus fuentes.* México: Universidad Nacional Autónoma de México.

León-Portilla, M. (1967). *Trece poetas del mundo azteca.* México: Universidad Nacional Autónoma de México, Instituto de Investigaciones Históricas.

León-Portilla, M. (1968). *Tiempo y realidad en el pensamiento maya.* México: Universidad Nacional Autónoma de México.

León-Portilla, M. (Ed.). (1971). *De Teotihuacán a los Aztecas: Antología de fuentes e interpretaciones históricas.* México: Universidad Nacional Autónoma de México, Instituto de Investigaciones Históricas.

León-Portilla, M. (1988). *Time and reality in the thought of the Maya.* Norman: University of Oklahoma Press.

León-Portilla, M. (1992a). *The Aztec image of self and society: An introduction to Nahua culture.* Salt Lake City: University of Utah Press.

León-Portilla, M. (1992b). *Fifteen poets of the Aztec world.* Norman: University of Oklahoma Press.

León-Portilla, M. (1992c). *Literaturas indígenas de México.* México: Fundo de Cultura Económica.

León-Portilla, M. (1994). *Quince poetas del mundo náhuatl.* México: Editorial Diana.

León-Portilla, M. (1995). *Toltecáyotl: Aspectos de la cultura náhuatl.* México: Fondo de Cultura Económica.

Leslie, C., & Young, A. (Eds.). (1992). *Paths to Asian medical knowledge.* Berkeley: University of California Press.

Leslie, J. (Ed.). (1991). *Roles and rituals for Hindu women.* Rutherford, NJ: Fairleigh Dickinson University Press.

Levesque, J. (2001). Let's return ASL to deaf ownership. In L. Bragg (Ed.), *DEAF-WORLD: A historical reader and primary source book* (pp. 116–117). New York: New York University Press.

Lévi-Strauss, C., & Eribon, D. (1988). *De près et de loin.* Paris: Editions Odile Jacob.

Levinson, B., Foley, D., & Holland, D. (Eds.). (1996). *The cultural production of the educated person: Critical ethnographies of schooling and local practice.* Albany: State University of New York Press.

Levinson, B., & Holland, D. (1996). The cultural production of the educated person: An introduction. In B. Levinson, D. Foley, & D. Holland (Eds.), *The cultural production of the educated person: Critical ethnographies of schooling and local practice* (pp. 1–54). Albany: State University of New York Press.

Lhuillier, A. (1963). El pensamiento náhuatl respecto de la muerte. *Estudios de Cultura Náhuatl* 4: 251–261.

Liégeois, J. (1987). *Gypsies and travellers: Socio-cultural data, socio-political data.* Strasbourg, Germany: Council for Cultural Co-operation.

Lincoln, Y., & Guba, E. (1985). *Naturalistic inquiry.* Newbury Park, CA: Sage.

Lings, M. (1983). *Muhammad: His life based on the earliest sources.* Rochester, VT: Inner Traditions.

Linton, S. (1998). *Claiming disability: Knowledge and identity.* New York: New York University Press.

Lippman, T. (1995). *Understanding Islam: An introduction to the Muslim world* (2nd rev. ed.). New York: Meridan.

Liu, J. (Ed.). (1974). *Political institutions in traditional China: Major issues.* New York: Wiley.

Liu Ts'un-Yan. (1970). Taoist self-cultivation in Ming thought. In W. de Bary (Ed.), *Self and society in Ming thought* (pp. 291–330). New York: Columbia University Press.

Llasera, I. (1987). Confucian education through European eyes. In R. Hayhoe & M. Bastid (Eds.), *China's education and the industrialized world* (pp. 21–32). London: Sharpe.

Locust, C. (1988). Wounding the spirit: Discrimination and traditional American Indian belief systems. *Harvard Educational Review* 58, 3: 315–330.

Loewe, M. (1965). *Imperial China: The historical background to the modern age.* New York: Praeger.

Loewe, M. (1990). *The pride that was China.* New York: St. Martin's Press.

Loimeier, R. (1997). *Islamic reform and political change in northern Nigeria.* Evanston, IL: Northwestern University.

lo Liyong, T. (1969). *The last word.* Nairobi, Kenya: East Africa Publishing House.

Lomawaima, K. T. (1994). *They called it prairie light: The story of Chilocco Indian school.* Lincoln: University of Nebraska Press.

Lopez, D. (Ed.). (1995). *Religions of India in practice.* Princeton, NJ: Princeton University Press.

Lopez, D. (2001). *The story of Buddhism: A concise guide to its history and teachings.* New York: HarperSanFrancisco.

Lowe, L. (1991). *Critical terrains: French and British orientalisms.* Ithaca, NY: Cornell University Press.

Lucas, C. (Ed.). (1989). *The sociolinguistics of the deaf community.* San Diego, CA: Academic Press.

Lucas, C., & Valli, C. (1992). *Language contact in the American deaf community.* San Diego, CA: Academic Press.

Luis de Rojas, J. (1988). *México Tenochtitlan: Economía y sociedad en el siglo XVI.* México: El Colegio de Michoacán, Fondo de Cultura Económica.

MacMillan, N. (1993). Indigenous peoples test the waters. *IDRC Reports* 21, 1: 6–8.

Magadla, L. (1996). Constructivism: A practitioner's perspective. *South African Journal of Higher Education* 10: 83–88.

Mahlangu, D. (1988). *Imiraro:* Ndebele riddles. *South African Journal of African Languages* 8 (Suppl. 1): 147–172.

Manglapus, R. (1987). *Will of the people: Original democracy in non-Western societies.* New York: Greenwood.

Mannan, M. A. (1989). The frontiers of Islamic economics: Some philosophical underpinnings. In *Toward Islamization of disciplines* (pp. 295–311). Herndon, VA: International Institute of Islamic Thought.

Maqsood, R. (1994). *Islam.* London: NTC.

Marcus, J. (1992). *Mesoamerican writing systems: Propaganda, myth, and history in four ancient civilizations.* Princeton, NJ: Princeton University Press.

Margalit, G. (2002). *Germany and its Gypsies: A post-Auschwitz ordeal.* Madison: University of Wisconsin Press.

Markus, M. (1963). Estudio comparativo entre la educación nahuatl y la griega. *Estudios de Cultura Náhuatl* 4: 281–292.

Martin, C. (1994). Ethnohistory: A better way to write Indian history. In A. Hurtado & P. Iverson (Eds.), *Major problems in American Indian history: Documents and essays* (pp. 23–33). Lexington, MA: Heath.

Martin, J. R. (1982). The ideal of the educated person. In D. DeNicola (Ed.), *Philosophy of education: 1981* (pp. 3–20). Normal, IL: Philosophy of Education Society.

Martin, J. R. (1985). *Reclaiming a conversation: The ideal of the educated woman.* New Haven, CT: Yale University Press.

Martin, P., & O'Meara, P. (Eds.). (1995). *Africa* (3rd ed.). Bloomington: Indiana University Press.

Martín del Campo, B., & Poveda, D. (2002). Las narraciones de los niños y las niñas gitanas: Un análisis de géneros discursivos. *Discurso y Sociedad* 4: 53–80.

Mascaró, J. (Trans.). (1965). *The Upanishads.* Harmondsworth, England: Penguin.

Maspero, H., & Escarra, J. (1952). *Les institutions de la Chine: Essai historique.* Paris: Presses Universitaires de France.

Matras, Y. (Ed.). (1995). *Romani in contact: The history, structure, and sociology of a language.* Amsterdam, The Netherlands: John Benjamins.

Matsunaga, A. (1969). *The Buddhist philosophy of assimilation: The historical development of the Honji-Suijaku theory.* Tokyo: Sophia University.

Mazrui, A. (1980). *The African condition: The Reith lectures.* London: Heinemann.

Mazrui, A., & Wagaw, T. (1985). Towards decolonizing modernity: Education and culture conflict in Eastern Africa. In *The educational process and historiography in Africa* (pp. 35–62). Paris: UNESCO.

Mbiti, J. (1989). *African religions and philosophy* (2nd ed.). Oxford, England: Heinemann.

McCloud, A. B. (1995). *African American Islam.* London: Routledge.

McEvedy, C. (1980). *The Penguin atlas of African history.* Harmmondsworth, England: Penguin.

McGovern, S. (1999). *Education, modern development, and indigenous knowledge: An analysis of academic knowledge production.* New York: Garland.

McIvor, M. (1990). Research into traditional First Nations healing practices: A beginning. *Canadian Journal of Native Education* 17, 2: 89–95.

McKay, A., & McKay, B. (1987). Education as a total way of life: The Nisga'a experience. In J. Barman, Y. Hébert, & D. McCaskill (Eds.), *Indian education in Canada, Volume 2: The challenge* (pp. 64–85). Vancouver: University of British Columbia Press.

McKnight, B. (1989). Mandarins as legal experts: Professional learning in Sung China. In W. de Bary & J. Chafee (Eds.), *Neo-Confucian education: The formative stage* (pp. 493–516). Berkeley: University of California Press.

McMullen, D. (1988). *State and scholars in T'ang China.* Cambridge, England: Cambridge University Press.

Medicine, B. (1987). My elders tell me. In J. Barman, Y. Hébert, & D. McCaskill (Eds.), *Indian education in Canada, Volume 2: The challenge* (pp. 142–152). Vancouver: University of British Columbia Press.

Menzies, G. (2003). *1421: The year that China discovered America.* New York: Morrow.

Mernissi, F. (1987a). *Beyond the veil: Male–female dynamics in modern Muslim society.* Bloomington: Indiana University Press.

Mernissi, F. (1987b). *The veil and the male elite: A feminist interpretation of women's rights in Islam.* Reading, MA: Addison-Wesley.

Meskill, J., with J. Gentzler (Eds.). (1973). *An introduction to Chinese civilization.* New York: Columbia University Press.

Miller, C. (1975). American Rom and the ideology of defilement. In F. Rehfisch (Ed.), *Gypsies, tinkers, and other travellers* (pp. 41–54). London: Academic Press.

Miller, D. (1988). Hopi education: Before schools and teachers. *Tennessee Education* 18, 2: 28–32.

Miller, D., & Wertz, D. (1976). *Hindu monastic life and the monks and monasteries of Bhubaneswar.* Montréal: McGill-Queen's University Press.

Miller, M. E. (1986). *The art of Mesoamerica from Olmec to Aztec.* London: Thames and Hudson.

Milton, S. (1991). Gypsies and the Holocaust. *The History Teacher* 24, 4: 375–387.

Mitchell, B. (1995). *An invitation to Old English and Anglo-Saxon England.* Oxford, England: Blackwell.

Mitchell, B., & Robinson, F. (1992). *A guide to Old English* (5th ed.). Oxford, England: Blackwell.

Mitchell, D. (2002). *Buddhism: Introducing the Buddhist experience.* Oxford, England: Oxford University Press.

Mitchell, P. (2002). *The archeology of southern Africa.* Cambridge, England: Cambridge University Press.

Moctezuma, E. (1987). Symbolism of the Templo Mayor. In E. Boone (Ed.), *The Aztec Templo Mayor: A symposium at Dumbarton Oaks* (pp. 185–209). Washington, DC: Dumbarton Oaks Research Library and Collection.

Moll, L. (Ed.). (1990). *Vygotsky and education: Instructional implications and applications of sociocultural psychology.* Cambridge, England: Cambridge University Press.

Mookerji, R. (1969). *Ancient Indian education.* Delhi: Motilal Banarsidass Publishers.

Morales-Gómez, D. (1993). Knowledge, change and the preservation of progress. *IDRC Reports* 21, 1: 4–5.

Morton, W. S. (1995). *China: Its history and culture.* New York: McGraw-Hill.

Moses, W. J. (1998). *Afrotopia: The roots of African American popular history.* Cambridge, England: Cambridge University Press.

Mote, F., & Twitchett, D. (Eds.). (1988). *The Cambridge history of China, Volume 7: The Ming dynasty, 1368–1644, part I.* Cambridge, England: Cambridge University Press.

Motoyoshi, M. (1990). The experience of mixed-race people: Some thoughts and theories. *Journal of Ethnic Studies* 18: 77–94.

Mottahedeh, R. (1998). Traditional Shi'ite education in Qom. In A. Rorty (Ed.), *Philosophers on education: New historical perspectives* (pp. 451–457). London: Routledge.

Moumouni, A. (1968). *Education in Africa.* New York: Praeger.

Moyo, S., Sumaili, T., & Moody, J. (Eds.). (1986). *Oral traditions in Southern Africa, Vol. 6.* Lusaka, Zambia: Division for Cultural Research, Institute for African Studies, University of Zambia.

Mudimbe, V. (1988). *The invention of Africa: Gnosis, philosophy, and the order of knowledge.* London: Currey.

Mulcahy, D. G. (2002). *Knowledge, gender, and schooling: The feminist educational thought of Jane Roland Martin.* Westport, CT: Bergin & Garvey.

Muller, C. F. J. (1986). *Five hundred years: A history of South Africa* (5th ed.). Pretoria: Academica.

Muslim Public Affairs Council. (2002). Action alert: Keep contacting President Bush regarding Fallwell's bigotry. (14 October).

Myburgh, A. (Ed.). (1981). *Anthropology for Southern Africa.* Pretoria: van Schaik.

Mzolo, D. (1988). Social function of clan praises. In A. Nkabinde (Ed.), *African linguistics and literature* (pp. 132–138). Johannesburg: Lexicon.

Nadel, S. (1942). *Black Byzantium: The kingdom of the Nupe in Nigeria.* London: International African Institute.

Nakosteen, M. (1964). *History of Islamic origins of Western education, A.D. 800–1350.* Boulder, CO: University of Colorado Press.

Nason, J. (2000). "Our" Indians: The unidimensional Indian in the disembodied local past. In *The changing presentation of the American Indian: Museums and native cultures* (pp. 29–46). Seattle and Washington, DC: National Museum of the American Indian, Smithsonian Institution, in association with the University of Washington Press.

Nasr, S. H. (1984). Islamic education and science: A summary appraisal. In Y. Haddad, B. Haines, & E. Findly (Eds.), *The Islamic impact* (pp. 47–68). Syracuse, NY: Syracuse University Press.

Nasr, S. H. (1987). *Traditional Islam in the modern world*. London: Routledge & Kegan Paul.

Nayyar, A. H. (1998). Madrasah education frozen in time. In P. Hoodbhoy (Ed.), *Education and the state: Fifty years of Pakistan* (pp. 215–250). Karachi, Pakistan: Oxford University Press.

Nee-Benham, M., with Cooper, J. (Eds.). (2000). *Indigenous educational models for contemporary practice: In our mother's voice*. Hillsdale, NJ: Lawrence Erlbaum Associates.

Needham, J. (1981). *Science in traditional China: A comparative perspective*. Cambridge, MA: Harvard University Press.

Nelson-Barber, S. (1990). Considerations for the inclusion of multiple cultural competencies in teacher assessment: A Yup'ik Eskimo case study. *Canadian Journal of Native Education* 17, 2: 33–42.

Neusner, J. (Ed.). (1994). *World religions in America*. Louisville, KY: Westminster/John Knox.

Nicholson, H. (1967). The efflorescence of Mesoamerican civilization: A resume. In B. Ball (Ed.), *Indian Mexico: Past and present* (pp. 46–71). Los Angeles: University of California at Los Angeles, Latin American Center.

Nkabinde, A. (Ed.). (1988). *African linguistics and literature*. Johannesburg: Lexicon.

Nkara, J. (1992). *Bisisimi* or the language of the wise. *South African Journal of African Languages* 12, 4: 144–149.

Noddings, N. (1990). Constructivism in mathematics education. In R. Davis, C. Maher & N. Noddings (Eds.), *Constructivist views on the teaching and learning of mathematics* (pp. 7–18). Reston, VA: National Council of Teachers of Mathematics.

Noddings, N. (1995). *Philosophy of education*. Boulder, CO: Westview.

Norman, J. (1988). *Chinese*. Cambridge, England: Cambridge University Press.

Nover, S. (1993). *Our voices, our vision: Politics of deaf education*. Paper presented at the CAIS/CEASD convention in Baltimore, Maryland.

Nwosu, S. (1986). Pedagogic problems in Africa today. In J. Okpaku, A. Opubor, & B. Oloruntimehin (Eds.), *The arts and civilization of Black and African peoples, Volume 6: Black civilization and pedagogy* (pp. 102–118). Lagos, Nigeria: Center for Black and African Arts and Civilization.

Nyembezi, C. (1974). *Zulu proverbs*. Johannesburg: University of the Witwatersrand Press.

Obanewa, O. (1973). *Education of the children and youth in Ile-Ife: A comparison of formal and non-formal systems of education*. M.Ed. thesis, University of Ife, Nigeria.

O'Flaherty, W. D. (Trans.). (1981). *The Rig Veda: An anthology*. Harmondsworth, England: Penguin.

Ogbalu, F., & Emenanjo, E. (Eds.). (1982). *Igbo language and culture, Vol. 2*. Ibadan, Nigeria: Ibadan University Press.

Ogundijo, M. (1970). *Indigenous education in the Ejigbo District of Oshun Division in the pre-colonial days and the coming of the missionaries*. B.A. thesis, Faculty of Education, University of Ife, Nigeria.

Okeke, A. (1982). Traditional education in Igboland. In F. Ogbalu & E. Emenanjo (Eds.), *Igbo language and culture, Vol. 2* (pp. 15–26). Ibadan, Nigeria: Ibadan University Press.

Okely, J. (1983). *The traveler-gypsies*. Cambridge, England: Cambridge University Press.

Okepwho, I. (1992). *African oral literature: Backgrounds, character, and continuity*. Bloomington, IN: Indiana University Press.

Okpaku, J., Opubor, A., & Oloruntimehin, B. (Eds.). (1986). *The arts and civilization of Black and African peoples, Volume 6: Black civilization and pedagogy*. Lagos, Nigeria: Center for Black and African Arts and Civilization.

Olaniyan, R. (1982). African history and culture: An overview. In R. Olaniyan (Ed.), *African history and culture* (pp. 1–12). Lagos, Nigeria: Longman.

Olaniyan, R. (Ed.). (1982). *African history and culture*. Lagos, Nigeria: Longman.

Olivelle, P. (1993). *The Ashrama system: The history and heurmeneutics of a religious institution.* New York: Oxford University Press.

Oliver, R. (1999). *The African experience.* London: Phoenix Press.

Olson, D. (1998). *El mundo sobre el papel: El impacto de la escritura y la lectura en la estructura del conocimiento.* Buenos Aires: Editorial Gedisa.

Olson, D., & Torrance, N. (Eds.). (1998). *Cultura escrita y oralidad.* Buenos Aires: Editorial Gedisa.

Opland, J. (1983). *Xhosa oral poetry: Aspects of a Black South African tradition.* Cambridge, England: Cambridge University Press.

Opland, J. (1990). Xhosa *izibongo:* Improvised line. *South African Journal of African Languages* 10, 4: 239–251.

Opland, J. (1998). *Xhosa poets and poetry.* Cape Town: David Philip.

Orellana, C. (1997). *Historia de la educación en Guatemala* (5th ed.). Guatemala: Editorial Universitaria, Universidad de San Carlos de Guatemala.

Organ, T. (1970). *The Hindu quest for the perfection of man.* Athens, OH: Ohio University Press.

Orr, D. (1992). *Ecological literacy: Education and the transition to a postmodern world.* Albany: State University of New York Press.

Ortega, M. (1988). *La Inquisición y los gitanos.* Madrid: Taurus Ediciones.

Ortiz de Montellano, B. (1990). *Aztec medicine, health, and nutrition.* New Brunswick, NJ: Rutgers University Press.

Ortiz de Montellano, B. (1995). Multiculturalism, cult archaeology, and pseudoscience. In F. Harrold & R. Eve (Eds.), *Cult archaeology and creationism: Understanding pseudoscientific beliefs about the past* (Exp. ed., pp. 134–151). Iowa City: University of Iowa Press.

Otayek, R. (Ed.). (1993). *Le radicalisme islamique au sud du Sahara: Da'wa, arabisation et critique de l'Occident.* Paris: Éditions Karthala.

Othón de Mendizábal, M. (1971). La cultura azteca y los sacrificios humanos. In M. León-Portilla (Ed.), *De Teotihuacán a los Aztecas: Antología de fuentes e interpretaciones históricas* (pp. 208–214). México Universidad Nacional Autónoma de México, Instituto de Investigaciones Históricas.

Oxendine, J. (1988). *American Indian sports heritage.* Champaign, IL: Human Kinetics.

Ozmon, H., & Craver, S. (1995). *Philosophical foundations of education* (5th ed.). Englewood Cliffs, NJ: Prentice-Hall.

Padden, C., & Humphries, T. (1988). *Deaf in America: Voices from a culture.* Cambridge, MA: Harvard University Press.

Pai, Y., & Adler, S. (2001). *Cultural foundations of education* (3rd ed.). Upper Saddle River, NJ: Merrill Prentice-Hall.

Palter, R. (1996). *Black Athena,* Afrocentrism, and the history of science. In M. Lefkowitz & G. Rogers (Eds.), *Black Athena revisited* (pp. 209–266). Chapel Hill: University of North Carolina Press.

Pandey, S. N. (1991). Vedic mathematics: An appraisal from the perspective of modern mathematics. In H. C. Khare (Ed.), *Issues in Vedic mathematics* (pp. 103–104). Delhi: Motilal Banarsidass Publishers.

Pandit, B. (1993). *The Hindu mind: Fundamentals of Hindu religion and philosophy for all ages* (2nd ed.). Glen Ellyn, IL: B & V.

Paramhans, S. A. (1991). Glimpses of mathematical tradition of ancient India and its transmission to other countries. In H. C. Khare (Ed.), *Issues in Vedic mathematics* (pp. 105–116). Delhi: Motilal Banarsidass Publishers.

Parasnis, I. (Ed.). (1998). *Cultural and language diversity and the deaf experience.* Cambridge, England: Cambridge University Press.

Parrinder, G. (1969). *Religion in Africa.* Harmondsworth, England: Penguin.

Patton, M. (1978). *Utilization-focused evaluations.* Beverly Hills, CA: Sage.

Patton, M. (1990). *Qualitative evaluation and research methods* (2nd ed.). Newbury Park, CA: Sage.

Paul, D. Y. (1985). *Women in Buddhism: Images of the feminine in the Mahayana tradition.* Berkeley: University of California Press.

Paul, P., & Jackson, D. (1993). *Toward a psychology of deafness: Theoretical and empirical perspectives.* Boston: Allyn & Bacon.

Paulston, C., & Peckham, D. (Eds.). (1998). *Linguistic minorities in central and eastern Europe.* Clevedon, England: Multilingual Matters.

p'Bitek, O. (1967). *Song of Lawino and Song of Ocol.* Ibadan, Nigeria: Heinemann.

p'Bitek, O. (1971). *African religions in Western scholarship.* Nairobi, Kenya: East African Literature Bureau.

Pei-yi Wu. (1989). Education of children in the Sung. In W. de Bary & J. Chaffee (Eds.), *Neo-Confucian education. The formative stage* (pp. 307–324). Berkeley: University of California Press.

Pelikan, J. (Ed.). (1987). *Sacred writings, Volume 6: Buddhism, The Dhammapada.* New York: Quality Paperback Book Club.

Pennock, R. T. (1999). *Tower of Babel: The evidence against the new Creationism.* Cambridge, MA: MIT Press.

Peters, F. E. (1994). *The Hajj: The Muslim pilgrimage to Mecca and the holy places.* Princeton, NJ: Princeton University Press.

Pettitt, G. (1946). *Primitive education in North America.* Berkeley: University of California Press.

Phillips, D. C. (1995). The good, the bad, and the ugly: The many faces of constructivism. *Educational Researcher* 24: 5–12.

Phillips, D. C. (1996). Response to Ernst von Glasersfeld. *Educational Researcher* 25: 20.

Phillips, H. (1975). *Basic education: A world challenge.* New York: Wiley.

Piaget, J. (1979). *L'epistémologie génétique* (3rd ed.). Paris: Presses Universitaires de France.

Ping-Ti Ho. (1962). *The ladder of success in imperial China.* New York: Columbia University Press.

Pollak, S. (1983). *Ancient Buddhist education (Papers from the Bernard Van Leer Foundation Project on Human Potential).* Cambridge, MA: Harvard Graduate School of Education.

Prakash, G. (1990). Writing post-orientalist histories of the third world: Perspectives from Indian historiography. *Comparative Studies in Society and History* 32: 383–408.

Preston, P. (1994). *MOTHER FATHER DEAF: Living between sound and silence.* Cambridge, MA: Harvard University Press.

Pretorius, W. J. (1990). A comparative look at the development of heroic poetry in Northern Sotho. *South African Journal of African Languages* 10, 3: 125–131.

Puri, N. (1991). An overview of Vedic mathematics. In H. C. Khare (Ed.), *Issues in Vedic mathematics* (pp. 41–59). Delhi: Motilal Banarsidass Publishers.

Puri, N. (1992). *Higher applications of Vedic mathematics.* Bareilly, India: Prakash Book Depot.

Quintela, D., Ramírez, I., Robertson, X., & Pérez, A. (1997). ¿Por qué una educación bicultural bilingüe para las personas sordas? *Revista de la Universidad Metropolitana de Ciencias de la Educación* 3: 43–52.

Radhakrishnan, S. (Ed.). (1994). *The principal Upanishads.* New Delhi: Indus.

Radhakrishnan, S., & Moore, C. (Eds.). (1957). *A sourcebook in Indian philosophy.* Princeton, NJ: Princeton University Press.

Rahman, F. (1979). *Islam* (2nd ed.). Chicago: University of Chicago Press.

Rampal, A. (1992). A possible "orality" for science? *Interchange* 23, 3: 227–244.

Ramsey, S. R. (1987). *The languages of China.* Princeton, NJ: Princeton University Press.

Raper, P. (Ed.). (1986). *Names 1983: Proceedings of the Second Southern African Names Congress.* Pretoria: Human Sciences Research Council.

Raum, O. (1967). An evaluation of indigenous education. In P. Duminy (Ed.), *Trends and challenges in the education of the South African Bantu* (pp. 89–105). Pretoria: van Schaik.

Raval, S. (1958). *Basic education in modern India: A critique of Gandhian educational philosophy.* M. A. thesis, The American University, Washington, DC.

Rawski, E. (1979). *Education and popular literacy in Ch'ing China.* Ann Arbor: University of Michigan Press.

Ray, B. (1976). *African religions: Symbol, ritual, and community.* Englewood Cliffs, NJ: Prentice-Hall.

Raymond, J. (1982). Medicine as patriarchal religion. *Journal of Medicine and Philosophy* 7: 197–216.

Reagan, T. (1990a). Cultural considerations in the education of deaf children. In D. Moores & K. Meadow-Orlans (Eds.), *Educational and developmental aspects of deafness* (pp. 73–84). Washington, DC: Gallaudet University Press.

Reagan, T. (1990b). The development and reform of sign languages. In I. Fodor & C. Hagège (Eds.), *Language reform: History and future, Vol. 5* (pp. 253–267). Hamburg, Germany: Buske Verlag.

Reagan, T. (1990c). Philosophy of education in the service of apartheid: The role of "fundamental pedagogics" in South African education. *Educational Foundations* 4, 2: 59–71.

Reagan, T. (1993). Educating the "reflective practitioner": The contribution of philosophy of education. *Journal of Research and Development in Education* 26, 4: 189–196.

Reagan, T. (1995a). Neither easy to understand nor pleasing to see: The development of manual sign codes as language planning activity. *Language Problems and Language Planning* 19: 133–150.

Reagan, T. (1995b). A sociocultural understanding of deafness: American Sign Language and the culture of deaf people. *International Journal of Intercultural Relations* 19: 239–251.

Reagan, T. (2000). But does it *count?* Reflections on "signing" as a foreign language. *Northeast Conference on the Teaching of Foreign Languages* 48: 16–26.

Reat, N. R. (1994). *Buddhism: A history.* Berkeley, CA: Asian Humanities Press.

Reé, J. (1999). *I see a voice: Deafness, language and the senses—A philosophical history.* New York: Metropolitan Books.

Réger, Z. (1998). A preliminary typology of genres in the oral culture of children living in a traditional Gypsy community. Paper presented at the Fourth International Conference on Romani Linguistics held at the University of Manchester, England, 2–5 September.

Réger, Z., & Gleason, J. (1991). Romani child-directed speech and children's language among Gypsies in Hungary. *Language in Society* 20: 601–617.

Regnier, R. (1995). Bridging Western and First Nations thought: Balanced education in Whitehead's philosophy of organism and the sacred circle. *Interchange* 26, 4: 383–415.

Rehfisch, A., & Rehfisch, F. (1975). Scottish travelers or tinkers. In F. Rehfisch (Ed.), *Gypsies, tinkers, and other travelers* (pp. 271–283). London: Academic Press.

Reissner, J. (1984). Die innerislamische Diskussion zur modernen Wirtschafts-und Sozialordnung. In M. Ursinus (Ed.), *Der Islam in der Gegenwart* (pp. 155–169). München, Germany: C. H. Beck.

Renfrew, C. (1987). *Archeology and language: The puzzle of Indo-European origins.* Cambridge, England: Cambridge University Press.

Revel, J. (2002). *L'obsession anti-américaine: Son fontionnement, ses causes, ses inconséquences.* Paris: Editions Plon.

Reynolds, P. (1986). The training of traditional healers in Mashonaland. In M. Last & C. Chavunduka (Eds.), *The professionalization of African medicine* (pp. 165–187). Manchester, England: Manchester University Press.

Richardson, V. (Ed.). (1997). *Constructivist teacher education: Building a world of new understandings.* London: Falmer.

Ricoeur, P. (1965). *History and truth.* Evanston, IL: Northwestern University Press.

Riddell, P., & Cotterell, P. (2003). *Islam in context: Past, present, and future.* Grand Rapids, MI: Baker Academic.

Roberts, J. A. G. (1999). *A concise history of China.* Cambridge, MA: Harvard University Press.

Robins, R. H. (1979). *A short history of linguistics* (2nd ed.). London: Longman.

Rodinson, M. (1966). *Islam et capitalisme.* Paris: Éditions du Seuil.

Rodinson, M. (1974). *Mohammed.* New York: Vintage.

Rodinson, M. (1993). *L'Islam: Politique et croyance.* Paris: Fayard.

Rogers, J., & Wilson, S. (Eds.). (1993). *Ethnohistory and archaeology: Approaches to postcontact change in the Americas.* New York: Plenum.

Ronan, C. (1978). *The shorter science and civilisation in China, Volume 1: Volumes I and II of the major series.* Cambridge, England: Cambridge University Press.

Ronan, C. (1981). *The shorter science and civilisation in China, Volume 2: Volume III and a section of volume IV, part I of the major series.* Cambridge, England: Cambridge University Press.

Ronan, C. (1986). *The shorter science and civilisation in China, Volume 3: A section of volume IV, part I and a section of volume IV, part 3 of the major series.* Cambridge, England: Cambridge University Press.

Ronan, C. (1994). *The shorter science and civilisation in China, Volume 4: The main sections of volume IV, part 2 of the major series.* Cambridge, England: Cambridge University Press.

Ron-guey Chu. (1989). Chu Hsi and public instruction. In W. de Bary & J. Chaffee (Eds.), *Neo-Confucian education: The formative stage* (pp. 252–273). Berkeley: University of California Press.

Ropp, P. (Ed.). (1990). *Heritage of China.* Berkeley: University of California Press.

Rosander, E., & Westerlund, D. (1997). *African Islam and Islam in Africa.* Athens, OH: Ohio University Press.

Rosenthal, F. (1992). *The classical heritage in Islam.* London: Routledge.

Ross, K., Derman, D., & Dakovic, N. (Eds.). (2001). *Mediated identities.* Istanbul: Istanbul Bilgi University Press.

Ross, N. W. (1980). *Buddhism: A way of life and thought.* New York: Vintage.

Rousseau, J.-J. (1971). *Discours sur l'origine et les fondements de l'inégalité parmi les hommes.* Paris: Garnier-Flammarion.

Rousseau, J.-J. (1966). *Émile ou de l'éducation.* Paris: GF Flammarion.

Rubin, V. (1976). *Individual and state in ancient China: Essays on four Chinese philosophers.* New York: Columbia University Press.

Ruthven, M. (2000). *Islam in the world* (2nd ed.). Oxford, England: Oxford University Press.

Ryan, D., & Schuchman, J. (Eds.). (2002). *Deaf people in Hitler's Europe.* Washington, DC: Gallaudet University Press, in association with the United States Holocaust Memorial Museum.

Rycroft, D., & Ngcobo, A. (1981). *Say it in Zulu.* Pietermaritzburg: Language and Reading Laboratories, University of Natal.

Sacks, O. (1989). *Seeing voices: A journey into the world of the deaf.* Berkeley: University of California Press.

Sáenz, J. (1988). Reto y educación en el México prehispánico. In J. Josserand & K. Dakin (Eds.), *Smoke and mist: Mesoamerican studies in memory of Thelma D. Sullivan, Part II* (pp. 681–695). Oxford, England: B.A.R.

Safford, P., & Safford, E. (1996). *A history of childhood and disability.* New York: Teachers College Press.

Sagan, E. (1993). *Cannibalism: Human aggression and cultural form.* Santa Fe, NM: First Drum.

Sahadat, J. (1996). Divine revelation and the status of the Qur'an. *Muslim Education Quarterly 13,* 4: 4–17.

Sahagun, B. (1981). *El Mexico antiguo: Selección y reordenación de la historia general de las cosas de Nueva España.* Caracas: Biblioteca Ayachucho.

Sahlins, M. (1995). *How "natives" think: About Captain Cook, for example.* Chicago: University of Chicago Press.

Said, E. (1978). *Orientalism.* New York: Vintage.

Said, E. (1993). *Culture and imperialism*. New York: Vintage.

Sakai, T. (1970). Confucianism and popular educational works. In W. de Bary (Ed.), *Self and society in Ming thought* (pp. 331–366). New York: Columbia University Press.

Salazar, P. (2002). *An African Athens: Rhetoric and the shaping of democracy in South Africa*. Hillsdale, NJ: Lawrence Erlbaum Associates.

Salo, M. (1979). Gypsy ethnicity: Implications of native categories and interaction for ethnic classification. *Ethnicity* 6: 73–96.

Salo, M., & Salo, S. (1977). *The Kalderas in eastern Canada*. Ottawa: National Museums of Canada.

Sarwar, G. (1989). *Islam: Beliefs and teaching*. London: Muslim Educational Trust.

Saud, M. A. (1989). Toward Islamic economics. In *Toward Islamization of disciplines* (pp. 265–270). Herndon, VA: International Institute of Islamic Thought.

Saunders, C. (1988). *The making of the South African past: Major historians on race and class*. Cape Town: David Philip.

Schacht, J. (1964). *An introduction to Islamic law*. Oxford, England: Clarendon.

Schapera, I. (1965). *Praise-poems of Tswana chiefs*. Oxford, England: Oxford University Press.

Schein, J. (1984). *Speaking the language of sign: The art and science of signing*. Garden City, NY: Doubleday.

Schein, J. (1989). *At home among strangers: Exploring the deaf community in the United States*. Washington, DC: Gallaudet University Press.

Schein, J., & Stewart, D. (1995). *Language in motion: Exploring the nature of sign*. Washington, DC: Gallaudet University Press.

Schele, L., & Freidel, D. (1990). *A forest of kings: The untold story of the ancient Maya*. New York: Morrow.

Schele, L., & Mathews, P. (1998). *The code of kings: The language of seven sacred Maya temples and tombs*. New York: Simon & Shuster.

Schimmel, A. (1992). *Islam: An introduction*. Albany: State University of New York Press.

Schlagintweit, E. (1968). *Buddhism in Tibet* (2nd ed.). London: Susil Gupta.

Schmidt, P. (1997). *Iron technology in East Africa: Symbolism, science, and archeology*. London: Currey.

Scholten, D. (2000). *Sprachverbreitungspolitik des nationalsozialistischen Deutschlands*. Frankfurt, Germany: Peter Lang.

Schwartz, B. (1985). *The world of thought in ancient China*. Cambridge, MA: Harvard University Press.

Scott, D., & Doubleday, T. (1992). *The elements of Zen*. Shaftesbury, England: Element.

Seager, R. (1999). *Buddhism in America*. New York: Columbia University Press.

Sells, M. (1999). *Approaching the Qur'an: The early revelations*. Ashland, OH: White Cloud.

Semali, L., & Kincheloe, J. (1999a). Introduction: What is indigenous knowledge and why should we study it? In L. Semali & J. Kincheloe (Eds.), *What is indigenous knowledge? Voices from the academy* (pp. 3–57). New York: Falmer.

Semali, L., & Kincheloe, J. (Eds.). (1999b). *What is indigenous knowledge? Voices from the academy*. New York: Falmer.

Sen, K. M. (1961). *Hinduism*. Harmondsworth, England: Penguin.

Senese, G. (1991). *Self-determination and the social education of Native Americans*. New York: Praeger.

Shalabi, A. (1954). *History of Muslim education*. Beirut, Lebanon: Dar Al-Kashshaf.

Shankar, D. (1996). The epistemology of the indigenous medical knowledge systems in India. *Indigenous Knowledge and Development Monitor* 4: 13–14.

Shapiro, J. (1993). *No pity: People with disabilities forging a new civil rights movement*. New York: Times Books.

Sharer, R. (1994). *The ancient Maya* (5th ed.). Stanford, CA: Stanford University Press.

Sharer, R. (1996). *Daily life in Maya civilization*. Westport, CT: Greenwood.

Sharer, R. (1998). *La civilizatión Maya*. México: Fondo de Cultura Económica.

Sharma, A. (1993). Hinduism. In A. Sharma (Ed.), *Our religions: The seven world religious introduced by preeminent scholars from each tradition* (pp. 1–67). San Francisco: Harper.

Sharma, A. (Ed.). (1993). *Our religious: The seven world religions introduced by preeminent scholars from each tradition*. San Francisco: Harper.

Sharma, A. (2000). *Classical Hindu thought: An introduction*. New Delhi: Oxford University Press.

Sherzer, J. (1991). A richness of voices. In A. Josephy (Ed.), *America in 1492: The world of the Indian peoples before the arrival of Columbus* (pp. 251–275). New York: Vintage.

Shipps, J. (1985). *Mormonism: The story of a new religious tradition*. Urbana: University of Illinois Press.

Shunchiu Yau. (1982). Creation d'anthroponumes gesuels par une sourde amérindienne isolée. *Amérindia: Revue d'Éthnolinguistique Amérindienne* 7: 7–22.

Shunchiu Yau. (1990). Lexical branching in sign language. In S. Fischer & P. Siple (Eds.), *Theoretical issues in sign language research: Linguistics* (pp. 261–278). Chicago: University of Chicago Press.

Shunchiu Yau, and Jinxian He. (1990). How do deaf children get their name signs during their first month in school? In E. Edmondson & F. Karlsson (Eds.), *SLR '87: Papers from the Fourth International Symposium on Sign Language Research* (pp. 242–254). Hamburg, Germany: Signum.

Siddiqi, M. N. (1989). Islamizing economics. In *Toward Islamization of disciplines* (pp. 253–261). Herndon, VA: International Institute of Islamic Thought.

Siddiqui, A. H. (1991). *Life of Muhammad*. Des Plaines, IL: Library of Islam.

Siegel, H. (1997). *Rationality redeemed? Further dialogues on an educational ideal*. New York: Routledge.

Silverman, C. (1982). Everyday drama: Impression management of urban Gypsies. *Urban Anthropology* 11, 3/4: 377–398.

Siméon, R. (Ed.). (1889). *Annales de Domingo Francisco de San Anton Muñon Chimalpahim Quauhtlehuanitzin sixiéme et septiéme relations*. Paris: Maisonneuve et Ch. LeClerc.

Siméon, R. (1963). *Dictionnaire de la langue Nahuatl ou Mexicaine*. Graz, Germany: Akademische Druck U. Verlagsanstalt.

Sinclair, H., Berthoud, I., Gerard, J., & Venesiano, E. (1985). Constructivisme et psycholinguistique génétique. *Archives de Psychologie* 53: 37–60.

Sirayi, M. (1996). Oral African drama in South Africa: The Xhosa indigenous drama forms. *South African Theatre Journal* 10, 1: 49–61.

Smith, H., & Novak, P. (2003). *Buddhism: A concise introduction*. New York: HarperSanFrancisco.

Smith, J. (1999). *Islam in America*. New York: Columbia University Press.

Smith, K. (1988). *The changing past: Trends in South African historical writing*. Johannesburg: Southern.

Smith, R. (1983). *China's cultural heritage: The Ch'ing dynasty, 1644–1912*. Boulder, CO: Westview.

Snelling, J. (1991). *The Buddhist handbook: A complete guide to Buddhist schools, teaching, practice, and history*. Rochester, VT: Inner Traditions.

Snively, G. (1990). Traditional Native Indian beliefs, cultural values, and science instruction. *Canadian Journal of Native Education* 17, 1: 44–59.

Sokal, A., & Bricmont, J. (1998). *Fashionable nonsense: Postmodern intellectuals' abuse of science*. New York: Picador.

Solana, N. G. (1985). *Códices de México: Historia e interpretación de los grandes libros pintados prehispánicos*. México: Panorama Editorial.

Soustelle, J. (1961). *Daily life of the Aztecs on the eve of the Spanish conquest*. Stanford, CA: Stanford University Press.

Soustelle, J. (1979). *The Olmecs: The oldest civilization in Mexico.* Norman: University of Oklahoma Press.

Soustelle, J. (1991). *Les aztéques* (6th ed.). Paris: Presses Universitaires de France.

Soustelle, J. (1996). *El universo de los aztecas.* México: Fundo de Cultura Económica.

Spiro, M. (1970). *Buddhism and society.* New York: Harper & Row.

Spores, R. (1984). *The Mixtecs in ancient and colonial times.* Norman: University of Oklahoma Press.

Sprenger, A. (1991). Confucius and modernization in China: An educational perspective. In S. Krieger & R. Trauzettel (Eds.), *Confucianism and the modernization of China* (pp. 454–472). Mainz, Germany: Hase & Koehler.

Spring, J. (1995). *The intersection of cultures: Multicultural education in the United States.* New York: McGraw-Hill.

Staiger, B. (1991). The image of Confucius in China. In S. Krieger & R. Trauzettel (Eds.), *Confucianism and the modernization of China* (pp. 116–125). Mainz, Germany: Hase & Koehler.

Stanton, C. (1990). *Higher learning in Islam: The classical period, A.D. 700–1300.* Savage, MD: Rowman & Littlefield.

Stewart, M. (1997). *The time of the Gypsies.* Boulder, CO: Westview.

Storey, J. (1998). *An introduction to cultural theory and popular culture* (2nd ed.). Athens, GA: University of Georgia Press.

Stover, L. (1974). *The cultural ecology of Chinese civilization: Peasants and elites in the last of the agrarian societies.* New York: Pica.

Stuart, G. (1981). *The mighty Aztecs.* Washington, DC: National Geographic Society.

Stumpfeldt, H. (1991). Confucius and Confucianism: On their history and status and on their present theoretical and practical potential. In S. Krieger & R. Trauzettel (Eds.), *Confucianism and the modernization of China* (pp. 18–28). Mainz, Germany: Hase & Koehler.

Suárez, J. (1983). *The Mesoamerican Indian languages.* Cambridge, England: Cambridge University Press.

Subramuniyaswami, S. (1993). *Dancing with Siva: Hinduism's contemporary catechism.* Concord, CA: Himalayan Academy.

Sudarkasa, N. (1982). Sex roles, education and development in Africa. *Anthropology and Education* 13, 3: 279–288.

Sullivan, T. (1963). Nahuatl proverbs, conundrums and metaphors collected by Sahagun. *Estudios de Cultura Náhuatl* 4: 93–178.

Sultan, T. (1997). The role of Islamic universities in the Islamization of education. *Muslim Education Quarterly* 14, 3: 57–63.

Sumner, W. G. (1940). *Folkways.* Boston: Ginn & Co. (Original publication 1906)

Supalla, S. (1992). *Name signs: Naming in American Sign Language.* San Diego, CA: DawnSign Press.

Sutherland, A. (1975). *Gypsies: The hidden Americans.* Prospect Heights, IL: Waveland.

Suzuki, D. T. (1949). *An introduction to Zen Buddhism.* New York: Philosophical Library.

Swarup, R. (2002). *Understanding the Hadith: The sacred traditions of Islam.* Amherst, NY: Prometheus.

Swartz, L. (1998). *Culture and mental health: A Southern African view.* Cape Town: Oxford University Press.

Sway, M. (1988). *Familiar strangers: Gypsy life in America.* Urbana: University of Illinois Press.

Szasz, M. (1974). *Education and the American Indian: The road to self-determination, 1928–1973.* Albuquerque: University of New Mexico Press.

Talbani, A. (1996). Pedagogy, power, and discourse: Transformation of Islamic education. *Comparative Education Review* 40, 1: 66–82.

Tanahashi, K., & Schneider, T. D. (1994). *Essential Zen.* San Francisco: HarperCollins.

Tayob, A. (1999). *Islam: A short introduction.* Oxford, England: OneWorld.

Tebbutt, S. (Ed.). (1998). *Sinti and Roma: Gypsies in German-speaking society and literature.* New York: Berghahn.

Telushkin, J. (1992). *Jewish humor.* New York: Morrow.

Temple, R. (1986). *The genius of China: 3,000 years of science, discovery, and invention.* New York: Simon & Schuster.

Thien-An, T. (1975). *Zen philosophy, Zen practice.* Berkeley, CA: Dharma Publishing.

Thomas, N. W. (1969). *Proverbs, narratives, vocabularies and grammar: Anthropological report on the Ibo-speaking peoples of Nigeria, Part III.* New York: Negro Universities Press. (Original work published 1913)

Thompson, J. (1933). *Mexico before Cortez: An account of the daily life, religion, and ritual of the Aztecs and kindred peoples.* New York: Scribner's.

Thompson, J. E. (1962). *A catalog of Maya hieroglyphs.* Norman: University of Oklahoma Press.

Tibawi, A. L. (1972). *Islamic education: Its traditions and modernization into the Arab national systems.* London: Luzac & Co.

Tibi, B. (1990). *Islam and the cultural accommodation of social change.* Boulder, CO: Westview.

Tong, D. (Ed.). (1998). *Gypsies: An interdisciplinary reader.* New York: Garland.

Townsend, R. (1992). *The Aztecs.* London: Thames and Hudson.

Tozer, S., Violas, P., & Senese, G. (1998). *School and society: Historical and contemporary perspectives* (3rd ed.). New York: McGraw-Hill.

Trigg, E. (1973). *Gypsy demons and divinities: The magic and religion of the Gypsies.* Secaucus, NJ: Citadel.

Tritt, R. (1992). *Struggling for ethnic identity: Czechoslovakia's endangered Gypsies.* New York: Human Rights Watch.

Tucker, M., & Williams, D. (Eds.). (1997). *Buddhism and ecology: The interconnection of Dharma and deeds.* Cambridge, MA: Harvard University Press.

Turner, B. (1994). *Orientalism, postmodernism, and globalism.* London: Routledge.

Turner, N. (1988). Comparison of the *izibongo* of the Zulu royal women, Mnkabayi and Nandi. *South African Journal of African Languages* 8, 1: 28–33.

Tu Wei-ming. (1989). The Sung Confucian idea of education: A background understanding. In W. de Bary & J. Chaffee (Eds.), *Neo-Confucian education: The formative stage* (pp. 139–150). Berkeley: University of California Press.

Tu Wei-ming. (1990). The Confucian tradition in Chinese history. In P. Ropp (Ed.), *Heritage of China: Contemporary perspectives on Chinese civilization* (pp. 112–136). Berkeley: University of California Press.

Tu Wei-ming. (1993). Confucianism. In A. Sharma (Ed.), *Our religions: The seven world religions introduced by preeminent scholars from each tradition* (pp. 139–227). San Francisco: Hnarper.

Twitchett, D. (Ed.). (1979). *The Cambridge history of China, Volume 3: Sui and T'ang China, 589–906, part I.* Cambridge, England: Cambridge University Press.

Twitchett, D., & Loewe, M. (Eds.). (1986). *The Cambridge history of China, Volume 1: The Ch'in and Han empires, 221 B.C.–A.D. 220.* Cambridge, England: Cambridge University Press.

Twumasi, P., & Warren, D. (1986). The professionalization of indigenous medicine: A comparative study of Ghana and Zambia. In M. Last & C. Chavunduka (Eds.), *The professionalization of African medicine* (pp. 117–135). Manchester, England: Manchester University Press.

Tyrnauer, G. (1991). *Gypsies and the Holocaust: A bibliography and introductory essay* (2nd ed.). Montréal: Montréal Institute for Genocide Studies, Concordia University.

Übelhör, M. (1989). The community compact (*Hsiang-yüeh*) of the Sung and its educational significance. In W. de Bary & J. Chaffee (Eds.), *Neo-Confucian education: The formative stage* (pp. 371–388). Berkeley: University of California Press.

Uka, N. (1986). Continuity and change: A challenge to African educators. In J. Okpaku, A. Opubor, & B. Oloruntimehin (Eds.), *The arts and civilization of Black and African peoples, Volume 6: Black civilization and pedagogy* (pp. 129–144). Lagos, Nigeria: Center for Black and African Arts and Civilization.

UNESCO. (1985). *The educational process and historiography in Africa.* Paris: UNESCO.

Ungar, S. (1986). *Africa: The people and politics of an emerging continent* (Rev. ed.). New York: Simon & Schuster.

Ursinus, M. (Ed.). (1984). *Der Islam in der Gegenwart.* München, Germany: C. H. Beck.

Vaillant, G. (1995). *La civilización azteca.* México: Fondo de Cultura Económica.

Valli, C., & Lucas, C. (2000). *Linguistics of American Sign Language: An introduction* (3rd ed.). Washington, DC: Gallaudet University Press.

Van Cleve, J. (Ed.). (1993). *Deaf history unveiled: Interpretations from the new scholarship.* Washington, DC: Gallaudet University Press.

Van Cleve, J., & Crouch, B. (1989). *A place of their own: Creating the deaf community in America.* Washington, DC: Gallaudet University Press.

van der Vliet, V. (1974). Growing up in a traditional society. In W. Hammond-Tooke (Ed.), *The Bantu-speaking peoples of Southern Africa* (pp. 211–245). London: Routledge & Kegan Paul.

van Jaarsveld, F. A. (1975). *From Van Riebeeck to Vorster, 1652–1974.* Pretoria: Perskor.

van Nieuwenhuijze, C. (1985). *The lifestyles of Islam: Recourse to classicism, need of realism.* Leiden, The Netherlands: Brill.

van Zantwijk, R. (1985). *The Aztec arrangement: The social history of pre-Spanish Mexico.* Norman: University of Oklahoma Press.

Vansina, J. (1985). *Oral tradition as history.* Madison: University of Wisconsin Press.

Vernon, M., & Andrews, J. (1990). *The psychology of deafness.* New York: Longman.

Veytia, M. (1944). *Historia antigua de Mexico,* 2 vols. México: Editorial Leyenda.

Viergever, M. (1999). Indigenous knowledge: An interpretation of views from indigenous peoples. In L. Semali & J. Kincheloe (Eds.), *What is indigenous knowledge? Voices from the academy* (pp. 333–343). New York: Falmer.

Viswanathan, E. (1992). *Am I a Hindu? The Hinduism primer.* San Francisco: Halo Books.

Vogel, A., & Elsasser, N. (1981). Rom (Gypsy), merimé, and the schools. *Theory into Practice* 20, 1: 70–72.

Voll, J. (1994). *Islam: Continuity and change in the modern world* (2nd ed.). Syracuse, NY: Syracuse University Press.

von Däniken, E. (1968). *Chariots of the gods: Unsolved mysteries of the past.* New York: Berkley.

von Däniken, E. (1995). *The return of the gods.* Shaftesbury, England: Element.

von Däniken, E. (1996). *The eyes of the Sphinx.* New York: Berkley.

von Däniken, E. (1997). *Arrival of the gods.* Shaftesbury, England: Element.

von Glasersfeld, E. (1984). An introduction to radical constructivism. In P. Watzlawick (Ed.), *The invented reality: How do we know what we believe we know?* (pp. 17–40). New York: Norton.

von Glasersfeld, E. (1989). Cognition, construction of knowledge, and teaching. *Synthese* 80: 121–140.

von Glasersfeld, E. (1993). Questions and answers about radical constructivism. In K. Tobin (Ed.), *The practice of constructivism in science education* (pp. 23–38). Hillsdale, NJ: Lawrence Erlbaum Associates.

von Glasersfeld, E. (1995a). *Radical constructivism: A way of knowing.* London: Falmer.

von Glasersfeld, E. (1995b). A constructivist approach to teaching. In L. Steffe & J. Gale (Eds.), *Constructivism in education* (pp. 3–15). Hillsdale, NJ: Lawrence Erlbaum Associates.

von Glasersfeld, E. (1996). Footnotes to "The many faces of constructivism." *Educational Researcher* 25: 19.

Vygotsky, L. (1978). *Mind in society: The development of higher psychological processes.* Cambridge, MA: Harvard University Press.

Vygotsky, L. (1986). *Thought and language.* Cambridge, MA: MIT Press.

Waghid, Y. (1996). Why a theory of Islamic education cannot be epistemologically "neutral." *Muslim Education Quarterly* 13, 2: 43–54.

Waines, D. (1995). *An introduction to Islam.* Cambridge, England: Cambridge University Press.

Waley, A. (Trans.). (1938). *The Analects of Confucius.* New York: Vintage.

Wall, S. (1994). *Shadowcatchers: A journey in search of the teachings of Native American healers.* New York: HarperCollins.

Walker, B. (1968). *The Hindu world: An encyclopedic survey of Hinduism, Vol. 1.* New York: Praeger.

Walton, L. (1989). The institutional context of neo-Confucianism: Scholars, schools, and Shu-yüan in Sung-Yüan China. In W. de Bary & J. Chaffee (Eds.), *Neo-Confucian education: The formative stage* (pp. 457–492). Berkeley: University of California Press.

Wang Gungwu. (1991). *The Chineseness of China.* Hong Kong: Oxford University Press.

Warder, A. K. (1970). *Indian Buddhism.* Delhi: Motilal Banarsidass.

Warraq, I. (2002a). Introduction. In I. Warraq (Ed.), *What the Koran really says: Language, text, and commentary* (pp. 23–106). Amherst, NY: Prometheus.

Warraq, I. (Ed.). (2002b). *What the Koran really says: Language, text, and commentary.* Amherst, NY: Prometheus.

Warren, D., Slikkerveer, L., & Brokensha, D. (Eds.). (1995). *The cultural dimension of development: Indigenous knowledge systems.* London: Intermediate Technology Publications.

Watson, B. (Trans.). (1961). *Records of the grand historian of China,* 2 vols. New York: Columbia University Press.

Watt, W. M. (1953). *Muhammad at Mecca.* Karachi, Pakistan: Oxford University Press.

Watt, W. M. (1956). *Muhammad at Medina.* Karachi, Pakistan: Oxford University Press.

Watt, W. M., & Bell, R. (1970). *Introduction to the Qur'an.* Edinburgh: Edinburgh University Press.

Weaver, M. (1981). *The Aztecs, Maya, and their predecessors: Archeology of Mesoamerica* (2nd ed.). New York: Academic Press.

Weckman, S. (1998). Researching Finnish Gypsies: Advice from a Gypsy. In D. Tong (Ed.), *Gypsies: An interdisciplinary reader* (pp. 3–10). New York: Garland.

Weibust, P. (1989). Tradition as process: Creating contemporary tradition in a rural Norwegian school and community. *International Journal of Qualitative Studies in Education* 2, 2: 107–122.

Weinreich, M. (1999). *Hitler's professors: The part of scholarship in Germany's crimes against the Jewish people.* New Haven, CT: Yale University Press. (Original publication 1946)

White, F. C. (1983). *Knowledge and relativism: An essay in the philosophy of education.* Assen, The Netherlands: Van Gorcum.

White, J. (1971). *Cortés and the downfall of the Aztec empire: A study in a conflict of cultures.* New York: St. Martin's Press.

Wilcox, S. (Ed.). (1989). *American deaf culture: An anthology.* Burtonsville, MD: Linstok Press.

Wilkinson, E. (2000). *Chinese history: A manual* (Rev. and enlarged ed.). Cambridge, MA: Harvard University Press.

Willard, T. (1993). I've had enough of the I-LOVE-YOU sign, thanks. *Silent News* 25: 2.

Williams, P. (2003). *Gypsy world: The silence of the living and the voices of the dead.* Chicago: University of Chicago Press.

Williams, R. (1983). *Keywords.* London: Fantana.

Williams, S. W. (1907). *The Middle Kingdom: A survey of the geography, government, literature, social life, arts, and history of the Chinese empire and its inhabitants,* 2 vols. New York: Scribner's.

Williamson, A. (1997). Decolonizing historiography of colonial education: Processes of interaction in the schooling of Torres Strait Islanders. *International Journal of Qualitative Studies in Education* 10, 4: 407–423

Willms, A. (1984). Nordafrika. In M. Ursinus (Ed.), *Der Islam in der Gegemeart* (pp. 561–569). München, Germany: C. H. Beck.

Winefield, R. (1987). *Never the twain shall meet: Bell, Gallaudet, and the communications debate.* Washington, DC: Gallaudet University Press.

Wing-tsit Chan. (1989). Chu Hsi and the academies. In W. de Bary & J. Chaffee (Eds.), *Neo-Confucian education: The formative stage* (pp. 389–413). Berkeley: University of California Press.

Witherspoon, G. (1977). *Language and art in the Navajo universe.* Ann Arbor: University of Michigan Press.

Wolfe, M. (Ed.). (2002). *Taking back Islam: American Muslims reclaim their faith.* New York: Rodale.

Woodcock, K. 1992). Cochlear implants vs. deaf culture? In M. Garretson (Ed.), *Viewpoints on deafness: A Deaf American monograph, Vol. 42* (pp. 151–155). Silver Spring, MD: National Association of the Deaf.

Wright, R. (1992). *Stolen continents: The "new world" through Indian eyes.* Boston: Houghton Mifflin.

Wyatt, D. (1990). A language of continuity in Confucian thought. In P. Cohen & M. Goldman (Eds.), *Ideas across cultures: Essays on Chinese thought in honor of Benjamin I. Schwartz* (pp. 33–61). Cambridge, MA: Harvard University Press.

Xinzhong Yao. (2000). *An introduction to Confucianism.* Cambridge, England: Cambridge University Press.

Yellow Bird, R. (1990). Position paper on Native Education. *Humanity & Society* 14, 3: 297–301.

Young, R. (1990). *White mythologies: Writing history and the West.* London: Routledge.

Young, R. E. (1981). The epistemic discourse of teachers: An ethnographic study. *Anthropology and Education Quarterly* 12: 122–144.

Yuan Zheng. (1994). Local government schools in Sung China: A reassessment. *History of Education Quarterly* 34, 193–213.

Yu Dunkang. (1991). The concept of "great harmony" in the Book of Changes (*Zhou Yi*). In S. Krieger & R. Trauzettel (Eds.), *Confucianism and the modernization of China* (pp. 51–62). Mainz, Germany: Hase & Koehler.

Zaehner, R. C. (1962). *Hinduism.* London: Oxford University Press.

Zelliot, E., & Bernsten, M. (Eds.). (1988). *The experience of Hinduism.* Albany: State University of New York Press.

Zimmermann, M. (1996). *Rassenutopie und Genozid: Die nationalsozialistische "Lösung der Zigeunerfrage."* Hamburg, Germany: Christians.

Zürcher, E. (1989). Buddhism and education in T'ang times. In W. de Bary & J. Chaffee (Eds.), *Neo-Confucian education: The formative stage* (pp. 19–56). Berkeley: University of California Press.

Author Index

Subject Index

A

A Brief Introduction to Hinduism (Herman), 185
Accuracy, 8, 20
Acoli (Africa), 66
A Concise History of China (Roberts), 155
Africa in History (Davidson), 82
African Civilization Revisited (Davidson), 82
African education
  Acoli, 66
  Afrocentric worldview, 78–79
    romantic nationalism, 79, 81
  Ashanti (West Africa), 55–56
  Benin (West Africa), 55–56
  Bissimi, 66–67
  community role, 62–63, 70–71, 72, 73, 80
  conclusions, 80
  cultural commonality, 56
  cultural diversity, 55–56
  cultural misrepresentation, 79
  East Africa, 63
  educational goals
    character formation, 61, 70–71, 81
    conformity, 61
    effectiveness, 62
    features, 61–62
    good person development, 61
    play activities, 62–63
    seven cardinal goals, 60–61
    vocational skills, 62–63
  elders, 71
  ethnic diversity, 55–56

family role, 70–71
gender distinctions, 63, 72, 74, 75–76,
  86n.84
geographical diversity, 55–56
Hausa (West Africa), 55–56, 69
Igbo (Nigeria), 62, 64, 65, 71
initiation ceremonies, 71–73, 86n.84
  age-set, 72
  schools, 73, 81
introduction, 55–56
!Kung (Kalahari), 55–56
linguistic diversity, 55–56
Masai (Kenya), 74
Masai (Tanzania), 74
morality, 70–71, 81
Ndebele, 67
Négritude movement, 79
Nupe (Nigeria), 75
oral tradition
  dilemma tales, 68–69
  fables, 69
  folktales, 68
  games, 66–67, 68
  language, 63–68, 70
  legends, 69
  mathematics, 68–69
  myths, 69
  praise-poems, 70, 77–78
  proverbs, 64–67, 81
  puzzles, 67, 68–69
  riddles, 67, 68
  tongue-twisters, 67
  word games, 66–67, 68

B

C